Other Books by Richard Tanner Pascale

Managing the White House: An Intimate Study of the Presidency

The Art of Japanese Management, co-authored with Anthony G. Athos

MANAGING
ON THE EDGE

How the
Smartest Companies
Use Conflict to Stay Ahead

Richard Tanner Pascale

SIMON AND SCHUSTER

New York   London   Toronto   Sydney   Tokyo   Singapore

Simon and Schuster
Simon & Schuster Building
Rockefeller Center
1230 Avenue of the Americas
New York, New York   10020

Designed by Irving Perkins Associates, Inc.
Manufactured in the United States of America

2   3   4   5   6   7   8   9   10

Library of Congress Cataloging in Publication Data

Pascale, Richard Tanner
Managing on the edge : how the smartest companies use conflict to
stay ahead / Richard Tanner Pascale.
p.   cm.
1. Organizational change.   2. Organizational effectiveness.
3. Conflict management.   I. Title.
HD58.8.P365   1990
658.4—dc20   89-48997
ISBN 0-671-62442-3   CIP

Acknowledgments

I am grateful and indebted to many people who helped make this book possible. First, I wish to thank Shafiq Naz, who parented the book from its early drafts to completion and added wisdom, encouragement, and first-rate editorial comments. Second, I am indebted to Ann Carol Brown, who read and commented on the earliest drafts when the going was rough, provided support, and made many valuable suggestions that have added coherence and concreteness to this work. Third, I wish to express particular thanks to Jim Moore, who coined the terminology "fit, split, contend, transcend" and contributed to the underlying conceptualization of the book. Special gratitude goes to Charles Butt, who both read and commented on early chapters and whose generosity eased some of the pressures that writing and simultaneously earning a living can entail.

Beyond these four individuals there have been a number who read, commented, encouraged, and criticized. Among these are several colleagues: Rhoda DuBois, Robert Jaedicke, Dean of Stanford's Graduate School of Business, Jerry Sternin, Professors Joseph Bower and Thomas Rohlen. Lifelong colleague and friend Anthony Athos provided inspiration and ideas in the earlier drafts and contributed particularly to the final chapter. In addition, a number of executives contributed a real world perspective. Foremost among these was David Shrigley, General Manager of Intel and Andy Grove, CEO of Intel; Donald R. Petersen, CEO of Ford Motor Company; Jack Welch, CEO of General Electric, who made time in his demanding schedule to invest dozens of hours probing, challenging, and ultimately improving the argument presented here; others include John Olds, Managing Director, J. P. Morgan; Robert Allen, CEO of AT&T; and Robert Kohler, General Manager of the Applied Systems Group, TRW. I also wish to thank Greg Crawford, Gary Shirts, and Curt Berrien of The Bay Group, whose collaboration on the essentials of contention management was invaluable.

A few individuals at the companies which I have written about in depth played a major role in supporting this work. At Ford, Nancy Badore, Vice President of Executive Development, has been a colleague for a decade, a source of input and inspiration, and one of the leading thinkers in the United

States on large systems change. Her counterpart at General Electric, James Baughman, along with former GE staff member Donald Kane, contributed many hours to my education and set high standards of insight and accuracy.

In the final year of this writing, two extraordinary men who gave their personal attention and support to this book have died. To Konosuke Matsushita I am indebted for the hours spent with me in interviews when his voice was feeble and my questions wearying. Honda's Takeo Fujisawa provided time, personal example, and a philosophy which embraced contention. From that seed this book was born. Others at Honda contributed immensely—among them Shin Tanaka, Shoichiro Irimajiri, and Messrs. Ueda, Fujiwara and Anderson.

Finally, I want to thank Sheila Griffin, who husbanded the drafts and perfected this manuscript with her energy, editorial improvements, and dedication. Researchers Rajiv Sabharwal, Rafi Kassarjian, Jim Mayer, and Pauline French assisted in data collection. I wish to also thank Wes Jenkins and Alicia Williamson for support on graphics, and my editors, David Shipley and Alice Mayhew.

RICHARD TANNER PASCALE
Five Star Ranch
Pescadero, California
August 1989

For Regina:
Who learned . . .
then taught . . .
and changed the course of a lifetime.

Contents

Introduction

The world that we have made as a result of the level of thinking we have done thus far creates problems that we cannot solve at the same level as they were created.

ALBERT EINSTEIN

Nothing fails like success. Winning organizations—whether the Israeli Army, the U.S. Olympic Committee in its heyday, expanding young enterprises or established global corporations—are locked in the embrace of a potentially deadly paradox. This is because great strengths are inevitably the root of weakness. Organizations have a tendency to do what they best know how to do; they are, if you will, the ultimate conservatives. Couple this with the tendency of dedicated and energetic leadership to drive an organization to be still better at what it already does well, and we propel ourselves on a trajectory toward excess. Results may be positive and profitable in the short run, but excesses are fatal over time. The golden adage "Stick to your knitting" becomes an epitaph. This is because our fixation on "what is" obscures that other aggravating necessity of worrying about "what isn't" and "what might be."

Let me clarify. Organizations *do* need to drive themselves toward perfection. But the pursuit of operational excellence is often mistaken as an end in itself. It is an easy trap to fall into, since doing such things as pushing manufacturing quality toward perfection and achieving very high levels of customer satisfaction are extremely demanding tasks. But in a larger context, these ongoing tasks are the *means* of building muscle tone for future, unseen trials. Like calisthenics and scrimmages, they build intensity and discipline that *can* serve the cause of agility and staying power. Just as easily, a company's attributes become the objects of overweening pride and organizational narcissism. Of the corporations in the Fortune 500 rankings five years ago, 143 are missing today. (By comparison, in the twenty-five years, 1955 to 1980, only 238 companies dropped out.[1]) While it is by no means true that all of these companies foundered for the same reason, the foible common to most was that they took a good thing too far.

11

The statistics above underscore the discomforting fact that despite the vast arsenal of modern management techniques we don't do very well at keeping successful companies healthy. A second source of embarrassment is that we are unable to imitate successful organizations. This is especially frustrating because managers generally excel at emulating a winning formula. Companies reverse-engineer products and technology with relative ease. New advances in finance, marketing, and production are replicated with alacrity. But when the core essence of competitive advantage turns on *people* and *organization,* we are thwarted by an invisible barrier.[2] We may see clearly what we lack, but we can't bridge the gap. Examples abound. Burger King strives unsuccessfully to match the quality and disciplined service ethic of McDonald's. Rival banks seem consigned to a destiny of being weak imitators of Citicorp's pace of innovation and marketplace aggressiveness. We study companies such as 3M and Sony, yet few can match their sustained record of new product breakthroughs. We invest in training and team-building, modify the reward structure, and experiment with a variety of other devices—but somehow it doesn't quite take. Try as we might, a gap remains.

COMPLACENCY?

Conventional wisdom has it that as organizations grow large and successful, they grow fat, happy, and decadent. This research argues otherwise. True, at a distance, complacency seems to contribute to the downfall of many companies, but the problem for the executive who has to deal with the ever-present danger of stagnation in real time is that "complacency" is most apparent in hindsight. Insiders of the many companies that declined or disappeared this past decade rarely characterized themselves or top management as "complacent" while they were living the drama through. Most of these firms employed intelligent and dedicated executives, who were giving it their best. Only *after* decline was well under way and danger stalked the corridors did it become clear that they had been coasting on past success. Only in hindsight, in all of the random noise that existed at what later was regarded as the "critical" juncture, could we clearly discern those first weak signals that foretold the environment was changing. For those who lived in the swim of the situation as it unfolded, the company seemed on track: people were working hard, various signs of success marked the flow of events, and finances were strong.

TRANSFORMATION?

The incremental approach to change is effective when what you want is more of what you've already got. Historically, that has been sufficient because our advantages of plentiful resources, geographical isolation, and absence of serious global competition defined a league in which we competed with ourselves and everyone played by the same rules. Campaigns to become "more automated," "more productive," "more participative," "more dedicated to quality" made sense and, in aggregate, yielded some improvement. For over one hundred years we grew accustomed to improving things without having to alter the mindset upon which the improvements were predicated. It is not surprising that organizational theorists and managers who observed and practiced during this era came to regard the assumptions that undergird our success as fundamental truths that no longer warranted questioning and reexamination.

But when the competitive environment pushes an organization to its limits, the old mindset no longer holds. If we ignore this fact, we subject ourselves to the spinning wheel that prevails today. Our industrial landscape is littered not only with many failed attempts at change, but with many partially successful and mediocre attainments. No doubt there have been gains when measured against *our* prior standards of performance. But what is disheartening is how slowly we are closing the gap between ourselves and our ever-improving global competitors. While we get better, so do they. A *discontinuous* improvement in capability is needed, and that entails transformation.

The trouble with "transformation" is that it has been relegated to the questionable status of muddled, New Age thinking. In part, this is because we keep trying to apply the *tools* of transformation without a corresponding shift in our managerial *mindset*. From the vantage point of the old mindset, the "technology" of transformation is not that new. But when approached with a new way of thinking, systematic application of the right tools and techniques yields transformation. It's really not as mysterious as it sounds. As described in Chapters Five and Six, Ford is proof that this can take place.

MENTAL MAPS AND INQUIRY

The discussion above alludes to an inherent tendency of the human mind (and organizations) to perceive patterns: over time, these patterns form a mental infrastructure—or mindset. Scientists call it a *paradigm*. Danger arises when our mental maps cease to fit the territory. The problem with mindsets or paradigms is that we tend to see *through* them, and so the degree to which they filter our perception goes unrecognized. To counter this threat, individuals and organizations must build mechanisms (i.e., checks and balances) that cause them to question and update their mental maps. Let me underscore this. *The* essential activity for keeping our paradigm current is persistent questioning. I will use the term *inquiry*. Inquiry is the engine of vitality and self-renewal.

Much will be said in Chapters Two and Three about constructive contention. Contention fuels the "engine of inquiry," and is a cheap and abundant fuel. Yet contention carries a stigma: managers are uncomfortable with it, and it is often misconstrued as a sign of organizational ill health. This need not be the case. Internal differences can widen the spectrum of an organization's options by generating new points of view, by promoting disequilibrium and adaptation. There is, in fact, a well-known law of cybernetics—the law of requisite variety—which states that for any system to adapt to its external environment, its internal controls must incorporate variety. If one reduces variety inside, a system is unable to cope with variety outside.[3] The innovative organization must incorporate variety into its internal processes. This book suggests seven domains of contention as one way of mapping the tensions that stimulate questioning, experimentation, and variety so that they can be mined for adaptive purpose.

HYPER-MANAGEMENT

To summarize, this book has two basic aims. The first pertains to how we think, and the second prescribes actions that support a new way of thinking. With respect to the first objective, the paradox that confounds us is that successful organizations *must* build paradigms—and having done so, are inevitably imperiled by them. A central premise of this book is that the ultimate, and largely ignored, task of management is one of creating *and* breaking paradigms. The trouble is, 99 percent of managerial attention today is devoted to the techniques that squeeze more out of the existing paradigm—and it's killing us. Tools, techniques, and "how-to" recipes won't do the job without a higher order, or "hyper" concept, of management. Second, it is by no means enough to be mindful of these pitfalls, nor even to think about management differently, if our quest ends there. Forewarned is not forearmed. Thus our second task: to suggest explicit checks and balances that provoke inquiry and sustain vitality. This is to resist the inherent tendency toward overdetermination and closed-loop thinking. Applications of these prescriptions will be bolstered by extensive examples, out of the conviction that experience isn't always the best teacher—someone else's often is.

It is to these tasks that we now turn.

CHAPTER ONE

Unlocking the Mystery
of Self-Renewal

*In evolution, [the saying] "nothing fails like success" is
probably always right. A creature which has become perfectly adapted to its environment, an animal whose whole
capacity and vital force is concentrated and expanded in
succeeding here and now, has nothing left over with which
to respond to any radical change. Age by age, it becomes
more perfectly economical in the way its entire resources
meet exactly its current and customary opportunities. In the
end it can do all that is necessary to survive without any
conscious striving or unadapted movement. It can, therefore, beat all competitors in the special field; but equally,
should the field change, it must become extinct.*

ARNOLD TOYNBEE

Few of us have heard of Tycho Brahe. Yet as most books on the history of
science record, it was Brahe, in the sixteenth century, who was the first modern
astronomer—not Johann Kepler or Galileo Galilei. Brahe was the first to observe the stars systematically and to precisely record their nightly movements
across the sky.[1] Unfortunately, while Brahe amassed facts, he totally missed
the point of their meaning. An analyst of great discipline, he clung to the
prevailing theory of his day that the planets, sun, and stars circled the earth,
which his own observations increasingly showed to be wrong. It took thirty
years of accumulated frustration with these inconsistencies before Kepler,
Brahe's protégé, reexamined the evidence and confirmed Copernicus's radical
view of the universe that the planets orbited the sun.[2]

ORGANIZATIONAL SUCCESS

It has occurred to me that those of us who manage, consult with, and study organizations may be a lot like Tycho Brahe. We assume we know what's going on—yet empirical evidence suggests the contrary. If we stand back and look, the accumulating evidence compels us to acknowledge that we simply don't understand the forces that sustain organizational success. Consider the evidence:

Demise of Excellent Companies

In summer 1982, *In Search of Excellence,* by Thomas J. Peters and Robert H. Waterman, was published.[3] A runaway best-seller, the book sold more than five million copies and was on the *New York Times* best-seller list for over two years. It based its conclusions on a study of forty-three "excellent" companies, all of which for twenty years had demonstrated superiority over competitors as measured by six financial yardsticks;* each had been an industry leader in innovation and adaptability.

Only five years after the book's publication, two-thirds of the companies studied had slipped from the pinnacle. Some, such as Atari and Avon, were in serious trouble. Others, among them Wang and DuPont, no longer shine with the same luster. Of the original forty-three, only fourteen are, as of this writing, still regarded as "excellent." We can further assume that some of today's survivors will fall from grace. Others may regain their former stature. In every case we can be virtually certain that management was trying *very* hard to succeed. Why do such efforts so often come to naught? What can be done to improve our batting average?

We can, of course, learn from excellent companies, but *how* to learn from them is far more complicated than might first be supposed. Simply identifying attributes of success is like identifying attributes of people in excellent health during the age of the bubonic plague. A study of the "survivors" during the Middle Ages might have identified any number of spurious patterns: perhaps some drank only wine (or only water), were married (or celibate), were devout Catholics (or atheists). All of those patterns were foolishness, of course, yet hundreds of thousands of desperate citizens amassed like lemmings behind one credo or another in hopes of being spared.[4] Sound familiar? The true path of insight, of course, required a study of both the sick and the healthy. Painstaking effort was necessary to trace the plague to rat-borne fleas, the final link in the chain

---

* The six financial yardsticks: twenty-year averages of (1) compound asset growth, (2) compound equity growth, (3) ratio of market value to book value, (4) return on capital, (5) return on equity, and (6) return on sales.

FIG.1–1

Status of the 43 "Excellent" Companies Five Years Later*

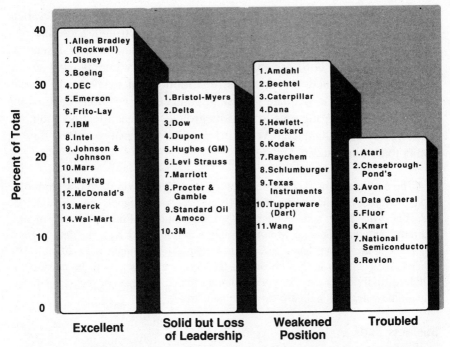

Percent of Total

Excellent
1. Allen Bradley (Rockwell)
2. Disney
3. Boeing
4. DEC
5. Emerson
6. Frito-Lay
7. IBM
8. Intel
9. Johnson & Johnson
10. Mars
11. Maytag
12. McDonald's
13. Merck
14. Wal-Mart

Solid but Loss of Leadership
1. Bristol-Myers
2. Delta
3. Dow
4. Dupont
5. Hughes (GM)
6. Levi Strauss
7. Marriott
8. Procter & Gamble
9. Standard Oil Amoco
10. 3M

Weakened Position
1. Amdahl
2. Bechtel
3. Caterpillar
4. Dana
5. Hewlett-Packard
6. Kodak
7. Raychem
8. Schlumberger
9. Texas Instruments
10. Tupperware (Dart)
11. Wang

Troubled
1. Atari
2. Chesebrough-Pond's
3. Avon
4. Data General
5. Fluor
6. Kmart
7. National Semiconductor
8. Revlon

* The 43 "excellent companies" were identified in *In Search of Excellence,* by Thomas J. Peters and Robert H. Waterman, published 1982.

communicating the illness to human beings. The painstaking and disciplined work that has largely eliminated this pestilence from our planet bears a message to those of us who manage or study organizations. We should expect no shortcuts.

Slippage of Industry Leaders

Another way of gauging how difficult it is to sustain organizational vitality (even when a company has tremendous resources, advantages of scale, and dominant market position) is to focus on major industries and trace the leading American company within each. Figure 1–2 depicts the trajectory of the industry leader in thirteen large nonregulated industries in the United States.[5] To avoid overstating the recent impact of global competition, let us take the twenty-year period 1962–1982, which straddles a tranquil decade and includes most of a turbulent one, but excludes the intense international competition of the eighties. (I avoided the eighties to sidestep arguments that our poor showing in global competition was the result of the dollar being overvalued during most of the decade, of ill-defined U.S. government trade policy, and so on.) At the end of this period, only two companies, IBM and Boeing, had held, or had seen gain in, their position in terms of market share and comparative advantage.* In eleven of the thirteen industries, the previous leader experienced a deterioration in position, and in most instances, was displaced by a U.S. or Japanese rival. Seemingly impregnable advantages such as production economies, distribution efficiencies, and market dominance proved inadequate to sustain competitive position. Each of the firms made diligent attempts to hold its ground, yet each lost position.

McKinsey consultant Tom Woodard provides this analysis of the flow of events that culminate in decline:

> The undisputed market and technology leader coasts on the momentum of past successes, failing to react strongly to the "weak signals" of impending decline. Analogies, none of them perfect, might include Pratt & Whitney in jet aircraft engines, General Motors in automobiles, and Xerox in plain paper copiers. One reason that successful management teams find it so difficult to heed weak signals is that no one in the organization *seems* to be coasting. Indeed, individuals may be working harder than ever, signs of progress punctuate the calendar, and cash flows remain strong.[6]

Business Fads

In the face of sagging fortunes, companies become notably more willing to experiment with new ideas. It might even be argued that an indicator of managerial panic is the consumption rate and shelf life of business fads. Over two dozen managerial techniques have waxed and waned since the 1950s. More interesting, half were spawned in the past five years.[7] The list reads like a Who's Who of business hype: Theory Z, Matrix, Managerial Grid, T Groups, Intrapreneurship, Demassing, and One-Minute Managing. To be sure, there are valid aspects to most of these ideas. What's wrong is that, overwhelmingly, companies apply them in a piecemeal fashion and shift from one to another too frequently. What is lacking is a grasp of the larger context in which they must be embedded. A marketing manager at a large Midwestern equipment manufacturer captures the sentiment: "In the past eighteen months, we have heard that profit is

---

* Both IBM and Boeing have since lost ground.

FIG. 1–2

Market Share and Comparative Advantage: Trends in Thirteen Key Industries, 1962–1982

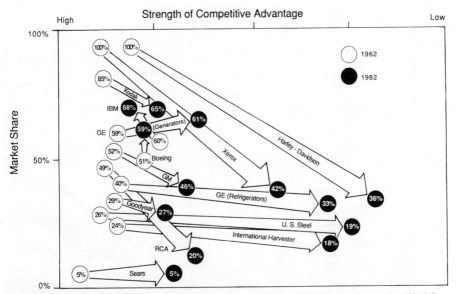

Markets defined as follows: Xerox: plain paper copiers; Harley-Davidson: motorcycles, Kodak: photographic film; IBM: mainframe computers; GE (General Electric)₁: generators; GE₂: electrical appliances (refrigerators); GM: passenger cars; Boeing: commercial widebody jet aircraft; RCA: color TVs; Goodyear: OEM ties; U.S. Steel: finished steel; International Harvester: farm tractors; Sears: mass-market retailing.

more important than revenue, quality is more important than profit, that people are more important than profit, that customers are more important than our people, that big customers are more important than our small customers, and that growth is the key to our success. No wonder our performance is inconsistent."[8]

Managerial ideas began to acquire the velocity of fads after World War II. The ascendance of professional management diminished reliance on up-from-the-ranks managerial wisdom developed and passed on within an industry or a company. The very notion of "professional management" rests upon the premise that a set of generic concepts underlies managerial activity anywhere. Such presumed universal concepts lend themselves to mass marketing techniques; new ideas can thus be rapidly disseminated. In America, "managerial techniques" are a packaged goods industry. One unintended consequence of this situation is that it has fostered superficiality.[9] It has become professionally legitimate in the United States to accept and utilize

FIG. 1–3

Ebbs, Flows, and Residual Impact
of Business Fads, 1950–1988*

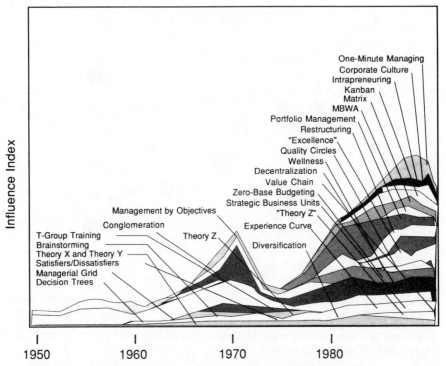

* Curves shown are for illustrative purposes. Empirical foundation of chart based upon frequency of citations in the literature. However, increased interest in business topics in the past
decade tends to exaggerate amplitude of recent fads when compared to earlier decades. As a
result, the author has modified curves to best reflect relative significance of trends over entire
period.

ideas without an in-depth grasp of their underlying foundation, and without
the commitment necessary to sustain them.

Not surprisingly, ideas acquired with ease are discarded with ease. Fads
ebb, flow—and even change by 180 degrees. Business journalist John Byrne
observes: "Business fads have always been with us. What's different—and
alarming—today is the sudden rise and fall of so many conflicting fads and
how they influence the modern manager."[10] Interestingly, fads are largely
an American phenomenon. While faddish books sell abroad, they are taken
as grist for thought, not as prescriptions to be acted upon. In the rare
instances in which ideas such as Deming's notions of "statistical quality

control'' and ''quality circles'' stimulate serious consideration, as has been the case in Japan, they are adopted as an enduring way of doing business.* Meanwhile, in the United States, 75 percent of all quality circles begun with enthusiasm in 1982 had been discontinued by 1986.[11]

All of this suggests that a sequence unfolds as a company starts to falter. These patterns are true for companies big and small. During successful years, managers perfect the formula that made their achievements possible. If the firm begins to lose momentum, efforts are made to reinvigorate the slackening pace—usually based on what has worked in the past. That's what the ''excellent companies'' and industry leaders did. When this proves insufficient, gimmicks are introduced. In most instances, these have little lasting impact.

What distinguishes a fad or gimmick from earnest experimentation? The acid test isn't whether efforts to implement a new idea are initially successful. The bedrock issue is commitment and follow-up, *whether or not* the initial attempt is a success *or* a failure. Our tendency, however, is to try things out capriciously. When a new idea fails, we give up instead of investigating the causes of failure and addressing them systematically. Under the simplistic and misapplied principle that ''experimentation is good for organizations,'' many otherwise thoughtful executives become management gimmick junkies.[12]

Owing to the inadequacy of our understanding as to what sustains success, we are unable to help organizations sustain performance with any reliability. This is evident when we take stock of how poorly our assessments and predictions stack up with results. Harvard's Paul Lawrence, a well-known organizational theorist and one of the most savvy judges of corporate performance, devoted a chapter to the automotive industry in *Renewing American Industry* (written in 1983 with historian Davis Dyer). He concludes with a paragraph on General Motors:

> In part, GM owes its relatively steady performance to advantage of size . . . But GM was also quicker to recognize a changing environment and to adapt to a long-term strategy which better balances innovation and efficiency. Moreover, GM (by both recognizing differences among units and integrating them to overall corporate strategy) adapted project centers at the managerial level (i.e., to design the J-car, and so on) and quality of work life (QWL) programs for hourly workers. As a result, GM is the only American auto company entering the 1980s with much reason for optimism.''[13]

---

* W. Edward Deming first gained notoriety in Japan in the 1950s introducing statistical tools to improve quality in the production process. ''Quality circles'' pertains to small groups of employees who engage in quality improvement activities.

In fact, General Motors stalled out through much of the eighties and is only now showing some signs of renewed life. Massive recentralization led to each of its major divisions (Chevrolet, Buick, Oldsmobile, and Cadillac) converging on near-identical styling of their respective cars. Persistent focus on financial results sacrificed quality and manufacturing excellence. An over-ambitious modernization strategy cost, in excess of $60 billion (enough to acquire Nissan and Honda), has resulted in significant overcapitalization for GM in a period of massive global overcapacity.[14]

Even today's most careful students of organizations will readily admit that they lack adequate models to predict sustained corporate success. Recall how widely we celebrated such New Age cultures as People Express, Atari, and Rolm. Ardent supporters included academics, consultants, business journalists, and seasoned executives. Our former enthusiasm becomes a source of embarrassment when we hold ourselves accountable for predictive accuracy.[15]

It is no longer permissible to dismiss these reversals lightly, acknowledging once again that "management is an art," and excusing ignorance by giving it another name. The sobering truth is that our theories, models, and conventional wisdom combined appear no better at predicting an organization's ability to sustain itself than if we were to rely on random chance.

Costly Distractions

The grim picture of declining fortunes and failing fads presented thus far needs to be placed in a larger context. American corporations are emerging from a decade that business historians may well regard as one of the most trying in our industrial history. The industrial democracies have matched us as competitive equals. Equally significant, the past few decades have imposed a good number of burdens on corporations, burdens that have exacted a cost—both fiscal and psychological. These include:

1. Adjusting to high inflation—then disinflation.
2. Coping with high interest rates and high costs of capital.
3. Funding pension programs through ERISA; this entailed a significant redirection of cash flow.
4. Meeting OSHA and environmental standards—a costly burden in terms of both dollars and management energy in some industries.
5. Stringent tightening of accounting standards affecting disclosure, how funds are utilized, and the manner in which firms portray their future prospects.
6. Dramatic increases in insurance rates, and greater financial exposure through litigation.
7. Roller coaster stock prices.

8. Defensive maneuvers against hostile takeovers, driving increased borrowing, leveraged buyouts, and other short-term behavior that reduces resilience against competitive threats.

The list goes on and on. It would be foolish to argue that all of these trends have peaked, or that challenges will not arise in the decade ahead. Let us assume, for purposes of discussion, that the decade of the nineties will at least begin with a period of less traumatic change. We see a small but growing number of U.S. firms holding their own against foreign (particularly Japanese) competitors. The global economic environment seems relatively stable. There are increasing examples of management and unions working together in a less adversarial, more cooperative fashion—particularly in industries threatened with extinction.

One thing is clear. In crude, quantitative terms, the United States has an industrial infrastructure that should be unbeatable. America has fifteen million companies (no other nation comes close) and 5.5 million scientists and engineers (two times the number in Japan), and we have won more Nobel prizes than the rest of the world together. We spend twice as much on R&D as Germany and Japan combined. We are no longer a high-cost production nation (over half or our trade deficit comes from countries that pay their workers higher wages than we do).[16]

The decade of the nineties might be one of reconstruction and regeneration. If we are to seize the moment, we need organizations capable of exploiting our industrial base and mobilizing their employees effectively. Above all, once initial success is achieved, we need to sustain it; exploring the mechanisms for doing so is the central aim of the pages that follow.

FIRST STEPS IN SEARCH OF A NEW MINDSET

The thrust of this exploration of mechanisms that sustain success begins with four key ideas. First, our current managerial mindset (or paradigm) is inadequate. We have no basis whatsoever for our confidence that we know how to manage a corporation in a fashion that sustains its vitality and that engenders adaptation.

Second, in the face of this situation, a good place to start is by identifying the factors that drive stagnation and renewal in organizations. I identify four, which, for brevity's sake, I term *fit, split, contend,* and *transcend.*

1. *Fit* pertains to an organization's internal consistency (unity).
2. *Split* describes a variety of techniques for breaking a bigger organization into

BOX 1–1.

Fit/Split/Contend/Transcend

Fit   Refers to the consistencies and coherence of an organization. When fit is absent, organizational life can be confusing. For example, a new strategic thrust may direct us to improve customer service, yet (1) the organizational chart relegates customer service to a weak and undermanned staff function, (2) the reward systems drive exclusively for profitability and cost containment, (3) the personnel department regularly utilizes this function for cast-offs from other departments, and so on. This is an example of poor fit. When the gears engage and all of these elements mesh, fit is attained.[17]

Split   In contrast to fit, split pertains to a variety of techniques used to sustain autonomy and diversity. Common among such vehicles are decentralized profit centers and stand-alone subsidiaries. Typically, these entities are assigned responsibility for specialized products and markets outside the parent company's mainstream. Other types of split rely less on structure, and more on human networks. Multi-functional task forces and new venture teams are examples. Many corporations today utilize a variety of such approaches to build special capabilities that a customer or a particular technology demands.[18]

Contend   Draws attention to the presence and value of constructive conflict. There are some tensions in organizations that should *never* be resolved once and for all (such as between cost control and quality, or between manufacturing efficiency and customer service). The functional disciplines that advocate these points of view rub up against one another and generate debate. Contention across these boundaries is inescapable. Moreover, it can be productive. We are almost always better served when conflict is surfaced and channeled, not suppressed. The contend factor pertains to this management task.[19]

Transcend   An approach toward management that can cope with the complexity entailed in orchestrating fit, split, and contend. This is not just an incremental increase in the difficulty of the management task. It requires a different mindset. It looks to the tension (or dynamic synthesis) between contradictory opposites as the engine of self-renewal. It is predicated on the notion that disequilibrium is a better strategy for adaptation and survival than order and equilibrium.[20]

smaller units and providing them with a stronger sense of ownership and identity (plurality).

3. *Contend* refers to a management process that harnesses (rather than suppresses) the contradictions that are inevitable by-products of organizations (duality).

4. *Transcend* alerts us to the higher order of complexity that *successfully* managing the renewal process entails (vitality).

For more detailed definitions, see Box 1–1. More will be said about these factors shortly.

Third, much more needs to be said about the role of conflict in organizations. Many readers are familiar with the idea of constructive conflict, but we remain in the Dark Ages in grasping the value of contention, the specific domains in which it arises, and how it can be constructively harnessed.* Contention provides a fuel for self-renewal.

Fourth, and perhaps most significant, we will see that the reconciliation of fit, split, and contend factors contains a paradox, and that a new, higher-order (I use the term *transcendent*) approach to management is necessary to juggle them effectively. The challenge arises in coping with the *relatedness* of fit, split, and contend. As we strive to relate them to one another in a coherent fashion, we grapple with a higher order of complexity.[21] This leads again to our managerial mindset, or "paradigm." It lays the foundation for exploring the limitations of the old, and for charting the frontiers of the new.

Management must contain the energy that fit, split and contend produce. The idea is analogous to the shift from conventional turbine engines to atomic reactors; more was involved than a change of fuel. Almost every element in the containment housing had to be altered. In the same vein, juggling fit, split, and contend so overloads conventional methods of management, that "meltdown" is likely to occur. An example might help.

HONDA'S "MAGIC"

Honda Motor Company is arguably the best-managed company in the world.[22] Like any organization, it could stumble, but as of this writing, it defies the organizational equivalent of the law of gravity by doing all things well and achieving profit margins that rivals envy. It is a low-cost producer (second only to Toyota, which is three times its size),[23] it is a leading innovator in the automotive and motorcycle fields,[24] its quality is rated tops

---

* One of the best resources on contention management is The Bay Group of San Raphael, California.

(superior to Mercedes for three years running),[25] and its sales and marketing of both automobiles and motorcycles rank with the very best in these respective industries.[26] Subsequent chapters will delve into these mysteries in greater depth, based on observation of Honda over the past ten years. But even the most cursory acquaintance with this company leads the visitor to suspect that they are marching to a different drum—a different mindset, or paradigm, to use our nomenclature. On one hand, Honda is a very coherent organization. Its set of overarching values, called The Honda Way, influences day to day decisions on the shop floor. Honda is buttoned down in other ways. Costs are tightly controlled, and efficiency and productivity are pursued relentlessly. Honda sustains its advantage through research, engineering, and manufacturing. These priorities are meticulously supported by every leverage point available—how the company is organized, how employees are selected, trained, and rewarded, and so on.[27] In short, Honda has a lot of fit.

Yet early in Honda's evolution its founders worried about too much fit.[28] Their solution was to break the company apart in a far more radical fashion than had ever occurred in their industry. R&D and Engineering were split as separate companies. While Honda Motor Company (with sales and manufacturing responsibility) is the parent, and primary customer, each of the three companies has its distinct identity and organizational character. Why did Honda decentralize to such an extreme? Because, in Honda's view, too much fit breeds complacency. The tension between these three companies, each highly independent, yet each *inter*dependent, was the best way of arresting decay.

Not surprisingly, Honda's extraordinary degree of decentralization generates a lot of internal heat. To cope with the conflict, Honda dedicated itself to explicitly surfacing and managing contention in a constructive way.[29] Honda simmers with contention by holding sessions in which subordinates can openly (but politely) question bosses and challenge the status quo. This is not an empty ritual but a vital force in keeping Honda on its toes. It sustains a restless, self-questioning atmosphere that one expects to see in new ventures—yet Honda is into its fourth generation of management. Its founders retired in 1970.

Honda embraces contradictions that one might expect would blow the company apart: (1) strong values and tightly disciplined management control systems (i.e., fit), (2) proud and highly independent companies that must nonetheless produce a single, highly integrated automobile (i.e., split), and (3) a contention-management system that facilitates, rather than suppresses, conflict (i.e., contend). Yet Honda's cultural fabric is strong enough to handle the stress without tearing. Here is where the mysterious "transcendent" element enters the equation. Honda thrives within this intense field by adopting a different paradigm, or mindset. Honda managers have a different notion of what a healthy organization feels like, and they focus on different variables. Honda executives not only live with the paradox of these contradictions, but consciously and explicitly embrace it as an operational tool of self-renewal.[30]

THE NEW MINDSET

The Honda example draws us deeper into assessing the limitations of an old mindset, and puzzling over what a radical new mindset might contain. The contrasting notions of scientific management (as set forth by Frederick Taylor early in this century) and the modern thinking underlying Japanese management amplify this point. Taylor once wrote:

> Hardly a competent workman can be found who does not devote a considerable amount of time to studying just how slowly he can work and still convince his employer that he is going at a good pace. Under our system a worker is told just what he is to do and how he is to do it. Any improvement he makes upon the orders given to him is fatal to his success.[31]

Compare Taylor's words, which still have wide application today, with those of Konosuke Matsushita—founder and, until his death, leader of one of Japan's largest firms, Matsushita Electric Ltd.—and we begin to discern the hidden mindset:

> We are going to win and the industrial West is going to lose out; there's not much you can do about it because the reasons for your failure are within yourselves. Your firms are built on the Taylor model. Even worse, so are your heads. With your bosses doing the thinking while the workers wield the screwdrivers, you're convinced deep down that this is the right way to run a business. For you the essence of management is getting the ideas out of the heads of the bosses and into the hands of labor.
>
> We are beyond your mindset. Business, we know, is now so complex and difficult, the survival of firms so hazardous in an environment increasingly unpredictable, competitive and fraught with danger, that their continued existence depends on the day-to-day mobilization of every ounce of intelligence.[32]

Most people think a "managerial mindset" is easy to spot. But mindsets are more perceptual than tangible. The filters through which we perceive are seldom, if ever, explicit. Our mindset is composed of unquestioned, tacit understandings, transmitted by "folklore" and "war stories"—and internalized unknowingly through behaviors that surround us day to day.

Our mindset plays a role in shaping what we pay attention to, and what we ignore. Consider the evidence presented in the opening paragraphs of this chapter. Our lack of success in sustaining the vitality of corporations has been there to see all along, but we ignore it, rarely discussing or acknowledging this reality. For a pragmatic people, this is a remarkable state of affairs. Then again, perhaps our problem is pragmatism taken to extremes. If something doesn't work immediately, we abandon it for fear of having waited too long. Our pragmatism is too tactical and too narrow. We don't confront the deeper issues squarely.

Consider the books that have been written about what successful companies do. Contemplate the thousands of visits by executives to leading firms in Japan, Europe, and within the United States. Notwithstanding the sincerity of these efforts, the commitments made, the diligent follow-up on lessons learned, a near-universal outcome of these endeavors is that not much happens. We readily borrow technology, reverse-engineer products, and copy manufacturing processes, but when that mysterious "software" that drives superior performance is the object of our quest, mastery always seems to escape us. Part of the problem is that American executives don't like to tangle with the complex interdependencies that managing the "software" entails. We prefer small, digestible bites.

It is useful as we proceed to have a few images in mind as to the nature of the challenge we face. We are separated from the "secrets" of outstanding organizations by an invisible barrier, the "old mindset." Think of it as a very clear pane of glass—so clear that we cannot discern that we are separated from the phenomenon we observe. The visitor to Honda "sees" employee involvement, quality circles, effective teamwork, constructive handling of contention, excellent service, productivity, and so forth. On the face of it, there is not much that is new, but the visitor is taking still photographs—observations made on the day of the tour. He would be better served using a movie camera to capture, as in time-lapse photography, how gradually, day by day, the things observed in his first visit evolved into better, faster, more perfected versions. Time-sequenced photography would expose the continual learning that is occurring. Continual learning is synonymous with self-renewal. By a process of deduction, one comes to suspect that there is an invisible force at work. That "invisible" force is a managerial mindset that, among other things, ignites a lot of little fires, and then harnesses their thermal energy.

As will be discussed in the final chapter of this book, the subtle but distinct quality of the survivors is that their organizations become *engines of inquiry*. Yes, they solve problems, but what they do best is harness the forces of organization so that they constantly and obsessively question their modus operandi. It is this continual questioning that generates the next paradigm . . . and the next . . . and the next.

SUBTLE CONTRADICTIONS: IBM

A close look at IBM takes us one step beyond the earlier Honda example in revealing a cluster of subtle contradictions.

1. IBM has sustained itself in a fast-changing industry, and has proven more adaptive than any other company of its size in this century.[33] A great deal of tension, experimentation, and self-questioning drives this behavior. Yet IBM also has a reputation for "white shirts and company songs"; in other words, continuity and consistency.[34]
2. IBM fusses over its customer service while struggling to be the low-cost producer in the industry.
3. Although IBM appears to be a large, monolithic entity, its independent divisions compete for customers and resources. IBM pioneered the notion of "independent business units," the most successful of which is its personal-computer subsidiary, Entry Systems. Led by maverick Don Estridge, this unit defied its parent's policies and norms, and generated a lot of conflict. It also delivered a 63-percent market share.[35]
4. IBM blends job security and good working conditions with relatively hardball personnel policies, such as sending errant managers off to "Siberia" or to the "penalty box." ("Siberia" entails long-term purgatory in obscure, dead-end positions from which some executives do not return. The "penalty box" entails a short-term—six months to two years—assignment out of the mainstream, during which ruffled feathers smooth out and peccadillos are forgotten.)[36] The firm has socialized its professionals to handle intense cross-examinations in their briefings of senior managers (called *probing* at IBM).[37] An inordinately high degree of socialization enables IBM to command a great many sacrifices from its employees. For example, IBMers endure an extraordinary number of moves and family dislocations (second only to the U.S. Army). Between 1986 and 1988, IBM downsized its workforce by 16,200 through voluntary programs. An additional 45,000 employees were retrained; 21,000 of these were relocated—some to lesser-paying jobs. Yet morale and commitment to IBM remain high.[38]

5. IBM promotes openness in communication, but expects a great deal of self-censorship. There are powerful strictures against airing dirty linen with outsiders.

The points enumerated above suggest that Big Blue has many of the attributes of a tough, hardball company, but it is precisely because IBM has mastered hardball that it can play softball. We are only misled by the high visibility given to its endearing softer qualities if we fail to recognize the constructive tension between IBM's human resource policies and its attention to basic business fundamentals.

As was true at Honda, IBM's managerial approach somehow embraces the conflicting demands of fit (emphasis on uniform values, coherence of systems and strategy), split (rivalry among divisions, and the creation of independent business units), and an abundance of contention (customer versus cost, valuing employee dignity versus disciplined approaches to the business and demands of employee sacrifice).

If we delve more deeply into IBM, we begin to discern the managerial mindset that undergirds its approach. First, IBM does not rely exclusively on the hard-edged tools of conventional management—namely, strategy, organizational structure, and systems. To be sure, these are not ignored, but we note how aggressively IBM employs the softer forms of control—such as its emphasis on values, which prevents its strong, bottom-line orientation from sacrificing its commitment to employees. In a similar vein, IBM's socialization process is meticulously tuned to replicate its culture across successive generations. IBM has a unique style of managing, selling, handling contention—and thinking.

Second, IBM avoids extremes. Along each of the three coordinates (fit, split, and contend), IBM extracts a great deal of leverage—but it never takes one dimension to excess. While there is a lot of fit, for example, most employees view IBM's protocols as fostering a common "grammar" of "the way we do things" throughout a global enterprise, not rigid doctrines that prevent taking reasonable actions. There are independent business units, but somehow they are reined in just as they threaten to spin out of orbit. There is a lot of constructive contention, but one seldom hears of destructive turmoil and internecine strife.

Third, IBM blends control with a climate that tolerates individual initiative.[39] IBM attracts and retains first-rate employees because it gives them a great deal of responsibility. IBM management does *not*, in Mr. Matsushita's words, "do the thinking while workers wield the screwdrivers." Skeptics may discount this, but most IBMers steadfastly insist that opportunity for individual initiative exists—no small feat given the size and complexity of this global company of some 400,000 employees. Clearly, a global corporation is bound to be bureaucratic in many respects, but IBM strives to generate a tension between its rules and routines, and a model of management that generates employee initiative through empowerment and through rewards tied to performance. People who make waves and spark contention (provided they do it in IBM style) are regarded as assets, not liabilities.[40]

This is not to say that IBM is not hierarchical and autocratic. Like all companies, its managers seek to reduce problems to core causes and solve them. But in a day-to-day practice, one sees an emphasis on relationships, networks, and interpersonal skill. IBM's style of management is more typically as coach and facilitator than as doer and heroic decision maker. As high a priority as IBM places on getting things done, the company reveals a remarkable tolerance of "contradiction."[41] Instead of solving problems at all costs, IBM often engages in paradoxical activities (e.g., caring personnel policies versus demanding expectations and discipline) that solve the problem in due course.

IBM is far from perfection, as its executives would readily testify. (In fact, in recent years it has wrestled mightily with its size and institutional metabolism.)[42] Nonetheless, it generates many paradoxical pressures for self-renewal, which sets it apart from most conventional firms. While not always perfect in practice, IBM, like Honda, appears to have established a different context, in which a new "species" of management has evolved.

These contextual shifts, as summarized in Table 1-1, suggest the managerial challenges with which the new mindset must cope.[43] While no individual trend is earthshaking, the aggregate impact of the whole cluster imposes more of a burden than our traditional approach to management can bear. The old focuses on managerial "hardware" (specific techniques and financial objectives); the new encompasses "software" (restlessness and creative tension). It is not that the "hardware" is unimportant, but that it is insufficient. This relationship between the old and new can be likened to the Mobius strip (a strip of paper twisted 180 degrees before its two ends are joined). At first glance we think of a Mobius strip as "two-sided," but as we trace one side it becomes the other. It isn't one versus the other, it's "holistic." For example, in the 1960s Honda "planned" to enter the U.S. market, was highly "opportunistic" once there, then reverted to careful planning again to expand in the U.S. once the initial beachhead was secured. The critical point isn't to leave the old mindset behind entirely, but to realize that excessive reliance upon the old mindset causes us to fall short of meeting the challenges that are implied in the new situation.

TABLE 1–1.

Contextual Shifts in Management

From Exclusive Reliance On	To Include As Well
Organizations as "machines"; emphasis on concrete strategy, structure, and systems	→ Organizations as organisms; emphasis on the "soft" dimensions—style, staff, and shared values
Hierarchical model; step-by-step problem solving	→ Network model; parallel nodes of intelligence which surround problems until eliminated
Fit to ensure consistency	→ Fit, split, and effective contention management
Managers think; workers do what they're told	→ Managers as "facilitators"; workers empowered to initiate improvements and change
Military model	→ Commitment model
Emphasis on "vertical tasks" within functional units	→ Emphasis on "horizontal tasks"; hand-offs and collaboration across units
"Content"; specific tools and techniques	→ "Process"; holistic synthesis of techniques
Putting matters to rest; "solving the problem at all costs"	→ Sustaining restlessness; "avoiding overkill while solving the problem in due course"
Resolving tension	→ Maintaining a constructive level of tension
"Truth" based on fundamental laws and principles	→ Approximations of reality; coexisting with ambiguity and paradox

FROM *EITHER/OR* TO *AND/ALSO*

In 1960, Douglas McGregor used the terms *Theory X* and *Theory Y* to highlight the contrasting assumptions underlying autocratic versus participative styles of management. Seven years later, having seen executives regard his theories in either/or terms, McGregor introduced Theory Z to encourage executives to embrace the paradox reconciling the X and Y opposites.[44] Theory Z, however, was soon forgotten (so much so that when UCLA's William Ouchi introduced Theory Z as an archetype of pseudo-Japanese management, few, including Ouchi, were aware that the term had been used before).[45] The extent to which McGregor's ideas have been misapplied and misunderstood lies in the well-worn grooves of our minds. It is almost impossible to think certain thoughts because our minds haven't been trained to work that way. We continue to polarize choice in terms of Theory X *or* Theory Y because we are wedded to a simpler intellectual framework. We can't readily conceive of things in and/also terms.

An example might help. At the dinner table, some of us are able to say we've had enough before our appetite is satisfied. Experience tells us we've had enough to eat, even though our body hasn't caught up yet, and still feels hungry. It's counterintuitive. We start working on the offsetting activity (i.e., remaining a little bit hungry) *before* we've accomplished the initial objective of getting full. While such behavior is smart, it doesn't feel good. We never experience the momentary pleasure of feeling full because we know that in twenty minutes we'll feel like someone in an Alka-Seltzer commercial if we do.[46]

DON'T CALL IT "BALANCE"

At this juncture it might appear that what we're seeking is a "balance" between opposites, as between Theories X and Y, or between the old and new mindsets. However, in discussing these ideas with managers, one discovers that the term *balance* creates a great deal of confusion. For Westerners, balance means equilibrium. Of course, from a purely rational standpoint, one *can* have dynamic forms of balance (such as unstable equilibrium), but our associations with the term *balance* evoke images of rest and stability, not tension and instability.

The problem, from a managerial point of view, is that if you want to stay in balance, you need to live out of balance. McGregor's Theory Z isn't a static compromise between Theory X and Y. Rather, it entails being *both* X and Y over time. That's one reason balance is so difficult to see when you look for it. You can't capture it in a snapshot—it requires a movie camera. In the pages that follow, whenever possible I will use such terminology as *orchestrating tension* and *harnessing contending opposites* to signal the dynamic relationship between opposites that the new mindset requires.

This leads to a final point. A major objective of this book is to challenge managers to think at a higher level of intellectual complexity. That, in the last analysis, is what the new managerial mindset entails. The necessity for a mindset shift applies whether you manage an organization of 200 people, or of 200,000. Problems of self-renewal confront us, and their remedies are complex *regardless* of an organization's size.

The point here is not that American executives aren't smart and analytical. Rather, our minds aren't accustomed to dealing with paradoxical relationships. Compounding the problem, a great deal of what has been written for managers recently is wrong-minded in so far as it demands *less,* rather than more, of our thought processes. For example, the thrust of some recent literature has called upon managers to be more "passionate" and "obsessive" with respect to customers, quality, and so forth.[47] It seems difficult to quarrel with such aims. Indeed, if such terminology only heightens managerial intensity and commitment, there can be no argument, but passionate and obsessive behavior is often single-minded behavior—seeing the world in either/or terms, and going after the "either" or the "or" with a vengeance. Passion and obsession frequently degenerate into simplistic formulae; e.g., acronyms such as KISS (Keep it simple, stupid).[48] This book advocates wisdom and coolness at a higher level of complexity. The pages that follow ask executives to make decisions of the moment that "feel" wrong, but that are ultimately right. This requires discipline—a discipline against the excesses of passion.

This book will elaborate on the themes sketched briefly above. Chapter Two focuses on the first two factors—fit and split. Chapter Three identifies the specific vectors of contention, and develops a context for further thinking about the new mindset. Chapter Four takes on the very important matter of where our traditional managerial mindset comes from. Only as we come to see the way in which our biases are hidden everywhere among our foundational beliefs are we apt to truly internalize that our way of thinking *really* has to change. Without an alteration in mindset, the full challenge of self-renewal will not be met.

The second section of the book, Chapters Five and Six (Ford), Seven (General Electric), and Eight (Citicorp and Hewlett-Packard), details how several very different companies struggle with the task of renewal. None is offered as a textbook solution. In fact, throughout this book, the underlying assumption is that there are no great companies insofar as "great" implies a lasting state of attainment. There are, however, companies that, with varying degrees of success, struggle mightily to sustain their vitality and to adapt appropriately to competitive challenges.

The third, and concluding, section of the book turns to the question of "how to do it." The contrast of Honda Motor Company and General Motors provides a provocative juxtaposition and reveals the benefits and hazards of the techniques proposed here. The objective of Chapter Nine is to illuminate the nuances of "social engineering"—harnessing values, attitudes, and behavior to fine-tune organizational performance. Yet, as we see from this discussion, Honda and General Motors' ability to grow and sustain vitality is tied closely to the vitality of their leadership. The concluding chapter turns to the issue of leadership and the shifts in mindset at the personal level that are required to meet the challenge that these ideas entail.

CHAPTER TWO

The Fit/Split Paradox

STAGNATION AND RENEWAL

The past ten years have provided me with the opportunity to study, and in several instances, consult extensively with, the top management of a dozen of America's largest companies. The list includes AT&T, GE, GM, Ford, IBM, Apple, Chrysler, Coca-Cola, Hewlett-Packard, American Medical International (the third largest for-profit health care company), HEB Stores (the nation's twelfth largest supermarket chain), The New York Times, Marriott, Intel, General Motors, McKinsey (the consulting firm), British Petroleum and J. P. Morgan Bank. In addition, having a long-standing interest in Japan, I have engaged in research at Honda, Mazda, Sony, and Matsushita.

There was a quality common to all of the firms in the study. Each had a tradition of success. Yet each was struggling with the task of revitalization. The challenge in each case was for management to capitalize on their market position and reinvigorate their institution. The unseen hindrances were subtle, underlying beliefs about management, closed-loop organizational habits, and, in some instances, an appetite for quick fixes. In Chrysler's case, with urgency self-evident, it was imperative that it unshackle itself from the past. For Coca-Cola, the challenge was more subtle because Pepsi's encroachment occurred gradually. In the instances of General Electric, Hewlett-Packard, and Marriott, the competitive threats were not life-threatening, but there was evidence of each institution drifting off target, looking too much inward and losing competitiveness, or being far too internally oriented. Studying the predicament of top management in each of the latter three examples, I participated in, and observed, success and failure in the task of revitalization.

The twenty-two previously mentioned companies provided extensive interview opportunities and permitted me to observe the cycle of stagnation and renewal over many months—often over years. In many instances, circumstances permitted exposure to behind-the-scenes management issues not generally visible. As a means of broadening reach, a second, and much larger, sample of eighty-eight firms was tracked over the past five years.* (See Box 2–1.) This effort relied primarily on a literature review and structured interviews of managers at each of these companies.

Finally, this work has been deeply influenced by my prior research on Japanese management. The original efforts, 1972–1978, entailed an in-depth study of fourteen Japanese firms with major facilities in the United States. Each was paired with a closely matched (and high performing) American competitor. This research shed considerable light on the management practices of Japanese firms, and on the ways in which they exported their practices to their facilities here. This work culminated with the book *The Art of Japanese Management,* written with Anthony Athos. The central thrust of this work was to identify the practices and subtle assumptions that characterize Japanese management, and to explore their relevance to the West.[1]

As noted earlier, this book is based on thousands of hours of interviews and observation. Interviews focused broadly on the competitive environment, on the organizations' purposes and internal functioning, and on the process through which continuous improvement was attained. The most difficult aspect of the work emerged when I began to focus on the important domains of contention, whether, and how, conflict served the cause of renewal and, most difficult of all, how organizations dealt with contention within their own ranks. Organizations often conceal or avoid conflicts. Fine-grained questioning and observation was necessary to penetrate the veil.

THE SEVEN S FRAMEWORK REVISITED

I was assisted in these interviews by the Seven S Framework.† The framework (see Figure 2–1) is nothing more than seven important categories that managers pay attention to—strategy, structure, systems, style and shared values, skills (an organization's distinctive competence) and people (to

---

* The firms listed were not selected to be representative of U.S. industry. Rather, the bias was toward "the action"—in particular, toward companies reported to be doing extremely well or very poorly.

† I had a hand in developing this model as a consulting tool for the firm McKinsey & Co. in 1979—along with Anthony Athos, then at Harvard Business School, and Robert Waterman and Tom Peters, both then at McKinsey.

BOX 2–1.

Research Base

A. Adidas
  Allen Bradley
  AMD
  Amdahl
  Amoco
  Anheuser-Busch
  Apple*
  Atari*
  AT&T*
B. Bank of America*
  Bechtel
  Black & Decker
  Boeing
  Bristol-Myers
  British Leyland
  British Steel
  Bulova
  Burroughs

F. Fairchild
  Federal Express*
  Firestone/Michelin
  Fluor
  Ford*
  Frito-Lay*
G. Genentech
  General Electric*
  General Foods*
  General Motors*
  Gerber
  Goldman, Sachs*
  Goodyear
H. Hallmark
  Harley-Davidson
  Harvard Business
    School*
  Head Ski/Prince

M. Macy's*
  Marriott*
  Mars
  Martin Marietta*
  Mary Kay
  Matsushita*
  Maytag
  Mazda*
  McDonald's*
  McDonnell Douglas
  McKinsey*
  Merck
  Merrill Lynch
  Microsoft
  Miller Lite
  J.P. Morgan*
  Motorola
N. National Semiconductor

S. Sainsbury's*
  Schlumberger
  Sears
  Selectron
  Shearson Lehman
  Sony*
  Sun Microsystems*
  Supermarkets (HEB*,
    Safeway)
  Syntex*
T. Tandem
  Tandy
  Texas Instruments
  Time Warner
  Timken
  Toyota*
  Toys "R" Us

C. Campbell Soup
Canon
Chesebrough Pond's
Chrysler*
Coca-Cola*
Continental Illinois Bank
Control Data
Cummins Diesel

D. Dana
Dart & Kraft
Data General
DEC*
Delta
Disney
Dow
Dun & Bradstreet
DuPont

E. EDS*
Emerson Electric
Esprit
Exxon

Hewlett-Packard*
Hilton
Hitachi
Honda*
Howard Johnson
Hughes
EF Hutton
Hyatt
Hyundai

I. IBM*
Indian Head Mills
Intel*
International Harvester
ITT*

J. Johnson & Johnson
Joseph Magnin

K. Kentucky Fried Chicken
K mart
Kodak
Kyowa Hakku

L. Levi Strauss
Lockheed
Lucasfilm*

NCR
Nike
Nissan
Nordstrom's*

P. Pan Am
J.C. Penney*
Pepsi-Cola
Polaroid
Procter & Gamble*

Q. Quaker Oats

R. Raychem
Reebok
Rent-A-Wreck
Revlon
Rockwell*
ROLM*

TRW*
Tupperware*
TWA

U. United Airlines*
United Technologies
UPS
USX

W. Wang
Wells Fargo*
Western Union
Westinghouse
Weyerhaeuser*

X. Xerox

Y. YKK*

Z. Zales*
Zenith

* First tier research sites

FIG. 2–1

The Seven S Framework

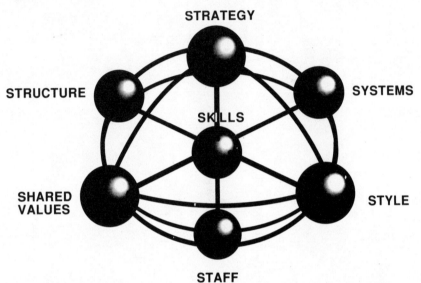

maintain the alliteration, we called the people category "staff"). There is nothing sacred about the number seven. There could be six or eight S's. The value of a framework such as the Seven S's is that it imposes an interviewing discipline on the researcher. It forces one to audit an organization from all perspectives, both "hard" (strategy, structure, and systems) and "soft" (style, staff, and shared values).[2] Behind each of the dimensions is a history that is important to understand—strategies that have been tried, organizational structures that have been imposed and cast aside, shared values that have been announced and then abandoned, and so on. Above all, it is a superb vehicle for assessing fit. Learning as much as one can about each of the seven dimensions and *assembling* what one has collected invariably reveals a lot. Readers wishing a quick refresher on the Seven S's may wish to glance at Box 2–2.

PLUSES AND MINUSES OF FIT

When an organization hangs together, when its strategy is reinforced by its organizational structure, and this, in turn, is supported by its measurement and reward systems, its style, its values, and so on, then the gears mesh. The resulting coherence contributes mightily to focus. If the company's strategy is sound, the result is usually success in the marketplace.

McDonald's illustrates the point. The fast-food chain assigns its success to a strategy that emphasizes quality control and efficiency. (McDonald's doesn't just sell hamburgers, it sells a predictable experience.) Anywhere you go, you can count on McDonald's to provide you with a Big Mac, and French fries that look and taste like they're supposed to. In support of McDonald's strategy are (1) disciplined management control systems, (2) stringent standards of cleanliness and equipment maintenance, and (3) a complementary set of values and personnel systems. When all of these elements are in sync, exceptional organizational performance is possible. That's what fit is all about.

But the 1980s witnessed changes in consumer tastes that impacted the fast-food industry. Americans stopped eating as many meats, sweets, and fried foods. Parents learned that a hamburger and French fries contained the equivalent of ten tablespoonfuls of grease. A new factor entered the equation—namely, to innovate. McDonald's response was the Egg McMuffin, Chicken McNuggets, and the salad bar. It appears straightforward because they responded appropriately, and it worked. But, as will be seen, history demonstrates how easily fit could have caused McDonald's to narrowly stick to "hamburgers."[3]

It may seem an exaggeration to imagine McDonald's defining their business so narrowly as to have gotten fixated on hamburgers. Yet UPS defined its business as "moving parcels by trucks"—resisting for over a decade the inroads of Federal Express (which moved parcels by air). I could cite a dozen, similar examples. The reason it happens so frequently is that what appears to be a minor adaptation (from hamburgers to a range of breakfast, chicken, and salad offerings; from a parcel delivery system reliant primarily on trucks to one dependent primarily on airplanes) requires fundamental shifts in an organization's skills. After the fact we are wont to say that an organization made a "bad decision" or was "too slow" to decide to do things differently. But underlying this superficial explanation is the tendency for organizations to do what they best know how to do. Decisions are largely determined by existing skills. As noted in Box 2–2, skills are the product of the other six S's. When an organization is *exceptionally* skilled, it is, in a sense, overadaptive. In the short run, this may provide superb performance, but concomitantly, fit magnifies the difficulty of any type of change. UPS's inability to compete successfully against Federal Express stemmed from its lack of key skills.

Consider what UPS lacked. It needed a "real time" information system

BOX 2–2.

The Seven S Framework

Strategy   Plan or course of action leading to the allocation of a firm's scarce resources, over time, to reach identified goals

Structure   Salient features of the organization chart (i.e., functional, decentralized, etc.) and how the separate entities of an organization are tied together

Systems   Proceduralized reports and routinized processes (such as meeting formats), etc.

Staff   "Demographics" description of important personnel categories within the firm (i.e., engineers, entrepreneurs, MBA's, etc.). "Staff" is not meant in line-staff terms

Style   Characterization of how key managers behave in achieving the organization's goals; also the cultural style of the organization

Shared Values   The significant meanings or guiding concepts that an organization imbues in its members

Skills   Distinctive capabilities of key personnel and the firm as a whole

Strategy pertains to a firm's plan of action that causes it to allocate its scarce resources over time to get from where it is to where it wants to go. *Structure* refers to the way a firm is organized—whether it emphasizes line of staff—in short, how the "boxes" are arranged. *Systems* refers to how information moves around within the organization. Some systems are the "hard copy" variety—computer printouts and other ink-on-paper formats that are used to keep track of what's going on. Other systems are more informal—such as meetings. These three elements—*strategy, structure,* and *systems*—are probably quite familiar to most readers.

The next three factors are what we call the "soft" S's. *Staff* pertains not to staff in the line/staff sense, but to demographics characterizations of the kind of people who collectively comprise "the organization." In some instances we encounter an "engineering culture" (Hewlett-Packard). In other cases we note that a company is dominated by a cadre of current and former salesmen (Tupperware), governed by flinty-eyed MBA's (Goldman, Sachs), or populated by computer jocks (Microsoft).

Style refers to the patterns of behavior of the top executive and the senior management team. For example, ITT's Harold Geneen and his team had a tough, facts-oriented style. *Style* also refers to distinct traits of an organization as a whole. Clearly, General Motors has a different style than Apple Computer.

Shared values pertains to the overarching purposes to which an organization and its members dedicate themselves. These are never bottom-line secular goals (such as growing 10 percent a year or obtaining a 20-percent return on investment). *Shared values* tend to "move men's hearts" and knit individual and organization purposes together.

The last of the Seven S's, ***skills,*** is both "hard" and "soft." *Skills* refers to those things which the organization and its key personnel do particularly well—the distinctive capabilities that truly set a company apart from competition. For example, at the *organizational* level, Apple is skilled at marketing computers. At the *individual* level, at least historically, it has had one of the most skilled cadre of software developers in the business.

The most significant aspect of *skills* (and the reason it is always listed last) is that it is the *dependent* variable. In other words, *skills* is the derivative of the other six S's. More often than not, managers are charged with the task of improving a skill (such as building a marketing capability, upgrading quality or reinvigorating customer service). The Seven S framework reminds us that to achieve these ends we must systematically fine-tune the other six S's to get the dependent variable, *skills,* to shift accordingly.

to deal with much shorter delivery cycles. It needed a higher-caliber work force geared to faster response times. The easiest part was purchasing a fleet of airplanes and the linear programs necessary to route them efficiently. What UPS couldn't overcome was the massive overhaul of virtually all aspects of its organization that would have been necessary to match the courtesy, service levels, and response times that Federal Express provides.[4] UPS was a trained marathoner in a world of sprinters.

It is of interest to study how McDonald's escaped the perils of too much fit. Somewhere amongst the cost accountants and kitchen operations experts at McDonald's headquarters there was a new-product-development function with adequate capability to rise to the challenge. Most significantly, McDonald's 7,907 independently owned franchises comprise a high-quality cadre of successful entrepreneurs. They represent a powerful voice in the McDonald's system—indeed, they are often an irritant and source of tension to corporate staff. The franchisees' identification of shifting consumer tastes was communicated forcefully enough to pierce complacency at the corporate level. It broke through attachment to the status quo. In short, contention came to the rescue; it challenged the smug comfort of fit. Contention prodded the chain to life once the market began to change.[5]

SPLIT

Simply put, when things get too big or too homogeneous, it is generally helpful to break organizations into smaller units. Multidisciplinary task forces, subsidiaries, or decentralized profit centers are often best suited for addressing special customer needs, niche market segments, or difficult technological challenges. As noted in Chapter One, IBM utilized split when it established its personal computer subsidiary, Entry Systems, in 1980. In so doing, it cut the new entity free from the overhead, red tape, and operating assumptions that had prevented IBM from gaining a foothold in this rapidly growing market. The new cross-disciplinary team violated IBM norms, borrowed components from outside, and delivered a 63-percent market share within three years.[6]

IBM reorganizes frequently, using split to stir things up, refocus the organization in a changing marketplace, and reenergize employees to rethink their jobs. This was the rationale behind the massive decentralization effort in 1988 that split the company into seven loosely autonomous businesses and four worldwide regions. IBM maintains that a reorganization of this scope is not so disruptive that the costs outweigh the gains. It takes at least six months—often much longer—for essential informal networks to be rebuilt, and before a new entity starts to really work effectively. IBM gets away with frequent, and large-scale, reorganizations (split) because it is working from a solid foundation of fit (e.g., IBMers often identify themselves with statements such as "I work for IBM and am currently in the XYZ division"). This identification with *the company* generates coherence. Each "card" knows it belongs to a common "deck," even though the deck is continually reshuffled. Results tend to reaffirm IBM's view. Since the reorganization, IBM has reduced overhead by 20 percent, launched a vastly improved networking product, and reduced its development time for mainframes from three years to eighteen months.[7]

The idea of decentralization, or splitting off self-contained units from their monolithic parents, was pioneered by General Motors and DuPont in the early decades of this century.[8] It has long since entered the mainstream of management thinking. The concept reached its apogee in the 1960s when dissatisfaction with large, bureaucratic organizations spawned a wave of decentralization. Sometimes it worked—many times it did not.[9] The breakdowns occurred when the separated units became so far removed from the parent culture that necessary levels of connectedness and synergy were lost. There has been a resurgence of this decentralization wave in the past decade. Over a dozen best-sellers have championed the virtues of split. These include E. F. Schumacher's *Small Is Beautiful,*[10] and a variety of books on innovation, including Gifford Pinchot's *Intrapreneuring.*[11]

A variety of factors make split an attractive recourse: economists point out competitive and market necessities; technologists remind us that discontinuities in technology require it; behaviorists have shown that people are more motivated and productive in small clusters. There is even an ideological argument built on the premise that society would be more humane if our organizations were on more of a human scale.[12]

A compelling case for split is provided by Michael J. Piore and Charles Sabel in *The Second Industrial Divide.*[13] They argue for "flexible specialization" (i.e., having the organizational capability to remain agile and to focus on niche markets). They document how the world's industrial economies have generated ever-increasing demands for more specialized goods. Concomitantly, technological advances in information management have made it feasible to produce specialty products economically. Robotics enable us to customize products that formerly had to be mass produced. Apple Computer, for example, carries near-zero inventory, and routinely manufactures computers and workstations to order in less than five days. Clearly, high degrees of market segmentation do not necessarily require organizational decentralization (i.e., split), but smaller market niches combined with technology have placed small manufacturers on an equal footing with larger ones. Piore and Sabel trace the inroads of small, flexible producers in industries such as steel, chemicals, textiles, and computers that a mere decade ago were regarded as impervious to small-scale competition. Ironically, in almost all cases, the smaller players are the most profitable.

We would not do justice to the rationale for split without addressing its role in coping with technological discontinuity. Peter Drucker's book *The Age of Discontinuity* describes the commercial era in which we live.[14] Under steady-state conditions, large, monolithic units can perform well, but when a technological breakthrough comes along, it is often better to be small. Consider the electronics industry. In twenty-five years there have been eight step-function shifts in technology—in almost every case pioneered by a small spin-off. Some of these units operated at least initially under the umbrella of larger companies. Most were start-ups.[15]

It is not nearly as surprising that the new entrants did well as it is that the former leaders almost always fell out of the race. Across the past two and a half decades there has been an almost complete turnover of leadership. The leader in the earlier generation of technology failed to provide the next era with the resources and autonomy required to execute a meta-shift into the new technology.

The organizational rationale for split is not hard to grasp. First, a dedicated entity can focus on the key success factors of a new market or technology. Second, new expertise often requires different people (e.g., electrical instead of mechanical engineers). New units that start from scratch can staff themselves more easily to meet such needs. Third, the cross-disciplinary nature of new markets or technology often requires talent from several functional disciplines. In established firms, individuals are often *borrowed* from preexisting departments on a part-time basis. This seldom works. Full-time commitment to the new stand-alone entity is the preferred approach. Finally, smaller, more manageable entities perform better as innovators. A National Science Foundation survey found that small firms produced about four times as many innovations per research and development dollar as medium-sized firms, and about twenty-four times as many as large firms.[16]

BEING BIG, ACTING SMALL

The case for split might lead us to conclude that small entities are good at almost all things, and that large companies, like the dinosaurs of ages past, are candidates for extinction. Yet a little reflection suggests that this is a vast oversimplification. We see examples of companies such as McDonald's, IBM, or Honda for whom size, deep pockets, and market clout represent a major competitive advantage. The trick is to combine advantages of size with an ability to generate focus and commitment at the subunit level. Throughout this decade, we have witnessed dedicated efforts by companies to be big, and yet to act small. Success turns, in large measure, on rather subtle organizational arrangements. Dana, for example, redefined its plant executives as "store managers," and instituted systems and incentives toward creating a sense of entrepreneurship at the plant level.[17] 3M does similar things with its venture teams,[18] as does Texas Instruments with over

TABLE 2-1.

Technological Transitions and Leadership Shifts from Vacuum Tubes to Microprocessors

| Technology | Inventing Company | Year of Innovation | Market Leaders (Ranked by 1988 Market Share*) | | | | |
			#1	#2	#3	#4	#5
Vacuum Tube	Bell Labs (AT&T)	1915	RCA	Sylvania	GE	Raytheon	Westinghouse
Transistor	Bell Labs (AT&T)	1950	Hughes	Transitron	Philco	Sylvania	Texas Instruments
Semiconductor	Texas Instruments	1960	Texas Instruments	Motorola	Fairchild	RCA	GE
Static Random Access Memory (RAM)	Intel	1969	Hitachi	NEC	Toshiba	Fujitsu	Mitsubishi
Dynamic RAMs (DRAM)	Intel	1970	Toshiba	NEC	Mitsubishi	Texas Instruments	Hitachi
EPROM	Intel	1971	Intel	Fujitsu	Hitachi	Mitsubishi	Toshiba
8- and 16-Bit Microprocessors	Intel	1971–1974	Intel	NEC	Motorola	Hitachi	Mitsubishi
Microcontroller	Intel	1976	Mitsubishi	Hitachi	Motorola	NCR	NEC
32-Bit Microprocessor	National Semiconductor	1982	Motorola	Intel	National Semiconductor	INMOS	AT&T

* Market share rankings by revenues for 1987, with the exception of vacuum tubes, transistors, and semiconductors. (*Courtesy Dataquest*)

ninety Product Customer Centers.[19] New words have been coined to capture the informal processes that go hand in hand with these arrangements. Our everyday business vocabulary includes terms such as *champions, performance shoot-outs* (among rival teams), and *skunkworks.*

IDEOLOGICAL UNDERTOW?

A cautionary note is in order. Split is a valuable link in the renewal chain, but it is not a panacea. In particular, be on the watch for the ideological undercurrent that submerges the thoughtful application of split in a sea of indiscriminate euphoria. Illustrative of the phenomenon is this quote from Thomas J. Peters' and Nancy Austin's *A Passion for Excellence:*

> When it comes to innovation, small, as we have seen, is more beautiful than even we had ever imagined. Virtually all successful innovation comes from or is markedly enhanced by decentralization and disrespect.[20]

The populist appeal of such quotes is almost irresistible. It champions the little guy against the system. It is macho, and it resonates with American ideals. Many of the terms used interchangeably with split (*autonomy, profit centers, entrepreneurship,* and so on), have an ideological undertow— especially in America, where constitution and custom hold these values dear. The result: our ideological affinity for split fuels a great number of ill–thought through decentralization efforts. Most of us have experienced the disruption that occurs when such blind leaps of faith lack substance.

THE PERILS OF SPLIT

Hewlett-Packard is an enthusiastic proponent of split. Size and "bureaucratization" have been historically regarded as grave threats to HP's entrepreneurial spirit. Policy dictates that every time a head count in a parent division exceeds 1,200, a new division is created. But too much split, like too much fit, causes trouble. HP's tradition of hiving off divisions works well when each unit is dedicated to a distinct market segment, but in the 1980s HP found itself designing and manufacturing computers. Excessive decentralization proved crippling in this new area. Hewlett-Packard has repeatedly taken too long to move its products from the design stage to the market.[21]

Computers are made of microprocessors, memory units, disk drives, key boards, CRT screens, and software. All must integrate into a coherent system that constitutes the final offering. At HP, each of these components was made by a separate entity, each jealously guarding its prerogatives. In due course, a consensus can be hammered out among these stakeholders, but almost always after arduous negotiation. The price paid is a long product development cycle, and sometimes not the best results (some HP computers have had awkward interfaces, which might have been avoided had the original design been driven by one, powerful guiding vision).

The costs of overdifferentiation have been significant. HP was ideally positioned to pioneer, and to be the dominant participant in, the sixteen-billion-dollar workstation market. Instead, they came to market five years late—long after Sun, Apollo, and a host of competitors had grabbed the lead.

Hewlett-Packard's response has been to somewhat hesitantly reverse course. Through several reorganizations, HP has tried to loosely couple the errant divisions into a "Systems Group." So doing, it has sought to restore fit and deemphasize split. Such rebalancing is usually a necessary, but insufficient, remedy. It can result in the worst of both worlds—burdening formerly independent units with what feels like onerous bureaucracy, sacrificing their entrepreneurial spirit and sense of ownership. HP's remedies to date have not been particularly effective. As will be seen, striking the right tension between fit and split takes more than a compromise between the two factors.[22]

THE CONTEND FACTOR

Fit contributes to coherence—but too much of it risks overadaptation. Split helps instill vitality and focus—but too much of it diffuses energy. That's where the third factor, contend, enters the equation. Contention management is essential to orchestrate tensions that arise. Why? Because you can never engineer just the right blend of fit and split without dealing with the human element. Making an organization tick isn't like wiring a circuit board. Recourse to the hard levers—strategy, structure, and systems—takes you only so far. Inevitably, one must deal with the passion and perspiration of human interaction. Organizations are, in the last analysis, interactions among people. These interactions often generate disagreements of one type or another. At HP these disagreements arose whenever the key divisions convened to hammer out a final computer design. Each sought to optimize at the other's expense. The software designers imposed hardships on hardware, an elegant innovation by the storage technology division fouled up the microprocessor unit. Trade-offs had to be made, and could only be made effectively by facing the contention and channeling it constructively. Unfortunately, Hewlett-Packard's emphasis on congeniality at all costs tended to "smooth and avoid."

Hewlett-Packard's inability to "engineer" the perfect blend of fit and split confirms what we know intuitively—namely, that there are no static prescriptions that will keep organizations vital. Problems of administration are never "solved" the way things dissolve in water or are resolved in mathematics. The problem you solve today creates the opportunity to solve the next problem that your last solution created. Chapter Three identifies the dimensions along which this eternal juggling act takes place.

Vectors of Contention

ORDER VERSUS DISEQUILIBRIUM

Managerial behavior is predicated on the assumption that we should rationally order the behavior of those we manage. That mindset needs to be challenged.[1] The earlier cited law of cybernetics noted that a system requires "internal variety" to cope with external change. The trouble is, "internal variety" is most often experienced within organizations as contention. The central thrust of this thinking is that internal differences can widen the spectrum of an organization's options by generating new points of view.[2] This, in turn, can promote disequilibrium; under the right conditions, self-renewal and adaptation occurs.[3] Herein lies the impetus for our focus on contention. The forces that we have historically regarded as locked in opposition can be viewed (through a different mindset, or paradigm) as apparent opposites generating inquiry and adaptive responses. This is because each point of view represents a facet of reality, and these realities tend to challenge one another and raise questions. If we redefine the manager's job as maintaining a constructive level of debate, we are, in effect, *holding the organization in the question.* This leads to identifying blind spots and working around obstacles.

PERPLEXING FINDINGS

I have mentioned earlier that a surprising, and initially perplexing, finding was that corporations with a high degree of fit among parts had a lot of focus—but concomitantly, they were often threatened with stagnation.[4] Companies for whom the organizational parts meshed together less well were plagued with contradictions and tensions; while their performance was less than outstanding, their deviant strains made them somewhat more adaptive. In a few instances, this research identified companies with *both* qual-

51

ities; that is, a high degree of coherence (i.e., fit) and a lot of internal tension. (Ford, IBM, DEC, Federal Express, and Honda fell into this category.) These companies fostered a restless, self-questioning quality, yet retained focus. Each had demonstrated an ability to pull itself back from the brink of stagnation and renew.[5]

Examining these companies in detail revealed that contention in organizations tends to arise in very predictable domains. Somewhat arbitrarily, I will map this territory as seven specific domains, or vectors of contention, each corresponding to one of the Seven S's. Each of these domains captures a paradox, or polarity, that needs to be reconciled—a "dialectic," as one manager put it.[6] The polarities provide an ongoing vehicle for sustaining constructive disequilibrium.

It is reassuring to note that these seven "domains" map closely with the trade-offs that command attention in the academic literature and in many of the classic books on management. For example, (while terminology may differ) a great deal of attention among those who study strategy formulation has been focused on the appropriateness of the somewhat academic-sounding terms *purposive* and *emergent*.[7] (I have used the terms *planned* and *opportunistic* to capture this dichotomy.) Similarly, a commonly addressed structural issue among organizational theorists is "differentiation and integration."[8] While few managers use such cumbersome terminology, most wrestle with the problem of building strong functional competence in key, elite functions—yet try to prevent these units from becoming so overpowering that they undermine efforts to get the entire organization to work (I use the terms *elitist* and *pluralist* to capture this trade-off). The pages that follow will define the polarities listed in Figure 3–1, and will illustrate them with practical examples. What has been missing is that we have treated these trade-offs in a disjointed fashion—as "irreconcilable dilemmas" or "nuisances to be dealt with."[9] I am proposing, instead, that all of these paradoxical qualities of organizations be viewed as a whole—if you will, as powering the engine of an inquiry-generating system. Properly channelled, they fuel enough pain to stimulate change and adaptation. Whether we divide them into seven or seventeen domains misses the point. The critical insight is that what have heretofore been regarded as hardships (owing to their paradoxical nature) or chronic sources of aggravation to managers are, in fact, the wellspring of organizational vitality. Yet to harness this fuel, as will be discussed in Chapter Four, requires a different mindset—a shift in paradigm.

STRATEGY: PLANNED VERSUS OPPORTUNISTIC

Most Fortune 500 companies engage in some type of strategic planning. Business schools devote many semester credits to strategic analysis, and

FIG. 3–1

Contending Opposites

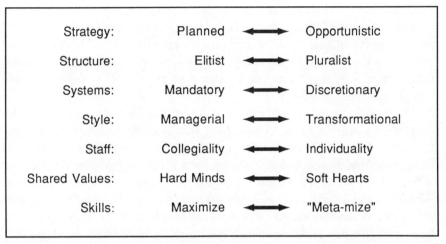

Strategy:	Planned	⟷	Opportunistic
Structure:	Elitist	⟷	Pluralist
Systems:	Mandatory	⟷	Discretionary
Style:	Managerial	⟷	Transformational
Staff:	Collegiality	⟷	Individuality
Shared Values:	Hard Minds	⟷	Soft Hearts
Skills:	Maximize	⟷	"Meta-mize"

consultants develop elaborate matrices to advance thinking in this realm. There are, of course, instances in which strategic analysis played an important role in shaping a corporation's actions, but more often than not, strategic planning and formal strategic analysis plays a secondary role in explaining the home runs that occur now and then. Many business breakthroughs result from an opportunistic response: someone has a new idea, it matches a market niche, and soon a new business is budding. Only after the fact are premeditated designs attributed to these outcomes. Conversely, companies that are opportunistic to the extreme often wind up like Atari: managerial umbrellas for a loose band of entrepreneurs. There was a lot of energy and initiative, but the organization as a whole didn't cleave together.

Neither "planned" nor "opportunistic" *extremes* alone provide the long-term answer. Organizations need both. The answer lies in a "dynamic synthesis"—not a compromise or mathematical halfway house of strategic and opportunistic tendencies, but a *paradoxical embrace* that contains both poles.

Context Is Key

Opportunistic responses often shape the content of a new thrust. Strategic thinking identifies the underlying context. By examining a new development strategically, we come to realize its full implications. An example will help. When Howard Head "invented" the metal ski, he was focusing on the *content* (i.e., skis made of metal had superior performance features over skis made of wood). What he failed to recognize was that he had redefined an entire industry (i.e., changed the *context*—or mindset—or paradigm). No longer was athletic equipment relegated to traditional materials. The idea gradually dawned on others that new technology could be introduced into virtually every facet of the industry—boots, bindings, poles, camping equipment, clothing, tennis rackets, and so forth. And since technology tends to evolve, this opened the additional possibility of transforming the staid once-in-a-lifetime-purchase athletic equipment industry into a fashion-driven business with planned obsolescence; again, a change of context. It fell to other companies, more strategic minded than Head Ski, to seize upon and exploit this context shift.[10]

"Strategic" planning, at best, is about *posing* questions, more than attempting to answer them. (I will treat this important matter much more broadly in Chapters Nine and Ten.) As suggested in the previous example, strategy formulation entails the search for a different frame of reference.[11] When Walter Wriston envisioned the shift in banking from a money-moving business to an information-moving business, he was changing the frame of reference. When McDonald's envisioned the hamburger business as shifting from a fragmented taste experience business to a nationwide franchise selling quality, reliability, and a predictable taste experience, they too were changing the frame.

These observations force to the surface a rather critical point that has been overlooked or deemphasized in recent years. As we have focused on the *mechanics* of industry and competitive analysis, we have taken our eye off the ball: Strategic thinking *is*, in the last analysis, the quest for a new business paradigm. To avoid confusion, we need to distinguish between the two types of paradigms that apply to management. First, there are business (or strategic) paradigms through which a company defines its position in the marketplace with respect to technology, products, and customers (e.g., the Citibank and McDonald's examples). The bulk of this book addresses a second class of paradigms, which are organizational, or managerial. These pertain to assumptions concerning how we inspire and coordinate collective activity; they entail our fundamental assumptions about human beings at work, and our expectations concerning their capabilities.

Strategy is the king of business disciplines because, at its best, it causes us to question the fundamental premises on which all else rests. To be sure, strategic thinking also involves understanding the basic economics of a business: identifying one's sources of competitive advantage, and allocating resources to insure that one's distinctive capabilities remain strong. But these are the tactical aspects of strategy. To repeat, *strategy's most important contribution is searching for, and redefining, context (ie., the business paradigm*). Since most context shifts are stumbled into inadvertently by an opportunistic experiment of one type or another, an essential strategic capability is that of perceiving, articulating, and exploiting the changes in context that opportunists discover, but frequently overlook.

Strategic thinking also creates a readiness to exploit unforeseen opportunities when they arise. Consider GE. The conglomerate's strategic planning department did not foresee nor trigger one of the most significant events in GE's recent history: the acquisition of RCA. This opportunity increased GE's revenues by 30 percent, strengthened its aerospace business, and added NBC to GE's portfolio. The strategic planners' analysis of opportunities both inside and outside GE's lines of business gave management the foundation and conviction to move quickly when the opportunity presented itself.

HONDA'S OPPORTUNISM

One of the greatest examples of an opportunistic strategy is provided by Honda's Supercub in the U.S. motorcycle market. An understanding of Honda's iconoclastic approach to business must, at the outset, take into account the unusual character of its founder, Soichiro Honda, and his partner, Takeo Fujisawa. Soichiro Honda had a childlike, spontaneous nature, which was reflected in his personal life as well as in business. In the formative stages of his company, Honda is variously reported to have tossed a geisha out a second-story window, climbed inside a septic tank to retrieve a visiting supplier's false teeth (washed and subsequently placed the teeth in his own mouth to prove they were clean), appeared drunk and in a pirate costume before a formal presentation to Honda's bankers requesting financing vital to the firm's survival (the loan was denied), hit a worker on the head with a wrench, and stripped naked before his engineers to assemble a motorcycle engine.[12] Honda embodied a rare combination of inventive ability and ultimate self-confidence. His motivation was not primarily commercial. Rather, the company served as a vehicle to give expression to his inventive abilities. A successful company would provide a resource base to pursue, in Fujisawa's words, Honda's "grandiose dream."[13]

Notwithstanding these idiosyncrasies, Mr. Honda raised his sights to the international arena and committed the firm to winning, at Great Britain's Isle of Man, the "Olympics" of motorcycle racing. Again, Honda's inventive genius was called into play. Shifting most of the firm's resources into this racing effort, Honda embarked on combustion studies that led to a new configuration of the combustion chamber that doubled horsepower and halved weight. Honda leapfrogged past European and American competitors—winning in one class, then another, winning the Isle of Man manufacturer's price in 1959 and, by 1961, sweeping the first five positions.[14]

Following these victories, Mr. Honda was pressed by Fujisawa's business priorities to adapt his racing technology to a commercial motorcycle. Fujisawa had a particular segment in mind. Most motorcyclists in Japan were male, and the machines were used primarily as an alternative form of transportation to trains and buses. There were, however, a vast number of small commercial establishments in Japan that still delivered goods and ran errands on bicycles. Trains and buses were inconvenient for these activities. The purse strings of these small enterprises were controlled by the Japanese wife—who resisted buying conventional motorcycles because they were expensive, dangerous, and hard to handle. Fujisawa challenged Honda: Can you use what you've learned from racing to come up with an inexpensive, safe-looking motorcycle that can be driven with one hand (to facilitate carrying packages)?[15]

In 1958, the Honda 50cc Supercub was introduced—with an automatic clutch, three-speed transmission, and the safe, friendly look of a bicycle (without the stigma of the outmoded mopeds). Owing almost entirely to the feat of combining high horsepower with an inexpensive lightweight 50cc engine, it was affordable. Overnight, the firm was overwhelmed with orders. Honda skyrocketed into first place among Japanese motorcycle manufacturers. The stage was now set for exploration of the U.S. market.[16]

On September 10, 1982, the six Japanese executives responsible for Honda's entry into the U.S. motorcycle market in 1959 assembled in Honda's Tokyo headquarters. They had gathered at my request to describe the sequence of events that had led to Honda's dominance in the U.S. market. All were in their sixties; three were retired. The story that unfolded, greatly abbreviated here, highlights miscalculation, serendipity, and organizational learning.

Mr. Kihachiro Kawashima, who would soon be named president of American Honda, first arrived in the United States in 1958. His account traces Honda's unfolding adventures in the U.S. market.

My first reaction after travelling across the United States was: How could we have been so stupid as to start a war with such a vast and wealthy country! My second reaction was discomfort. I spoke poor English. We dropped in on motorcycle dealers who treated us discourteously and, in addition, gave the general impression of being motorcycle enthusiasts who, secondarily, were in business. There were only 3,000 motorcycle dealers in the United States at that time, and only 1,000 of them were open five days a week. The remainder were open on nights and weekends. Inventory was poor; manufacturers sold motorcycles to dealers on consignment; the retailers provided consumer financing; after-sales service was poor. It was discouraging.

My other impression was that everyone in the United States drove an automobile—making it doubtful that motorcycles could ever do very well in the market. However, with 450,000 motorcycle registrations in the United States, and 60,000 motorcycles imported from Europe each year, it didn't seem unreasonable to shoot for ten percent of the import market. I returned to Japan with that report.

In truth, we had no strategy other than the idea of seeing if we could sell something in the United States. It was a new frontier, a new challenge, and it fit the "success against all odds" culture that Mr. Honda had cultivated. I reported my impressions to Fujisawa—including the seat-of-the-pants target of trying, over several years, to attain a ten-percent share of U.S. imports. He didn't probe that target quantitatively. We did not discuss profits or deadlines for breakeven. Fujisawa told me if anyone could succeed, I could, and authorized one million dollars for the venture.

The next hurdle was to obtain a currency allocation from the Ministry of Finance. They were extraordinarily skeptical. Toyota had launched the Toyopet in the United States in 1958 and had failed miserably. "How could Honda succeed?" they asked. Months went by. We put the project on hold. Suddenly, five months after our application, we were given the go-ahead—but at only a fraction of our expected level of commitment. "You can invest $250,000 in the U.S. market," they said, "but only $110,000 in cash." The remainder of our assets had to be in parts and motorcycle inventory.

We moved into frantic activity as the government, hoping we would give up on the idea, continued to hold us to the July 1959 start-up timetable. Our focus, as mentioned earlier, was to compete with the European exports. We knew our products at the time were good, but not far superior. Mr. Honda was especially confident of the 250cc and 305cc machines. The shape of the handlebar on these larger machines looked like the eyebrow of Buddha, which he felt was a strong selling point. Thus, after some discussion and with no compelling criteria for selection, we configured our start-up inventory with twenty-five percent of each of our four products—the 50cc Supercub and the 125cc, 250cc, and 305cc machines. In dollar value terms, of course, the inventory was heavily weighted toward the larger bikes.

The stringent monetary controls of the Japanese government together with the unfriendly reception we had received during our 1958 visit caused us to start small. We chose Los Angeles where there was a large second and third generation Japanese community, a climate suitable for motorcycle use, and a growing population. We were so strapped for cash that the three of us shared a furnished apartment that rented for eighty dollars per month. Two of us slept on the floor. We obtained a warehouse in a run-down section of the city and waited for the ship to arrive. Not daring to spare our funds for equipment, the three of us stacked the motorcycle crates three high by hand, swept the floors, and built and maintained the parts bin.

We were entirely in the dark the first year. We were not aware the motorcycle business in the U.S. occurs during a seasonable April-to-August window—and our timing coincided with the closing of the 1959 season. Our hard-learned experiences with distributorships in Japan convinced us to try to go to the retailers direct. We ran ads in the motorcycle trade magazine for dealers. A few responded. By spring of 1960, we had forty dealers and some of our inventory in their stores—mostly larger bikes. A few of the 250cc and 305cc bikes began to sell. Then disaster struck.

By the first week of April 1960, reports were coming in that our machines were leaking oil and encountering clutch failure. This was our lowest moment. Honda's fragile reputation was being destroyed before it could be established. As it turned out, motorcycles in the U.S. are driven much farther and much faster than in Japan. We dug deeply into our precious cash reserves to air freight our motorcycles to the Honda testing lab in Japan. Throughout the dark month of April, Pan Am was the only enterprise in the United States that was nice to us. Our testing lab worked twenty-four-hour days bench testing the bikes to try to replicate the failure. Within a month, a redesigned head gasket and clutch spring solved the problem. But in the meantime, events had taken a surprising turn.

Throughout our first eight months, following Mr. Honda's and our own instincts, we had not attempted to move the 50cc Supercubs. While they were a smash success in Japan (and manufacturing couldn't keep up with demand there), they seemed wholly unsuitable for the U.S. market where everything was bigger and more luxurious. As a clincher, we had our sights on the import market—and the Europeans, like the American manufacturers, emphasized the larger machines.

We used the Honda 50s ourselves to ride around Los Angeles on errands. They attracted a lot of attention. One day we had a call from a Sears buyer. While persisting in our refusal to sell through an intermediary, we took note of Sears' interest. But we still hesitated to push the 50cc bikes out of fear they might harm our image in a heavily macho market. But when the larger bikes started breaking, we had no choice. We let the 50cc bikes move. And surprisingly, the retailers who wanted to sell them weren't motorcycle dealers, they were sporting goods stores.

The excitement created by the Honda Supercub began to gain momentum. Under restrictions from the Japanese government, we were still on a cash basis. Working with our initial cash and inventory, we sold machines, reinvested in inventory, and sunk the profits into additional inventory and advertising. Our advertising tried to straddle the market. While retailers continued to inform us that our Supercub customers were normal, everyday Americans, we hesitated to target toward this segment out of fear of alienating the high margin end of our business—sold through the traditional motorcycle dealers to a more traditional "black leather jacket" customer.[17]

Honda's phenomenal sales and share gains over the ensuing years have been previously reported. History has it that Honda "redefined" the U.S. motorcycle industry. In the view of American Honda's start-up team, this was an innovation they backed into—reluctantly. It was certainly not the strategy they embarked on in 1959. As late as 1963, Honda was still working with its original Los Angeles advertising agency, its ad campaigns straddling all customers so as not to antagonize one market in pursuit of another.

In the spring of 1963, an undergraduate advertising major at UCLA submitted, in fulfillment of a routine course assignment, an ad campaign for Honda. Its theme: You Meet the Nicest People on a Honda. Encouraged by his instructor, the student passed his work on to a friend at Grey Advertising. Grey had been soliciting the Honda account—which, with a $5 million yearly budget, was becoming an attractive potential client. Grey purchased the student's idea on a tightly kept nondisclosure basis. Grey attempted to sell the idea to Honda.

Interestingly, the Honda management team, which by 1963 had grown to five Japanese executives, was badly split on this advertising decision. The president and treasurer favored another proposal from another agency. The director of sales, however, felt strongly that the Nicest People campaign was the right one—and his commitment eventually held sway. Thus, in 1963, through an inadvertent sequence of events, Honda came to adopt a strategy that directly identified and targeted that large, untapped segment of the marketplace that has since become an inseparable part of the Honda legend.[18]

The Nicest People campaign drove Honda's sales at an even greater rate. By 1964, nearly one out of every two motorcycles sold was a Honda. As a result of the influx of medium income leisure class consumers, banks and other consumer credit companies began to finance motorcycles—shifting away from dealer credit, which had been the traditional purchasing mechanism available. Honda, seizing the opportunity of soaring demand for its products, took a courageous and seemingly risky position. Late in 1964, they announced that thereafter, they would cease to ship on a consignment basis, but would require cash on delivery. Honda braced itself for revolt.

While nearly every dealer questioned, appealed, or complained, none relinquished his franchise. In one fell swoop, Honda shifted the power relationship from the dealer to the manufacturer. Within three years, this would become the pattern for the industry.[19]

Honda's successful foray into the motorcycle market was later to be repeated in the yet more competitive arena of automobiles. More will be said about these developments in Chapter Nine. The critical capability in both instances was Honda's ability to combine the resolve that stems from planning with the capacity for opportunistic learning once an initial beachhead has been secured.

STRUCTURE: ELITIST VERSUS PLURALIST

Structuring an organization so that it *really* works is not as easy as drawing lines and boxes. There must be enough integrity and focus within each function (or business unit) to support functional excellence. At the same time, too extreme a functional emphasis prevents the pieces from working together.

Elites

Published organizational charts are often misleading. It is necessary to get behind the chart and ascertain how things *really* work. If the boxes were drawn to scale (in proportion to their relative influence in the organization), which would be the largest? If the solid and dotted lines *really* depict informal networks, what do they say about the loci of power and status? Who are the second-class citizens? *Elites,* as I shall define the term, describes specialized organizational units with proximity to power and/or superior competence when compared to competitive benchmarks.

It is highly desirable that certain functions be regarded as "elite" in that they represent a particular organization's distinctive capability (when compared to like functions of competitors). By the same token, it is important that two or more of such elites exist, and that they are complementary and hold one another in check.

A positive example is Honda, where R&D, Engineering, Manufacturing, and Marketing are all first-rate units and vital forces in the decisional calculus.[20] (I term this condition *pluralist*). Honda's performance benefits from the tensions that these strong players evoke; their disagreements stimulate thought, self-improvement, and competitiveness.

In contrast, Finance during the zenith of Harold Geneen's tenure at ITT exemplifies an "imbalanced elite." Finance spoke the primary language for decision-making; its competence and power (via proximity to Geneen) gave it the deciding vote. The financial managers planted within each division had far more allegiance to the head of corporate finance than to the division heads who were ostensibly their "bosses." In its auditing role, Finance was the investigator, policeman, judge, and jury. Not surprisingly, a short-term, bottom-line–oriented culture prevailed, and it gradually eroded the competitive edge of each of the divisions that had given the company a distinctive advantage in the marketplace.[21]

A third example is General Electric's marketing function. Here, in contrast, we find an organizational unit that is generally underpowered for the role it needs to play. General Electric's marketing efforts are "decentralized" across all fourteen businesses. While not necessarily bad, it deprives GE's marketing of functional integrity. The marketing units in each division are often small and understaffed—both in numbers and in quality of personnel. At the corporate level, the activity has little leadership or clout. Not surprisingly, GE has done very poorly in growing many of its existing product lines internally and has been forced to rely on major acquisitions (and protected markets such as defense and aerospace) to meet its financial objectives. Marketing at GE is an example of a unit that needs to be elevated in stature if it is to be effective.[22]

The existence of elites anchors one side of the organizational paradox. The stronger and more competent they are, the tougher it is to achieve cross-functional teamwork. Several examples make the point.

Marriott is a highly respected participant in the lodging industry. Its Architectural and Construction Division (nicknamed A&C) is a competent and all-powerful entity. Many in Marriott claim that its contracting procedures, cost parameters (e.g., allowable construction expense per square foot of lodging space), and architectural guidelines impose a stranglehold on innovation. It is important for a nationwide innkeeper of Marriott's size to have a strong A&C function, which is particularly evident when one realizes that three-quarters of Marriott's growth in revenues and profits over the past decade has come from building new units; only 2 percent of Marriott's 20-percent growth per year is from real growth; another 2 percent stems from inflation.[23] In effect, Marriott makes its money from building, then spins off its progeny to independent investors, who in turn subcontract the operations to Marriott.

But the lodging industry has changed dramatically in the last decade—from the soaring architectural innovations of Hyatt (putting pizazz into the lobbies of upscale convention hotels) to low-budget offerings such as Holiday Inn's Embassy Suites, which appeal to the cost conscious end of the continuum. In these two segments, Marriott's marketing staff and new-product development teams were well ahead of the industry in their thinking, but they were frustrated, unable to execute their plans. A&C objected to the additional architectural expense and lower space utilization that go hand in hand with the grandeur of a dazzling hotel lobby. Hyatt seized the advantage at the high end of the convention hotel market, and has relegated Marriott to second place.

Likewise, Marriott's "Suites" and "Courtyard" projects lost their leadership edge because A&C's tried and true construction formulas translated into building costs that were out of line for the low-end segment. An internal Marriott memo captures the problem.[24]

> As I reflect on the strategic issues facing Marriott, I have become convinced that Marriott is at an organizational cross roads, and that our future success requires major organizational change over the next two years . . . New lodging products (including Suites and Courtyards) must be set up as independent, autonomous business units in order to assure the entrepreneurial initiative required for their success . . . In Suites, Holiday Inn is moving out further and further in front of us and we struggle to get our first unit built. Embassy Suites (Holiday Inn's trademark) has thirty-seven properties now open, sixty more to be opened by the end of this year, and 200 slated by 1990. Meanwhile, our low end product, Courtyard, is eighteen months behind its original schedule. Bottlenecks have emerged in A&C.[25]

Marriott suffers from problems at both ends of the "elitist" versus "pluralist" functions. A&C is an elite function. Together with Marriott's other two elite entities (Finance and Operations), there is a strong imbalance favoring control at the expense of creativity and market agility. The forces for innovation, namely, Marketing and Product Development, have little chance to make headway. As we have seen, Marriott's future success depends heavily upon unit growth in the unsaturated segments of the market (i.e., in those new areas at the low and high end where Marriott has stumbled). Marriott's "imbalanced elites" trigger a compounding problem of defective cross-functional teamwork. The elite functions tend to stand aloof as jealous feudalities defending their turf. In the roll-out of a low-cost offering, such as Courtyard, each would have to bend a little and lend support. The product champion in charge of Courtyard complains:

> Marriott is short term. Finance likes hard, tangible things rather than soft, intuitive things. A new, unproven product is always at a disadvantage. It's death by pinprick. Finance asks, "Tell me again why and how?" Operations drives you nuts. Our hotel specs say we have to have short-pile carpet with flecks in the pattern. Why? Because short pile doesn't show footprints and vacuum cleaner tracks, and the pattern conceals stains. But the Courtyard

customer tests say they want the housekeeping units to feel like home. And that means deep pile carpet with no pattern or flecks.[26]

For Courtyard to be launched effectively, Finance would have to bend its ROI hurdle rates, Operations would have to make exceptions to its specs, A&C would have to build units at lower cost per square foot (meaning less sound proofing and lower-cost materials). The Marketing and Development functions would have to command a seat at the table to bring these and other adaptations to fruition.

Many American companies today are caught in the iron jaws of this "elitist versus pluralist" issue. They need each of their departments or business units to be strong enough to at least be at parity with competition. This requires intensity and focus. At the same time, the market demands that the companies respond in ways that cut across these functional compartments. Success demands shorter response times, higher levels of service, and the ability to solve customer problems. In product oriented industries, the need to shorten the product development cycle means that design, engineering, and manufacturing must work collaboratively from the inception of a new product idea. Honda, for example, requires only two and a half years to launch an entirely new model, whereas General Motors and Chrysler take seven.[27] The Japanese are well into their third-generation product, while we are still launching our first-generation vehicle. This is a formidable competitive advantage, and it stems almost exclusively from the superior Japanese organizational capability.

A final example pertains to the high technology arena. In the information field, customers increasingly demand solutions to their information management problems. These solutions require computers, networks, switches, terminals, telephones, and a host of other peripherals. Large companies such as AT&T—with business units offering parts of the whole—have to knit the pieces together to provide the package a customer needs. This requires an agonizing amount of teamwork. AT&T estimates that 80 percent of its energies in responding to a customer request for complex systems are expended fighting, negotiating, and jawboning internal stakeholders into line. Only 20 percent is devoted to actually listening to, and selling to, customers. These ratios are not atypical for many companies.[28]

SYSTEMS: MANDATORY VERSUS DISCRETIONARY

Systems include not only the "hard copy" reports and procedures, but a host of informal mechanisms such as meeting formats and conflict management routines. Systems need to relentlessly emphasize key themes—such as quality or cost management—and at the same time permit discretion and exception. They are powerful influencers of behavior. Well-managed firms try to eliminate inconsistencies—especially concerning key themes—but too much fit breeds a stultifying inward-centeredness.

Consider Macy's. As a premier department store, Macy's is struggling to redefine the balance within its systems. Confronted on the West Coast with serious inroads made by its competitor Nordstrom (a company noted for its excellent customer service), Macy's is striving to loosen its controls in order to give its sales force more freedom to serve its patrons. But systems-intensive Macy's, having historically gained strategic advantage from having things nailed down, controls costs vigilantly, strives to minimize inventory, polices shrink,* and rewards and punishes its sales staff for doing things by the book.[29] Macy's rule book is an inch thick; Nordstrom's rules can be summed up in two sentences: Rule 1: Use your good judgment in all situations. Rule 2: There will be no additional rules.[30]

For Macy's to respond to Nordstrom requires that more discretionary latitude be given the salesperson (called a "personal shopper") to respond to the customer, accompany her throughout the store, pull an ensemble together from various departments, and ring up the purchase on one tag. This seemingly simple procedure requires Macy's to alter dozens of systems: sales, selection, training, staffing ratios, billing, inventory management, and incentive systems among departments. Further, Macy's centralizes all buying in Atlanta, and this, too, would come under pressure if the sales force were given a greater voice in decisions regarding customer wants. Macy's historical position at the "mandatory" end of the continuum has, to date, frustrated efforts to establish a better balance between systems and their flexible application.[31]

We can build upon the example of Marriott cited earlier. Marriott prides itself on the consistency and predictability of its service at whatever Marriott establishment one visits. The food, and the room service, even down to the details of room cleanliness and check-out procedures, are specified with obsessive detail. But the trouble with Marriott is its sameness—and the inability of managers at each location to respond fully to local market conditions. It's small wonder that Hyatt, a small fraction of Marriott's size, repeatedly outscores its rival in consumer surveys of service, luxury, and style. A Marriott hotel manager comments: "Overcontrol is a problem here.

---

* "Shrink" is a term utilized in retailing for losses of merchandise due to spoilage, damage, misshipment, theft, etc.

I wanted to expand a ballroom to the tune of $400,000. The accounting area reviewed it for seven months, said it just met ROI requirements, but was so close we shouldn't do it. They missed the whole point that if we don't expand we'll fall to number three position in our market.[32] An assistant hotel manager at another Marriott echoes a similar theme: "The internal control systems are onerous. They smother you with detail . . . want a scenario of every possible contingency. Most hotel managers are simply unwilling to wade against the stream. Subtly, the systems signal: 'How can we reduce costs?' 'Why not take this out?' The balance is wrong. Somewhere in the system there needs to be an occasional exception where we squander a few extra resources to maintain market leadership."[33]

At Marriott, both strengths and weaknesses derive from its controls and superbly efficient operations. Yet managing the contention between Marriott's systems-driven discipline versus providing discretionary latitude for new format innovations is so alien to Marriott that a dynamic synthesis has little chance of arising. In contrast, McDonald's strikes this tension, primarily because McDonald's franchises infuse entrepreneurial independence into the system. The independent ownership of each McDonald's outlet assures some flexibility from the intimidating corporate hierarchy. Franchisees are more inclined than paid employees to buck the system whenever McDonald's is afflicted with tunnel vision. The result is varied architecture and a consistent flow of franchisee-initiated suggestions.

STYLE: MANAGERIAL VERSUS TRANSFORMATIONAL

You will have noted by now that each pair of the contending opposites is couched in terms that give validity to either end of the continuum. *Planning* is as essential as *opportunistic* behavior in the evolution of successful strategy, *elite* functions bring core strengths to an organization, but must cooperate with the whole (the *plurality*) to achieve collective results. The same is true for the next domain—*style*. The "managerial versus transformational" polarity constitutes a continuum in which both ends make essential contributions to performance.

WHAT ABOUT "LEADERSHIP"?

Recent books on leadership, most notably Warren Bennis and Bert Nanus's *Leaders: Strategies for Taking Charge*, carry an unmistakable meta-message: to "lead" is in vogue, to "manage" is passé. Some readers give up midway, feeling a little depressed.[34] Either they don't quite see themselves as meeting the "leader" profile, or the situation they're in doesn't call for it. When the previously mentioned authors assert, "managers do things right, leaders do the right things," the clear implication is that "managing" is not only different from, but maybe even the opposite of, "leading," and that it is more useful to "lead" than to "manage." Confusion arises when we reflect on the fact that some leaders do manage, and some managers lead. The dichotomy generates more heat than light because the roles are not mutually exclusive.

We enter a quagmire when our categories depend on stylistic qualities. There is always an exception to any rule; human personality is too diverse. We are on somewhat safer ground if we focus on the end states that are sought. End states are easier to classify.

I define *managerial* as an administrative orientation whose aim is to get the maximum out of the existing organization. Clearly, managers might *modify* a strategy, and improve organizational performance incrementally, but the managerial orientation works with what is there. In contrast, a *transformational* orientation aims at quantum leaps in performance. The focus is on creating an entirely new order of things.

TRANSFORMATION

Petersen's approach at Ford (examined in detail in Chapters Five and Six) illustrates the transformational style. He is low-key and low-profile. His strategy for revolutionizing Ford emphasized the comprehensive reform of reward and budgeting systems, reducing the overpowering role of corporate staff (particularly Finance), breaking down barriers between functions, and involving hourly employees.[35] Petersen would be the first to say that he had no master plan, but he has diligently fostered a broad attack on the institutional factors that contribute to higher costs, defects, and off-market automobiles. Ford consciously orchestrated so much pressure for change on so many fronts that it became, in the view of employees and outside observers, a different company. Petersen distrusts the concept of a strong, overpowering leader. Lasting transformation, he believes, requires employees to accept responsibility for, and contribute wholeheartedly to, the change that is sought. The executive's role is that of prodder, facilitator, and catalyst. This approach taps the collective genius of the organization in order to identify and solve problems. As such, it is not as vulnerable to the imperfections of a strong leader as is the charismatic style.

Charismatic Leadership

It may surprise the reader that I have selected a less colorful executive such as Don Petersen to exemplify transformational leadership. Why not a superstar such as Lee Iacocca?

There can be little argument that Iacocca led Chrysler in a full-blooded American fashion. He rebuilt a faith among Chrysler's diverse and divisive stakeholders. He substituted a common dream of the future for the disintegrating scenario of the past. His strong, decisive behavior resonated with employees', stockholders', and the general public's vision of what leadership stands for—inspiring commitment, loyalty, and confidence. His personal stamp was evident everywhere. He closed plants, reduced break-even, and played a major role in the design and marketing of automobiles. He turned Chrysler around from a demoralized firm at the brink of bankruptcy to a profitable, winning enterprise.[36]

Yet a subtle, but important, distinction needs to be drawn between a financial turnaround and a genuine organizational transformation. The operative definition of true transformation is a thoroughgoing alteration of values, behavior, and organizational process. When it has occurred, employees will invariably say: "This place is totally different; there is a discontinuity between the way we are today and the way we were before."

Iacocca's brand of leadership is charismatic to be sure. The same might be said of Jack Welch at General Electric, and Mayor Ed Koch of New York City. But charismatic leadership can apply to both transformational and managerial approaches. It has more to do with the power of personality than with a company transformation, and does not guarantee that an organization will change in a discontinuous (clean break from the past) fashion.

Research at Chrysler during, and following, the turnaround tends to support this point.[37] No doubt, Iacocca almost single-handedly restored Chrysler's solvency, but the Chrysler organization today, while better managed, less stratified, and more efficient and market focused, is only incrementally better than its pre-crisis incarnation. Few employees would assert that Iacocca has engineered a discontinuity in how the company functions. Iacocca's interests center on products, styling, and market segments. He adds value in those areas—but they operate within rather traditional parameters. Beyond those domains, Chrysler tends to run its engineering and manufacturing operations much as before. Strong schisms still exist between union and management. Plants operate with a traditional hierarchy. Boundaries between functional disciplines, while not impenetrable, are still real. A member of Iacocca's top management states:

> I was surprised by the absence of a Human Resources program when I arrived here in the mid-eighties. The turnaround was behind us but we were parochial. Unlike Ford, when the cost cutting was taking place, the basic strengths of the personnel system underwent serious attrition. It's a mixed signal environment; top management really does not like change. They don't walk like they talk. They discuss what's wrong but exhibit strong resistance when you try to do something about it. We had to do battle to institute an executive training program and employee surveys. We reduced employee health benefits on one hand, but simultaneously defend an executive compensation plan in which Chrysler's top six executives rank among the top fifty in U.S. executive compensation. Iacocca alone earned $17 million last year. We get complaints about this but no one dares discuss it with him.[38]

The "Managerial" Imperative

At the other end of the polarity stands day-to-day *managerial* activities. While not nearly as heroic, it is the mundane "to do" lists and attention to business fundamentals that provide an essential foundation for a successful, self-sustaining enterprise. The managerial approach tends to be more project than process focused.

Intel's Andy Grove exemplifies the *managerial* end of the continuum. A co-founder of the company in 1968, Grove has for twenty years maintained Intel's leadership position in a fiercely competitive industry. Intel's batting average is nothing short of astonishing. They commercialized the first static memory device; the first dynamic, random access memory (DRAM); the erasable, programmable memory (EPROM); and, in 1976, the first microprocessor (i.e., a computer on a chip). Intel's products form the backbone for all IBM and IBM-compatible computer equipment. Year after year, Intel continues to come up with state-of-the-art technology that leaves other competitors (e.g., Texas Instruments, Motorola, Fairchild, AMD, and even the first among Japanese rivals, NEC) in the dust.[39]

Grove's managerial strengths include a first-rate mind, and an ability to get to the heart of problems and to quickly break large, complex tasks into manageable chunks. He demystifies problems, and is an uncanny B.S. detector. He has built a lean, highly disciplined company that, despite its matrix organization,* strives for accountability and rewards individuals for

---

* A matrix organization is a structure in which each unit has two bosses. At Intel, one boss oversees technology and the other oversees a geographical region or a product group.

getting the job done. He has cultivated a system of contention management called Constructive Confrontation, which fosters straight talk and tough-minded problem solving. In short, Intel has enormous vitality given its age and the fact that it is now a $2 billion company with 20,000 employees.[40]

Watch Grove on a typical day, and you will observe a masterful grasp of both strategy and tactics. At 8:00 a.m. he will make a $50 million commitment to a new technology based on an oral presentation by a respected researcher. An hour later he will delve into the details of a training program for entry-level employees. Still later he will grapple with the arcane mysteries of why silicon chip yield rates are below target at one of Intel's dozen manufacturing facilities worldwide. It is this capacity to simultaneously see big and small that makes Grove one of the best "managerial" executives in America.[41]

Yet, as with any end of the continuum taken to excess, Intel's most significant weaknesses stem from Grove's great strengths. Intel's top tier of management faces the prospect of Grove's retirement in the early 1990s. If the pace of change in electronics slackens, or if Intel stumbles in some future generation of technology, the firm would be at risk. Intel's excellence in R&D has not been matched by strengths in manufacturing. In fact, Intel is mediocre in this regard. Once a product begins to mature, and other low-cost manufacturers enter the market, Intel inevitably fades. Reliance on Andy Grove's ability to "see around corners" has allowed the organization to avoid responding to this weakness.

Grove's likely successors have already faced the stark competitive realities and understand the levels of quality, service, and cost that Intel must achieve to hang onto its market share once products mature. They believe that Intel *must* learn to compete in these areas; it can no longer afford to walk away from its former markets (as it did in RAMs and DRAMs once those products became commodities). But to win at this game requires a *transformation*. In addition to being a scrappy, combative, fire fighting R&D company, Intel must enlist bottom-up initiatives of supervisory and hourly employees and generate obsessive commitment to continuous improvement. Intel would have to hold fewer "fire drills," and react somewhat less precipitously when crises arise. It would have to be less *project* and more *process* oriented to support the systematic approaches to quality that the Japanese have perfected. It would have to honor singles instead of home runs, as teams chip away at defect rates and inefficiencies. It would need to lessen its emphasis on individual performance and meritocracy and recognize team contributions. It would need to tone down its very direct, at times brutal, confrontational style in the interest of greater harmony. This is especially essential between manufacturing and marketing, where close coordination is necessary to achieve the high levels of service, delivery, and quality necessary to beat the Japanese. None of these individual challenges are beyond the scope of a manager. Together, they represent a massive change in Intel's culture—a transformation.[42]

Andy Grove, the brilliant *manager,* finds all of the New Age jargon—*teamwork, process, transformation*—extremely disquieting. Will he and his team be able to exploit (rather than eliminate) the tension between these contending philosophies? Intel's long-term vitality will depend on it.

Our discussion has portrayed the two extremes—Grove at the managerial end, Petersen at the other. Rarely do we encounter a figure versatile enough to do both. Perhaps IBM's Thomas Watson, Jr., was such an exception; Japan's Konosuke Matsushita is a contemporary example.[43] The problem is that there are not many "renaissance" executives in top management positions who are versatile enough to do it all competently. The solution, and one seen occasionally, is to achieve an effective synthesis through the pairing of complementary talents. This is best provided by offsetting strengths among top management teams—usually the CEO and COO. We saw such an arrangement at Ford, when Chairman Phil Caldwell (financial and strategic skills) and President Don Petersen (product and engineering background) joined forces. When Petersen became Chairman, he, in turn, chose to juxtapose his transformational strengths with the managerial skills of Red Poling, his numbers-oriented second in command.[44] The same type of successful marriage was found at Honda (between Mr. Honda and Mr. Fujisawa);[45] at HP (between Bill Hewlett and David Packard);[46] and at Sun Microsystems (between visionary Scott McNeally and pragmatist Bernie LaCroute—before his departure in 1989).[47] One of Great Britain's most admired companies, Sainsbury's, has for four generations consciously followed the practice of pairing opposites in the top two slots.[48]

It seems straightforward logic to combine managerial and transformational talents rather than to gamble on the miracle that one executive will be good at both, but its occurrence is more the exception than the rule. Perhaps we have not heretofore recognized the necessity for such combinations. A more likely explanation is the human tendency to surround ourselves with others who think as we do. Selecting one's counterpart in order to provide "a corrective tension" means hassles every day. It takes maturity—and a new mindset. Thus, a Jack Welch at GE chooses a Vice Chairman Larry Bossidy, who is more similar to Welch than different.[49] John Sculley (managerial) fights with, and ultimately eliminates, Steven Jobs (transformational), and happily pairs up with a COO who is managerial like himself.[50]

Managerial John Young of Hewlett-Packard selects Dean Morton as his COO—doubling HP's profile because both embody a very genteel contention management style. A rival candidate for COO, Paul Ely, whose style of conflict management was more direct (and would have provided the hard edge HP badly needs to face hard realities) was blocked careerwise and left the company.[51] Roger Smith, Chairman of General Motors (managerial), eliminated Ross Perot (transformational) and is reputed to have a bench filled with buttoned-down managers like himself.[52]

An extreme example of the tendency of executives to surround themselves with others like themselves is AT&T. Since the Bell System split up in 1984, AT&T spun off the regionally operating telephone companies and kept the technology-intensive businesses (communication networks, network switching, PBXs, computers, semiconductor manufacturing, and Bell Labs). Given such a portfolio, it is almost unthinkable that the top management team would not include a preponderance of executives with backgrounds in one or more of these fields. Guess again. The company is run by a team of five individuals, all but one of whom, the CFO, were groomed to run a regional telephone company. This latter task is more akin to running the American Chamber of Commerce—requiring PR skills, and the ability to deal with regulators, Congress, and other stakeholders. This might entail transformational or managerial skills, but none of these individuals scores highly in either category. Within AT&T's several businesses there is a strongly felt need for a Chairman, President, or COO who can grasp the intricacies of the technology and add value in competitive maneuvers. But top management's quest for stylistic comfort and camaraderie (within its club of similar backgrounds and personalities) appears to overshadow other considerations.[53]

STAFF: COLLEGIALITY VERSUS INDIVIDUALITY

Organizations such as GM, DuPont, and P&G socialize employees extensively—and pay a price.[54] Peer pressures at these firms are so compelling that heretics either leave or become homogenized by powerful organizational norms. At the other extreme, entrepreneurial firms, such as Apple Computer during the Steven Jobs era, and Atari under Noland Bushnel, foster individuality. But the autonomy of talented designers and narrowly focused design teams often becomes a problem when it comes time to tie separate contributions to a whole.

Consider Wozniak and Jobs' development of the Apple Computer and the

MacIntosh. The task itself was so complex that no single person could get his mind around it. Instead, a team composed of highly talented and autonomous individuals with intense goal identification collaborated so effectively that they almost seemed to merge into one mind and one body. Steven Jobs emphasized the team's self-identity with such a vengeance that it generated an adversarial relationship with the rest of the organization. This paradoxical phenomenon is highly correlated with success in many high-tech projects—from aerospace to microprocessors, from compact disc players to biotechnology.[55] Tension arises from the inevitable tendency of autonomous individuals and groups to foster a narrow, adversarial view. For example, Apple's extreme version of "individualism *über alles*" contributed to its controversial TV commercial depicting IBM users as lemming-like followers. (In the process, they antagonized many potential customers in the Fortune 500.) Excesses jeopardize success. As implied in the earlier discussion, Steven Jobs' zeal (in support of the second-generation MacIntosh) relegated the company's star product, the Apple II, to backwater status. Former winners were suddenly "outsiders" to the new MacIntosh "tribe." Morale dropped, performance plummeted, and a number of superb designers left the company.[56]

The term *collegiality* evokes images of warm, supportive relationships and teamwork. Collegial organizations have communal tendencies in the form of coherent social rules and common identities. Highly successful organizations such as Honda, as will be seen later, derive much of their magic from collegial networks. Such ties harness the social system—knitting people together in an invisible web. A well-constructed social system enables employees to feel both autonomous and part of a coherent whole. (Chapter Nine's discussion of Honda will focus on how to create such a social system.)

But a collegial, or communal, orientation, like the extremes of individuality cited earlier, has a dark side. General Motors illustrates the dangers at the communal end of the continuum. In its venture with Toyota in Fremont, California, GM placed sixteen of its high-potential managers within the Japanese-run entity to watch and learn first-hand how the Japanese manufacture automobiles. The results in Fremont have been astounding. The plant was notorious for the extraordinary number of grievances, slowdowns, and work stoppages that plagued the GM-UAW relationship. Its grievance rate ran on the order of 5,000 per year. In 1980–1981, absenteeism was in excess of 20 percent, and it ranked among the worst plants in the GM system for quality. Under Japanese management, grievances are down to thirty to forty per year, and absenteeism is less than 3 percent. Based on GM audits throughout 1986, it ranked highest among all GM plants for quality, scoring

140 out of a possible 145 points. With 2,500 employees, Fremont reached full capacity of 200,000 units per year in 1987, two years after reopening. These impressive dimensions of Japanese success on U.S. soil are not new. Parallel achievements have occurred at the Honda facility at Marysville, Ohio, and at the Nissan plant in Smyrna, Tennessee. Fremont's productivity is three times the best GM rate (at its most modern and highly automated factories); defect rates and capital costs are one-third of GM's best plants.[57]

To the GM managers on the scene, "the secret" is not hard to grasp: the Japanese do it primarily with *people*. Rehiring the union members, most of whom had worked at the plant prior to the venture, they inherited the worst UAW local in the GM family, having the highest level of member grievances and the worst quality record. Through an intensive retraining effort (which entailed sending 500 workers to Japan for thirty days of on-the-job training, and allowing workers at Fremont to set their own work standards, rotate jobs, and exercise major control over the assembly line design), they transformed the workers' mindset from an adversarial to a cooperative tone.

University of Michigan's Karl Weick has written extensively, as have many before him, about the social construction of reality.[58] An elaborate social system blinds management from exploiting opportunity within its grasp. By General Motors standards, the facility at Fremont is an enigma. It is low-tech. It uses simple devices such as household-type clocks, to record downtime on the line, as contrasted to the $100 million information system that GM has been unsuccessfully experimenting with for the same purpose. Managers and workers move around the large plant on bicycles rather than on automated self-guided vehicles. Despite the fact that GM managers on the scene were submitting detailed, and increasingly emphatic, reports on Toyota's "low-tech/high-motivation" formula, GM doggedly invested in technology ($60 billion over the period 1982–1985—enough to buy Honda and Nissan).[59] Why? Because the traditional rules at GM emphasize engineered solutions, not human or motivational solutions (except for a few cosmetic efforts at team building). GM rebuilt the suburban-Detroit Buick City plant from scratch, and constructed two $200 million "green field" facilities* elsewhere. These space-age installations are indeed breathtaking technological feats—advanced robotics, driverless delivery carts, vision systems,† and state-of-the-art computerized materials handling—but high technology doesn't work without people. Buick City opened soon after the Toyota venture; the plant has nearly identical

---

* Plants built brand-new on open country fields (as contrasted to remodeled older facilities).
† Vision systems are robotics and other automated production systems which actually "see" (via sensors) where to position a part before it is welded or bolted into place.

space, volume, and production parameters. Its work force is *larger* than the Japanese partnership, yet it produces *one-third* the cars per employee.[60]

In the face of an experiment so successful (occurring within a former GM facility with a former GM work force), one might expect General Motors to study it with keen interest. Instead, we discover a pattern of conduct that almost suggests covert sabotage.

First, GM steadfastly mismarketed the Fremont-produced Nova, despite its strong quality rating and inherent consumer appeal. Steve Bera, a GM manager, and a member of the start-up team at Fremont, states: "The Nova was built to sell as a $7,200 subcompact. The people who buy this car are usually women shopping for a second car, and they are very price constrained. The vehicle is manufactured without air conditioning, but the Chevy Division imposed a pricing policy on the Nova that required the customer who wanted air conditioning to buy an entire package, which included a rear window defogger and a number of other features. This kicked the price from $7,200 up to $9,000, and priced the vehicle outside of its segment."[61]

Notwithstanding this injudicious pricing strategy, the Nova sold reasonably well. States Michael Naylor, director of Strategic Planning: "One of the activities I must invest in is countering the current disinformation campaign against Fremont. The basis of this attack rests on the assertion that 'The Nova isn't a marketing success, therefore Fremont is a failure,' or 'They hand picked their employees, which is not the real world,' or 'It was a start-up situation, which is not true to life.' These are defenses that GM has erected against the learning that ought to occur."[62]

General Motors imposes tight restrictions on its employees' access to Fremont. This made it almost impossible for interested managers to study and comprehend what makes Fremont successful. Citing Federal Trade Commission sensitivities, GM has restricted all company visitors, including even the most senior GM executives, to a *one-day* tour. During that day, the visitor spends a maximum of three hours in the plant itself; the balance of the time is spent a mile away at briefings held by GM executives, who themselves are not, and have not been, members of the Fremont management team. Not surprisingly, the focus of the briefings, and of the plant tour, is on technology. Guides point to the various robots and feed systems that are in use. Little attention is directed to the most important ingredient—Fremont's managerial philosophy and its approach to people.[63]

A General Motors intern, who had taken part in a tour of GM executives through the Fremont facility, provides this powerful anecdote:

From the front of the line, the voice of the guide droned on, discussing the quality of the material-handling system, robotics, innovative painting, etc. But I had lost interest. I was fascinated by the workforce. I kept comparing them with my familiar world in the assembly plants in Flint, Michigan. What had they done to these people to make them care like this?

Now we were in the middle of the body shop watching a group of four men in an assembly operation. Several of the visiting GM managers had lagged behind the rest of the tour group to watch these men work.

"Have you ever seen anything like it?" marveled the one. "Look at 'em go!"

"How do they train them to work like this? It's unreal."

"They train each other. Remember, isn't that what they told us?"

"Yeah, but check that equipment. It's so damn primitive."

We were about to move on and catch up with the rest of the group, but one of the plant managers hesitated and scoffed, "It's probably an act. There's no way in hell those guys could keep this pace up all day. They probably pick up speed every time they take a tour through their area."

They pretended to move on along, but out of eyesight, eased behind a gravity rack and worked their way back to peer cautiously out at the men. I stayed with them. In front of us, the workers, unaware they were being observed, continued to move quickly and efficiently at their job.

The one manager turned to the other. "You know, I couldn't do that job with less than six men in my plant."

"You gotta give these Japanese credit," the other said. "How could they get those suckers to design their own work processes? And with no experience?"

They continued to watch in silence for another few minutes. The men before them never let up their pace. Finally, the plant manager could stand it no longer. He clapped his hands as he stepped out from behind his hiding place. "Bravo!" he yelled at the workers. "You guys are something else! If only I could have people like you!"

The workers turned and smiled at the men as they left, but I lingered behind to hear their reaction. One of them turned and said to the others:

"It's too bad, isn't it, that they don't realize that they already have people like that."[64]

Equally remarkable has been the way in which General Motors has repatriated its sixteen managers who served as part of the Fremont team. During 1986, as the tours of duty of most of these individuals came to an end, GM's car-of-the-future Saturn project was getting under way. Several other high-tech plants were about to open. GM was urged by many to move these individuals as a team (or, at most, as two or three teams) in order to retain a critical mass and to increase the likelihood of transferring the learning from Fremont to the new site. The opposite policy was pursued. The majority of GM executives were moved as individuals to plants in which they had little opportunity to initiate reform. Three GM executives were transferred as a team of "consultants" and allowed to work "on assignment" within plants at the request of the plant manager. Within the GM system, the "consultant" title, an ad hoc role, offers very little prospect of achieving impact.[65]

General Motors authorized two "in depth" studies of Fremont. While long on detail, these tended to pull their punches and reflect GM's biases in their conclusions. For example, GM's most exhaustive study imposed a sampling procedure in which for every worker interviewed who liked Fremont, there would be a matching interview with one who did not. In that only 3 to 5 percent of the current work force is regarded as even vaguely dissatisfied, this builds a significant bias into the findings (i.e., the sampling procedures portray more dissatisfaction with the Toyota approach than exists). The effort to make the findings fit with GM's traditional worldview sufficed to allay any fears among top management that dramatic change was needed. In summary, in a variety of ways GM's social system conspired to protect itself from disruptive change.[66]

How does one explain this persistent tendency of GM management to ignore compelling evidence and the testimony of their *own* managers on the scene at Fremont? The answer lies in its collective identity and deeply etched social rules. It is almost beyond comprehension for GM management to contemplate the full-blown changes in status, power, and worker relations that adaptation of the Toyota formula would entail. It is easier to install robots.

SHARED VALUES: HARD MINDS VERSUS SOFT HEARTS*

"Hard minds" pertains to a bottom-line orientation. Most frequently this boils down to financial performance, the lifeblood of private enterprise. If an enterprise cannot generate a profit, it is not, by definition, adding enough value to perpetuate its right to exist, but overemphasis on short-term profit frequently sacrifices a company's long-term competitive position. This pattern is widely evident among American corporations.

* I am indebted to Jack Welch, Chairman and CEO of General Electric, who coined this terminology in conversations that focused on revitalizing GE in 1986.

A hard-minded emphasis all too often spawns a short-term focus, and fosters organizations that treat their employees like robots. At the other extreme, preoccupation with soft-hearted values can lead to wastefulness and the loss of efficiency. Consider the U.S. Olympic Committee. The poor U.S. showing in the 1988 Olympics exposed an organization plagued by ethereal values, endless committee meetings, and bureaucratic self-importance. The bottom-line activity of cultivating world-class athletes was sacrificed. An audit of the four-year program that culminated in the 1988 U.S. Olympic participation established that only 1.5 percent of the Olympics Committee's hundreds of millions of dollars (much of it surplus from the Los Angeles Olympics) had trickled down to the athletes.[67] It's small wonder we had such a tough time in South Korea.

There is an essential tension between "hard minds" and "soft hearts." "Hard-minded" executives include more than those who drive for financial results (although this is the most common fixation by far). It is reflected in a preoccupation with concrete, bottom-line results of all types (e.g., achieving deadlines, or meeting a particular standard or quota). A common trait of hard-minded values is that they are tied to goals that are unambiguous and quantifiable. Realizing them is often tied to the compensation of senior executives. Not surprisingly, tangibility contributes to their receiving the lion's share of an organization's attention. In contrast, "soft-hearted" values pertain to intangibles that are tied to higher-order ideals affecting employees (e.g., treating them with dignity), customers (e.g., fairness), and society (e.g., making a social contribution). These often get short-changed. Soft-hearted values are essential because they act as a counterweight to tangible financial (and other such concrete) goals to which all else is sacrificed.

We need a new mindset that embraces this paradox. The major drawback in stating the pairings as contending opposites is that the old mindset insists on camping out at one end of the continuum or the other. That's wrong-headed. These polarities are not so much dichotomies as two sides of the same coin. Our problem is a failure of imagination. We don't see the possibility of doing both until we come upon hard evidence that the "impossible" can be done. It's like breaking the four-minute mile. No one could imagine it until Roger Bannister did it. Then a host of competitors suddenly found they could do it as well.

SLEIGHT OF HAND?

Meaningful values and guiding principles are essential because they serve to reconcile these paradoxical demands. They do so by being (1) lofty enough to legitimize an organization's role in the society it serves, (2) profound enough to touch both hearts and minds, tying organizational purposes to higher-order human aspirations, (3) pragmatic enough to focus a business on the key factors of day-to-day success, and (4) concrete enough to serve as a tiebreaker in day-to-day decision-making. Behaving in a caring fashion, while retaining toughness, is a type of managerial sleight of hand. Nonetheless, a number of companies—such as IBM—have articulated positions that meet this test. For such companies, values serve as a "compass," pointing employees in the right behavioral direction. If, as is the case at IBM, one deeply held "meaning" emphasizes customer service, this acts as "magnetic north," influencing employees to make correct, independent decisions. "Meanings" act as tiebreakers in making close calls. They eliminate uncertainty and help to make correct decisions clearer in situations that might otherwise be resolved the wrong way. Box 3–1 enumerates IBM's basic beliefs.

Experience teaches us that an effective statement of vision, values, and guiding principles cannot be hammered out by the public relations staff or the human resources personnel department. Nor do they blossom from crash efforts of an executive task force. Values are truly a "no pain, no gain" proposition. If top management doesn't agonize over them and regard them as a never-to-be-broken psychological contract between themselves and employees and society, such statements are little more than empty words. But if hewn from discussion and introspection, values come to be internalized as honored precepts of behavior. They serve like the North Star—valuable guiding lights that orient an organization and focus its energies.

A key ingredient in this quest is choice of language. Articulating what an organization stands for all too often results in the verbal equivalent of Cream of Wheat—bland, and homogeneous in texture. Many well-intended efforts

BOX 3–1.

IBM's Basic Beliefs

Service:	The best service organization in the world
People:	Respect for the dignity of the individual
Excellence:	Set high standards and strive for superior performance in all undertakings

to draft statements of vision, values, and guiding principles bog down in platitudes. The same weary words appear: *leadership, superior, teamwork, excellence, highest standards, rate of return.* The challenge is to use fresh language that inspires and connects.

An example makes the point. Dentsu is the largest ad agency in the world, and controls 35 percent of all advertising in Japan. Its guiding precepts (see Box 3–2) were articulated by its first Chairman, Hideo Yoshida. He titled these principles *The Ten Rules of the Demon.* The fresh quality of Dentsu's "rules" stems from their focus on a successful Dentsu *person.* Juxtaposing these statements with our tired clichés underscores the importance of putting old ideas in a fresh package. For example, Dentsu's Rule 1 reads: "Initiate projects on your own instead of waiting for work to be assigned." We would probably lump this under the generic term, *initiative.* Rule 5 asserts: "Once you begin a task, complete it—never give up." The sentence communicates more clearly than our overused word, *commitment.*

The hard minds/soft hearts dichotomy challenges companies to be caring yet engender realism. One of the pitfalls awaiting those who craft lofty vision and value statements is that they overreach. Swept away by rhetoric that stresses personal concerns and the company's commitment to society,

BOX 3–2.

Dentsu's Ten Rules of the Demon

---

1. Initiate projects on your own instead of waiting for work to be assigned.
2. Take an active role in all your endeavors, not a passive one.
3. Search for large and complex challenges.
4. Welcome difficult assignments. Progress lies in accomplishing difficult work.
5. Once you begin a task, complete it. Never give up.
6. Lead and set an example for your fellow workers.
7. Set goals for yourself to ensure a constant sense of purpose. This will give you perseverance, resourcefulness, and hope.
8. Move with confidence. It gives your work focus and substance.
9. At all times, challenge yourself to think creatively and find new solutions.
10. When confrontation is necessary, don't shy away from it. Confrontation is the mother of progress and the fertilizer of an aggressive enterprise. If you fear conflict it will make you timid and irresolute.

they ignore the imperatives to survival. So doing, they set themselves up to charges of hypocrisy when times get tough and the company's *enacted* behavior doesn't square with its *espoused* values.

WESTERN HISTORY AND SHARED VALUES

We in the West live in a culture that separates man's spiritual life from his institutional life. This has had a far-reaching impact on modern Western organizations. It is also an integral part of the old mindset, or paradigm. Our companies freely lay claim to mind and muscle, but they are culturally discouraged from intruding upon our personal lives and deeper beliefs.[68] This is part of what the earlier quote by Mr. Matsushita was alluding to.

The dilemma for modern Western organizations is that, like it or not, they play a very central role in the lives of many who work for them. Employees in all ranks of the hierarchy not only "work" at their jobs, but (1) derive much of their daily social contact there, and (2) often locate themselves in social relations outside the firm through their association with their company and occupation. (One of the first questions we are asked when we meet a person for the first time is: "What do you do for a living?") Splitting man into "personal" and "productive" beings makes somewhat artificial parts of what is the whole of his character. When we do so, our cultural heritage not only too strictly enforces this artificial dichotomization, but deprives us of two rather important ingredients for building employee commitment. First, companies are denied access to higher-order values, which are among the best-known mechanisms for reconciling one's working life with one's inner life. Second, the firm itself is denied a meaning-making role in society, and thus pays excessive attention to instrumental values such as profit, market share, and technological innovation.[69]

I recognize that some readers will resist the specter of a merger of "the Church and the corporation," but that is not what I am proposing. There is an important difference between religiosity and spirituality. In the West, because of the separation of the secular and the spiritual sides of man, spirituality tended to be the Church's domain. That is not so in Japan, for example, and it need not be so in the West.* This insight goes a long way

---

* There is more at work here than employees who are socialized to be loyal and dedicated. While these characterizations often hold true, in addition the company is often entrusted to serve as the vehicle through which individual efforts are seen to better mankind. Employees are therefore strongly encouraged to fulfill their own lives through work. This propensity to support employee self-realization through work emboldens Japanese companies to address "aspects" of their employees' spiritual lives. That would be plainly unacceptable in the West.

toward explaining why Japanese, Korean, and other Asian firms are able to derive much more leverage from their mission, vision, and shared values.

SKILLS: MAXIMIZE VERSUS "META-MIZE"

A company's skills represent special capabilities that truly set them apart from competition. McKinsey's Tom Woodard uses an excellent analogy to capture the essence of skills—a term that can be used interchangeably with the concept, "distinctive competence."[70] A former basketball player himself, he notes that a great many foundational skills, and assets, make up a championship-quality NCAA basketball team: they can shoot and dribble well, they can play zone and man-to-man defenses, and such teams usually have a good coach and a good athletic program. Many might think of "good shooting" or a "good zone defense" as a team's distinctive area of competence, but it is seldom that simple. If one looks at the college teams that rank near the top year after year—Kentucky, Georgetown, Duke—one discovers more than excellence at the fundamentals. The best teams "play smart" (i.e., they are steady and don't lapse into prolonged periods in which they make dumb mistakes). Statistics show that they achieve higher rates of turnovers against their rivals, and capitalize on their opponents' mistakes. It is these ineffable qualities—truly an organizational *synthesis* of the foundational skills noted earlier—that constitute distinctive competence. Many companies have an abundance of raw skills or assets (General Motors is a good example) but fail to establish the institutional capability that gives them a unique competitive edge.

Both Hard and Soft
This discussion of skills, or distinctive competence, warrants repetition of a point made earlier in this chapter; namely, that a company's skills can include "hard" assets, such as financial strength, dominant market share, and so forth. But these "hard" attributes achieve the status of a "distinctive competence" by virtue of *how* a company organizes and exploits these advantages (i.e., institutional capability). For example, General Motors has a decided advantage in the "hard" category (i.e., financial strength, dominant market share), but is sadly lacking today in the "softer" realm of institutional capability. Ultimately, it takes the human and managerial input to translate hard assets into a sustainable competitive advantage.

Maximize or "Meta-mize"?
The great challenge facing any company is whether to get better at what it is already good at, or to look toward a higher-order capability that goes

beyond the old. This is what is meant by maximize versus "meta-mize." An example will help.

Take Western Union. No one can argue that Western Union "stuck to their knitting" and maximized. Through modern technology they became more and more efficient, and competitively more dominant in sending telegrams, but they did so with such a vengeance that they were blind to the higher-order applications of their skills that might have bred new life into an aging product. Western Union became transfixed with maximizing the efficiency of their underlying strengths (i.e., sending telegrams); they failed to recognize the "meta"-possibilities that might have derived from different uses of these assets. In hindsight, product offerings such as those provided by Federal Express, or the advantages of fax technology, could have given new life to Western Union's businesses. In short, the "maximize" presentation led Western Union to fixate on "sending telegrams"; the "meta" orientation might have led to alternative concepts such as "moving information." Western Union defined its strategic context too narrowly, and failed to develop institutional capabilities outside its traditional realm.[71]

Owing to the intensity of competition among global, as well as domestic, players in this decade, companies need to think about their skills at both the "maxi" and "meta" levels. Examples abound. We see Citicorp maximizing (by driving for greater productivity and efficiency in its existing banking operations), but also "meta-mizing" by being the first to realize that success in modern banking would turn on moving information the fastest. Citicorp has been a leader in the use of information technology as a result.[72] We see a very different example in the motion picture industry. Disney both "maximized," through tighter management of film libraries and theme parks, and "meta-mized," by repositioning itself not only as a traditional producer of movies, but as the broker of limited partnerships for low-budget films such as *Splash* and *Big*. Disney's concept was to move from the high-risk front-line exposure of a traditional production company into the more financially lucrative "broker" role. Disney's "meta" skill has transformed it into a specialized, limited partnership "brokerage firm." The only difference between it and a monetary broker is that it matches investors with scripts and production budgets instead of apartment houses or oil wells.[73]

PITFALLS

This discussion of the domains of contention has identified critical dimensions along which conflict arises in everyday organizational life. It might seem an easy matter to put this conflict to constructive use, but this research would suggest quite the opposite conclusion. While all firms face these conflicts, very, very few harness it productively. Like the twin perils of Scylla and Charybdis facing Odysseus on his homeward voyage, two ever-present dangers seem to consume most corporate efforts to handle contention. The first is "overdetermination" (taking a good thing too far), and the second is seeking the "golden mean"—a safe middle-of-the-road solution.

OVERDETERMINATION

Pharmacists know that too big a dose of the "right" medicine inevitably becomes a "destructive" remedy. Executives often ignore this principle. Tupperware was so close to its traditional housewife customer that it missed fundamental shifts in female work force dynamics—and has suffered declines.[74] We earlier noted that Hewlett-Packard's "congeniality" interfered with effective contention management. HP has gotten so hooked on its people-oriented "Hewlett-Packard Way" that members of its six-man executive committee fret that "The Way" has become an institution in its own right.[75] We also observed that Hewlett-Packard shifted strategic focus from the protected world of instruments to the cold, cruel, competitive arena of computers. (Computers have also become an increasingly important component in HP's traditional instrument business). Along the way, every noteworthy aspect of HP's culture—highly autonomous divisions, nonconfrontational decision making styles, job security, and genteel values—stands in the way of the repositioning that is needed for it to compete successfully. As suggested in earlier discussions, HP needs to consolidate inefficient production facilities, regroup autonomous units that need to be closely integrated to be competitive (i.e., computers, software, and peripherals), and slash head count and unprofitable product lines (HP has 84,000 employees and 60,000 products, and its overhead ranks among the highest in the industry).

Clearly there is a paradox. In order to achieve excellence, organizations need to focus their energies on key themes. Tupperware is not "wrong" in concentrating on its traditional housewife, nor is HP "wrong" in emphasizing the value of "The HP Way." What is "wrong" is allowing the pendulum to swing so far that an organization becomes "overdetermined"—imbalanced in its emphasis to such an extent that any fluctuation in environmental conditions leaves it at risk. Like the tree at the timberline that survives for decades by leaning into the wind, such organizations find themselves in jeopardy when the wind blows from a different direction. The essence of the idea is to embrace a theme or area of emphasis, but to never let its opposite languish entirely. Overdetermination kills balance and eliminates healthy levels of tension and resilience in organizations.

Yet overdetermination abounds. The *Wall Street Journal* on a daily basis celebrates well-intentioned CEOs who march their companies toward one extreme or the other. It makes good press. It's "decisive." It rings of inspired leadership. And it almost always gets a company into trouble. Consider Coca-Cola. Having fought its way back into supremacy over Pepsi, Coca-Cola leapfrogged its rival by consolidating its 800 formerly independent bottlers into four very large, independent franchises that control 75 percent of its U.S. volume. The shift makes a lot of sense in that these mega-franchises are well capitalized; can better serve the needs of very large, regional retailers; have the wherewithal to advertise regionally; and tailor regional marketing programs and promotions. So far, so good, but like many companies, Coca-Cola lacks the organizational wisdom to check the pendulum swing before excesses become costly. Rather than live with the paradox of imposing "checks and balances" on its decentralization effort, Chairman Goizueta has pulled out all stops. Dismantling centralized personnel eliminates the mechanisms for common selection, training, and inculcation of values; likewise, there is no common approach to information systems. Finance remains the only thread of consistency among the four giant franchises and Coca-Cola corporate headquarters. There is a strong likelihood that in time the four franchises and Coca-Cola Corporate will evolve into five distinct companies. They will pursue different objectives (market share versus profit versus diversification), and will lose their common vision in such critical areas as problem solving and conflict management. Above all, they will lose their shared values concerning quality, and their pride in Coca-Cola as the preeminent soft drink in the world. Those values today serve as a tiebreaker, a type of magnetic north. Somewhere in the nineties, Coca-Cola will awaken with a migraine headache—namely, having dismantled one mighty national company and created five jealously independent companies with only a logo in common.[76]

THE GOLDEN MEAN?

Given the danger of overdetermination, the wisest course might seem to be to seek the middle ground. Some firms accept this, and the result is usually the blahs: organizations without distinction, and lacking in creative tension.

Companies such as General Foods, Chase Manhattan Bank, and Texaco come to mind. Too much equilibrium can lull an organization into a stupor of self-complacency. Ironically, the old mindset encourages us to devote a great part of management energy to maintaining equilibrium, eliminating tensions, enhancing consistency, and achieving a happy medium. But when you eliminate the polarities, you sacrifice vitality. The dialectic is lost. This simple Japanese saying grasps the point: "The moment two bubbles are united, they both vanish."[77]

Thus, a conundrum: too much coherence breeds complacency; too little yields diffusion of focus. What's the solution? Consider Citicorp's Darwinian culture, in which the focus is on individual contributions to profits and growth, or, at the other extreme, J. P. Morgan's conviction that the future is built on teamwork fostered by a nurturing culture. Both firms have experienced significant past success, with diametrically opposed policies. But over time, the Yin does not flourish in the absence of the Yang. Both Citicorp and Morgan, despite their distinctive character, have nurtured countercultural qualities to keep themselves from carrying a good thing too far. Citicorp supports a first-class Human Resources function, which ensures that due process is served in the treatment of employees. Genteel J. P. Morgan had a tougher time in 1984 as it attempted to reconcile its conflict-adverse style to the "hockey player" individualists in the Mergers and Acquisition group, staffed with "tigers" and headed by an extremely competitive and aggressive individual.[78]

In summary, a pronounced emphasis (i.e., *temporary* extreme) in an organization can contribute significantly to its competitive advantage, but if such an emphasis persists too long, an organization gets too committed to one ideology or approach and is vulnerable to sudden environmental shifts. To maintain constructive tension, any area of strong emphasis needs the counterweight of its opposite.[79] These relationships are suggested in Figure 3–2.

There is more to this prescription than meets the eye. As in controlling a nuclear reactor, the uranium rods need to be monitored carefully. We've had our share of "organizational Chernobyls": People Express and Atari are prime examples. Chapters Five through Nine will use specific company examples to illustrate how tension can be managed without "meltdown."

DYNAMIC SYNTHESIS

The preceding pages have described seven critical vectors of contention that organizations face. It is easiest to write about them as trade-offs, and to think

FIG. 3-2

Relation of Components in Constructive Tension

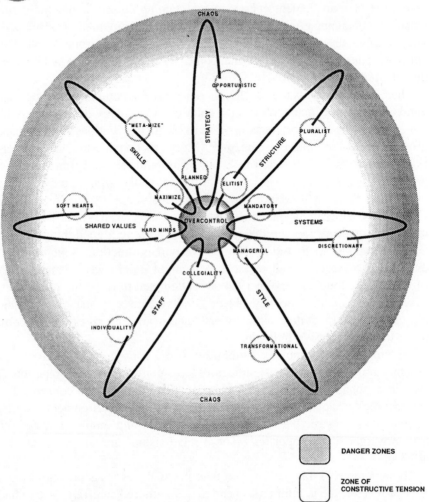

of the dilemmas they entail as polar opposites of a continuum. More consistent with the new mindset, we might better consider them as nodes of elliptical orbits—phenomena that never come to rest, like particles around a nucleus. Such imagery helps capture another important truth, namely, that no organization deals with one polarity at a time. Most are wrestling with several. It is for this reason that Figure 3–2 depicts these polarities as a set of dynamic relationships that are in simultaneous orbit, and that need to be monitored constantly. We can visualize these forces as perturbations pulsing at various amplitudes and frequencies, needing to be harnessed with skill and subtlety.

This discussion shifts the managerial focus from "static solutions" to "orchestrating dynamic synthesis or dialectic." We have come to regard this juggling act as a set of tensions simultaneously in dynamic play. So doing, we begin to grapple with a more complex mindset than the one that prevails in American corporations today: a more complicated mindset (as $E = mc^2$ was to the Newtonian physicists at the turn of the century), but hopefully a more accurate one. We turn now to tracing the origins of the old mindset, and to reflecting a bit further on the likely shape of the new.

CHAPTER FOUR

Disturbing Equilibrium

We must break the chains of the old mindset if we are to grapple success-fully with the task of managing adaptive organizations. Recall Konosuke Matsushita's chilling observation: "We are going to win and the industrial West is going to lose out; there's not much you can do about it because the reasons for your failure are within yourselves." The enemy "within our-selves" is the old mindset.

This chapter has three objectives. First, to introduce the mental models I have been calling "mindsets," which have been used and discarded over the centuries. Second, to explore the idea that the old managerial mindset springs from our traditional beliefs about America's industrial ascendancy and the ways in which it is embedded in organizational theory. Third, to suggest the broad parameters of the new mindset.

SCIENTIFIC REVOLUTIONS

Thomas Kuhn's *The Structure of Scientific Revolutions* is really a book about how mental models work. He calls them "paradigms." He defines paradigm as follows:

> A constellation of concepts, values, perceptions and practices shared by a community which forms a particular vision of reality that is the basis of the way a community organizes itself.[1]

For some readers, the term *paradigm* is too esoteric and academic. I have, up to now, substituted the word *mindset*. Whichever word one prefers, it is important to recognize that paradigm is the better term because it alone captures the *shared* nature of a belief system. That is what makes it at once so powerful and so difficult to discern. An individual can hold a "mindset" or a "worldview"—but a "paradigm" is always shared by a community. Box 4–1 presents an illustrative list of the hidden assumptions that tend to be taken as givens in the traditional management paradigm.

What gives paradigms their insidious power is that we generally don't distinguish between *what's* being thought and the paradigm it's being thought *through.* To demonstrate this point, Kuhn traces scientific disciplines in their shifting of mental gears over the past 400 years. In particular, he points out three surprising patterns. First, as noted earlier, a dominant paradigm is seldom, if ever, stated explicitly; it exists unquestioned. Second, paradigms, once accepted, are clung to tenaciously by our mental apparatus. When questions arise that the older belief system can't answer, the rationalization is: "We're not clever enough to figure out how it applies yet," or "We don't have the right measuring equipment." In Kuhn's scheme, normal science consists of mopping-up operations. The scientist is

BOX 4–1.

Illustrative Hidden Assumptions of the Old Paradigm

- Capital, technology, and labor are interchangeable and can be managed; rational analysis can be applied.
- Segmentation of human experience into the secular and the sacred. Business is secular and not an appropriate domain for the dynamics and sensitivities of the sacred.
- Profit is the ultimate measure of business performance.
- The "organization" as structure: chains of command, spans of control, centralization and decentralization are principal parameters.
- Focus on content (e.g., bottom-line results) yields greater impact than attention to process.
- Tendency to view organizations as personifications of strong leaders; corporate culture defined as personality of the company.
- Compensation system that rewards top executives at dramatically higher rates than rank and file employees.
- "Either/or" modes of cognition as contrasted to "and/also"; tendency to see alternatives as binary choices.
- The language of management borrows heavily from sports (home runs, blocks and tackles), the Wild West (shootouts, silver bullets), sex (in bed together, suitors), and Newtonian physics (mechanisms of control).

not a true innovator, but a solver of puzzles, and the puzzles upon which he concentrates are those that can be stated and solved within the existing scientific tradition. But slowly and steadily there accumulates a frustrating set of puzzlements that defy conventional wisdom. Eventually, the critical mass of unsolved problems creates a quiet uncertainty within the community. Third, the unfolding of a new paradigm is *always* discontinuous. Intellectual and emotional resistance inevitably arise when a radical way of looking at the world is presented.[2]

An example will help. Several experiments at the turn of the century found contradictions in classical Newtonian mechanics—contradictions that occurred as matter was seen to approach the speed of light.[3] Einstein's Theory of Relativity explained the contradictory results by showing that classical mechanics applied to a limited subset of situations within the broader General Theory of Relativity. It should be noted that Einstein didn't completely "refute" the old paradigm (i.e., Newtonian mechanics), but simply took the next logical step. But this is to miss the point. Einstein changed the context and upended the classical paradigm. It is difficult to overstate how thoroughly Einstein's Theory of Relativity, and subsequent formulations of quantum mechanics and particle physics, have disturbed the physicist's universe. For example, Einstein, by showing the relationship between mass, energy and velocity near the speed of light ($E = mc^2$) disproved the universality of Euclidean geometry. (Nearing the speed of light, time slows down and distance shortens). Von Neuman and Schrodinger demonstrated that subatomic phenomena can be considered *both* particles and waves depending on what the observer is measuring.[4] The universe isn't absolute (as Descartes believed); it is in the fullest scientific sense, "a matter of how we look at it."[5] The very terminology— particles and waves—is spurious, used primarily for mathematical purposes and linguistic convenience (creating pictures appealing for the imagination). More accurately, subatomic phenomena are "patterns of energy," sometimes appearing to coalesce into dense clusters (that can be investigated as "particles"), and at other times dissipating (exhibiting patterns that one can associate with "waves").[6] Thus the evolving paradigm had to reconcile itself to the fact that the fundamental building blocks of the universe are energy and organization. "Fundamentals" of the old belief system like space, time, and mass are only secondary derivatives.[7]

The reaction by fellow physicists to Einstein's shattering discovery is highly instructive in revealing how agonizing it can be to shift mental models. Fritjof Capra, in *The Turning Point,* writes:

The atomic and subatomic world brought scientists in contact with a strange and unexpected reality that shattered the foundations of their world view and forced them to think in an entirely new way. Every time they asked nature a question in an atomic experiment, nature answered with a paradox and the more they tried to clarify the situation, the sharper the paradoxes became. In their struggle to grasp this new reality, scientists became painfully aware that their basic concepts, language, and their whole way of thinking were inadequate to describe atomic phenomena. Their problem was not only intellectual but an intense emotional experience.[8]

We can expect that a new managerial paradigm will be as intellectually and psychologically wrenching to managers as paradigm shifts are to scientists. Many distinguished physicists of Einstein's day could not adjust to the more complex and problematic world of quantum mechanics and relativity. When you grope toward a new paradigm, you step into an abyss.

THE OLD MINDSET AND AMERICAN ASCENDANCY

Turning from science to the managerial realm, we can identify antecedents of our management paradigm in the evolution of ideas and assumptions surrounding America's remarkable ascendancy as an industrial power. The worldview associated with this history represents one of our most significant stumbling blocks today. Central to this is our abiding conviction that what American corporations have accomplished testifies to the validity of our methods. A great part of our reluctance to reevaluate stems from this illusion of past success—an illusion so pervasive that few see a reason to significantly alter course. "If it ain't broke, don't fix it," the adage says.

Not surprisingly, a common sentiment among executives today is to "get back to basics," and "get ourselves back on track." The underlying assumption is that, having up until recently been an invincible industrial power, we *have* the capacity to be innovative and competitive—it's merely a question of having "gotten sloppy" and lost our touch. If we can just "execute better," "listen to customers," "reduce (or eliminate) restrictive union practices," "restore the good old American work ethic," "get government regulators off our backs," "play hardball with foreign competitors engaged in unfair trading practices," and so on, everything will fall into place.

The fundamental mistake is believing that going "back" to something will bring us forward. One is reminded of the plight of utopian communities in the United States at the turn of the century—each endeavoring to turn back the clock to a more harmonious order.[9] Yet the encroachment of the future on the present is inevitable. The task of adjustment becomes more onerous the longer one postpones facing the discrepancy between the old worldview and the new reality; we desperately need to discard assumptions that are no longer valid.

The harsh truth is that we never were a *world*-class competitor—once the rest of the world developed the industrial infrastructure to compete with us on an even footing. Competitiveness in a *global* sense is not something America lost, but something we never had.[10]

Do I overstate the case? Probably not. An increasing chorus of industrial experts is pointing toward the problems which this book addresses. Notable among these voices are the recent findings of MIT's Commission on Industrial Productivity. Noteworthy because of its scope and the cross disciplinary expertise of the thirty distinguished professors involved, this two-year endeavor based its conclusions on in-depth studies of eight industries, 150 factory visits and 540 interviews. It asserts "that America is not producing as well as it used to produce, or as well as the industries of some other nations have learned to produce." The report's single most important recommendation is that *U.S. executives need to fundamentally rethink how they manage* and dwells at length upon "our deep reservoir of outmoded attitudes and policies." In the Commission's view, only one-half of one percent of American companies have transformed themselves sufficiently to embrace the higher order understanding of management that is required.[11]

Endowed with vast natural resources and an untapped and rapidly expanding domestic market, America's managerial history is largely inward-focused and self-congratulatory.[12] Throughout the latter part of the nineteenth, and through most of the twentieth century, as European economies alternately exhausted themselves with wars or stagnated economically, America imported cheap, and highly productive, immigrant labor and a vast array of European technology and innovation.[13] The steam engine, automobile, radar, and jet engine are examples. In addition, we imported the technological foundations of virtually every basic industry—rubber, steel, aluminum, glass, and petrochemicals. To be sure, America had its inventors, such as Thomas Edison and Alexander Graham Bell (a naturalized Scotsman), but not unlike claims currently made against Japan, it could be said that from the early 1800s through the 1960s, America borrowed a lot more than it lent.[14]

Most historians agree that the end of the Civil War ushered in the industrial age of America.[15] The engine of change was, quite literally, the steam engine. The railroads were America's first modern business enterprise, and they established the foundation for much that would follow.[16] First, they were geographically decentralized. Second, the systems they evolved emphasized impersonal controls (to keep things working without management being on the scene to direct matters personally). Third, as the rails spread across America, many small carriers were absorbed into mergers or trusts (an American pattern thereafter). The railroad not only created an industry, but its reach across the continent created the world's first, and largest, *mass-distribution* system. This, in turn, created opportunity for *mass marketing* of *mass-produced* products.[17] The importance of this chain of events (in giving America a distinctive competitive character as compared to Europe) cannot be overstated. In a real sense, geography was destiny. Peter Drucker writes: "The United States became the first 'continental economy.'"[18] This did not simply mean that it was a large trading area, rather, that this vast region shared the same economic values and spawned similar preferences and consumer tastes.

A set of providential factors shaped America's growing industrial self-confidence in the nineteenth century: abundance of raw materials and unskilled and semiskilled labor, no unions to restrain production, a continental landmass (supporting, as noted earlier, mass distribution, mass marketing, and mass production), and an immigrant population whose industriousness established a middle class that rapidly evolved homogeneous tastes as ancestral diversity was erased by transplantation.[19]

Archetypes

By the turn of the century, many archetypes of today's modern organizations had begun to evolve.[20] Joining the railroad as pioneers, among the earliest industries were agriculturally based companies such as American Tobacco Company (cigarettes) and Quaker Oats (cereals). Soon, Diamond (matches), Heinz and Campbell's (packaged foods), and Kodak (photographic equipment) joined the parade.[21] The speed with which such companies fed the huge continental appetite for goods shaped a uniquely American organizational paradigm. Markets were exploding and profits accruing for those who could build industrial capacity and consolidate market share rapidly. There was little need for finesse. First, standardization and control were key. The military metaphor had great appeal as early corporations literally assembled "armies" of employees and material to "conquer" market opportunities on a vast geographical scale.[22] Geography and complexity necessitated large headquarters staffs and the "invention" of middle management. Noteworthy, in terms of the evolving mindset, was the implicit emphasis on authority, chain of command, and the expectation that middle- and lower-level employees *do* what was directed from above. In effect, standardization in markets and products made it both effective and efficient to adopt a directive, do-it-according-to-company-policy approach.[23]

Adding impetus to this tendency, a number of early industries—railroad, telegraph, steel, and petroleum—were constructed via merger of collections of small, regional players. U.S. Steel, Standard Oil, Western Electric, and General Electric are examples. As with the All-Star Football game, one doesn't try fancy plays with a "team" assembled from heterogeneous backgrounds. Abstract quantitative measures were developed to inform "management" (often committees formed of independent owners) as to overall corporate performance. These senior managers behaved more like modern boards of directors than like true executives. Impersonal measures made sense for the same reason they do in modern-day conglomerates. Most of the top management hadn't grown up in the businesses they now ran; former owners understood a piece of the business, but not the whole. Senior executives were seldom personally acquainted with middle managers in the echelon below. Dependence on headquarters staffs evolved to fill this vacuum. Finally, top executives (as former owners of a "merged" company, or its financiers) had status needs and economic expectations that set them apart from the employee body. These status distinctions shaped our mindset, and are reflected in the status and salary distinctions awarded to American CEOs in corporations today.[24]

Management by Remote Control

These evolving managerial practices contributed to a mindset that was predicated upon "management by remote control." When organizational theorist Max Weber, industrial engineer Frederick Taylor, and other classicists codified mechanistic models for organizing companies and managing them, their ideas were readily grasped because they fit, and legitimized, what was already happening. What is significant is what was left out. There was almost a total absence of emphasis on building a corporate team.[25] There was little attention given to the importance of selection, training, and socialization.[26] There was little or no recognition that the "field infantry" composed of lower-level managers and workers could add value through initiatives and ideas if empowered to do so.[27] There was virtually no emphasis on close communications and internal networks, nor awareness that such networks tend to flourish when organizations break down functional barriers and status distinctions between the top and the bottom.[28] There was little grasp of the need to anchor a corporation in transcendent human and social purposes in order to make meaning for its employees.[29] All of these omissions were reflected in our assumptions about what it means to manage. A half-century would unfold before even a minority of U.S. executives would acknowledge these issues as vaguely relevant. Such is the power of our mindset.

Labor's Unique Role

A contributing ingredient to the evolving mindset was the tractable role of labor. American industry was built upon a low-skilled or semiskilled work force. Many were illiterate or semiliterate. In many respects this was common to European corporations at the time. What made the U.S. labor force unique was its diversity and ethnic heterogeneity. Unlike the several states of Europe (where labor was "cohesive" in socioeconomic terms), U.S. labor was ethnically splintered by custom, religion, and language; subgroups of employees in the same company often held themselves defiantly aloof from one another. From management's point of view, these qualities reinforced the general tendency to treat workers as units of production. A markedly directive and mechanistic philosophy for assigning and supervising work prevailed.[30]

This type of work force was not offered, and did not ask for, influence over managerial decisions. Even in the 1930s (and not withstanding powerful support for organized labor from the Roosevelt Administration), the heterogeneous American work force proved very difficult to organize.[31] Increasing literacy and rising economic expectations led to growing unrest, but unrest without organization left management practices unchanged. When labor inevitably organized, there was no clear-cut ideological center of gravity (as contrasted with the ideological clusters arising from social class distinctions in Europe). Union leaders in the late thirties and forties, faced with a rank and file of widely divergent interests, stuck close to basic wage issues, and rarely sought influence over matters other than those that directly impacted on the worker (i.e., safety, hours of work, and so on). These policies reinforced the tradition: U.S. management and workers operated in different spheres of influence.[32] Management did the thinking, and the worker did what he was told. Referring to this evolving philosophy, Harvard's Richard Walton recently commented: "A broad consensus has emerged that U.S. managers generally came to rely upon poor models for managing their work forces, to expect and accept much less from workers than is potentially available."[33]

Inventive Prowess?

Another facet of the evolving paradigm pertains to America's pride in "Yankee ingenuity, entrepreneurship, and technological leadership."[34] Interestingly, the facts present a far more modest profile of our inventive and entrepreneurial prowess. Table 4–1 traces the fifty significant commercial inventions from 1850 through 1950. It will be noted that over 80 percent of these breakthroughs originated abroad, and in the majority of cases the first significant commercial exploitation occurred in Europe as well.[35]

In the steel industry alone, the U.S. imported the Seimens open-hearth process, the Bessemer converter, the Gilchrist-Thomas basic lining, the electric furnace, the continuous rolling process, and the oxygen process—all from Europe. From 1900 to 1930, no American steel firm, including U.S. Steel, made significant investments in R&D. Virtually all technology was imported. Much the same could be said for radio, synthetic fibers, radar, refrigeration, antibiotics, and a host of other fields.[36]

Up through the end of World War II, the United States, while beginning to play a role in basic research, was not a leading player. In the period 1901 through 1945, Americans were awarded nineteen Nobel laureates as contrasted to thirty-five for Germany and twenty-two for Great Britain.[37]

Extenuating Circumstances

In the face of such evidence, where does our inventive and entrepreneurial self-confidence come from? The answer lies partly in the circumstances culminating with World War II. First, prior to the creation of the Common Market after World War II, European markets were splintered into the dozen or so nations constituting that marketplace. Even within nations, markets were more eclectic—owing, in part, to class distinctions and class tastes. American manufactured goods, such as Singer sewing machines, could achieve extraordinary economies of scale in the U.S. domestic market—then export to Europe at prices no one could match.[38] European companies, except those in bulk products such as dyes and raw materials, could not compete in the U.S. markets on the same basis because their domestic base was not large enough to achieve distinct manufacturing efficiencies. That perpetuated America's advantage.[39]

Second, almost continuously from 1859 through 1945, Europe was distracted by wars, regional tensions, and economic recessions. In the period 1859 through 1917 alone, there were four regional wars, followed by an economic depression, followed by World War I (which left continental industries destroyed and British capacity exhausted and antiquated). Then came the economic crisis that culminated in the Great Depression. Economic warfare between 1929 and 1937 (including competitive devaluations, exchange control, and tariffs) slashed world trade by two-thirds. While impacting the United States, these events were particularly felt in Europe.[40]

TABLE 4–1.

America as Borrower of Technology

INVENTION	INVENTING COUNTRY	1ST MAJOR COMMERCIAL EXPLOITATION	1ST MAJOR U.S. COMPETITOR
Aniline Dyes	Great Britain (1856)	Gr. Britain/Germany (1860's)	ALCOA
Atomic Reactor	U.S. (1942)	Gr. Britain/U.S. (1956)	Atomic Energy Comm./GE
Automobile	France (1769)	Germany (1885)	Oldsmobile (later GM)
Bessemer Converter	Great Britain (1856)	Great Britain (1860s)	U.S. Steel Co.
Catalytic Cracking	U.S. (1915)	U.S. (1935)	Sun Oil Company
Computer	U.S. (1946)	U.S. (1956)	IBM
Continuous Steelcasting	Germany (1927)	Germany (1946)	Continuous Metal Casting Co.
Dynamite	Swede working in Germany (1867)	Nobel (Sweden) (1870s)	Dupont
Electric Generator	Gr. Britain for DC (1831) France for AC (1832)	U.S. (1882)	Edison (later GE)
Electrolytic Process of Aluminum	U.S./France (1886)	U.S. (1865)	Alcoa
Fluorescent Lighting	Great Britain (1852)	France (1934)	General Electric
Helicopter	France (1935)	France (1941)	Sikorsky
High Grade Steel	Great Britain (1777)	U.S. (1956)	U.S. Steel Co.

INVENTION	INVENTING COUNTRY	1ST MAJOR COMMERCIAL EXPLOITATION	1ST MAJOR U.S. COMPETITOR
Polyethylene	Great Britain (1933)	Great Britain (1939)	Philips Petroleum
Portland Cement	Great Britain (1824)	Great Britain (1873)	Universal Atlas Cement Co.
Radar	Great Britain (1935)	Great Britain (1940)	Raytheon
Radio	Italian working in Great Britain (1896)	U.S. (1921)	Westinghouse/GE/RCA
Refrigeration	Great Britain (1834)	Great Britain (1876) or Germany (1890s)	Wolf/Linde or Frick
Rockets	U.S. (1926)	Germany (1928)	Convair (later General Dynamics)
Steam Turbine	Great Britain (1884)	Great Britain (1884)	General Electric
Sulfa Drugs (Antibiotics)	Germany (1908)	France/Germany (1935)	Pfizer
Synthetic Detergents	Germany (1886)	Germany (1928)	Procter and Gamble
Synthetic Fibers (Rayon)	Great Britain (1883)	France or Great Britain (1892)	American Viscos Co. or Dupont
Telegraph	Gr. Britain (1837)	U.S. (1846)	Western Union

INVENTION	INVENTING COUNTRY	1ST MAJOR COMMERCIAL EXPLOITATION	1ST MAJOR U.S. COMPETITOR
High Voltage Generator	Germany (1820)	Germany (1820)	General Electric
Incandescent Lightbulb	Great Britain (1800)	U.S. (1879)	General Electric
Internal Combustion Engine	France (1860)	Germany (1884-86)	Oldsmobile (later GM)
Jet Engine	Great Britain/Germany (1923)	Great Britain (1941)	GE/Protisahutrem
Locomotive	France (1759 or Great Britain (1803)	Great Britain (1825)	Baldwin
Neoprene	Belgium (1906)	U.S. (1932)	Dupont
Oxygen Steelmaking	Great Britain (1856)	Germany (1939)	Bethlehem Steel
Pharmaceutical (Aspirin)	France (1853)	Germany (1899)	Sterling Drug Company
Photography	France (1827)	France (1854)	Eastman Kodak
Plastics (Bakelite)	Belgian working in U.S. (1907)	U.S. (1910)	Dupont

INVENTION	INVENTING COUNTRY	1ST MAJOR COMMERCIAL EXPLOITATION	1ST MAJOR U.S. COMPETITOR
Telephone	U.S. (1876)	U.S. (1881)	Bell/AT&T
Television	Gr. Britain (1924)	U.S./Great Britain (1936)	RCA
Transformer	Germany (1831)	Germany (1885)	General Electric
Transistor	U.S. (1940)	U.S. (1950)	Bell Labs
Vulcanized Rubber	U.S. (1841)	U.S. (1852)	Goodyear
Xerography	U.S. (1938)	U.S. (1949-50)	Haloid Co. of New York*
Vacuum Tube	U.S. (1915)	U.S. (1930)	RCA
Zipper	U.S. (1891)	U.S. (1923)	Talon

*Later Xerox Co

Aside from the eight years lost to the Great Depression, America thrived during the first half of this century. Success reaffirmed and solidified our managerial mindset. Harvard's Skinner states: "The Great War provided step-function impetus to industrial production and induced the initiation of many new technologies, processes, products, and markets. By 1920, modern industry, as we know it today—with immense productive facilities, multi-unit, multi-product, line and staff management, paperwork planning, scheduling, accounting and controlling—was flourishing.[41]

Growing in step with these developments was a set of techniques that gave rise to the concept of "professional management."[42] In 1919, the first general management association was founded. Senior executives at General Motors published detailed accounts of Sloan's control and accounting procedures. Harvard established the first graduate business school. Paralleling the mass marketing of products, professional writers and consultants broadly disseminated their ideas in such subjects as factory management, time and motion study, engineering, and organizational structure.[43] In the 1920s, DuPont adopted diversification as an explicit strategy for growth. (They did so initially in order to employ the surplus of managerial staff and facilities that had been greatly enlarged by World War I.)[44]

The central point here is threefold: first, America found herself in a fortuitous global context. Second, the unique geographical and untamed circumstances of the American frontier made a military model of management quite appropriate, and fostered a wide variety of practices that are with us to this day. Third, human nature being what it is, we attributed much of our success not to circumstances but to our own managerial prowess. So believing, we have elaborated endlessly upon our managerial techniques out of faith that therein lies the source of our industrial genius. In essence, not only did we evolve a managerial paradigm, but have come to worship it. It was firmly installed as America began to take itself seriously as a world-class industrial power, and it has changed little since. "By the end of World War I," observes historian Alfred Chandler, [American managerial thinking] had come of age . . . A businessman of today would find himself entirely at home [with the precepts that existed seventy years ago]."[45]

World War II marked the zenith of America's industrial ascendancy. Prior to that time, Europeans had dominated the majority of key technologies, including atomic physics, synthetic fuels, plastics, aeronautics, radar, synthetics, and petrochemicals. World War II precipitated the wholesale transfer of know-how—this time with allied help. America was virtually placed in the driver's seat and asked to husband all of the new technologies that would shape the second half of the twentieth century. It's not surprising that the United

States assumed leadership in these fields.[46] Between the end of World War II and 1982, the United States won 109 Nobel prizes for science; the closest runners-up were the United Kingdom, with forty, and Germany, with fourteen.[47] Scientific ascendancy was accomplished by leadership in major commercial innovations. The most reliable measure, a European Common Market source, credits the United States with seventy-four during the 1945–1982 period, as contrasted to eighteen for the United Kingdom, and fourteen for Germany. However reassuring these statistics, we must acknowledge them for what they truly represent—namely, America's windfall flowing out of World War II. Evidence that these achievements are temporary in nature is suggested by America's declining role in recent years. For example, Table 4–2 tracks patent activity among leading companies around the world. The slippage in U.S. leadership is self-evident. These data parallel other, more general measures of innovative activity worldwide.[48]

World War II included another watershed that shaped the industrial and geopolitical landscape. It was becoming clear that territorial gain was no longer the only, or even the best, means of advancing a nation's interest. World War I had nearly proved the point that fighting no longer served a rational purpose. The winners emerged not appreciably better off than the losers. Germany and Japan had banked on this lesson in their gambles leading to World War II. They bet, erroneously, that the Allies lacked the will to effect another Pyrrhic victory. While they were guessing wrong,

TABLE 4–2.

Issued U.S. Patents 1960–1982

	General Electric (U.S.)	IBM (U.S.)	Philips (Eur.)	Siemens (Eur.)	Hitachi (Japan)	Toshiba (Japan)
1960	773	296	234	96	2	3
1965	1,063	537	321	161	14	14
1970	1,000	631	290	231	102	80
1975	839	519	411	451	386	90
1980	770	386	332	369	409	257
1982	741	439	386	477	544	301
CAGR*(%)	−0.2	1.8	2.3	7.6	29.0	23.3

* Compound annual growth rate

defeat confirmed the fallacy of territorial expansion. Since World War II, the technology of the nuclear age has made warfare not only more devastating, but unacceptably risky to belligerents and nonbelligerents alike.[49]

As the lesson gradually dawned, an industrial strategy supported by an international trading system offered an increasingly appealing alternative. With the International Monetary Fund in place (augmented by what, in hindsight, has proven to be the longest period of political and economic stability in three hundred years), Germany and Japan set their sights on becoming major industrial powers.[50] For the first time, the playing field was level. For the first time, foreign competitors were on an equal footing with their American counterparts in terms of market size and capital availability. It is only in this context that the term ''world-class competitor'' has come to have true meaning. And for the first time the veracity of our *assumptions* about management (and our underlying mindset) was truly tested. It has been found wanting.

THE OLD MINDSET AND ORGANIZATIONAL THEORY

A second major force in shaping the old paradigm has been our evolving theories about organizations. An irreverent, but useful, way of examining this literature is to think of it as falling into two categories. Some of it is logical enough, but misleading. Alfred Chandler, Frederick Taylor, and Max Weber belong in this first category. These ideas tend to be mechanistic. The second group is that body of research that maps quite accurately with reality, but is unable to explain the exceptional things organizations do (such as generating energy to remain adaptive, and breaking with tradition to truly transform themselves). For example, they would have difficulty explaining the discontinuous changes at Ford in this decade.

Exemplifying the mechanistic tendencies of the traditional mindset, Alfred Chandler, in *Strategy and Structure* (1962), concluded that form follows function.[51] Once a company's strategy was in place, its structure would follow (i.e., its organization would evolve to support it). The underlying assumption is that organizations act in a rational, sequential manner. Yet most executives will readily agree that it is often the other way around. The way a company is organized, whether functionally focused or driven by independent divisions, often plays a major role in shaping its strategy. Indeed, this accounts for the tendency of organizations to do what they best know how to do—regardless of deteriorating success against the competitive realities.

An example will help. The dominant role of financial controls at General Electric made it difficult to generate new revenue and pursue entrepreneurial opportunities within its core businesses. (Chapter Seven will discuss this at greater length.) The elite status that Frito-Lay gives to its marketing department goes a long way toward explaining why this company overwhelms competition with new product introductions and product extensions. At Frito-Lay, Marketing hires the MBAs, pays the highest salaries, recruits the top talent, and is the undisputed pacesetter. (At the same time, the production and sale functions are powerful and consistent constituencies that act as checks and balances against the onslaught of "too many good ideas.") Yet Marketing's status as first among equals in Frito-Lay's *structure* is the engine of its *strategy*. No one thought it out that way. Rather, through historical accident, marketing became preeminent. The result drove a strategy based on product differentiation and innovation.[52]

Another important pillar of our organizational inheritance stems from Max Weber. One of the first to codify what was known about organizations,[53] Weber relied extensively on the rational and mechanistic tradition prevalent in his time. He is regarded as the father of the "military metaphor," with its emphasis on coordination and control. Other writers—Fayol, Gulick, Urwick (since labeled the classicists)—expanded this tradition. The classicists believed that organizations succeeded primarily by dint of their ability to reduce diversity and ambiguity. They emphasized clear lines of authority, and formal and systematic procedures for control and integration. This tradition is clearly at variance with contemporary themes stressing empowerment, cross-functional teamwork, employee initiative in identifying and solving problems, and so forth.[54]

Weber's second contribution was his notion of organizational behavior as a network of individual, yet reciprocal, human interactions. Talcot Parsons dubbed this approach "action theory," and formalized it as an underlying paradigm for social science.[55] As with all of this classical thinking, it paralleled the Newtonian worldview in which "every action has an equal and opposite reaction." To be sure, a great deal of behavior is reciprocal. It gets confusing, however, because while individuals may act (and elicit reactions from others) with some degree of purpose, the sum total of an organization's collective efforts is often seriously out of whack. Interactions have side effects. It seems surprising that human beings interact with a definite purpose in mind, yet wind up, in aggregate, frustrating their overall purpose. Yet it happens all the time.

It might be said that Frederick Taylor simply took Weber's command and control theories (applied at the organizational level) down to the micro level of the workplace.[56] Taylor pioneered the science of industrial engineering, carving up each job into a finite set of tasks. His four precepts were (1) find the "one best way" (using industrial engineering and scientific methods), (2) match people to the task (again, scientifically), (3) supervise, reward, and punish, and (4) use staff to plan and control. In effect, like Weber, he sought to reduce ambiguity. His focus was the workplace and the worker. He sought to tighten up the linkage between worker behavior and managerial intentions through procedures, control systems, and clear assignment of responsibility and chains of command. Earlier discussion has noted that the most far-reaching influences of Taylor's work stemmed from his assumptions concerning how people behave on the job. Recall his observation "Hardly a competent workman can be found who does not devote a considerable amount of time to studying just how slowly he can work and still convince his employer that he is going at a good pace . . ."

We recall, from Chapter One, the words of Konosuke Matsushita to the effect that the industrial West is going to lose out because the reasons for our failure are within ourselves. Matsushita chides us because "For you the essence of management is getting the ideas out of the heads of the bosses and into the hands of labor."

The chasm separating the Matsushita and Taylor quotes extends far beyond a simple quarrel over willingness to trust in worker initiatives.[57] The bedrock difference is the differing mindsets. It emerges throughout the writings of Chandler, Weber, and Taylor—a subtle "topspin" in how they view reality. The organizational precepts tend to be couched in mechanistic terms (i.e., "chains of command," "hierarchical structures," "reciprocal linkages"). Further, the translation of these ideas into practice has been shaped by managers whose disposition is more akin to an engineer than a composer. This is what Konosuke Matsushita (and the Japanese generally) are pointing to. Our problem lies with assumptions so deeply internalized that they are truly "within us." That's why our efforts to emulate the Japanese seldom close the competitive gap. That's why, as will become increasingly clear, nothing short of a shift in our thinking, discontinuous with the past, is necessary. As we come to understand the old mindset and the conventional wisdom in which it is embedded, we discover how powerfully it filters our thinking. This is not to suggest that the Japanese have the new paradigm all locked up, but that our evolving paradigm needs to embrace a set of ideas that theirs has already encompassed.

Following upon the heels of the classicists are the works of more contemporary researchers whose understandings map more closely with newer ways of thinking, but who leave tantalizing questions unanswered. Chester

Barnard, writing in 1939, defined an organization as "a system of consciously coordinated activities of forces of two or more persons."[58] Essential to the survival of an organization is the willingness of its members to cooperate and to ensure the continued integrity of organizational purpose. Barnard focuses on the tasks of the executive, highlighting the importance of the informal social properties of organizations and the leadership role in harnessing those forces and in shaping and guiding values. Barnard advocates coherence among such elements as values, informal social networks, formal systems, and purposes. The better they are orchestrated, the better the organization performs. His limitations are twofold. First, like Weber, he doesn't deal with unintended behavior that is counter to avowed purpose. Second, as champion of the " 'fit' school," Barnard doesn't address the observable fact that coherence and fit are insufficient to ensure *adaptation* and *vitality*—in fact, they often detract from it over time.

Elton Mayo was a contemporary of Chester Barnard. Mayo and his Harvard colleague, Fritz Roethlisberger, tinkered with working conditions in an assembly room of Western Electric's Hawthorne plant.[59] The original intention was to show that better workplace hygiene would result in higher worker productivity. So, they improved illumination, and productivity went up as predicted. Then, in order to restore baseline conditions before experimenting with another factor, they routinely turned the lights back down. Productivity went up again! Lightbulb: Simply paying attention to employees, whether or not it improves working conditions per se, can have a significant positive impact on productivity.

That the Hawthorne experiment has validity is indisputable, but its implications have often been trivialized and misinterpreted. (In fact, an oft cited justification for "just trying out" many of the fads noted earlier is that they're "an endless stream of Hawthorne effects.") The result is usually a lot of wheel spinning and cynicism. At a more fundamental level, we need to look at the Hawthorne experiments from "outside the box." In the context of the earlier Matsushita quote, the Hawthorne experiments are a parable about researchers (and managers) manipulating and "playing tricks" on employees. (While this may not have been the researchers' motivation, it is one implication of the research.) "There is nothing wrong with the findings," the Japanese plant manager of Sony's Color TV production facility in San Diego once told me. "But the Hawthorne experiments look at human behavior from the wrong perspective. Your thinking needs to build from the idea of empowering workers, placing responsibility closest to where the knowledge resides, using consistently honored values to draw the separate individuals together. The Hawthorne experiments imply smug superiority, parent-to-child type assumptions. This is not a true understanding.'' Again we catch the shadow of our traditional mindset.[60]

More recent researchers Herbert Simon, Richard Cyert, and Jim March devoted their energies to studying how managers think and make decisions. They noted how decision-makers tended to use limited problem solving and research strategies. Specifically, they conclude: (1) ''the cause of a problem will be found 'near' its effect,'' and (2) ''the new solution will be found 'near' the old one.''[61] (For example, if there is a problem on a production line, the tendency is to look at the specific station that is in trouble, and to try to fix that problem, rather than looking at the overall manufacturing system in which the station is embedded.) Organizations learn and adapt v-e-r-y slowly, and adhere to traditional rituals and cues long after practical value has lost all meaning. These ideas, too, are imbedded in the old mindset. Why is it that some American companies, consulting firms in particular, are masterful at moving past ''presenting problems'' and identifying core issues, rejecting superficial solutions in favor of more fundamental solutions? How can entire enterprises—not only consulting firms such as McKinsey, Bain, and BCG, but mainline manufacturers such as IBM, DEC, and Honda—largely escape the iron law of limited rationality? They do so because they are not bound by the old mindset. They don't expect people to react within the confines of assigned authority and responsibility. Rather, they expect them to think outside the box and do what's right. (Seemingly, if your mindset, or paradigm, cues people to think *in*side the box, they do. If you expect them to think *out*side the box, they do.) The ideas sound simple enough, but behaving like an IBM or Honda is not in any respect ''simple.'' As noted in Chapter One, these organizations operate from a different set of managerial assumptions. It is virtually impossible to copy them unless you adopt their mindset—and that, as stated earlier, requires transformation.

The extent to which Herb Simon and ''limited rationality'' were honored and celebrated says still more about our unstated assumptions. Simon (an economist by training, who received a Nobel prize for his contributions in the organizational area) published *Administrative Behavior* in 1947.[62] His joint work with Jim March, *Organizations*, was written in 1958.[63] (The latter book presented 450 interrelated propositions about organizing; none of their work is based on the systematic study of the general management of large organizations.) The idea of *limited rationality* came thirty years after the classicists had published their work. In the interval, Barnard had called attention to social and behavioral networks, and the Hawthorne experiments had underscored irrational behavior in response to managerial attention.

Thus, Simon's contributions did not, in fact, represent a particularly great leap. His primary contribution was to formalize the proposition that man is governed by other forces than pristine rationality.[64] What, then, was all the fuss about?

Simon, the economist, wrote about "limited rationality" in a highly rational way. He dignified and legitimized the study of organizations, which had been struggling for a seat at the table as a respected academic discipline. It wasn't that Simon (or his followers) in the limited rationality school truly made an intellectual quantum leap in our knowledge about organizations. Rather, they gave it the rigorous trappings of self-contained theory, all in the interest of fashioning "soft" science to look like the "hard," physical sciences. Ironically, this endeavor (consuming prodigious amounts of the energy of organizational research in the four decades since Simon's book was published) has crossed paths with "hard" sciences heading the other way.[65] While organizational research persists with largely reductionistic, quantitative, and deductive metaphors, the hard sciences have shifted to more organic concepts of reality.[66] Physicists talk of "charm," depict the universe as "energy and organization," and demonstrate mathematically that there can never be *one* organizing theory of the cosmos.[67]

This is not to say that these contributions have not made incremental improvements to the old mindset, but we are still bound to the old; it continues to establish a powerful mental and psychological bias in how we view organizations and manage them. Still, the question remains: If man and organizations are creatures of limited rationality, forever finding new solutions near old answers, moving in incremental fashion, why do some organizations consistently generate discontinuous breakthroughs (Bell Labs), or repeatedly reform themselves (IBM's radical shift to the stand-alone Entry Systems subsidiary)? How can some (Ford) totally reform their culture? Discontinuous shifts in organizations should never happen—but they do.

A leading thinker in the field, University of Michigan's Karl Weick, reflects on his own work and the shortcomings of contemporary organizational theory: "People repeatedly overlook a different kind of organization, one that values improvisation rather than forecasting, dwells on opportunities rather than constraints, discovers new actions rather than defends past actions, values arguments more than serenity, and encourages doubt and contradiction rather than belief."[68] Interestingly, there is little in the prevailing organizational theory of the Western world that would explain or predict the organizational behavior that Weick describes. Yet, literally hundreds of Japanese companies, and many American firms, especially small ones, behave this way year in and year out.

Now we enter a transitional period that bridges the old paradigm with the new. A key contribution was the research of Paul Lawrence and Jay Lorsch.[69] Both at Harvard, they published in 1960 one of the most elegant empirical studies of this century. They investigated the ways in which companies "organize" to fit with their environment. They looked at organizational structures and management systems and contrasted the top performers in a fast-moving business (specialty plastics) with the top performers in a stable business (containers). They were among the first to document the presence and value of paradox, namely, that the star performers in both volatile and stable businesses permitted the functional units within their organizations to specialize (differentiation), while at the same time drawing them back into the whole (integration). Lawrence and Lorsch first identified the "loose-tight paradox"—the need both to give the parts of an organization freedom and to pull them together.[70]

Their work also flagged the significance of "elite" functions within an organization in shaping its distinctive competence. While acknowledging the existence of elite groups, they left unaddressed the need for checks and balances among elites so that one function does not dominate all others. They also noted the importance of empowering managers to make decisions and take initiative at the level of the organization in which the operational knowledge resides. (They concluded, however, that it was only warranted in volatile industries in which events are moving too fast for senior management to maintain more traditional degrees of control. This is in contrast to Japanese, and some American, companies that devolve large amounts of responsibility to employees at all levels, even in stable businesses.)

Having accepted the necessity of tension and paradox, Lawrence and Lorsch embraced the importance of conflict management. While moving from the prior tradition of "conflict as bad" to the position of "conflict as inescapable but manageable," they stopped short of recognizing the need to nurture it under controlled conditions.

Some of the most refreshing ideas in organizational theory come from the pioneering work of younger, lesser known authors. Robert E. Quinn and Kim Cameron,[71] both of the University of Michigan, have aggressively expanded our understanding of organizational paradox. Quinn, writing with John Kimberly[72] of the Wharton School, inventoried a wide range of tensions (or contradictions). They distilled them to four basic dimensions (flexibility versus stability, internal versus external, means versus ends, individual versus organization). Investigating the circumstances under which paradox is appropriate, they suggest that given an organization's place in its life cycle, companies emphasize one or the other polarity. Companies can thus be profiled at any point in their evolution in terms of (1) where the balance is struck, and (2) which balance issues need particular attention. What is most significant about this stream of research is that it challenges the old mindset. For the first time in the century-long study of organizations, it calls attention to a new source of energy and begins to explain why some organizations renew themselves.

Quinn sees the usefulness of unresolved tensions within organizations, and extols the virtues of striving for a synthesis of opposites. Indeed, the inherent tension within organizations is the primary, if not the only, vehicle for self-regeneration. Almost all other forces tend to drive toward equilibrium and stability. A great deal of empirical evidence testifies to the surprising finding that environmental threats breed excessive conservatism and retrenchment (except under the most extreme circumstances, such as Chrysler's near bankruptcy and its fortuitous selection of Iacocca as a radically different type of leader).

PUNCTUATED EVOLUTION

Several strands of an argument are being woven together as we proceed. First, we have developed a deepening appreciation for the power of the "hidden mindset" by tracing the paradigm shifts we have come to understand. Second, we briefly noted the "paradigm shifts" in physics and their impact on the generation of scientists who straddled the era during which the paradigm shift took place. Third, we have traced the old mindset to hidden assumptions in American industrial history and organizational theory. The final strand of this inquiry broaches the topic of organizational self-transformation. Whereas in substance physical changes of state occur as the result of tangible triggers, social systems (such as organizations) rely on a more ephemeral process. They must lift themselves by their own bootstraps.

The field of biology provides an interesting point of departure. In 1977 Stephen Jay Gould and Niles Eldridge[73] challenged Darwin's assumption that random mutation and natural selection lead to *gradual* evolution. They argued, instead, that fossil evidence showed that evolution was discontinuous—a series of relatively quick jumps that somehow produce new species without a transitional stage. Most missing links are missing, they say, because they never existed. The human brain is an example. It did not evolve through tiny next-logical increments, but jumped during the Neanderthal to Cro-Magnon transition (20,000 years ago). The result: we are equipped with a brain that has far greater capacity than any current use requires. It's as if we've been endowed with a mainframe, and we're using it for word processing. (Some scientists speculate that human beings need to evolve another 50,000 years before the capability of the brain will be fully utilized.)[74]

Over the past fifteen years, natural scientists have grappled with a "paradigm shift" because evolutionary processes testify to the paradoxical way in which fluctuation creates equilibrium. Traditionally, fluctuation was seen as disturbing equilibrium. Yet, as the previously cited findings suggest, order based on equilibrium is vulnerable to destruction (owing to the stagnation and absence of adaptation), whereas order based on disequilibrium has a much higher probability of being maintained.[75]

These ideas do not in themselves make the case for disequilibrium as an essential ingredient in *organizational* renewal, but they provide a provocative metaphor for questioning it. Systems theorist Kenneth Boulding observes: "We are in the middle of a quiet revolution in virtually all sciences, which is largely the development of what might be called 'post-Newtonian science.' It involves recognition that equilibrium systems are extremely rare. The universe has been a big disequilibrium process since its inception. The new trend in science also recognizes the importance of rare, impossible, even unique events. We see this in the strangeness of twentieth century physics; in the development of chemistry 'far from equilibrium'; in the development of 'punctuational' rather than 'gradualist' evolutionary theory; and *in the increasing dissatisfaction with the equilibrium theory in economics and sociology.*"[76]

When disruption occurs, our managerial response is generally to impose order as quickly as possible. The old mindset is predicated on the virtues of stability. Organizations are structured to reduce ambiguity; systematic procedures and a variety of other formal and informal mechanisms are employed to provide focus and coherence.[77] But does an organization's short- and long-term health benefit from these measures? Analogies to the natural sciences cause us to consider that the *most* beneficial course of action to ensure long-term survival might be to foster disequilibrium. The idea is counterintuitive.

Stability and Resilience
The previous discussion challenges a long-standing belief; namely, that stability is a desired state. But is it? Far better than stability is the attribute of resilience. *Stability* can be defined as the capacity of a system to return to equilibrium after it has been disturbed; the more rapidly it returns, the less

it fluctuates and the more stable it is. *Resilience* may be viewed as the "measure of the persistence of a system and its ability to absorb change and disturbance." Resilience entails the ability to continue to function, to survive, and to absorb disturbances. Resilience entails an adaptive strategy, not a stabilizing one.[78] Under this scenario, breakdowns produce breakthroughs—an idea with wide relevance for organizations as well as organisms.

University of Pennsylvania Wharton School's Kenwyn Smith makes these interesting observations: The distinction between resilience and stability highlights two radically different ways for thinking about how to manage organizations. Since the stability view emphasizes equilibrium, within this framework it becomes all important to pour resources into maintaining a predictable world (a *fail-safe* world). On the other hand, a resilience view suggests the energy be focused on resilience, with the emphasis upon keeping one's options open (a *safe-to-fail* world). The assumption here is that the future will be unexpected rather than expected.[79] The reader may note that these latter conditions more closely resemble today's competitive situation. The picture emerging from the natural sciences suggests that for an entity to survive, it must not only be in relation to its environment (i.e., the earlier discussed notion of "fit"), but it must be ever-vigilant and adaptive. In natural phenomena, this process is driven by largely unexplained incidents that trigger discontinuous change (or transcendence).

Social entities, in contrast, cannot rely on "chemical or geological triggers." Discontinuous change entails "self-transcendence." Sounding a little like expecting an organization to jump over its own shadow, self-transcendence may be viewed as the capacity of an organization to change its point of view and therefore explore its situation from a different angle. Clearly, self-transcendence is very difficult, but it is essential. Survival requires that organizations periodically "step out" of well-worn routines created and reinforced by past success.[80]

Kenwyn Smith writes:

> For a social entity such as an organization to reflect on itself, it must have a system representing both itself and the *context* in which it is imbedded. That's where nonequilibrium comes in. A social system that promotes paradox and fosters disequilibrium (i.e., encourages variation and embraces contrary points of view), has a greater chance of knowing itself (as the by-product of continually reexamining its assumptions and juggling its internal tensions). This in turn generates a reasonable likelihood of being aware of the context in which it operates.[81]

THE ROLE OF PARADOX

Paradox serves us by setting up polar opposites and affirming both sides. Two factors, mutual exclusivity and simultaneity, are essential for a genuine paradox. If neither side can win, a conceptual "launching pad" is readied for blasting beyond the "gravitational field" in which the original paradox is framed.[82]

Paradoxical qualities within an organization have value because they force people to *think* outside the box, and to break away from convenient categories and patterns. The puzzle in a paradox serves as an impulse; it energizes our minds to "jump the rails" in search of a reconciling insight.[83]

When we transcend a paradox there is often a quality of obviousness that produces a shock of recognition. No longer held captive by the old way of thinking, we are liberated to see things we have known all along, but couldn't assemble into a useful model for action.[84] Peter Elbow, in his thoughtful book, *Embracing Contraries,* states: "The surest way to get hold of what your present frame blinds you to is to adopt the opposite frame. A person who can live with contradiction and exploit it—who can use conflicting models—can simply see and think more."[85]

IS PARADOX ALWAYS HELPFUL?

It is useful to draw a distinction between two types of problems: *convergent* problems (such as balancing your checkbook) that deal with distinct, quantifiable problems amenable to logic, and *divergent* problems (how to reorganize the production department) that are not quantifiable or verifiable, and that do not lend themselves to a single solution.[86] When one solves a convergent problem, one literally eliminates it. There is nothing wrong with that. Divergent problems, however, cannot be permanently eliminated, and benefit from the lateral thinking that paradox evokes.

Paradox has had a pervasive role in creative activities of all types. One pioneering investigation into the essence of creativity studied the milestone contributions of fifty-eight famous scientists and artists, including Einstein, Picasso, and Mozart. They shared a common pattern: *all* breakthroughs occurred when "two or more opposites were conceived simultaneously, existing side by side—as equally valid, operative and true." The research report continues: "In an apparent defiance of logic or physical possibility, the creative person consciously (embraced) antithetical elements and developed these into integrated entities and creations."[87]

Nowhere is paradox more visible than in poetry and the dramatic arts.

Chaucer, Shakespeare, and Eliot develop paradoxical situations of heroic proportions, from which the reader's only escape is to achieve a deeper level of insight.[88] Consider poetry. The language and structure of a poem is often somewhat inscrutable. The poet writes in code. The function of a poem is not to disclose but to conceal its kernel of truth from the lazy-minded, and to reveal it only to those who read carefully and reflect. Paradoxes are presented with complexity and irony so that only those with the right sensibilities get "inside."[89] Illustrative are T.S. Eliot's masterful lines from "East Coker" of his *Four Quartets:*

> *I said to my soul, be still, and wait without hope*
> *For hope would be hope for the wrong thing; wait without love*
> *For love would be love of the wrong thing; there is yet faith*
> *But the faith and the love and the hope are all in the waiting.*
> *Wait without thought, for you are not ready for thought.*
> *So the darkness shall be light, and the stillness the dancing.*[90]

Once hooked, we wrestle with the irreconcilable until we discover a higher-order frame of reference. Only then is intellectual tension released.

THE "INCREMENTALISTS" DISAGREE

Mainstream organizational thinking is a long way from embracing paradox. Charles Lindbloom's 1959 article "The Science of Muddling Through" is an early, and well-known, contribution in a long parade of literature that both documents and legitimizes the *incremental approach*. He writes: "Policy making is typically a never-ending process of successive steps in which continual nibbling [is better than] a good bite."[91] The "limited rationality" school discussed earlier joined this chorus, arguing that organizations change and adapt best by a succession of incremental steps. As Stanford's Jim March put it:

> Managers and leaders propose changes, including foolish ones; they try to cope with the environment and to control it; they respond to other members of the organization; they issue orders and manipulate incentives. . . . Organizational leaders are not likely to behave in strikingly unusual ways. And if a leader tries to march toward strange destinations, an organization is likely to deflect the effort . . . Neither success nor change requires dramatic action. The conventional, routine activities that produce most organizational change require ordinary people to do ordinary things in a competent way.[92]

In short, the "incrementalist school" holds that organizations can avoid the costs of hostilities, demotivation, wasted energy, and foolish risks by limiting themselves to small disruptions and piecemeal progress—that evolution is superior to revolution.

There is much to be said for this point of view. Many organizations have crippled themselves through ill-advised efforts to do too much, too soon. People Express comes to mind. But the key phrase is "ill-advised efforts." Discontinuous change need not be ill-advised.

The earlier overview of America's industrial evolution may help bring the point into focus. The incremental approach to change is very effective when what you want is more of what you've already got. From the Civil War through the end of the 1960s, American industry enjoyed very special circumstances. Campaigns to become "more automated," "more efficient," "more participative," "more stakeholder-oriented," "more environmentally sensitive" were all relatively productive incremental efforts. But each of these shifts of emphasis operated within the existing mindset. Nothing fundamental was changed. It is not surprising that organizational theorists and managers who observed and practiced during this era concluded that incremental change was the wisest approach.

But when the competitive environment pushes a social system to the boundaries of its paradigm, we witness the type of wheel spinning that prevails today. We note the discouraging aftermath of so many self-improvement efforts that lead nowhere.

The overwhelming pattern of almost all efforts for change within American industry in the last decade (aimed at closing the gap between ourselves and the Japanese and other world-class competitors) has resulted in improvements in terms of *our* prior standards of performance, but little narrowing of the gap between ourselves and our ever-improving competition. While we have improved, so have they. It seems impossible to get there from here.

To quote Karl Weick again:

> The more one delves into the subtleties of organizations, the more one begins to question what order means and the more convinced one becomes that prevailing preconceptions of order (that which is efficient, planned, predictable and has survived) are suspect. Simply pushing harder within the old boundaries will not do.[93]

DISCONTINUOUS VERSUS INCREMENTAL CHANGE

A common thread runs through almost all of the organizational theories covered earlier in this chapter: each is predicated on seeking or maintaining order. Weber, Taylor, and Chandler clearly belong in this school. The same is true of the writings of Chester Bernard, Herbert Simon, and the Hawthorne Experiments as reported by Roethlisberger and Mayo. While the latter group noted ways in which social behavior and cognitive limitations detract from order and stability, their aim was to restore equilibrium through closer management of social systems, cognitive processes, and informal group norms. The contingency theorists, such as Harvard professors Lawrence and Lorsch, while acknowledging fluctuations in the environment, propose multiple strategies to retain coherence in the face of environmental uncertainty.

As noted earlier, developments in physics and the natural sciences led some recent organizational theorists to consider that disequilibrium might be a better strategy for survival than coherence and order. A central thrust of this thinking is that internal differences can widen the spectrum of an organization's options by generating new points of view. These, in turn, can promote disequilibrium; under the right conditions, self-renewal and adaptation occur. Herein lies the impetus for our focus on contention. The specific vectors of contention are simply one way of identifying the domains in which conflicts reliably occur and of stating them in operational terms. The seven vector framework is predicated on the notion of a "dialectic." The forces that we have historically regarded as locked in opposition and conflict can be viewed through a different mindset, or paradigm, as apparent opposites generating adaptive responses through a cycle of circulating energy.

In 1984, two professors of McGill University, Danny Miller and Peter Friesen, embarked on a careful, empirical study that lends significant support to the advocates of discontinuous change.[94] A study of twenty-six companies over a prolonged period provided organizational evidence that is both as compelling and surprising as was the fossil evidence in supporting punctuated evolution and challenging Darwin. Significant change, they discovered, occurs in *revolutionary* ways.

Organizations possess a great deal of momentum, or "drift," which inhibits alteration or reform. Increased centralization, for example, leads to more of it, and the same holds true for decentralization (i.e., the familiar "pendulum swings"). But their most startling conclusion is as follows:

> Organizational adaptation is likely to be characterized by periods of dramatic revolution in which there are [changes] in a significantly large number of variables [like] strategy and structure. Organizations seem to evolve in a manner that is quite similar to the development of scientific knowledge. Kuhn

portrays programs in science as "a succession of tradition bound periods punctuated by noncumulative [revolutionary] breaks." In the same way, organizations evolve consistently in accordance with a perspective, strategy, ideology, and mission of their own until some stimuli prompt a revolution.[95]

An interesting theater in which one can observe the interplay of the "incrementalist" and "discontinuous" theories of organizations is provided by the extensive research on competitiveness in manufacturing. These findings, as will be seen, have broad applicability to organizations of all types.

In their pioneering studies, Harvard's Robert Hayes and Stanford's Steven Wheelwright classified manufacturing operations into four distinct stages: (1) reactive, (2) competitively neutral, (3) strategic contributor, and (4) source of world-class competitive advantage.[96] Following the publication of this classification system, the researchers worked extensively with companies eager to upgrade their capability. They discovered some interesting things. First, companies tended to hold inflated views as to where they stood on the four-stage continuum. Second, no company ever succeeded in skipping a stage (which seems to support the incrementalist view). Organizations keep getting in their own way. Third, *very* few companies succeeded, despite great dedication, in evolving into a full-blown Stage 4 competitor. Most companies muscled their way forward, and then slid back.[97]

In sharp contrast is Ford Motor Company. While far from perfect, and faced, like all organizations, with the risks of slipping back into old ways, it worked as systematically as any company in the decade of the eighties to reach Stage 4. Unlike Chrysler (which devoted its primary energies to lowering the breakeven point), and General Motors (which invested $60 billion in plant modernization and robotics), Ford reached a different conclusion. Heavily influenced by the visit of senior executives with their joint venture partner, Mazda, in Japan, Ford concluded that the *key* to building a world-class car was "getting their organization to work." Ford was persuaded that their "manufacturing problem" wasn't a *manufacturing* problem alone. For manufacturing to work effectively, it had to be tied closely to the other organizational functions. What was necessary was a thoroughgoing transformation of virtually all aspects of the company—including a greater involvement of sales, marketing, design, engineering, and finance; a rebalancing of power between line and staff functions; increased levels of participation by individual workers and their union; and the redesign of central control systems, communications networks, corporate values, and strategy. Ford regarded these shifts as requiring *discontinuous* change. As described in Chapters Five and Six, Ford launched a full-court press on every identifiable aspect of these organizational deficiencies. In the process, Ford appears to be making real progress in changing the paradigm.

The earlier cited Hayes and Wheelwright findings were on target, but they didn't go far enough. The four stages of manufacturing have much broader relevance than to shop floor operations alone. In the fullest sense, the four stages apply to the phases of an *organization's* development. Unless the *organization* transcends to the fourth stage, neither manufacturing nor marketing, nor virtually any function with strong interdependencies to other parts of the company, can progress. *Organization* is the common denominator.

Thus a second key insight supporting the discontinuous view: Stage 4 is *not* a natural incremental extension of Stage 3. Stage 4 requires a transformation. The old paradigm creates an "invisible wall" between the first three conventional stages and the last. This is the same barrier that Konosuke Matsushita referred to. It took a concerted frontal assault for Ford to break through the wall. Let us now turn to trace the events that unfolded there.

CHAPTER **FIVE**

Crisis and Transformation: Ford

On a dark day in 1980, Donald Petersen, the newly chosen President of Ford Motor Company, visited the company's Detroit design studios. That year, Ford would lose $2.2 billion, the largest loss in a single year in U.S. corporate history. Petersen could see no light at the end of the tunnel.[1]

The 1970s, with two oil crises and recessions, had weakened Ford. Consumers flip-flopped from wanting fuel economy to seeking sleeker styling, and better acceleration and quality. Ford lagged behind the competition in responding to these trends. Stringent governmental regulations on emissions and safety raised costs.[2] So did a thirty-year-old system of labor-management relations that kept both union and management from working productively.[3] While Ford hemorrhaged, labor costs had risen to in excess of $20 per hour (65 percent more than the average American worker).[4] In some facilities, workers loitered about antiquated and malfunctioning assembly lines reading papers, playing cards, and even lying down and sleeping.[5]

Like GM and Chrysler, Ford had attempted to purchase labor peace with wage, benefit, and work practice concessions that were not competitive by world standards. It tried to make up these added costs by (1) cutting costs on repairs and capital improvements in the factories and (2) pushing workers to close the cost per unit gap with higher volume.[6] Ford's quality levels were the worst in Detroit, and its problem rate per hundred cars was three times higher than the Japanese.[7]

Managerially, Ford was fraught with the turf wars and Byzantine politics portrayed in such books as *Iacocca*.[8] The company was financially focused. Cost accounting drove suboptimal design decisions at the front end of the product development process. In the factories, a system tied a large percentage of plant managers' compensation to volume, driving plants to build cars as rapidly as possible and worry about the defects later.[9] In short, by virtually any measure, Ford was enmeshed in the death grip of inter-locking forces. The problems seemed insurmountable, and the solutions remote.

Petersen had come to the design center to review proposals for a new Thunderbird. Once a breath of fresh air in Ford's line, the Thunderbird had become about as exciting as a cement truck. "He was shown the customary sketches of the big boring boxes," said one source. "Ford designers, truth be told, hated their own designs. They had come to the unhappy state through attrition; year after year they had championed daring ideas and been shot down by top management. There was only one kind of car headquarters wanted: A Car Just Like Last Year's."[10]

After reviewing several prototypes, Petersen probed: "Is this the car you would like to drive?" There was a long silence. Generally, people at Ford learned not to say what they thought. "Absolutely not. I wouldn't want that car parked in my driveway," Ford's Chief Design Executive, Jack Telnack, answered frankly. Petersen inquired further. Encouraged, the designers rolled out their clay models, their dream designs. Functionality, taking the driver seriously, appealing to the consumer's better judgment rather than to the market research department's lowest common denominator: headquarters was bound to hate it. Instead, Petersen gave the go-ahead to design a radically new car.[11] Emboldened, Design showed him their ideas for a daring mid-sized car design—where Ford sells most of its automobiles. Petersen liked what he saw, eventually investing $3.2 billion in the now famous "jellybean" cars—the Taurus and the Sable.[12]

Ford went on to lose $3.3 billion from 1980 to 1982, much more than Lockheed and Chrysler (whose recoveries via bailout sparked public scru-tiny and debate).[13] Had Ford failed, its impact on the U.S. economy would have been far more severe, but Ford's brush with disaster slipped by with little public attention—despite, or perhaps because of, the fact that Ford ranks second among the Fortune 500 in revenues, profits, and assets and is the seventh-largest industrial corporation in the world.[14] Though at one point its cash reserves could keep the company solvent for only forty-five days, the world never allowed itself to acknowledge that Ford teetered on the brink.[15]

In the years since those dark moments, Ford has executed a remarkable turnaround. Its 1986 profits surpassed those of GM for the first time since 1924. In 1987 it broke all previous industry records for profitability and surpassed GM for the second year in a row.[16] In product quality, Ford moved to Number One among the Big Three, and was ranked third in quality among *all* U.S. companies.[17] Its bold designs have gained 6 percent in a market in which each percentage point is worth \$1.5 billion in revenues.[18] Ford's gains have come at a time when many other competitors, including GM and some of the Japanese and German manufacturers, were losing, or barely holding, position. All faced tougher competition both from low-end entrants such as Hyundai, and the convergence of many established American, Japanese, and European manufacturers on the upscale market. Still better news, over 15 percent of Taurus and Sable buyers were owners of imports who were initially looking to purchase another foreign car.[19] Taurus won the "triple crown" in 1987: it was selected as Car of the Year, Best Domestic Car, and Top Car—a first for any American automobile in the decade.[20]

The media has covered this turnaround extensively. Ford's success has been attributed to: (1) making product quality the single most important priority; (2) shifting from an autocratic bureaucracy to a participative, reinvigorated culture; (3) involving the worker as a thinking problem solver rather than simply as an automaton; and (4) investing in Taurus and Sable. But explaining "turnarounds" is a little like defining pornography: "We can't pin it down in words," as a Supreme Court judge once observed, "but we know it when we see it." The trouble is, we have usually already classified a company as having successfully turned around before we look for the causes. Then we settle for superficial explanations that sidestep deeper understanding. Let us test our understanding:

1. How does one of the most autocratic and politicized companies in America shift to a participative style of management, and pull it off with such seeming ease? Cultural change takes time—a decade we are told. Yet Ford made major strides in five years without (1) reorganizing, (2) a house cleaning of "old style" executives, or (3) an infusion of outsiders.

2. In the midst of the \$3.3 billion loss between 1980 and 1982, how does top management make a decision to spend \$3.2 billion on a risky new Taurus/ Sable design? Were they prudent or lucky? Certainly, Ford needed to do *something*—but the cultural change and product quality efforts, both under way and safer bets, were challenges enough. Why take an unnecessary gamble on a bold new design when better execution of a safer design would avoid exposing the company to a possibly fatal risk?

3. Ford had historically been a finance-oriented company. CEO Phillip Caldwell came from Ford's purchasing ranks, and Red Poling (head of North American Automotive Operations, called NAAO) was an alumnus of the Finance fraternity. Given the predisposition of these key players at the top, what explains the emergence of Design, Engineering, and Manufacturing in the turnaround?

4. By 1984, long before the big success of Taurus and Sable, Ford turned the

corner and posted $2 billion in earnings for the year. Why not ease off? Why pursue change with such vigor? By 1984, the programs of Employee Involvement and Participative Management were still taking root. None had become part of the mainstream of the Ford culture. What held the company on course once the urgency was gone?

5. Much is said about hourly workers' enthusiasm for Employee Involvement, but Ford, GM, and Chrysler had all experimented with near-identical programs in the 1970s, and each experiment, after basking in media attention, either died a quiet death or remained an isolated success story. Why did it "take" this time?

6. How does a company sell employees on "involvement" and "cooperation with management" at the very same time they are eliminating 43 percent of hourly jobs and 23 percent of salaried positions? How did Ford elicit cooperation instead of cynicism and sabotage?

7. Finally, theory tells us that strong leaders tend to emerge in time of crisis: Britain had its Churchill, France its de Gaulle, Chrysler its Iacocca. How, then, does an individual such as Don Petersen—reticent and unassuming— execute a daring turnaround of such magnitude? How can Petersen flourish with a style so different from what the situation seemed to warrant?

Herein lies the problem. Many readers are acquainted with the turnaround at Ford, but most will concede that no account of what happened there answers these questions. It points up how easy it is to entertain the illusion of understanding without real understanding. Ford succeeds where, without hindsight, we would surely have predicted it would fail. Our task then is to get beneath the surface explanations. The true answer lies with transformation and the new paradigm.

DISCONTINUOUS CHANGE

The transformation of the Ford Motor Company commands center stage in our quest to understand organizational renewal. As noted earlier, this book is based on descriptive research involving a sample of over 100 companies. Ford stands alone in appearing to have truly transformed itself. There are two risks in making such an assertion. First, like any living entity, there is no guarantee that Ford will not stumble and lose momentum. Renewal is a never-ending struggle. Second, there is no scientifically established standard for "transformation." I have somewhat arbitrarily defined it as "a step-function increase in capability."

Evidence of discontinuous change at Ford is available through both external and internal sources. Objective marketplace criteria document dramatic and sustained performance shifts over a ten-year period.[21] In addition, Ford has brought its production times for some vehicles, in terms of the man-hours it takes to manufacture a car, down close to Japanese levels.[22] The same is true of its warranty costs, which have plunged from $1,100 in 1981 to $100 today. Again, this is comparable to some of the Japanese car makers, and better than any American producer.[23] A similar pattern of step-function improvement is corroborated by Ford's employee surveys: (1) employee job satisfaction has skyrocketed, (2) employee involvement is widely accepted as "a way of life," and (3) quality as Priority One, teamwork, and effective contention management have become major features of the new climate.[24] Based on these external and internal measures, Ford *has* "transformed" itself. While some may quarrel with the criteria applied, few will argue that organizational changes of this magnitude and duration are an *extremely* rare occurrence.

The sticky question is how did Ford do it? Was success the result of improbable coincidences, or can it be replicated? Answers are frustrating because, at first blush, Ford did no more than apply a set of techniques that have been around for some time. Our reaction to many accounts in the media is "So what?" The obstacle to true understanding is the old mindset, or paradigm. As will be seen in the pages that follow, what distinguishes Ford is not *what* they did, but *how* they went about it.

The overarching quality of Ford's approach is that they have been far more *process*-oriented than GM or Chrysler (i.e., they have focused on getting the organization to work, not exclusively on costs or technology).[25] This distinction may seem underwhelming to some—until we reflect on the extent to which a *results* orientation dominates managerial thinking. It was Peter Drucker who first coined the phrase "management by objectives."[26] In so doing, he legitimized an already pervasive facet of American conventional wisdom: focus on the bottom line. Drucker argued that since businesses live or die by results, management should approach the setting of goals and results in a methodical way. Broad corporate goals should be subdivided into component objectives, and assigned as clearly as possible to each unit and individual in the firm. If taken seriously, and defined specifically, the negotiation of these objectives establishes a cascading set of contracts that tighten up ambiguities in the delegation of responsibility. Management by objectives ensures that each link in the chain of command does its part. But as we have seen, too much of a good thing is a bad thing. The central theme of the new mindset is its advocacy of a *synthesis* of, rather than a *choice* between, means and ends, between projects and process.

FORD AS CORNERSTONE

The transformation at Ford is a cornerstone of this book. As I tried to unscramble the complex set of events that unfolded there, several patterns emerged.

First, rather early in its turnaround, Ford began to focus on business fundamentals, sharpen its strategic positioning, and eliminate internal contradictions in how the organization functioned. The pieces began to *fit* together.

Second, Ford moved to lessen the burdens of overcentralization, and used a variety of techniques to *split* up the organization and infuse a sense of autonomy and ownership.

Third, Ford addressed its problem of widespread and unproductive *conflict*. These three basic activities inspired the labels fit, split, and contend.

I was personally involved in one of Ford's organizational change efforts— the 1983 Change Task Force that developed an "architecture" to improve organizational fit. Ford used the Seven S framework for this purpose. The Task Force made over one hundred presentations of its findings throughout the organization. Using the findings as a stimulus, management teams at the corporate, division, and plant levels hammered away at the impediments that had prevented the organizational elements from meshing.

CRISIS AND TRANSFORMATION

The most controversial link in the renewal chain centers on the notion "transcend." Several points warrant comment.

First, there is no prescribed sequence of steps that guarantees a step-function improvement in performance will occur when a certain threshold of change is reached. Yet we observe at Ford that change appears to have reached a critical mass and generated a metamorphosis.

Second, while there were general goals, there was no master plan. A set of tributary actions began to flow into a river of change. But many of these were, for the first several years, largely independent and coincidental activities. Only in hindsight does a pattern appear that might be construed as a "systematic change effort."

One Ford executive observes:

There are several ways to achieve change. One approach is charismatically induced. A single, strong leader like Jack Welch can provide the personal force to reach through to the rank and file and make his priorities felt. In such circumstances, everyone from the first line foreman through top management assigns the success to their leader. A second type of change is environmentally induced. The financial service industry is a great example; not a lot of charismatic leadership, but a lot of change. Our type of change was neither of these. After it happened, even the participants asked: 'How did it start? Where did it come from?' Ours was certainly not a top-down effort—in fact, it occurred almost despite the people at the top. Top management in the sixties and seventies hypersaturated us with fads. Their support of the EI program (as with its predecessors) came in the form of "a memo." The point here isn't to disparage or to discredit top management. Rather, I believe that the most profound and lasting change occurs when the rank and file want it so badly that *they* take the initiative and manage upward.[27]

Third, the common point of agreement among participants in Ford's transformation is that they shared a deep sense of *crisis*. It was the "sink-or-swim," "do your best today or there won't be a tomorrow" variety. One executive vice president states: "You can never underestimate how scared we were in 1980 and 1981. We *really* believed Ford could die. From top executives through middle management and down to hourly employees, a lot of people got religion. It enabled us to deal with the turf, the egos and the "not invented here" attitudes that were killing us. This shared sense of impending disaster was so deeply etched that we did not lose intensity in 1984 when things began to look better."[28]

Crisis does not guarantee redemption. In fact, more often than not, organizations mismanage it. Many companies, as noted in Chapter One, endeavor to repackage their past success formula. This was true of General Motors' reaction to the breakthroughs at Fremont. Others try "anything that's new" and diffuse their energies. People Express is a good example.[29] While most crises stimulate *individuals* to do their utmost, their efforts are not coordinated, the ensuing confusion usually undermines resolve, and a fog of cynicism and helplessness descends.

TOO MANY "COINCIDENCES"

The remarkable occurrence at Ford was that, somewhat mysteriously, a set of independent initiatives flowed together and became mutually reinforcing. Ford succeeded despite missteps. It encountered the normal impediments that plague large corporations. There were turf wars, resource constraints, "personalities," and serious political obstacles. Some of these represented

FIG. 5-1

Confluence of Change Initiatives at Ford

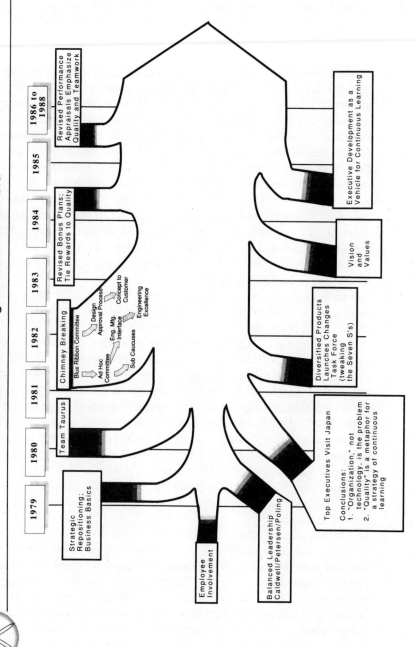

formidable barriers and seemed *certain* to block progress. Yet, miraculously, most cancelled one another out. In the ordinary course of field research, one finds, and overlooks, a few "discrepancies." Ford surmounted at least five.

1. Ford's CEO, Phil Caldwell, ". . . did not get along with . . ." Donald E. Petersen.[30] In most companies, this would guarantee political gridlock and paralysis. This problem persisted until well into 1983. It was during this critical period that Ford did much to regain its footing. Fortuitously, Henry Ford II remained active just long enough to ensure Petersen's succession.[31]

2. For the reasons noted above, it was not clear until the last moment whether Don Petersen, the product man, or Red Poling, the finance man, would be named the next chairman and CEO of Ford. These candidates were described as "in a horse race," with loyalists attached to their respective coattails. Such battles for succession can paralyze a company. At the least, what one aspirant advocates is often subtly or overtly opposed by another. Not so at Ford. At times it appeared that Petersen and Poling both aimed to outdo each other in promoting change. When one discovered a process that worked, it was reverse-engineered by his rival.[32]

3. The most likely sponsors of Ford's most ambitious change efforts were antagonists. The Human Resources function was headed by an individual who viewed novel programs as unproven and possibly injurious to the preservation of managerial rights. The Ford executive heading Labor Relations and his counterpart, the UAW official assigned the top role in representing the union at Ford, did not openly support the early employee involvement experiments begun at the plant level. But within six months, these obstacles vanished. The UAW official retired and was replaced by one of the most progressive thinkers in the UAW—Don Ephlin. The latter had firsthand experience with General Motors' successes with worker participation at Tarrytown, and was eager to try them at Ford. More remarkable, Henry Ford II had grown restive with his Industrial Relations chief, who subsequently retired. For the first time in Ford's history, the company went outside. Pete Pestillo, hired from Goodrich, was a champion of worker participation. Still more remarkable, Ephlin and Pestillo got along.[33]

4. The first collective effort by Ford's senior executives (known as the Blue Ribbon Committee) got off to a v-e-r-y slow start. Created in early 1980, it wrestled with its assignment of delayering and downsizing the engineering ranks for six months . . . then decided to enlarge its membership from beyond the engineering functions to include Design, Manufacturing, and Truck Operations. It also invited in a facilitator. Reconstituted as a truly cross-functional group, it took two years from inception to recommend (1) a reduction from five layers to three within the engineering hierarchy and (2) the identification of more than two hundred middle managers whose positions could be elimi-

nated. There was a hitch, however. The Committee stipulated that none of the redundant individuals be laid off and that, should their jobs be downgraded, they be protected at their current compensation and benefits levels for four years. (Attractive early retirement packages were proposed to encourage individuals to leave voluntarily.) While top management ultimately accepted these recommendations, many at the periphery viewed this endeavor with skepticism. The highly visible effort had consumed a lot of executive time and produced underwhelming results. Poling himself chided the Committee for taking too long. Yet curiously, this endeavor did not become the object of derision and scorn. To the contrary, it was regarded as a valiant first try from which others could learn. The Blue Ribbon Committee's members reconstituted themselves, learned from their mistakes, and have spearheaded some of Ford's most ambitious change initiatives in the years since.[34]

5. By 1983, as Ford's various initiatives began to show signs of paying dividends, the earlier-mentioned UAW officer, Ephlin, moved on to a new assignment at General Motors. His successor, the new UAW vice president assigned to Ford, regarded EI as "mostly a local matter." Notwithstanding this loss of a champion within the UAW, rank-and-file support of EI was strong enough to maintain the program's momentum.[35]

AGGREGATE CONSCIOUSNESS?

Nancy Badore makes this observation:

Where is the "consciousness" of a learning organization? Where is its head? There was no single node of intelligence at Ford. Top management certainly wasn't on top of all that was going on. In the formative stages their role was largely one of policy support. What happened instead is that you had a number of change efforts tackling things that were central to the business. These efforts were not coordinated in any way; in fact, there was a kind of jealousy between the various internal change efforts—gossip about whose program was the best "grounded." But we shared two common goals—crisis and a drive for quality. Crisis heightened our "consciousness." "Quality" was a wonderful unifying objective because it tied everyone from the Chairman to the hourly workers together. These shared values were so compelling that the false starts weren't fatal. They overcame the politics, sloppy training and mistakes.[36]

As suggested in this quote, Ford's "collective consciousness" stemmed from the intensity of a shared vision. This generated dozens of initiatives, and tapped into thousands of "nodes of intelligence." It guided people, operating in relative isolation, to march to the same drum. Carl Jung coined a term for this phenomenon: *synchronicity*.[37] The term rings true as applied to events at Ford. Some may dismiss the unfolding events as happy coincidence, but, as shown in Figure 5–2, the sheer number of activities underway, and formidable nature of the earlier-mentioned obstacles, made success unlikely. *Without hindsight,* it is difficult to envision that the various change initiatives would progress in the same direction and culminate in a change of such magnitude.

FORGING THE RENEWAL CHAIN

Fit

In the 1970s, Ford suffered from a double jeopardy of ills. On one hand, it had swung toward extremes in the control direction. Hard-edged, numbers-driven, and strategically rigid, it was a caricature of a large, mechanistic bureaucracy.[38] Ford was fixated on "control." There was also a lot of conflict—most of it misdirected toward internecine turf wars.[39] Like an academic seminar gone amok, an enormous amount of energy was devoted to one-upmanship. This tangle showed little prospect of self-renewal.

A stimulus for reexamining old assumptions occurred in the late 1970s and early 1980s when various task forces visited Japan. Chrysler and GM had also made such journeys to the Far East, but Ford drew different conclusions. Whereas Chrysler had focused exclusively on stark economics (closed plants, accelerated outsourcing, laid off employees, and reduced break-even by 50 percent), and GM sought to sidestep the Japanese onslaught through automation and technology, Ford's managers, and the UAW officials who accompanied them, reached a different conclusion: Yes, much could be borrowed from the Japanese in terms of techniques—such as just-in-time inventory control and lower-cost facilities planning—but the secret to Japanese success, in Ford's view, was *humans and organizations.* There, companies thrived on a wave of ideas that accumulated drop by drop. The genius of the Japanese methodology was in constructing organizations that motivated and then harvested tiny improvements in a thousand places. As difficult as this challenge was, the growing consensus at Ford was that there was no way to avoid it. Unlike General Motors, they did not have the financial resources nor the unlimited faith in the "technological silver bullet." Thus, they turned to the painstaking task of systematically fixing the organization.[40]

Change flourishes in a "sandwich." When there is consensus above and pressure below, things happen. While there was no operational consensus on

FIG. 5-2

Activity at Ford

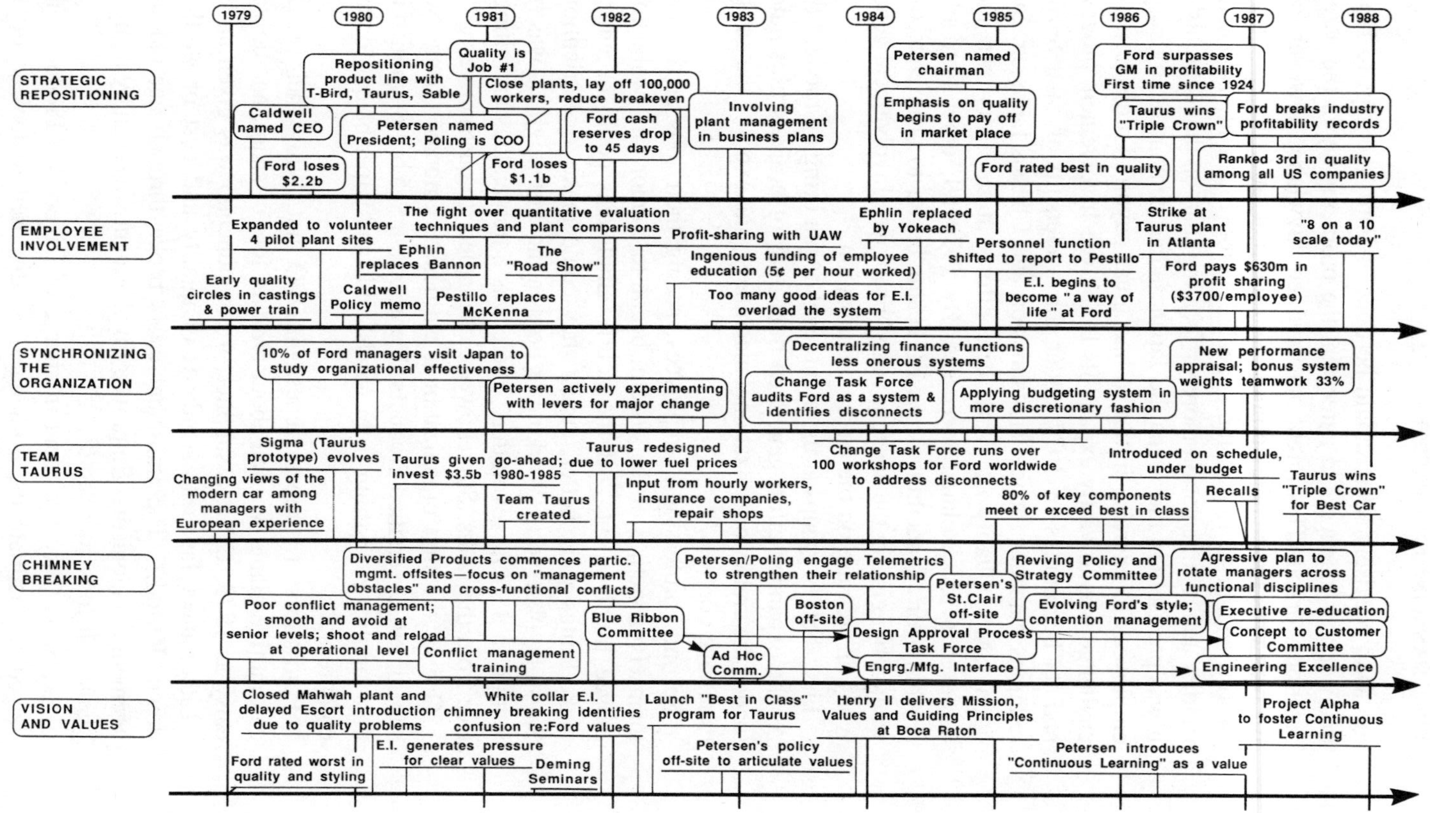

Timeline years: 1979 | 1980 | 1981 | 1982 | 1983 | 1984 | 1985 | 1986 | 1987 | 1988

STRATEGIC REPOSITIONING
- Caldwell named CEO
- Ford loses $2.2b
- Repositioning product line with T-Bird, Taurus, Sable
- Quality is Job #1
- Petersen named President; Poling is COO
- Close plants, lay off 100,000 workers, reduce breakeven
- Ford cash reserves drop to 45 days
- Ford loses $1.1b
- Involving plant management in business plans
- Petersen named chairman
- Emphasis on quality begins to pay off in market place
- Ford surpasses GM in profitability First time since 1924
- Taurus wins "Triple Crown"
- Strike at Taurus plant in Atlanta
- Ford pays $630m in profit sharing ($3700/employee)
- Ford rated best in quality
- Ford breaks industry profitability records
- Ranked 3rd in quality among all US companies

EMPLOYEE INVOLVEMENT
- Early quality circles in castings & power train
- Ephlin replaces Bannon
- Caldwell Policy memo
- The "Road Show"
- Pestillo replaces McKenna
- Expanded to volunteer 4 pilot plant sites
- The fight over quantitative evaluation techniques and plant comparisons
- Profit-sharing with UAW
- Ingenious funding of employee education (5¢ per hour worked)
- Too many good ideas for E.I. overload the system
- Ephlin replaced by Yokeach
- Personnel function shifted to report to Pestillo
- E.I. begins to become "a way of life" at Ford
- New performance appraisal; bonus system weights teamwork 33%
- "8 on a 10 scale today"

SYNCHRONIZING THE ORGANIZATION
- 10% of Ford managers visit Japan to study organizational effectiveness
- Petersen actively experimenting with levers for major change
- Decentralizing finance functions less onerous systems
- Change Task Force audits Ford as a system & identifies disconnects
- Applying budgeting system in more discretionary fashion

TEAM TAURUS
- Changing views of the modern car among managers with European experience
- Sigma (Taurus prototype) evolves
- Team Taurus created
- Taurus given go-ahead; invest $3.5b 1980-1985
- Taurus redesigned due to lower fuel prices
- Input from hourly workers, insurance companies, repair shops
- Change Task Force runs over 100 workshops for Ford worldwide to address disconnects
- 80% of key components meet or exceed best in class
- Introduced on schedule, under budget
- Recalls
- Taurus wins "Triple Crown" for Best Car

CHIMNEY BREAKING
- Diversified Products commences partic. mgmt. offsites—focus on "management obstacles" and cross-functional conflicts
- Poor conflict management; smooth and avoid at senior levels; shoot and reload at operational level
- Conflict management training
- Blue Ribbon Committee
- Ad Hoc Comm.
- Petersen/Poling engage Telemetrics to strengthen their relationship
- Boston off-site
- Petersen's St. Clair off-site
- Design Approval Process Task Force
- Engrg./Mfg. Interface
- Reviving Policy and Strategy Committee
- Aggressive plan to rotate managers across functional disciplines
- Evolving Ford's style; contention management
- Executive re-education
- Concept to Customer Committee
- Engineering Excellence

VISION AND VALUES
- Closed Mahwah plant and delayed Escort introduction due to quality problems
- Ford rated worst in quality and styling
- White collar E.I. chimney breaking confusion re:Ford values
- E.I. generates pressure for clear values
- Deming Seminars
- Launch "Best in Class" program for Taurus
- Petersen's policy to articulate values off-site
- Henry II delivers Mission, Values and Guiding Principles at Boca Raton
- Petersen introduces "Continuous Learning as a value"
- Project Alpha to foster Continuous Learning

top as to precisely *what* should be done at Ford, the trips to Japan caused many senior managers to agree that the problems lay in the way the organization worked. This might not have led anywhere, however, were it not for pressures for change coming from the rank and file.

Ford sought to loosen the shackles of too much fit. Nowhere was the rigidity and regimentation more suffocating than on the assembly lines. Yet it was precisely in this arena the Japanese had demonstrated that permitting employees to exercise initiative had great payoff. Ford's response to this challenge was to vastly expand its Employee Involvement program, which had its beginnings in 1977 under the leadership of Stan Surma, labor-relations manager for the Transmission and Chassis Division. Surma built upon GM's Quality of Work Life efforts at its Tarrytown facility and achieved a few isolated successes. By 1979–80, other Ford plants were reaching for "something." As EI Teams began to proliferate they underwent debugging in the ensuing years. Employee Involvement generated two types of pressure on the larger organization.[41]

First, hourly groups at the plant level began bringing forward their ideas. As the expanded effort generated thousands of projects, this quickly overloaded the creaky organizational machinery, and exposed the turf games and excessive controls.[42]

Second, professional employees, seeing their jobs at risk and feeling themselves victims of the system, began to clamor for "white collar" Employee Involvement.[43] If the hourly employees could be empowered to make things work better, surely they could make a contribution as well. Says one observer: "Working at Ford in the early eighties was like participating in a social revolution. There was a tremendous upwelling of initiative from the ranks. Somehow we channeled it constructively."[44]

One of the first organizational entities to embrace change was Ford's subsidiary, Diversified Products Operations, a $15 billion miniconglomerate that supplies everything from windshields and wiper blades to castings and compressors.

Ford's loss of competitiveness hit DPO first. While their brethren in the automotive plants worried about *gradual* loss of share, and downsizing, as early as 1979, DPO (a supplier of components) was given an ultimatum: "Either meet Japanese standards of quality and cost or we'll close you down. Period." The imminent crisis broke through age-old union/management antagonisms. Employee Involvement was seen by many as the *last chance*. It took root rapidly.[45]

Executive Vice President in charge of Diversified Products, Tom Page, helped to facilitate these changes. Predisposed to look at organizational problems systematically, Page was an effective and courageous champion of change. He also had a close working relationship with the new President, Don Petersen. He states: "Neither of us had a plan, but Petersen's support was clear. He regarded DPO as an ideal place to try some things out. If it worked, we might be able to extend success to the automotive side of the business."[46]

Page decided he had to reform the way his managers behaved. He felt organizational barriers were stifling the energy and initiative flowing from Employee Involvement at the hourly level. He sponsored a series of executive workshops, one for each of his ten business units. The open identification of problems, and subsequent improvements in productivity, flowing from these five-day sessions was extraordinary.

Over a four-month period, ten such workshops were held, each attended by the top 100 to 120 people of the respective business units. In each instance, rival functions within the businesses faced each other and identified the operational problems that prevented them from working together productively and creatively. States one executive present: "This was EI at the white-collar level. The roll-out of workshops on this massive scale generated tremendous momentum, and built a critical mass for change."[47]

By the time five of his business units had passed through the process, Page decided he needed to run a special session for his own staff. The ten executive committees were invited, as was Petersen. The time was ripe to examine the *system-wide* obstacles facing DPO and Ford as a company.[48]

It is tempting, in the interest of economy, to simply state that this unfolding of events addressed Ford's significant problem of oppressive fit. While such was the case, the indirection through which ultimate reform was achieved is an important dimension to any true and faithful account.

Page's organization could only achieve a limited degree of reform before it ran headlong into the barrier of Ford's corporate-wide controls. The challenge was how to bring this to top management's attention in a politically palatable way. There were *very* strong prohibitions at Ford against "meddling" in matters outside one's own area of responsibility. Initiatives to change corporate policies would be regarded as presumptuous, or worse, inspired by political ambition.[49]

Page's solution was to create a Change Task Force, whose *official* mission was to improve DPO's performance. To repeat: the work product was *strictly* for DPO's own internal consumption. But, as noted earlier, Page held an ace. Petersen had agreed that if something worthwhile was to surface, the findings would somehow be disseminated outside DPO.[50]

The Change Task Force approached its task by surveying well-run companies and identifying ideas that worked. When I met with them they were struggling to make sense of the mountain of information they had collected. Once introduced to the Seven S Model, the group decided to organize its findings into those categories. A Task Force member recalls:

> It became evident to us that Ford's organization was the obstacle and fixing ourselves was far more important than trying out a gimmick that we had picked up here and there. The problem was: we were greatly exceeding our charter. Instead of a report on well-run companies, we wanted to get people thinking about Ford. Our report presented instead a systematic picture of successful organizations. We didn't say anything bad about Ford but left it to the listeners to draw their own conclusions.[51]

Early in its deliberations, the Task Force met alone with Petersen. The Task Force coordinator observes:

> The question on the table was how to disseminate our ideas outside of DPO into the automotive side of the business. Petersen shepherded us around the land mines.
> First, he pointed out that while our audience would include *very* different people, what they shared in common was (1) a poignant sense of the magnitude of the external threat, and (2) robust goals like quality. The payoffs were so compelling that these common concerns would cut through their divergent philosophies. The moral: keep the recommendations closely linked to business imperatives.
> Second, Petersen went to Poling in advance and ensured that we would get a fair hearing. Interestingly, the Task Force never presented its ideas to Chairman Phil Caldwell.[52]

Caldwell was thought to be skeptical of such endeavors and might have derailed the project.

Petersen arranged for the Task Force to present its conclusions to the top five executives. Poling attended. One participant recalls:

> I remember the presentation. I had eight words out of my mouth when Red [Poling] said: "You're telling me Dana [the corporation] is soft on accountability?" My answer: "No—in fact, there is tighter accountability at Dana and many of these companies than we experience at Ford. But there is a better balance." He asked lots of tough questions but we did well. When we were finished, each of these top executives invited us to present to their management team. Before it was over, we had given one hundred presentations cascading

through automotive operations in the U.S., Europe, Latin America, and the Pacific Rim.[53]

The Management Change Task Force exemplifies Ford's efforts to address the problems of oppressive fit. It resulted in higher sign-off limits, decentralization of staff functions, and a variety of moves consistent with initiatives that were being taken at the plant level. It generated pressures for a common set of values, a revised performance appraisal, and a reward system that was more consistent with the way the organization needed to operate. By 1985, Ford had gone a considerable distance in realigning fit.

Split

Split refers to the way in which organizations divide themselves up to make tasks more manageable. Whereas fit focuses on togetherness, split focuses on separateness—and the two go hand in hand. Ford could only go so far in alleviating its onerous controls by realigning fit. The reason: fit, by definition, seeks its ends through *common* policies and procedures; split, in contrast, spawns divergent approaches and experiments.

Ford effectively orchestrated split to recapture vitality. One consequence of the changes made was to reestablish constructive tension. While the tendency in many companies is to take a "good idea" such as split and drive it to illogical extremes, Ford made no such mistake.[54] In areas for which more autonomy was essential, they fostered *greater* degrees of split; in other cases, in which units needed to work more closely together, they *reduced* it.

The centerpiece in Ford's efforts to establish appropriate levels of split was Team Taurus. This highly visible, bet-your-company project required a strong mission and identity to succeed. The core included not only designers, but full-time representatives from engineering, manufacturing, and finance. A number of other critical disciplines participated on a part-time basis—Power Train, Purchasing, Castings—and external representatives from suppliers, dealers, insurance companies, and the automotive media.[55]

Taurus was not just the stalking horse for Ford's "new look," it was the prototype of Ford's transforming organizational culture. Team Taurus devised many day-to-day enablers necessary to getting its job done. As work got under way, it became clear that each of Team Taurus' representatives from their respective functional disciplines needed an *equal* voice. This was addressed by (1) shielding the team from the interference of the towering functional disciplines that were anxious about prerogatives and precedents, and (2) establishing norms within the team that fostered listening, problem solving, and sanctioned turfism. Team Taurus evolved a "soft" technology for giving operational integrity to cross-functional teams. Its seven basic tenets are summarized in Box 5–1:

The pressures that Taurus generated on the organization in which it was embedded triggered the fine-tuning of a variety of systems to reward teams and autonomous units for their accomplishments.[56] To avoid excess, Ford interjected a counterbalance by tying a significant percentage of rewards to *overall* corporate profitability and product quality.[57] Finally, and perhaps most significantly, Ford's Employee Involvement program was a powerful force for split. The mere existence of thousands of employee groups examining, recommending, and challenging the status quo provided visible testimony that the individual and the small working unit could take a stand and make a difference.[58]

Contend

Conflict at Ford was pronounced. Adversaries either fought openly and heatedly or avoided one another altogether. In the plants and on the assembly line, it was often hostile. One plant engineer states: "The games we played were amazing. We'd sabotage the other's projects. We'd freeze the other side out of discussions, sneer, blow up, ignore people, or simply not show up at meetings."[59]

BOX 5–1.

Team Taurus Principles

1. Clear-cut, nonconflicting goals and measurements for the program and its team members.
2. Company-wide recognition and prestige associated with membership on the team.
3. Empowerment of the team and its members, by top management, to officially represent the interests of their respective vertical organizations.
4. Acceptance of the customer, instead of the most powerful vertical organization, as the tiebreaker.
5. Core development team members reported directly to the program manager.
6. Continuity of key team members.
7. Joint responsibility for team success.

John Manoogian, Ford's former Director of Quality Assurance, recounts that each division within the company was (then) "chiefly concerned with its own performance and really didn't care about the other divisions—to say nothing of optimizing the product. One division would take delight in saying that another had fouled up, instead of trying to help. Of near-legendary status were the disputes between Design and Car Body Engineering (which had to translate style into metal). Though their buildings were adjacent on the Ford 'campus,' officials of the two departments communicated by memo, refusing to meet face to face."[60] Petersen is quoted as saying of this time: "I couldn't stand the infighting that was going on—the pointless jockeying for position."[61]

The outcome of such extreme forms of ineffective contention management showed up in the final product. One example was Ford's attempt to make the European-designed Escort a world car when it was introduced in 1980. Ford sought to build a vehicle with common parts that could be assembled in different global locations for a variety of local markets. What happened *in fact* was that each geographical region *re*designed the car. Most flagrant was the United States, where only six of the Escort's 5,000 parts remained in common with their European counterparts—and one of these six was the radiator cap![62]

At the top of the corporation, conflict was avoided. Paul H. Weaver, who for a short time was a Ford public relations executive, states: "There was no crusading zeal, and no interest in intellectual combat. The [top management team] moved by indirection, dissembled, obfuscated, and avoided, rather than sought, confrontation and resolution."[63]

One of top management's primary tools to avoid conflict was elaborate and interlocking memos. These, in effect, were treaties that staked out turf. Current CEO Don Petersen recalls: "At the topmost levels, confrontation was gentlemanly. It was mostly avoided: You *only* dealt with issues that the 'Statements of Authorities and Responsibilities' said were yours. You learned real fast to stay inside your limits."[64]

> When I was head of the truck division, [he continues,] I went to the company product planning sessions for the first time. You quickly got the message that you shouldn't even dream of saying anything out loud about cars, even though I'd spent virtually my entire career working on product development in the automotive line. But once assigned to the truck division, I lost all credibility as a source. It was as if I was brain dead or spoke a different language. This same phenomenon held true when I went from product planning to marketing. I lost all credibility as a source of good ideas for products when I was wearing the marketing hat. We really compartmentalized one another.

So the "gentlemanly" way of dealing with conflict was basically by ignoring you, not taking your input, pretending that you hadn't even spoken at all. This, of course, led to communication flows that were compartmentalized and sequential: "You design it, stylist, I'll engineer it!" Still later, "I'll engineer it, damn it, you manufacture it!" Still later, Manufacturing would tell Product Development, "We'll make it, damn it, don't bother us. We'll fix your mistakes."

There was little or no interaction, and no problem solving. The stylists would say, "If you guys were half-decent engineers, you could make it like we designed it," and the engineers would say, "If you guys were half-decent industrial designers, you'd be able to design something that could be built." There were loggerheads everywhere, and, of course, we didn't push leading-edge technology. The only way to get a new idea in place was to be able to point out that some competitor already was doing it. Then you could say, "See, I told you so." It was all a game of "gotcha," a lot of distrust, lack of faith, and accusations that the other guy wasn't "professional." It was built on a series of negative concepts and negative thinking. It was an atmosphere in which rationality had a hell of a time flowering.[65]

Most companies ignore conflict. Very few have formal systems, or even effective informal norms, for contention management. Very few train managers and employees in the skills necessary to deal with conflict constructively. Contention is the "skeleton" in the organizational closet.

Beginning in the early eighties, Ford attempted to use its internecine strife as a source of constructive energy. This was a major priority of Diversified Products. DPO's senior executives engaged in a novel contention-management exercise in which each functional discipline was asked to identify the positive and negative impacts of the other functional departments on its ability to fulfill its role. These were brief, written messages, affectionately termed "valentines."* At the conclusion of the exercise, participants delivered their "valentines" to one another. Next, each function was asked to analyze its feedback, identify patterns, and share publicly what it had heard and how it intended to move forward to respond to perceived problems.[66]

"The first step in training people to deal with conflict," states the designer and lead facilitator of the exercise, "is to acknowledge it. The 'valentines exercise' got people to own up to what they were doing to each other. The ah-ha was the realization that no one was working toward a common goal but toward narrow, functional goals. Conflict that had been

---

* This process has much in common with General Electric's much-heralded "Work-Out" process but preceded it by five years.

latent was exposed, conflict that had been attributed to personalities was seen as having its roots in the system. It became demystified, depersonalized, and much more manageable."[67]

The inroads toward more constructive conflict management made by DPO were paralleled by a variety of efforts elsewhere within Ford. Petersen took his top team to an off site in St. Clair, Michigan, for team-building. The Blue Ribbon Committee, as noted earlier, spawned a number of highly successful cross-functional study groups. The same individuals, now much more skilled at collaborative work, addressed the Design Approval Process and have spearheaded one of Ford's major thrusts of the 1990s—Concept to Customer. Subordinates of the Blue Ribbon Committee formed the Ad Hoc Committee to handle the day-to-day breakdowns that cross-functional teamwork revealed. Later those same subordinates moved on to address the Engineering/Manufacturing Interface and are the main drivers behind the current campaign for engineering excellence.

All the above-noted in-the-trenches experience vastly improved executive skills in healthy conflict management.[68] Underscoring the importance of valuing differences and turning them to advantage, Ford's two top managers, Petersen and Poling, completed a personal-style profile and subjected themselves to one-on-one coaching to improve their working relationship.[69] Here were individuals who were almost mirror opposites in style choosing to actively engage and complement one another, rather than divide up turf so they would not have to interact. In concert, these various efforts sent strong signals that conflict could be healthy if managers would develop the skills to channel it constructively.

CHIMNEY BREAKING

Pre-Petersen, Ford had divided itself like the Italian city states, each at war with the others. Someone at Ford used the term *chimneys*—an allusion to tall, vertical structures (and playing off the image of the automotive business as a smokestack industry).[70] Every chimney was a self-contained unit. The task of breaking into these vertical structures and developing an ability to work across them horizontally became known as *chimney breaking*. One Ford executive states:

> Within its major operational divisions—North American Automotive Operations (NAAO), International Automotive, and Diversified Products—Ford was vertically organized by function. The vertical organizations had become so

parochial and self-contained that they were referred to as "chimneys" of power. Each function had its own goals and perspectives, and each tended to view the others as part of any problem, rather than as part of its solution.

What's more, the financial rewards were geared to results in managing your own chimney. If a guy in engine development came up with a way to make a lighter engine, or one that was more fuel efficient, there was little incentive to consult with manufacturing so they could prepare themselves for different assembly parameters. So the car would come together and the pieces wouldn't fit.

Top management knew this was a problem, but there were historical barriers in the way. An entire layer of people at the chimney tops—the equivalent of divisional presidents—had come up through their respective chimneys and had enormous loyalty to their former colleagues. It was civil war at the top. The question was never, "Are we winning against the Japanese?" but rather, "Are we winning against each other?" You had to reach your objectives, even if they were in conflict with the other chimneys, or in conflict with the broader objectives of the company.[71]

One clarification is in order here. The image of "breaking chimneys" could evoke images of disruption and the destruction of functional discipline. "Nothing could be further from the truth," says Mike Easton, internal Ford facilitator for the Blue Ribbon Committee. "True, we used the terms 'chimneys' and 'pipes' as code words for our tall functional departments. But the purpose wasn't to destroy them but to achieve better working relationships between them."[72]

THE BLUE RIBBON MYSTERY

It is difficult to pinpoint the exact origins of the chimney breaking process. As early as fall 1981, the new head of NAAO, Red Poling, put himself and the top twelve officers in the NAAO Executive Committee through a process aimed at assessing individual styles and building teamwork. The conviction was that if the top couldn't work together, it would be difficult to expect the levels below to do so. While this first try was far from a total success, one participant, Stuart Frey, in charge of automotive planning, design, and engineering, stepped forward as the champion of improving cross-functional teamwork. Frey had a monkey on his back: Poling wanted costs reduced dramatically and a far more efficient design and engineering process.

Rick Albertson, head of Human Resources for the group and a major support person to the efforts which were to follow, recalls:

Poling was putting financial pressures on Frey to get costs down. But instead of edicting cuts he asked: "What are the ways you can do that?" Poling, Frey, and a number of top executives had been heavily influenced by what they had seen in Japan. They had all concluded that our challenge was to avoid layoffs insofar as possible, and to keep the crew on board so that we could operate like our *real* competitors, the Japanese. But the heat was on. Frey definitely knew he had to come across with something. His style is very much like Petersen's— he listens well and has a knack for drawing people out and getting them committed.[73]

One of the most important insights into the nature of "continuous learning" is that you often don't know what is "learned" until after the fact. Bill Broussard, outside consultant and a facilitator within NAAO during this period, comments:

> The Blue Ribbon Committee began in a very traditional mode. The HR department came in and proposed a "new" organization chart to eliminate layers. Frankly, I think that's what Poling expected. And in many people's minds, committees like this were suspect—top management's window dressing to syndicate the inevitable edict of layoffs. But someone at the session spoke up: "Is this process we're proposing consistent with all the talk about participation at Ford?" The discussion began to heat up. The Committee decided it had to take real ownership of the problem. This led to an expanded membership to include the seniormost representatives from Manufacturing, Design, and Truck Operations. It also meant they needed to listen to the professionals in the ranks below.[74]

Frey surveyed all twelve thousand salaried employees under his command. The question was: What do we need to do to make engineering efficient and effective? The responses revealed some very clear patterns: Ford needed faster, higher-quality communications and to drive decisions down to lower levels.[75]

The story of the Blue Ribbon Committee is a microcosm of the mystery of Ford's transformation. Its members saw their role as seminal and are immensely proud of what was accomplished.[76] Yet, as noted earlier, many onlookers within Ford felt the Committee got bogged down in process and bit off too much in frontally attacking the layers of engineering's hierarchy.[77] Two years would pass before the Committee would recommend the elimination of two layers, identify more than two hundred redundant senior slots, and propose that surplus executives be guaranteed four years' protection at current compensation and benefit levels.[78] But in many respects, this "bottom line" assessment misses the "big picture."

First, the Committee members walked a tightrope. With pressure to "downsize and delayer" from above and cynicism from below, ninety-nine out of one hundred such groups would have opted for those two silver bullets—restructuring and layoffs. But the Committee members knew from hard experience that such measures would paralyze their organizations for months . . . and with the crisis at hand and the need to roll out Taurus and a sequence of follow-on products in rapid succession, they needed to *build* morale and elicit extraordinary levels of sacrifice and inspiration. So they took the heat, proceeded slowly, listened, and generated buy-in. In last analysis, top management was won over to this "go slow and keep the troops on board" approach.

Second, the *most* revolutionary achievement of the Blue Ribbon Committee was that the chimney heads of archenemy functions chose to meet every Thursday evening from 5 to 7 P.M. for two years![79] Recall that this was a time of crisis; everyone was working long hours under great stress. Imagine the impatience and frustration that these senior executives (with little initial mutual respect for one another) experienced as they struggled to find a way out of the box.[80] Here was the real revolution: in the sincerity and persistence of men who recognized that *they* needed to change if Ford was going to change. This is the rarest, yet most essential, ingredient in successful change: top executives who are willing to suffer and change themselves.

The example set by Stu Frey and the Blue Ribbon Committee had a cascading effect throughout NAAO. Most noteworthy, the subordinates of the Blue Ribbon Committee members were asked to form the Ad Hoc and Engineering/Manufacturing Interface Committees. These were the groups that went to work on the nitty-gritty operational problems and which, over a twenty-four-month period, nearly halved Ford's product development cycle from six to four years.[81] Later, by designing products with ease-of-manufacturing in mind, they brought the labor hours per vehicle for some Ford cars down to very near Japanese levels.[82]

As had occurred on Team Taurus, the experience of these groups shaped a set of ground rules for effective collaborative work. One such rule stipulated that members could not send delegates. While there were no explicit sanctions for nonattendance, it was understood that should the group reach a decision in one's absence, all participants were bound by its decision. Another feature was formal recognition of the value of facilitators. Many were internal Ford employees, some were outside consultants; all served to call attention to the games being played and were dedicated to eliciting straight and effective communication. Some played an invaluable role in tracking accountability. One executive recalls: "At the end of every meeting, the facilitator would pin people down as to who was going to do what. And at the beginning of the next meeting, there would be that ugly flipchart with everybody's name and action item."[83]

TRANSFORMATION

We turn again to reflect on the phenomenon of transformation. Ford's achievements were not natural extensions of what it already knew how to do. Understanding Ford is more than a linear extrapolation of cause and effect. I have earlier cited a set of astonishing statistics concerning Ford's renaissance. (Statistics such as the company's quality jumping from an annualized rate of increase of 2 to 3 percent a year to 57 percent over three years.)[84] Whereas in the past quality improvements were engineered into the product, and muscled through by management, fully 80 percent of Ford's improvements in quality and productivity over the past eight years have come from the human factor—not automation.[85] These are discontinuities. No trend line or prior pattern at Ford would predict them.

Why didn't Ford's change efforts bog down into a paralysis of meetings? Why didn't participants just filibuster and avoid tough choices? One Ford executive comments:

First, top management, beginning with Petersen, was really practicing what they preached. If people were avoiding conflict down below, it got up to the top quickly, and it was addressed. This is rare in most corporations. Secondly, the external facilitators kept us honest. I am puzzled how most companies use external consultants. They let them dabble in the most sensitive areas—what strategy to pursue, how to organize. That seems a *real* abdication of the manager's job. On the other hand, if your *process* is defective, external consultants can really help you. They surface the "unmentionable" topics and smoke out hidden "agendas."[86]

Ford protected its successes. As the various initiatives gathered momentum, Ford tried studiously to avoid the overzealous and premature rollout that had killed its earlier attempts at change in the 1970s. Says one manager deeply involved in the effort:

We identified the key individuals whose support (to the problem we were trying to solve) was critical. We put them on a team, or task force. We trained them and provided protected opportunities to experiment. Line managers were the focal point. Staff played a background role—conducting surveys and interviews, developing a facts base, steering a team toward "winnable" opportunities, and sourcing and training facilitators.[87]

Another internal facilitator states:

> As management engaged in these cross-functional tasks, their commitment was modified by their common experience. Impatient managers learned that the process resisted shortcuts or speedups. Wary managers formed sufficient positive results that their skepticism was allayed. Political managers found that lip service was insufficient and that the facilitators and their peers smoked out their sentiments. As the process progressed, managers, including senior managers, moved from being targets of the change strategy to its leaders and advocates.[88]

Not all executives made it. Ford retained an outside service to counsel with executives as to (1) their sympathy with the cultural change under way and (2) their willingness to engage in the personal work necessary to be a part of it. Most agreed with the change in principle, but some simply couldn't see themselves mastering the new, less "expert," more "facilitative," style. In these instances, attractive severance packages or lateral transfers (to less critical slots) were made.[89]

This holistic approach is a critical ingredient in two respects. First, a holistic (or systematic) approach to change reinforces itself owing to the fittedness, or harmony, among the parts. One chord resonates with the next. Second, by proceeding with a coordinated attack on many fronts, a critical mass is achieved that alters the state of things.

When a social system reaches a critical mass, participants sense that the old rules may no longer apply. Prior calculations of self-interest and cause-and-effect become suspect. When we sense the possibility of a true break-through (and begin to share the excitement of creating a better, less constrained world), we are often willing to take chances we would otherwise pass by. It is at this moment that people, indeed entire companies, set aside narrower transactional considerations and go for broke. The decision to "gamble" $3.2 billion on Taurus might be explained in these terms. Perhaps top management wasn't simply weighing risks against rewards. Winning teams hit a lot of base hits and occasional home runs. Taurus represented a swing for the fences—a chance to make history, betting that a "homer" (stemming from a design success) would accelerate the momentum of change at Ford. If successful, Team Taurus could be multiplicative, not just additive.

In nuclear fission, temperature and pressure follow a predictable curve until fission takes place. Since the physicist's objective is fission, he engineers his temperature and pressure increases to achieve that end. Although the change at Ford was not engineered with the same forethought, the multiple efforts under way kept increasing the temperature and pressure on the old system until it could no longer sustain itself. To repeat a key idea from Chapter Four, *breakdowns* can, under the right conditions, produce *breakthroughs*. Management orchestrated the *content* (e.g., Team Taurus, Quality is Job 1, and Employee Involvement) and this, in turn, forced a transformation in the *process* of how Ford functioned.

CHAPTER SIX

Ford: Resolving
the "Dialectic"

Earlier chapters have made fleeting reference to a cumbersome word with too many vowels: *dialectic*. Some may recall Georg Wilhelm Friedrich Hegel, the nineteenth-century German philosopher who introduced the notion of "a synthesis of opposites." His central idea, shown schematically on the next page, is that one entity (which he called a "thesis"), when juxtaposed with its opposite ("antithesis"), can generate a new configuration that both includes and transcends the foundational elements. This phenomenon is known as a "Hegelian dialectic."[1]

At first glance, the possibility of arriving at a synthesis of opposites seems feasible. It's like observing yoga. We are easily convinced that the body can assume unlikely postures when we observe a skilled practitioner in action, but it is quite another matter when we attempt to do it ourselves. Dialectic is intellectual yoga. It's easy to *imagine* a paradoxical synthesis until you try it.

The stumbling block is our Western mindset. We have been trained since childhood to think in absolute categories: good/bad, either/or, black/white. We are taught to argue positions "for or against"; the middle ground is suspect. Acknowledging the value of both sides is wishy-washy. By one's early twenties, these intellectual habits are deeply ingrained. When we encounter situations that might benefit from "and/both" thinking, we usually miss the opportunity to do so and drift into the comfortable groove of choosing one or the other. Either/or thinking lies at the heart of the old paradigm, and it cripples our ability to manage effectively.

If a single word can describe the engine that revitalized Ford, it is *dialectic*. Ford harnessed constructive tension to foster adaptation and continuous learning. To be sure, they did not conceive of this as a dialectic. No one specifically thought in terms of exploiting the Seven Vectors of Con-

FIG. 6–1

Hegel's "Dialectic"

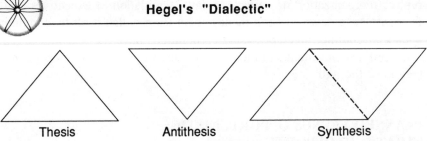

Thesis   Antithesis   Synthesis

tention, but the model fits. By the late 1980s, Ford had established a healthy tension in each domain, and went further. Addressing each of the contending opposites, Ford achieved its own unique *resolution*. These are shown in Table 6–1:

Subsequent pages describe the techniques that Ford used to reach this dialectic. It should be noted that these solutions were geared to Ford's unique history, and the competitive challenges it faced. There is nothing sacrosanct about these "resolutions."

Every organization must, to some extent, reconcile its opposites in its own way. It is nonetheless instructive to examine Ford's approach because their experience provides the practical details of how an organization used these ideas to achieve meaningful change. While the pages that follow contain many specifics about Ford, the general principles are applicable to companies large and small. These illustrations are particularly instructive because Ford (1) built on preexisting strengths, but reinjected constructive tension to build new strengths, (2) tapped into the entire organization, from

TABLE 6–1.

Resolving the "Dialectic" at Ford

Thesis		Antithesis	Synthesis
Planned	versus	Opportunistic ⟶	Strategic Opportunism
Elitist	versus	Pluralist ⟶	Interdependent Superstars
Mandatory	versus	Discretionary ⟶	Regulated Latitude
Managerial	versus	Transformational →	Enlightened Discipline
Collegiality	versus	Individuality ⟶	Socialized Activists
Hard Minds	versus	Soft Hearts ⟶	Compassionate Pragmatism
Maximize	versus	"Meta-mize" ⟶	Evolving Excellence

top to bottom, to fuel the change effort, and (3) succeeded without a disruptive reorganization or "Black Friday" liquidation of executives. Quite the contrary, a down-to-earth management team pulled it off by combining talents and pulling together. Many corporations have the potential to replicate Ford's achievements in their own unique way. The real question is: do they have the will?

PLANNED VERSUS OPPORTUNISTIC: STRATEGIC OPPORTUNISM

Throughout the seventies, most observers would agree that Ford was long on structured *planning* and short on *opportunistic* capability. There was little constructive tension, and no distinctive competence in the latter realm. Strategic planning had devolved into an econometric routine; the analysis was solid, but for the most part, Ford reacted to market changes rather than initiating them.[2]

One of Caldwell's, and later, Petersen's, first tasks was to reenergize the planning function and, through it, pioneer new strategic directions. Once strength was established in this arena, counterbalancing capability at the opportunistic end of the continuum was cultivated. By the end of the eighties, Ford had restored tension—albeit one that decidedly emphasized planning and analysis over opportunism and agility. Such a trade-off is inescapable in a capital intensive industry in which long lead times are necessary, and in which resource commitments are large.[3]

Ford's planning function had atrophied as a by-product of living under the shadow of General Motors. With massive resources, GM was able to underwrite costly market research, incur the major risks that styling changes entailed, and drive the industry with its economic models and pricing strategies.[4] The Big Three maintained large amounts of depreciated capacity. The good times lasted as long as they could pump out cars, load them on dealers' lots, and get the system to push them through to the customer.[5] The unsavory reputation of car salesmen stems in no small measure from these pressures. Detroit was driven by the demon "volume." Quality and other considerations took a secondary role.

In the 1970s, Ford's faith in this formula began to be shaken. At the heart of the problem was Ford's product concept. Designs never varied much: vehicles were medium to large in size, with plenty of horse power for acceleration, and had a pillowy ride. Henry Ford II was personally enamored with this product concept, and clung to it through the two energy crises of that decade. In each instance, Ford had no viable small car in its line. It suffered a catastrophic loss of 6 percent of its market share in the period 1978–1980 alone.[6]

The "dialectic" between effective *strategic planning* and the capacity for agile *opportunistic response* was in serious disarray when Caldwell, Petersen, and Poling stepped to the forefront. While the three didn't agree on all things, they were convinced that Ford could not survive through the next decade unless a new strategic course was charted. Crisis forced them to abandon the GM "paradigm." Quality, distinctive styling, and handling ability, not volume, were to be their paramount concerns.[7]

Pressures on Ford to assume control of its own strategic destiny pierced decades of complacency like an arctic wind across Lake Michigan. From the MacNamara days, Ford had built a competent stable of product planners; it was a rotational assignment for high-potential MBAs from Finance.[8] As such, there was talent on the bench, despite its underutilization. Now the unit was asked to think outside the box: Where should Ford place its bets? A process of deductive thinking led inevitably to the necessity for a very different car—the Taurus. While it would take Team Taurus the better part of two years to put flesh on the skeleton of these convictions, by 1980, Ford had come face-to-face with a most significant decision.[9]

It is almost impossible to overstate the magnitude of the risks the Taurus project entailed. Ford's challenge was not simply one of copying the imports—since the import buyer was *not* the primary target. Ford's bread and butter customers were still buying Fords. Could Ford build a car with some of the imports' features and styling pizzazz? Would Ford's traditional buyer agree with Ford's new thrust? Ford had never designed, engineered, or manufactured a car that could hold its own against the imports. This task alone was daunting. "We recognized that the learning curve was going to be steep and scary," recalls one Ford engineer. "It felt like skipping from high school football to the NFL. We were gambling on our ability to first *produce,* and then *persuade* our traditional purchaser to buy, a very different car. It's the sort of move you make when you have little left to lose."[10] And so it seemed for Ford in 1980 and 1981.

There is little indication that Ford *consciously* sought to "reestablish the tension" between strategic planning and opportunistic capability. Ford had always been strong at analysis and econometric modeling. These endeavors continued unabated, and some of it bore fruit. Forecasting 25-percent overcapacity in the world automotive industry by 1990, Ford closed eight plants in the United States, reduced hourly head count by 100,000 employees, and lowered break-even by 40 percent.[11] This was Ford in trauma—massive layoffs and cost cutting as never seen before. The new ingredient was Ford's renewed interest in product strategy. Petersen urged the product planners to make more aggressive use of customer survey data. Still dissatisfied, this quest led Ford to poll automotive mechanics and insurance companies for repair costs, seeking opportunities to add value.[12]

Most companies, having revitalized their strategic process, would pause and savor the results. But Petersen, the product man, had only limited faith in the capacity of planners to anticipate unforeseen events. As the Taurus project was launched, Petersen saw to it that it was not so closely tied to Planning's dictates that it would sacrifice its own good judgment.

The moment of truth occurred in April 1981. Planning had projected gasoline prices of $3.40 per gallon for the late eighties, and Taurus' configuration was based on that assumption. By spring 1981, fuel price projections were converging on $1.50 per gallon. Carefully marshaling the evidence at hand, the team reopened the debate. Did the revised projections point toward the feasibility of a larger car? Henry Ford II, historically an advocate of bigger vehicles, stepped forward to champion this proposal. Discarding an entire year's work, the team increased Taurus' wheel base, upped capacity from five to six passengers, widened its tread, and shifted from a four-cylinder engine to a V-6. In the circumscribed world of car design, this is like telling the carpenter you want a new kitchen in the place he's halfway through remodeling as a bathroom. Yet Ford was agile enough to make this shift and still meet Taurus' targeted introduction deadline. Here was dramatic evidence of the payoff of a constructive "dialectic." Taurus and Sable are, in this sense, concrete by-products of "strategic opportunism." States Lew Veraldi, executive with overall responsibility for Taurus:

> All members of Team Taurus knew the reason for this decision to change the architecture of this car. They all rallied around the change and gave their full support to make it happen. Had the team not been in place to do things simultaneously instead of sequentially, this decision would have delayed the car at least 18 months.[13]

Taurus' gains, while significant, offered no guarantee that Ford's opportunistic capabilities had become a part of its institutional fabric. Petersen knew all too well that Ford had hit home runs in the past with the Mustang and Thunderbird—only to lapse back into a backwater of "me too" products. He began searching for ways to prevent this regressive tendency from repeating itself.

Concept-to-Customer, a project aimed at streamlining the entire workflow of automotive development, was one significant outgrowth of this concern. At the core, it reflects Petersen's desire to institutionalize continuous learning. The logic behind Concept-to-Customer goes like this: industry success requires predicting consumer trends and shaping input into winning product concepts. If Ford concentrates on being the *best* at this process, it will both offer more marketable products and bring them to market more quickly.[14] In the years since Taurus was introduced, Ford has demonstrated a persistent dedication to both of these areas. It has won the Car of the Year award for the fourth year running. In addition, the product development cycle has been reduced from seven years to four; Ford is now best among the American producers.[15] Concept-to-Customer is Ford's way of focusing attention on the self-improvement *process*. In so doing, it is resisting the seductive influence of the two dark companions of success—excess conservatism and complacency.

ELITIST VERSUS PLURALIST: INTERDEPENDENT SUPERSTARS

The management team at Ford inherited an organizational structure that was seriously overdetermined. One "elite," Finance, overshadowed all others. At the "pluralistic" end of the continuum, things were in even greater disarray. Internecine conflicts and turf wars foreclosed any meaningful cooperation among the disciplines.

These problems were deeply etched into Ford's institutional psyche. There was a long history of dominant elites—first Engineering under Henry Ford I, then Manufacturing and, for more than thirty years, Finance.[16] The excesses of each of these dynasties had prohibited any type of meaningful cross-functional collaboration. Now management would have to create new norms of collaboration virtually from scratch.

The Rise of Finance
When Henry Ford II assumed leadership from his grandfather in 1950, he found a company in serious decline. Market share was declining, cash reserves were low, and the organization was heavily politicized. He sought to reverse Ford's fortunes by adopting a simplified version of General Motors' management system. GM was then drifting into the clutches of Finance, and Henry followed suit.[17] By the time MacNamara and his Whiz Kids had served their tour of duty at Ford, the company had swung from a

manufacturing dominated culture to a financially driven one.[18] David Halberstam, in his portrayal of the rise and decline of Ford, recounts the subsequent power shift: "Thereafter, the creative people and factory people systematically lost power for the next thirty-five years—while the financial people ascended—and formed a ferocious new cadre."[19]

George Romney, former CEO of American Motors, once observed that "nothing is more vulnerable than entrenched success."[20] Ford's legacy of overdetermined elites epitomizes Romney's point. From Henry Ford I's elite cadre of designers and engineers, to the operations dominated environment of the forties, giving way to a finance driven company from the fifties onward—Ford always took things to extremes. Each emergent elite had its "answer" for what would make Ford successful. Each demonstrated initial value. But disregarding the essentiality of constructive tension, each took its "solution" too far. Sound policy became rigid ideology.

Finance had historically derived its strength from recruiting the best—usually MBAs with backgrounds in engineering. It took care of its own, shepherded by a legendary figure, Ed Lundy, who personally interviewed every new finance-staff hire until his retirement from active management in 1979. He also shepherded their development via rigorous rotations through finance positions throughout the world. Under Lundy, Finance developed a string of capable generalists, such as Arjay Miller and Robert McNamara, each of whom subsequently ran the company.[21]

But unlike General Motors, Finance never gained absolute control. Henry Ford II was sensitive about his prerogatives as chairman. Having seen his grandfather stumble, he was leery of falling prey to the counsel of one interest group. As Finance became ascendant, Henry II experimented with pairing Finance and Product men in the top two slots reporting to him. Thus, Ford in the sixties and seventies assigned key leadership roles to men such as Semon E. (Bunkie) Knudsen and Lee Iacocca. These individuals served as valuable counterweights. Under Henry II's short leash, their tenure was short and precarious.[22]

Finance overshadowed the other "chimneys" in the Ford power structure not so much because of its overt status, but as a result of the pervasive nature of its influence.

First, there was an implicit value system that made volume and revenue supreme. Finance championed these goals. The product disciplines were always held suspect—prone to bungling product hand-offs, slipping schedules, and overrunning budgets.[23]

Second, Finance occupied the critical spot at the top of the pyramid of approval. In an organization in which initiatives were handled sequentially, a particular department would initiate a request for resources, and the proposal would work its way upward for approval. Finance, armed with the best, and most balanced, analysis, always held the trump card. States one executive: "They didn't win through blatant power plays. They just out-maneuvered the line by doing better homework."[24]

Not surprisingly, the line lost faith in their convictions. Over time, an obsessively financial focus led to suboptimal decisions. For example, Cost Accounting would press for a two-cent cost reduction in the price of a machine screw. Engineering would relent—only to have that decision show up as increased manufacturing and repair costs. A plant manager seeking to hold a factory-wide meeting to communicate details of a major assembly line reconfiguration would be prevented from doing so because the session translated into $100,000 in "lost" wages.[25]

Management's challenge in the 1980s was to sustain Finance's strengths yet upgrade the downtrodden domains of Engineering, Manufacturing, and Design. This was addressed through three major thrusts: (1) maintaining competence in Finance, but reducing head count and decentralizing some activities, (2) upgrading the product disciplines through investments in new tools such as computerized workstations, and giving these functions a greater voice in policy matters, and (3) reducing the number of management staff and shifting their role from policemen to a service organization to the line activities.[26]

By 1983, there were signs that this long legacy of financial dominance was coming to an end. Allan Gilmour, viewed by many as a close ally of Petersen, was named CFO. In that capacity he began to decentralize Finance and reduce head count at the corporate level. In Europe alone, Finance decreased its staff by 40 percent over a two-year period.[27] Gilmour also sought to give Finance a friendlier face, and made a variety of adjustments to lessen the onerous burden of controls. He agreed, for example, to close the books on each operating unit quarterly rather than monthly. This rep-resented a major shift for line executives. The very absence of an end-of-month numbers drill permitted the company to devote more time and energy to day-to-day business.[28]

There is little doubt that Petersen was a critical factor in realigning Fi-nance's influence. "Petersen feels very strongly about the balance between Finance and product priorities," observes one top executive. "He monitors it closely."[29]

Quality

Another major force for a healthier tension between Finance and the product disciplines was Poling's campaign for Quality.[30] As a former Finance "in-sider," he could champion Quality, and strengthen the product functions, yet never be seen as a threat to the Finance organization. He was one of them. An industrial relations manager of Body and Assembly Operations comments:

> There is no question that Red Poling has a tremendous commitment to the financial end of the business. To this day, we still fear that Finance rules the roost . . . a lot of decisions are still financially based. But not all. You don't see any financially driven decisions that undermine quality. Quality is the king now. It took time. By the mid-eighties, people started to think it might be real. Gradually, the audits and media attention forced people to acknowledge that Quality was the tiebreaker. It takes something measurable and concrete like Quality to hold Finance in check.[31]

Upgrading the Technical Elites

As Finance held steady, Engineering, Design, and Manufacturing were able to realize their full potential. The emphasis on Quality was especially important in enlarging their role, and in legitimizing the Engineering and Manufacturing disciplines. But there was more to be done than to simply elevate their status. The product disciplines had suffered from a serious loss of pride and energy. One executive remarks:

> Our problem in the functional disciplines wasn't just the overpowering role of Finance, but inherent weaknesses in line management. Going back to the twenties, these departments had always promoted from within. Some of these guys were pretty narrow and rigid—with caustic interpersonal styles. Petersen and Poling brought enough pressure to bear to force some of these old-timer chimney builders to retire. A few accepted less central assignments.[32]

The final ingredient in rebalancing Ford's elites was to downsize the white-collar ranks—both in numbers and status. Ford relied almost entirely on natural attrition to reduce its salaried employees. Between 1980 and 1988, staff ranks alone decreased by 47 percent.[33] There were few layoffs; a number of voluntary retirement programs accelerated exits. Rebalancing entailed more than numbers. "Beginning around 1983," recalls one corporate staffer, "we were strongly encouraged to visit the field rather than relying on the plant managers and engineers making their pilgrimages to Dearborn's version of Mecca. It was humbling. We ate a little crow. But it sent strong signals in a rank-conscious hierarchy like Ford. Staff had always held higher grade levels in the hierarchical structure. This too was changed so plant people of similar responsibility held the same rank. These were highly effective leveling agents."[34]

Promoting Interdependence

The danger of strong functional disciplines is that they create barriers to cross-functional cooperation. As noted earlier, Ford had a legacy of "chimneys." The disputes were legendary. For example, while Design and Engineering occupied adjacent buildings on the Ford campus in Dearborn, the protocol was such that officials of the two departments communicated by memo, and usually refused to meet face-to-face. *Strengthening* these functions might easily have made things worse.

Petersen lessened this risk by being very clear that he valued cooperation. One senior Ford executive states: "Petersen identifies people who can motivate others, and favors good team players. He reinforced these values through the simple expedient of promoting certain individuals and not others. The word spread fast."[35] Petersen is unabashed about his bias toward team play. He states:

> As I worked at Ford through the years, I just couldn't stand the infighting that was going on. There was all this pointless jockeying for position. Then I went to Truck Operations, which had a positive sense of self, lots of stability, and worked together as a group. After a while it struck me—those guys are having fun. They enjoy what they're doing. There is little petty bickering, and they are doing their jobs perfectly well, thank you, without a whole lot of complicated orders from the superstructure. It was clear they knew something I didn't know.[36]

A piece had fallen into place. Truck Operations convinced Petersen that given a conducive climate, managers at Ford could collaborate. Now the task was to create it company-wide.

Petersen and Poling joined forces to upgrade the product functions, simultaneously increasing emphasis on cross-functional teams. Taurus was an example of this. Its strategic importance to Ford's survival was so compelling that it overcame chimney loyalties. Yet even in Taurus' case, teamwork was no small task. One member observes:

> It took eighteen months before Team Taurus members really believed they could put what was right ahead of their loyalty to their chimney. Some of the delegates said openly at times they weren't sure they could deliver their area's commitment, or feared the wrath of their boss. We found we needed to manage upward a lot. But the clear-cut corporate priority to break down the barriers between chimneys and training aimed at surfacing conflict gradually won the day. We became new role models for the traditionalists within our chimneys. Gradually, our entire organizations adopted the new repertoire.[37]

Paralleling Team Taurus were a number of other cross-functional teams that demanded a "pluralistic" outlook. Chapter Five recounted the evolution of the Blue Ribbon Committee and the unfolding of "chimney breaking," as it is known today. Many top committees were spawned from those roots and had overlapping membership that permitted continuity of purpose.

It would create the wrong impression to suggest that these cross-functional efforts, learning from the Blue Ribbon Committee's tribulations, "lived happily ever after." Altering behavior and turf in organizations is never easy.

In 1984, after completing the Blue Ribbon effort, the same members formed a task force to address the cumbersome Design Approval Process. All went well insofar as they confined their discussions to the design approval steps that directly involved the individuals represented on their task force. Emboldened, they took a broader set of recommendations to the NAAO's Executive Committee (which included several non–task force members, most notably Marketing, Sales, and Service). The task force position: a step-function improvement in the Design Approval Process could not be achieved unless NAAO dealt with the entire approval chain from concept to customer. Their recommendation was not warmly received. The outside consultant/facilitator assisting them was summarily fired; for twelve long months the topic was considered "undiscussable." But under Petersen's subtle but relentless pressure, the now-well-seasoned Blue Ribbon veterans were recalled to duty in 1987 and charged with spearheading the Concept-to-Customer effort. The thrust now had the imprimatur of being a strategic priority. In this new incarnation, the group has been highly effective in reducing the product development cycle to within six months of Honda's best-in-class standard, improving quality and reducing cost.

Another of the more explosive spin-off groups was the Engineering/Manufacturing Interface Committee. Here, in particular, were several individuals with the most deep-seated prejudices toward one another. At some of the early meetings, some would have temper tantrums and endeavor to disrupt the process. One particularly vociferous individual was pressed into early retirement as a result of his unwillingness to collaborate.[38] Here we see an absolutely critical factor: top management didn't try to tell the Committee what to do, but they left *no* question that the *process* of working things through would succeed and that meaningful results were an imperative. One observer closely familiar with the Committee effort recalls:

> The dozen upper-level managers in charge of Engineering and Manufacturing were called into one room. Lou Ross, then senior vice president in charge

of factories, got right to the point. "Here's the problem," he said. "For twenty-five years, Engineering and Manufacturing have been fighting with each other. Enough is enough. We don't care how long it takes, but we want you to answer one single question: Will Engineering report to Manufacturing, or Manufacturing to Engineering?" Then he left the room. There was hell to pay.[39]

Now picture a meeting room eight months later. Many of the same guys from the Power Train and Engineering divisions are on hands and knees discussing the merits of the various organizational charts that cover the floor. There is a lot of give and take. Someone asks with an edge of frustration, "Which of these organizational charts is best?" Someone answers, "Maybe *this* (i.e., the process we're now engaged in) is?" A hush falls on the room. Then it dawns on us that the medium was the message. It was all about *how* we were working together, not finding the perfect organizational structure! We took the next month to put together an organization that didn't *reorganize* at all, but simply realigned the flows of communication across the chimneys.[40]

Ford's success in breaking down functional walls was supported by a great deal of senior management involvement. Poling's expectations were very clear. Unlike many top executives who create task forces only to forget them, Poling kept the heat on, constantly asking how things were going. Further, Poling encouraged his reports to reach outside NAAO and borrow ideas from other parts of the company—unheard of behavior in the past.[41]

Once seniors set the example, subordinates revealed their capacity to do the same.

MANDATORY VERSUS DISCRETIONARY: REGULATED LATITUDE

Ford had historically tilted toward the "control" extreme. Since the 1950s, its systems had been growing. By 1980, Ford had a towering pyramid of procedures and controls that "nailed down everything that moved," in the words of one victim of the system.[42] This systems orientation, which had originated in Finance, was adopted in kind by each of the functional disciplines. One senior executive states: "We seethed with frustration living within a labyrinth of rules and controls. There was a Finance manual, an Engineering manual, and so forth. We'd solve problems by issuing a new rule—which only solved the problem on paper. There wasn't any dialogue. It was bureaucratic gridlock. The edicts used to come from on high. You had to be nuts to argue anything."[43] Now, Ford sought to maintain the benefits of control yet loosen the "straitjacket" mentality that enshrouded it.

User Friendliness

The decentralization of Finance, mentioned earlier in this chapter, had the benefit of making Ford's control systems less formidable. As suggested by the comments in the following quote, when line managers were given a greater role in their financial destiny, ownership increased. As owners of the financial reports, they became more interested in the information the reports contained and made better use of it. The previously cited decision to close the books quarterly instead of monthly also had a positive impact. One executive states:

> Ford had a good budget system, but it was taken too literally. People didn't make intelligent decisions, they just kept within budget. Petersen began experimenting when he ran DPO in 1975. We had budgets, of course, but he kept saying, "Don't treat them as inflexible." After a while, we began to believe him. That philosophy has caught on today. Good decisions are expected to be driven by their merits—not the budget. To be sure, Poling holds people accountable, but top management has made it clear through the review process that while goals and budget are taken seriously, making good decisions is taken more seriously.[44]

Former head of Diversified Products, Tom Page, observes:

> Allan Gilmour played a vital role in putting a friendlier face on our control system. He is a respected member of the Finance organization, and one of Petersen's strongest allies. He was crucial in selling the Taurus concept through the financial hierarchy. When I wanted five million dollars for training during the rollout of EI and participative management, he urged me to budget for seven million dollars. But the big event was in 1984. I went to Gilmour and said, "Finance is not seen as very helpful." I had a list of twenty obstacles that my people had generated. Gilmour replied, "Let's try to attack this problem in a division or two." Within a year, the serious obstacles were gone. These are the kinds of changes that signaled a true willingness to trust in the discipline and discretion of line management.[45]

Other Systems Changes

Ford's other major thrust on the systems front entailed the addition of (1) competitive benchmarking, (2) conflict management, and (3) the fine tuning of performance appraisals, rewards, and bonuses.

Competitive benchmarking was an essential ingredient of Ford's active strategy. More often than not, systems foster an internal orientation. Ford needed an external focus to survive. The primary manifestation of competitive benchmarking was Ford's Best-in-Class program. Through it, each functional discipline identified industry leaders (e.g., in quality, marketing, supplier relations, and so on) and sought to emulate or exceed them.[46] For example, Team Taurus selected 400 key engineering features, and identified the Best in Class component for every car on the market in each category. Design and Engineering then committed themselves to meet or exceed 75 percent of those standards. In fact, Taurus surpassed these objectives.[47]

Ford's other major system addition was Contention Management.* We need only note that the ultimate purpose of such a system is to surface hidden conflicts and develop managers' ability to deal with them. Hank Lenox, a senior executive from Power Train, and an insider to Team Taurus, provides an overview of how these techniques were reinforced until they became the norm.

> In 1979 and 1980 we began attacking the relationships between the Engine Division's general staff and the eight plants they worked with. The opening round entailed intensive training in conflict management. We used a questionnaire. It revealed how we saw each other, and how others saw us. We engaged in role plays in which the objective was to disagree on an issue without pissing everyone off. Next came the opportunities to apply it. There were joint sessions between the plant teams and headquarters staff. The danger, of course, was forgetting the skills learned and lapsing into old habits. We met regularly as a joint team for the next two months. We worked on the most devisive business issues. Step by step we began to reach genuine resolution, and slowly built relationships that took into account who the other person really was.[48]

The strengthening of Ford's contention management system added both a discipline and a safety valve. With a more constructive format for disagreement, it was safer to disagree. Legitimacy made it easier for employees at all levels to surface concerns. States one employee: "Conflict management is our insurance policy against excesses of all kinds. It's a fail-safe system that prevents Ford's impersonal controls from riding roughshod over common sense."[49]

Ford made significant changes to its performance appraisals, bonuses, and rewards. The primary focus of these shifts was to encourage teamwork. Historically, Ford only gave it lip service. Under the revised system, collaborative contributions counted for one-third of a manager's performance rating. Bonuses and rewards were rebalanced between individual and group goals.[50]

Discretionary Latitude

The counterpoise to strong mandatory controls is discretionary latitude. A more intimate relationship between line management and their key mea-

---

* One of the best programs for training managers to manage conflict and channel contention constructively is provided by the Bay Group of San Rafael, California.

surements enhances intelligent interpretation. Understanding the logic behind systems improves one's ability to know how to treat results.

Ford made major efforts to blend mandatory controls and discretionary behavior in the realm of quality. States one observer: "Quality proved a seductive lure—it really piqued the interest of Ford's engineering-oriented culture. Quality problems were problems to be *solved*—and engineers love to solve problems. Only later did it become obvious that to solve these problems the organization needed to work differently. Inevitably, the focus on quality drove them to alter the way the system worked."[51]

The second benefit accruing from a focus on quality has been touched on earlier. It's a crisp enough concept to permit employees to safely buck the system on its behalf. Poling made Quality a safe value to defend by setting stringent quality targets, but also by demonstrating a willingness to delay the launch of new products if quality was not up to snuff. He was not punitive. He gave line management the time and resources necessary to close the gap. Here is a critical ingredient in achieving "regulated latitude":[52] systems must be seen as tools for improvement, not as weapons to punish.

Over a period of several years, Ford's Quality effort demonstrated what the proper tension between control and interpretation could accomplish. Quality standards could be quantified rather precisely, yet discretion was needed in determining how the operating units would work to achieve them. Plant managers could *choose* to train employees, buy new equipment, or assemble Employee Involvement teams to study defects. Employee Involvement teams could *choose* which source of defects to work on, and could subsequently initiate change. A worker on the plant floor could *exercise discretion,* and literally stop the line for quality. White collar workers could do the same.

A major factor in "the psychology of discretion" is the knowledge that recourse *is* available. It need not be exercised often. Ford's consistent commitment to quality assured each employee that initiatives taken on its behalf were always right. Quality was the vehicle through which the taking of initiative and the exercise of discretion were restored as important values.

MANAGERIAL VERSUS TRANSFORMATIONAL: ENLIGHTENED DISCIPLINE

One would be hard pressed to identify a more dramatic example of restoring constructive tension than in this domain as it unfolded at Ford. As suggested by earlier references, prior to the eighties, Ford was dominated by an intensely managerial orientation. This was highly consistent with its emphasis on control. Says one manager: "It was a buttoned-down culture and it extended to all facets of managerial behavior. In many ways, we operated like a civilian 'army.' There was an established repertoire for all things— even presentations. It extended to details like how chairs were to be arranged for briefings, black binders for each attendee, taping overhead projector cords to the floor (so no one could trip over them), and so forth. Little was left to chance."[53]

With the coming of the eighties, Ford suddenly found itself with an interesting mix of executives. Some had managerial strengths (Caldwell and Poling); others had transformational styles (Petersen, Page, Veraldi, Pestillo, as well as UAW Vice President Ephlin). Potentially, at least, Ford had strength at both ends of the continuum. What is remarkable is that these men did not kill one another off or gravitate toward stalemate and compromise. Instead, for the most part, they actively engaged one another. Petersen states: "Red Poling and I had different styles and different expertise. My role was to zero in on correcting the product offering. I supported some of the cultural change experiments getting underway in DPO. His was to zero in on reestablishing Ford's mastery of the business fundamentals within NAAO."[54]

Often in corporate life, the discussion of "roles" is a polite way of staking out turf. While this occurred to some degree at Ford, there was also a great deal of mutual respect. Petersen conveys the esteem with which he held his erstwhile rival:

> Poling reinstated control—I *really* mean discipline—when he took over NAAO. If you had made a commitment, you were obligated to meet it. His approach was to say, "You decide when your deadline's going to be, the timetable of your programs, the quality you're going to achieve, and then we'll hold you accountable." Red did the unthinkable. He went to Edison, New Jersey, where we were launching the Escort. This was a very scary time for us financially, and we all knew that the Escort had to be successful. Usually, the launch of a product like this is pro forma—top management comes out to cut a ribbon. But at the end of the day, after touring the plant, he said to the plant manager and program manager, "I don't think you're ready to start. When you're ready, tell me and I'll come back." From that day forward, things began to change.[55]

Business Fundamentals

As indicated above, Poling took the lead role in placing NAAO on a solid footing. The easiest problems to work on were the ones that did not require massive behavioral or cultural change. Given the losses of 1980, controlling costs commanded immediate attention. Ford was far too vertically integrated, with far too many underutilized manufacturing facilities. Poling closed plants and outsourced many more components (increasing external sourcing from 20 percent to 50 percent).[56] To enhance control over suppliers, he slimmed down the vendor ranks from 7,000 to 3,000, and required each survivor to meet much more stringent quality and delivery standards.[57] In 1978, Ford employed 506,500 employees worldwide, and produced 6.6 million cars and trucks. By 1986, it needed only 382,300 employees to produce six million vehicles.[58] In the United States, the number of UAW-represented hourly employees dropped 45 percent, from 191,000 in 1978 to 105,000 in 1986, and 47 percent of salaried employees left the ranks. Never satisfied, Ford has set a still tougher goal: it is striving to eliminate another $5 billion in costs by 1993.[59]

But Poling was far from one-dimensional. Reflecting the best of the managerial style, he sought to do more than downsize. The precedent of delaying the launch of a car due to a faulty transmission sent strong signals about Ford's new priorities. One of Ford's senior executives explains:

> Poling is a smart, pragmatic guy. He's also open-minded and aggressive. Until Henry II chose Petersen as chairman, he clearly saw Don as his rival. He was striving to do well, and Quality was his baby. When it came to Employee Involvement and Participative Management, he was a skeptic. But when it worked, he bought in and funded it. There is no pride in authorship with this guy. He will do what it takes to get something to happen.[60]

Transformational Leadership

On the transformational side of the ledger, Petersen had a knack for energizing people and permitting unforeseen possibilities to unfold. His words provide a glimpse into the man:

> I was in no one's mind as a candidate for president until my international assignment in the late 1970s. I have a hunch that one of the factors that led people to agree with Henry Ford that I should be named president was that the North American passenger car line was weak, and things were deteriorating at an alarming rate. Our market share was plummeting, and if you looked around at the top tier at Ford, I was the only one who had spent a lot of my life planning for new products. I think the fear factor plus relevant expertise played into my being chosen.
>
> All of this is to say that my dreams about how this company could be different organizationally played no role in my getting the president's job. I got

there for one reason: I strongly addressed product problems. But what I really did was to change how people thought about each other, and dealt with each other, from their chimney walls, shifting from a mode of confrontation to a sense of being a team.[61]

Whereas Poling exercises tight control and focuses on concrete objectives, Petersen's concept of leadership is to let things flow within certain parameters. "Some of the articles that have been written make me heroic," he states. "Believe me, no one person could do what some of the articles say I did." Tom Page describes Petersen in these terms:

He is an enabler. He doesn't make a lot of decisions. When you bring a quarrel to him, he'll say: "You two go off and see if you can't figure that out. Have dinner, have lunch—don't just write memos. Get your people together. Give me the alternatives, but see if you can't work something out."[62]

Understanding Petersen's role in the transformation is one of the most intriguing puzzles of this account. Petersen seems a highly improbable change agent for a turnaround of this magnitude. States one industry observer:

Picture the opposite of Henry Ford II, Lee Iacocca, and a host of other egotistical and dominating managers who have played significant leadership roles at Ford, and you get the man who could be Detroit's first Japanese-style executive. He lives and breathes participative management, taking to heart suggestions from vice presidents and assembly line workers. Most remarkably, he subordinates his ego to the needs of the company. Asked how he turned Ford around, he emphatically attributes the success to others. Says Petersen: "I want you to remember one thing. The credit here goes to our team, not me." So low is his profile that even after becoming chairman in 1985, the company proxy statement misspelled his name.[63]

It *is* inaccurate to single out Petersen as the hero who turned around Ford. Indeed, as noted earlier, there were no single heroes, rather, a widely shared need to save the company, and a coincidence of independent actions that culminated in massive change. While this, in the deepest sense, is the truth of Ford's transformation, it is also important to trace the role and philosophy of the man who permitted this metamorphosis to unfold.

Petersen had a degree in engineering, served in the Marines during World War II, and got his MBA from Stanford. He began at Ford at $300 a month, and immediately became a product planner lobbying Ford's future cars through Design, Engineering, Manufacturing, and Finance. In the fifties, he worked on the legendary Thunderbird team, and in the sixties he helped develop the Mustang and the LTD.[64]

But Petersen grew to despise the atmosphere at Ford, where fear and envy reigned. He recalls: "Those days built into me a strong desire to see things work differently, a strong desire to stop all the fighting, backbiting, and working to prove the other guy is wrong."[65] Petersen briefly quit twice out of these strong convictions, despairing of the overcontrolling bosses who were more worried about office politics than building cars.[66]

Petersen had been a peripheral member of MacNamara's Whiz Kids in the late fifties. He had witnessed what a man of substance could accomplish (even though MacNamara's skills were analytical and financial, whereas Petersen's favored the engineering side of things). With MacNamara's abrupt exodus, Petersen found himself without a mentor in a highly political company. He was exiled to Siberia—Truck Operations. Trucks represented big money to Ford, but despite their bottom-line contribution, trucks were traditionally low status for Ford's top management. So, while the Dearborn of the seventies contemplated its narcissistic navel, Petersen was free to think.[67]

In the late 1970s, Petersen was named head of Ford's International Automotive Operations. A man who knows cars and loves to drive them, he, as noted earlier, was exposed to the agility, clean designs, and quality construction of European vehicles. While abroad, he tried to sell Dearborn on these ideas. Instead, top management pegged him as something of an eccentric.[68] Yet Petersen was clearly the most highly qualified "product man" in the stable. When Caldwell became CEO, Henry Ford II insisted that Petersen become his president.

The most commonly used adjective for Petersen is "quiet." For relaxation he collects rocks—not exactly the profile of a revolutionary.[69] "People complain that Petersen is too quiet," says Joseph Kordick, a retired Ford Vice President. "That's because he's listening. They don't know how to deal with a CEO who actually listens to the people beneath him."[70]

To follow Petersen through a day is a study in minimalism. His factory visits, which are frequent, involve no fanfare, no bands, red carpets, or retinue of plant executives waiting outside in the cold for his arrival. He most typically meets in a conference room where supervisors and UAW members are assembled, speaks about the importance of employee participation and suggestions, and quickly gets into technical discussions of how the plant is doing.[71] In one such plant visit, the president of the local UAW presented him with the Union's blue and gold softball jacket. "At first we thought this employee involvement program was a lot of B.S.," the UAW representative commented, "but now we think it's for real."[72] The UAW local union president pointed to a wheel-making line. "See that? The hourly people control that whole line. There's no supervisor. I never would have believed I would see anything like that, or be saying such things about the company."[73]

Petersen spends considerable time poking around the plant, questioning workers. Then he heads to another conference room to meet with the Employee Involvement Committee. Fifteen hourly workers are assembled here, each with proposals to save the plant money. Petersen asks good questions, then delivers compliments. It is a slow, thoughtful session at which any Japanese manager would feel at home. Through these encounters, Petersen's humility and sincerity communicate his commitment more powerfully than any stirring speech or PR image. You trust him.[74]

A Synthesis of Opposites

Together, the Petersen/Poling team combines the best of two very different styles. The result, as stated earlier, is a marvelous synthesis of opposites. This is not to romanticize it as a partnership made in heaven. In the real world, it seldom works that way. Petersen and Poling (and their likenesses in the ranks below) do rub one another the wrong way from time to time. Currently, they engage in strenuous debates over such key issues as whether to delegate their line of compact cars to their Japanese partner, Mazda, and whether to build additional capacity. The issue of capacity is especially thorny because Ford is currently sacrificing 2 to 3 percent in market share by virtue of being unable to meet demand.[75] Yet there is the offsetting fear of the capacity glut in the decade ahead. The "miracle" at Ford is that this contention is channeled to the benefit, rather than the detriment, of the corporation.

COLLEGIALITY VERSUS INDIVIDUALITY: SOCIALIZED ACTIVISTS

Chapter Three noted that certain benefits accrue from creating a social fabric within an organization. When a culture is sufficiently coherent, organizations can safely support entrepreneurial activities without risk of disintegration. Historically, Ford scored poorly at both ends of this domain. Aside from a buttoned-down, military style, Ford had little in the way of a distinct identity. Its fractionalized chimneys created antagonistic tribes who resisted any hint of integration. The only positive attribute of Ford's culture was its flinty tenacity. This was retained, and served the corporation well in the early eighties.

Autonomous behavior was clearly proscribed. Readers familiar with Lee Iacocca's memoirs will recall the rare occasion when a champion's ideas coincided with a favorable political climate. But as a rule, backbiting and oppressive controls chopped down innovators. The few who attempted to run the gauntlet were written off as "politically motivated," and discounted accordingly. Powerful leveling agents undercut those who sought to make waves.[76]

A string of successes from the mid-eighties onward gradually gave rise to Ford's new concept of itself as a culture. A *collegial* identity began to flower.

There is little doubt that Petersen was a major contributor to this end. He set the tone by applying his philosophy to his own work group. As he readied himself for the chairmanship in 1984, he scheduled an off-site meeting in St. Clair, Michigan, for the top six executives who would report to him. The meeting focused on four key issues, one of which was a "people problem": How are we going to work together as a group to help address the problems facing Ford?[77]

In the flattering light of a now-established success story, Petersen's team-building session might seem an obvious thing to do. It was not. These six individuals (each with thirty years of experience in Ford's Darwinian environment) had boundaries around themselves to rival the Great Wall. They were, in the view of one manager, "dubious to the extreme."[78] The meeting would surely have failed were it not for the extensive planning and interviewing of each participant beforehand. "The participants made it clear that they thought the off-site for team-building was a really nutty idea," says the meeting planner. "But they also talked about the disconnects between them and the sources of distrust. When we finally got together, they were ready to do the work. Petersen is a very good group facilitator. He has strong intuition and great empathy for what's behind a person's words. He has the ability to ask piercing questions and then sit back and tolerate the squirming until the issues begin to be addressed. That first top-level team meeting set the tone for Petersen's tenure as chairman."[79]

Petersen invested energy in transforming other formalized decision bodies into meaningful vehicles for communication. Most critical was the Policy and Strategy Committee. Notwithstanding the high-sounding title, this entity had fallen prey to clogged agendas and laborious deliberations. Interactions were stilted, and its purpose was unclear. Petersen recalls: "The Policy and Strategy Committee had become ossified. We began by agreeing to get together informally at breakfast once a month. Gradually, things loosened up. Today it's almost the heart of where we make decisions. We can talk to one another in shirtsleeves about any subject, whether or not it involves the initiator's particular background."[80]

Ford's "collegial" sense of emphasizing teamwork was communicated through a few simple mechanisms.

First, work groups were physically integrated. Factories and offices that once segregated professional specialists began placing engineers, purchasing agents, and manufacturing superintendents side by side. Large bull pens were established to house networks of people who frequently interacted with one another. Even senior executives were moved from private offices into low-partition areas. States one engineer: "It's amazing what human nature does without barriers. It has made it easy to communicate, rather than difficult."[81]

Executive Reeducation

The second powerful vehicle for socialization was Ford's innovative approach to Executive Development. Unlike many counterparts in industry, Ford does a great deal more than offer its executives the usual smorgasbord of subjects and lectures. "Outwardly it looks like many corporate education centers," says Nancy Badore, currently head of Executive Education, "but at Ford it is recognized as an active agent of change. We challenge our executives more fully than almost any place you're going to see."[82] Petersen and Poling's commitment to this vehicle of change is evidenced by the time they invest at the center: they alternate spending the last half day of the week-long session.[83]

Each of Ford's 2,000 senior managers attends one of the Development Center's workshops. It takes two years for the cycle to repeat itself. They come in groups of fifty—a heterogeneous cross section of Ford's divisions around the world.[84] "The crucial dimension in these get-togethers," says Badore, "is that we treat the same issues that the chairman and president are grappling with. Participants are expected to add real value by working on these problems, often arguing—and along the way listening to markedly different points of view from different functions, levels, and markets around the world. As the nature of the problem requires, we bring in experts, and offer specialized briefings. Then the participants present their reactions and recommendations to Petersen and Poling. Both sides challenge each other with their most serious questions and concerns. It's very intense stuff."[85]

This format represented new rules for many. Learning to speak out frankly when Petersen and Poling were in the room was the biggest challenge. Executives who might normally try to assume a low profile are called upon.

Neal Dorsey, a twenty-five-year Ford manager from the tractor division, recounts: "At first I suspected it had to be some kind of trap. I thought, 'What? Am I nuts? Am I going to commit political suicide by telling bad news to the boss?' But they really do want you to say what you think, even if it's critical."[86]

The gains of such a program in creating a common culture are enormous. Participants learn to set their disciplinary biases aside and look at an issue from a larger perspective. They begin to grasp how the pieces of a complex issue fit together. Above all, they leave informed on major policy questions that are apt to affect the company in the months and years ahead. Indeed, participants are sought-after couriers of "the latest scoop" when they return home.[87]

"It's all aimed at reinforcing the shift from 'cults' to 'teamwork,' " says one senior manager. "What we learned from the Japanese is that if you're going to win in an industry with a complex, highly integrated product, you've got to get the organization to integrate. In the last analysis, that is our obsession here. If we can become 'best in class' at tackling problems, we will be one of the survivors."[88]

Job Rotation
The third ingredient in instilling a common culture at Ford has been to increase job rotations across functions. Petersen comments:

> The development of Ford's people had always been a very structured and segregated process. It went up through NAAO, DPO, or Europe, straight to the very top. Nothing occurred across. No discussions were held about people across chimneys. We now have a room in which we post pictures. We look into the future and assess needs for cross-functional development. We look especially at people in the thirty- to forty-year-old age range. Are there enough generalists here to manage a global company?[89]

Another manager comments about his organization: "A concerted effort was made to rotate staff personnel into line activities. Over five years, one-quarter of our white-collar professionals had switched jobs at all levels."[90]

Autonomy and Initiative
How does a company socialize extensively, yet encourage autonomy and initiative? Employee Involvement has been Ford's primary answer. While there was no grand plan from its inception to use Employee Involvement as

a leavening against smothering bureaucracy, it caught hold and served that purpose well.*

Bob Mueller, one of the staff members responsible for facilitating Employee Involvement at the salaried level within Ford's Engineering Center, states: "When Caldwell became Chairman, Ford was in deep trouble. He searched for every means available to turn the situation around. He knew the CEO of Cummins personally, and had heard favorable things about involving employees. So, in 1979, he promulgated a policy memo (the twenty-first in Ford's entire history) encouraging EI. It was a paper 'event'—a sanctioning document at best. Caldwell was, in fact, an invisible CEO. We never saw him. But the policy memo got managers to open their minds a little bit, and it gave our pilot experiments a better chance."[91]

An alternative point of view is provided by one labor-relations executive closely associated with the EI initiative. "Labor Relations initiated the idea of a policy memo to Caldwell. He reviewed our suggestion, paused, and then said: 'Gentlemen, we can't prove it but let's try it!' You can't know what a great assistance that memo was to giving us legitimacy—along with Caldwell's subsequent visits at the plant level."[92]

Notwithstanding its acclaim in recent years, Employee Involvement almost died several deaths. Ernie Savoie, regarded as one of the architects of Employee Involvement, recounts the precarious years of its beginnings:

> We were almost dying for lack of interest—then later from too much of it. In 1978, I went to Japan. The clear lesson was that if you involve the hourly worker, he'll willingly contribute far more than management could imagine. But I had no idea of how to execute this at Ford. We had a built-in assumption that no program like this could ever justify giving hourly workers paid time off to discuss what they did and how they did it. We called a conference of plant managers in late 1978. Sixty came, four volunteered to try EI. There was not much enthusiasm. In two of these plants the local unions said, "Sounds okay; it might help job security." The other two unions said, "We'll go along, but if it fails it won't be our fault."
>
> Lo and behold, in the next six months these four pilot plants started their efforts, and the results are pretty good. It was becoming visible enough that I thought we had to bring key UAW officials into the loop. This triggered our second brush with disaster. I never got a chance to talk. One official began by stating, "Okay, I know what's going on, and it's going to stop right now. EI is good for the employees, the union, and the company," he stated, "but in some companies it's been used as a device to keep unions out." Later, after

---

* The text highlights only a few aspects of EI. Arguably, more than any other, Employee Involvement altered the face of Ford. Appendix I delves into hourly Employee Involvement in greater detail.

being assured of the company's intent and after having an opportunity to help fashion the process, this official negotiated the 1979 letter that launched the UAW-Ford EI process. Six months later he retired and was replaced by a new leader, and Pete Pestillo was appointed as Ford's new head of Industrial Relations. The new union leader saw EI as an opportunity to improve product quality and therefore job security at a time when thousands were being laid off because of the 1980 recession. Suddenly, we had strong union and company advocates of EI.

The third near miss occurred once Employee Involvement started to gain momentum. Suddenly, senior executives began to take it seriously and wanted to manage it. For example, one executive wanted a pert chart so we could roll it out *nationally* within six months. Fortunately, the union's leadership killed this idea. "No way," they said, "you're oversystemizing it, you're taking away local initiative. The key is letting plant people participate in the development of the plan. We don't know enough to attempt a *national plan*." Another thrust was to establish *mandatory* teams of workers, and let the supervisors run everything. Again the union leadership said: "Far better to have eight volunteers who want to be there than twenty who don't. Let the workers run it. Don't impose the old hierarchy on them if you want them to behave differently."

No sooner did we head off these perils than a well-intentioned Finance organization, anxious over Poling's three-million-dollar investment in Employee Involvement training, wanted to impose measurements to track results. They proposed we count the number of suggestions, the savings realized, and so on. Our plant managers helped us kill this one. "Look," they said, "if you measure this I'll give you whatever I need to look good. But I won't manage in a way that this process needs to be managed to succeed. You'll be comparing EI teams, ranking plants, and so on. You'll destroy the program. You'll have to be content with anecdotal and descriptive evidence." With Caldwell's and Pestillo's help, we were able to stay on course.

Neither the UAW nor we had the answers. So neither one came from a place of imposing their solution on the other. Gradually, we felt our way.[93]

An observer offers this point of view: "Employee Involvement laid wonderful groundwork in the 1980 to 1982 period. But until management got *its* act together, the plants were not particularly well-led, and thus EI did not contribute as much as it could later on, when priorities and focus were clear."[94]

Whatever the interplay of causal factors, success stories flowed forth with sufficient frequency to convert the skeptics. As shown in Box 6–1, trial and error produced eight simple guidelines. When, in late 1984, Henry Ford II officially stated that "EI was a way of life at Ford," he was truly confirming a reality that had been achieved.[95]

BOX 6–1.

Eight-Step Model for Employee Involvement

1. Senior management commitment and support
2. Establishing a joint steering committee
3. Diagnosis of problem areas for productive collaboration
4. Selection of pilot projects
5. Preparation of the organization
6. Launching the pilot
7. Evaluation and fine-tuning
8. Generalization and diffusion

Initiative Is Key

An important factor contributing to EI's success at Ford was agreement that management would not dictate which projects employees worked on. Further, it was management's conviction that employees needed to be educated and trained to fully exploit the potential of worker involvement. In 1982, the company and union funded a development and training program, with Ford contributing five cents to it for every blue-collar hour worked.* These funds, which were subsequently increased, can be spent only with UAW concurrence; Ford cannot redirect or reclaim them if there is a stalemate. These restrictions, which *management* readily concurred with, seek to prevent Ford from abandoning the program if times get tough. Some might worry about a worst-case scenario in which a rebellious union engages in wasteful and counterproductive behavior and subverts the intent of the program, but this has yet to occur. The downside acts as an incentive. Ford has enormous stakes in preventing its relations with its hourly workers from deteriorating.[96]

The importance of EI is both substantive and symbolic. EI is credited with much of the quality improvement that has catapulted Ford from last to first place in quality.[97] EI is likewise regarded as an important factor in improving productivity. Ford squeezed out 400,000 more cars in 1988 than Ford's plants had rated capacity for. These are no small accomplishments.[98]

But EI's symbolic significance is equally great. The automotive industry, more than most, demands closely integrated processes. The overall system *must* drive close coordination. These imperatives create factories that at their best work like tightly meshed machines. It is difficult to encourage *auton-*

* This contribution has since risen to twenty cents per hour.

omous behavior in this context, but one can empower employees at all levels to work better within this context. The very act of *enabling* employees to push back on the system and realize their "strength of numbers," alleviates oppressiveness. Experiments have shown that people tolerate more stress when they believe they have the power to regulate it. Ford's EI proves this finding.

HARD MINDS VERSUS SOFT HEARTS: COMPASSIONATE PRAGMATISM

Notwithstanding the humanistic appeal of notions such as "Employee Involvement," "empowerment," and "teamwork," Ford of the early to mideighties had a decidedly hard-minded cast. Illustrative was Poling's ultimatum to the divisions of Diversified Products, such as Castings, Vinyl, and Carburetor: meet competitive cost and quality standards or else.

Hard-mindedness gets a bad rap in America—mostly because it is associated with a lopsided emphasis on financial results, and an insensitivity to people. Through the late seventies, Ford was as guilty as any company of these traits.

What made the eighties different is that "hard-mindedness" was successfully linked in employees' minds with imperatives such as "survival" and "quality." Even though profitability has returned, "quality" and "competitiveness" have remained rallying cries; Ford simply points to the capacity glut of the 1990s and the inevitable shakedown that will come.[99] Management has continued to squeeze the organization for efficiency—yet retains allegiance. The sine qua non is consistency.

Ford monitors itself scrupulously. When Ford jumped from worst to best in U.S. vehicle quality, it might have celebrated its triumph and returned to its traditional ways. When the number of vehicles arriving at dealers' lots needing repairs fell from 10 percent to 5 percent to 1 percent, there was ample reason for Ford to say it had done enough.[100] When corrective design changes (made once a car is in production) dropped from $135 million to $35 million per introduction, there was cause for elation.[101] But hardmindedness means that Ford is never good enough. While proud of its achievements, Ford management openly discusses its many shortfalls. For example, while Ford's warranty costs now run $100 per car (best among the Big Three), the Japanese cost is $55 per vehicle. Ford's dealer organization is, in Petersen's view, an embarrassment to both company and franchisees, causing Ford to be "universally castigated and criticized."[102] Ford sees itself as a major part of the problem, and thus surveys its dealers to identify the company's shortcomings and correct them. The company also rewards its good dealers, formally recognizes those who improve, and punishes the recalcitrant by withholding the hottest cars in the line.[103] This is "hard-mindedness" in its best sense.

Beyond these achievements, Ford has succeeded in making soft hard. It has devised a "technology" for managing cross-functional teams for chimney integration and conflict management. While many U.S. corporations still regard these techniques as fuzzy intangibles, Ford has come to regard them as concrete tools in its arsenal for sustaining operational excellence.

Soft Hearts

Notwithstanding its toughness, Ford has also made progress in strengthening the "softhearted" side of the continuum. Ford's values had their antecedents in policies begun by Henry Ford I. The founder adopted a very hard line toward the worker. The sprawling River Rouge plant became an industrial concentration camp in which assembly line workers were not permitted to talk or smile.[104] Embracing Taylorism with a vengeance, work was tightly programmed. Ford's legendary confrontation with the emergent UAW left deep scars. Henry I's aide, Henry Bennett, was notorious for his abuses of workers and managers alike. Over the succeeding thirty years Ford's employee policies were modified in line with the industry practice of hard bargaining and temporary accommodation.

Indeed, Ford's growing permissiveness in its worker relations was more the result of bargaining table concessions than enlightened management. As with each of the Big Three, layoffs were triggered at the slightest indication of a downturn. Workers were seen as units of production, hired for their legs and arms, not their brains.[105] Not surprisingly, Ford's occasional flirtations with various employee participation fads did not flourish in this climate.

At the managerial level, Henry Ford II's escapades and firings cast a long shadow within the salaried ranks. (Caldwell, succeeding Henry Ford II as chairman in 1980, was the first peaceful transition to that office in Ford's eighty-year history.) McNamara served only one year as president before retreating to relative calm as Secretary of Defense in the administration of John F. Kennedy. Between 1969 and 1978, Henry Ford II fired two presidents—Bunkie Knudsen and Lee Iacocca. A third president, Arjay Miller, had been kicked upstairs to the vice chairman slot. The ripple effect of these incidents instilled a fear mentality.[106] You did what you were told, trusted people sparingly, and never contradicted your superiors. Bob Mueller, former internal organizational consultant and one of the facilitators of the Blue Ribbon Committee, states: "In the late seventies, when Sperlich and Iacocca were dismissed, many executives at Ford started to talk openly about how unsatisfactory their working relationships were and how badly people were being treated. I think this heightened their readiness for a change in values."[107]

Mission, Values, and Guiding Principles

With all of the aforementioned changes underway, employees began to ask top management to take a stand and state the new values explicitly. In 1984, Petersen convened a team of three direct reports and three mid-level managers from different parts of the company to draft a response to this request. This produced a draft that triggered a major investment of time and energy by the top six executives in the company. Honed and rewritten several times, it resulted in Ford's simply worded statement of its mission, values, and guiding principles, as shown in Box 6–2.[108]

In hindsight, a major factor in the wide acceptance of this statement is that its principles were *enacted* for several years before they were formally announced. Most companies disseminate their value statements the other way around, and the product is dismissed as PR hype. Ford's hesitance to state what it stood for served it well. Waiting until employees were clamoring for clarity ensured a receptive audience.

Petersen's words capture much of what underlies Ford's philosophy:

> I want this company to be a place where we see the best in people, and not the worst. A place where we work cooperatively, not as adversaries. To recognize and seek and trust the professionalism of others. I believe in the power of teamwork. These are the lasting things about an institution—not the home run product of a particular model year, but a healthy process. It's a lot like parenting. It's not one event like a spanking or supporting your child to succeed on a particular project. It's the ongoing act of reinforcing, encouraging; it's operating from a positive framework, not a critical, negative framework.
>
> Finally, if you are truly interested in the human equation in industrial life you have to be driven to provide people with employment stability—and that only comes from being fully competitive on an international basis.[109]

BOX 6–2.

Ford's Vision and Values

MISSION

Ford Motor Company is a worldwide leader in automotive and automotive-related products and services as well as in newer industries such as aerospace, communications, and financial services. Our mission is to improve continually our products and services to meet our customers' needs, allowing us to prosper as a business and to provide a reasonable return for our stockholders, the owners of our business.

VALUES

How we accomplish our mission is as important as the mission itself. Fundamental to success for the Company are these basic values:

People—Our people are the source of our strength. They provide our corporate intelligence and determine our reputation and vitality. Involvement and teamwork are our core human values.

Products—Our products are the end result of our efforts, and they should be the best in serving customers worldwide. As our products are viewed, so are we viewed.

Profits—Profits are the ultimate measure of how efficiently we provide customers with the best products for their needs. Profits are required to survive and grow.

GUIDING PRINCIPLES

Quality comes first—To achieve customer satisfaction, the quality of our products and services must be our number one priority.

Customers are the focus of everything we do—Our work must be done with our customers in mind, providing better products and services than our competition.

Continuous improvement is essential to our success—We must strive for excellence in everything we do: our products, in their safety and value—and in our services, our human relations, our competitiveness, and our profitability.

Employee involvement is our way of life—We are a team. We must treat each other with trust and respect.

Dealers and suppliers are our partners—The company must maintain mutually beneficial relationships with dealers, suppliers, and our other business associates.

Integrity is never compromised—The conduct of our Company worldwide must be pursued in a manner that is socially responsible and commands respect for its integrity and for its positive contributions to society. Our doors are open to men and women alike without discrimination and without regard to ethnic origin or personal beliefs.

Values and the UAW

The most dramatic evidence of Ford's values in action is reflected in the company's relations with the UAW. In 1982, Ford negotiated a profit-sharing program as part of the contract. Caldwell and Petersen played a major role in this initiative, and it reflected the new philosophy of seeking ways to tie all employees to a common purpose. The program paid dividends, literally and figuratively. In 1987, Ford paid $630 million in bonuses—the largest payout in U.S. corporate history. That year, Ford's average hourly employee received a check for $3,700.[110]

With profit sharing, Ford workers are more attentive to the demands of the business; they too share an interest in maximizing production. No one disputes that the bonus program directly contributed to Ford's earlier-cited improvements in productivity. The astonishing achievement of producing 400,000 more cars out of plants that were already at rated capacity could not have been done without the worker. This is the equivalent of adding one and a half new factories.[111] As with labor relations in Japan, Ford has begun to weave worker and management into a fabric of goals and values.

MAXIMIZE VERSUS "META-MIZE": EVOLVING EXCELLENCE

The acid test of any company's revitalization rests on its ability to sustain its competitive advantage. Here too we note management's ability to work both ends of the "dialectic." Under Poling's strong direction, Ford has become a highly competitive manufacturer. It can produce some of its vehicles at close to the Japanese rate in terms of labor productivity.

But at the heart of Ford's ambition is another dimension. *Evolving excellence* for Ford means continuing learning. Ford continues to chip days off the development cycle. The Louisville truck facility churns out seventy-five trucks per hour—the highest productivity in the world.[112] Ford is equally obsessive about streamlining the flow from concept to customer. A recent study by the consulting firm of McKinsey and Company shows that products that come to market six months late but on budget earn an average of 33 percent less profit in their first five years; products coming out on time but 50 percent over budget cut profit only 4 percent.[113] Mindful of these factors, today Ford can develop a new automobile from scratch in three to four years for $1 billion; GM needs five to six years and $3 billion.[114] The 1986 Taurus was designed in four years and is only 6.7 percent more expensive in *constant* dollars than its 1976 LTD counterpart. Yet it is half the weight, gets nearly twice the mileage per gallon, and ranks among the highest-quality American cars.[115]

The Learning Organization

Petersen believes that Ford is at year eight of a twenty-year change process. As his tenure has worn on, "learning" has been added to Ford's list of values. "There is little to be complacent about," he says. "We have to purge from our minds the notion that there is an end point, a point where we will reach the best quality at lowest cost, or best products for our customers.[116] Petersen constantly stresses that the industry will face serious overcapacity by 1990. The only way to compete in the environment is to be obsessively vigilant, self-disciplined, and lean. Ford strives to spark this vigilance through its use of outward-looking surveys of customers, external benchmarks, and careful monitoring of competition. As one senior executive puts it: "MBO's are not helpful. We do not want static objectives. We want a process that is obsessed with constantly improving things."[117]

"In the last analysis," another executive comments, "Ford's continued ability to learn and adapt depends on our philosophy of management. There has been a radical change in the company's thinking regarding the managers' role. They are viewed today as change agents and facilitators—not just as experts and controllers. If we can internalize this mindset as a way of life at Ford, we may indeed have reason to hope that we can continue to revitalize ourselves."[118]

Ernie Savoie presents this view: "We're about halfway through our transformation; we've got a lot yet to do until this approach *really* becomes ingrained in us. There is no *one* magic transformation and it's over. Survival in the nineties requires ongoing transformation. That's why the deeply ingrained value of 'continuous learning' is so important. Most employees work for Ford for thirty years. It will be the mid-nineties before the majority of people here will have grown up in the post-1980 environment. We survived changes of UAW leadership and a change in top management when Caldwell and Henry Ford II left. If we can hold course through one more leadership rotation, I'll feel confident that we've really got this process sufficiently imbedded."[119]

CHAPTER SEVEN

Transformation without Crisis: General Electric

The Greeks had a word for it: *enantiodromia*. They used the term to capture the tendency of things to swing toward extremes and then return to the opposite.[1] This pendulum-like tendency of human nature, and human institutions, played a central role in Greek philosophy. Many since have sought to deny the wisdom of the ancients by shielding themselves from these taxing ebbs and flows. Their recourse was to plot a course down the "middle of the road." The result was humdrum equilibrium. They missed the central idea that *true* vitality flourishes only by (1) living in a state of continuous imbalance, yet (2) avoiding such extremes that overdetermination results. These themes are important keys to understanding the sustained vitality of General Electric.

The preceding chapters have begun to sketch the features of a new mindset—one that (1) entails a holistic rather than piecemeal view of organizations, (2) embraces contention as a source of energy and renewal, and (3) builds a climate that encourages people to identify with company goals and apply their full energies to achieving them. The net effect of these factors must be pronounced enough to prod an organization into a constant state of restlessness, yet not so rending that it becomes destructive. Clearly, this is a complex prescription. Ford is an example of how one management team has transformed an organization using these precepts. The following is a study of General Electric—a different kind of corporation that has employed a very different strategy for self-renewal. While both firms have undergone, and are in the midst of, transformation, GE faced a more difficult task. There was no clear and present crisis at GE to mobilize employees at all levels. Chairman Jack Welch had to "manufacture" a crisis—and it was resisted by employees who felt GE was already on a solid footing.

They regarded Welch's sense of urgency as exaggerated and resented his slashing of costs.

OVERVIEW

In business for over a century, GE has at times flirted dangerously with stagnation. Nonetheless, it thrives today and currently ranks among the top three American companies as measured by market value.[2] On average, it has earned a 15% return on investment and is the sixth most profitable firm in the world.[3] There is much to be applauded in this record of sustained achievement. Very few firms can match GE over so prolonged a period of time. GE is one of the best examples available to those who wish to discover the secrets of sustained vitality.

All human institutions have a past, however brief, and there are lessons embedded in it. We readily acknowledge, based on organizations we have known firsthand, that the newcomer cannot fully grasp what's going on without some understanding of what has gone before. Yet when it comes to reading about *another* organization's history, we are somewhat intolerant of the details and impatient to get to the bottom line. The reader is asked to contain this impatience. A good part of understanding how GE has renewed itself over successive generations stems from tracing its history and noting the compensatory actions that corrected its excesses—over time.

We should note at this juncture that GE is significantly different from Ford. Both are large global enterprises with revenues and numbers of employees of similar magnitude, but Ford is predominantly a single-product business, whereas GE is a highly diversified company. Its fourteen businesses—Medical Systems, Major Appliances, Aircraft Engine, Plastics, Financial Services, NBC, etc.—have very little in common. A *business* head at GE faces problems similar to those that Petersen faced at Ford. But at GE's *corporate* level, the management task is more complicated. GE's CEOs have steadfastly refused to play a passive role as banker and arm's-length caretaker. Instead, they have insisted upon an active role in (1) allocating financial, technical, and human resources, (2) helping shape business strategy, and (3) prodding businesses to remain competitive and adaptive.[4] GE has always been offended by the label "conglomerate." While highly diversified, its CEOs have sought to maximize the value of the portfolio by leveraging one business to help another and by exploiting common systems and shared values. Current Chairman Jack Welch has advanced these techniques a notch by aggressively installing common management processes and mechanisms for the sharing of best practices across business units.

A challenge faced in understanding GE across the generations stems from the complexities of "simultaneity" as discussed in Chapter Three. Simultaneity pertains to a number of paradoxical trade-offs that have to be kept in tension. It would be much easier if each of the domains of contention could be isolated and treated one at a time. Unfortunately, as our quest for the new mindset frequently confirms, isolating one effect, investigating an interlocking system by dissecting it into discrete parts, is illusory. Thus, in most real-life cases we see the combined effects of several imbalances. This makes our story harder to tell, but the additional complexity pays off in greater accuracy and a more trustworthy understanding of the factors that lead to sustained performance. This will be evident at GE as we note the trade-offs being managed within *and* between successive administrations.

The importance of this issue becomes clear as we observe GE's brushes with stagnation. The decade of the 1950s is of particular interest because it points out how the old mindset led us to cheer on management's actions at the very time they were driving GE to extremes. During the 1950s, GE was in a class by itself. Greatly admired and technologically formidable, it held much the same status as IBM held in the 1960s and 1970s. Yet almost any observer at the time, had we been clairvoyant enough to foresee that computers, semiconductors, and robotics could grow to become the major industries they are today, would have had a hard time imagining these developments without GE being a major participant. Indeed, GE's dominance in the field of electrical equipment, its early participation in electronics (audio products and semiconductors), deep pockets, established brand-name and worldwide presence virtually guaranteed it a place in these huge and evolving markets. Of course, GE could have elected not to participate in these fields and placed its bets elsewhere. But GE in fact made major strategic commitments to computers, semiconductors, and later to robotics, entered late, vacillated, and ultimately failed to establish a foothold.[5]

This is not to deny that GE succeeded in many other areas, but simply to point out that the halo that surrounded it in the 1950s masked danger signs. GE stumbled in several high-payoff fields in which smaller rivals were carving out profitable competitive positions. In computers, for example, late starters like DEC, Apple, Tandem, and Compaq have thrived notwithstanding the large capital requirements and stiff barriers to entry. In semiconductors, GE may be glad today that it has largely exited a field in which only a few make money. Yet it cannot be denied that GE tried here as well, hesitantly committing itself, withdrawing, unsuccessfully acquiring its way back in, and ultimately conceding to supply only in-house requirements. While GE zigged and zagged, unlikely start-ups, such as Intel and Texas Instruments, and old-line firms, such as Motorola, established profitable and defensible positions. Finally, in factory automation (still a GE strategic priority) old-line firms like Allen Bradley (today a division of Rockwell), Siemens, and Fanuc (a Japanese newcomer) have all flourished and profit handsomely, while GE is relegated to the status of a secondary player. T. S. Eliot wrote in *Four Quartets* about "having the experience but missing the meaning." Analogously, the 1950s was a time when GE had many of the modern tools of management, basked in the glow of media praise but, in significant ways, was missing the boat. More will be said of this later.

Bold-stroke actions and episodic attention spans are not altogether bad. But when excess is employed as a tool for revitalization, the seeds of stagnation are planted in the bargain. As we shall see, GE's CEO of the 1950s, Ralph Cordiner, decentralized the company with a vengeance and installed an iron system to enforce his programs. On the positive side, this enabled improbable start-ups such as GE's Plastics and Aircraft Engine businesses (neither of which had a chance of emerging under the former structure), to achieve their place in the sun. Both are global leaders today. By the same token, systems and "policing" mechanisms, installed to keep rein on this decentralized structure, devolved into a labyrinthine tangle that haunts the company to this day.

The majority of GE's seven CEOs swung the pendulum to extremes. And while, as suggested above, there are costs along with benefits in employing this technique, GE's vitality appears to have been served by these reinvigorating shifts in emphasis. Perhaps, in a very large, highly diversified firm, one must send very strong signals to ensure that employees many levels down get the message that change is necessary. While the pendulum swings have at times done "violence" to the organization, perhaps such violence is necessary to provoke an adaptive response. Many of GE's CEOs appear to have "sinned bravely" in taking harsh corrective actions. The pain inflicted at times threatens to overshadow the gains realized. Yet if we look at the *net* effect of the pendulum swings across a long period of time, a more tolerant perspective emerges.[6] GE's genius has been in its choice of *successive* CEOs, each of whom tended to counter the extremes of his predecessors.

One final point. Owing to its long history, General Electric provides an unparalleled opportunity to assess our managerial paradigm. We will see that the company has often been praised and celebrated when it was most at risk—and, ironically, ignored and criticized when it was most intensely engaged in self-renewal. Consider perceptions versus actualities over the past several decades. It may shock many readers to learn that GE's revenues in 1981, in constant dollars, were only double those of 1958. Its portfolio, as shown in Figure 7–1, had shown significant slippage as well.[7] Yet over this same time frame, GE was regarded as being in the vanguard of management. A 1981 Gallup poll ranked CEO Reginald Jones "CEO of the Year."[8] An article in the *New York Times* characterized the company as "a model of modern management techniques."[9] Normally understated *Barron's* concluded that "GE is a great company however you want to define great, and [its] management is superior."[10] Harvard Business School celebrated GE's contributions with over ninety flattering case studies.[11] As the 1980s unfolded, the tide of praise turned for a time and GE became the target of second-guessing and criticism. Ironically, it was during this time frame that revitalization and renewal were being pursued more rigorously than at any time in GE's history.[12]

In summary, GE contains several stories in one. It is a story of corrective pendulum swings, of stagnation and renewal, and, in the Welch era, of at least partial transformation. It is a story about the old paradigm and the new. The mystique that we have historically assigned to GE tells us more about *what we want to believe* about management than it tells us about GE. To repeat, this is not to say that GE is not a great company. But we have enshrouded it in an aura of invincibility, and this shroud conceals more than it illuminates.

HISTORICAL PERSPECTIVE

The corrective pattern of GE's pendulum swings can be fully understood only when viewed in historical context. The history begins in 1877. Thomas Edison's inventive contributions to the telephone, phonograph, and electric light bulb were secured with strong patent protection. Like a modern-day Silicon Valley entrepreneur, he sought to create a company in each of these technologies. To finance these start-ups, he assembled investors.[13] The group that underwrote Edison's fledgling electric lighting company included a farsighted individual, Charles Coffin, who recognized that Edison's concept of the incandescent lamp provided superior illumination to the alternative arc lamp technology.[14] But Edison was wedded to DC (direct current) applications, whereas rival firms were demonstrating greater efficiencies with AC (alternating current). Seizing the moment, Coffin headed a group that purchased Edison's patents, combined them with Thompson-Houston's

FIG. 7-1

STRATEGISTS: General Electric
Portfolio 1972–1981

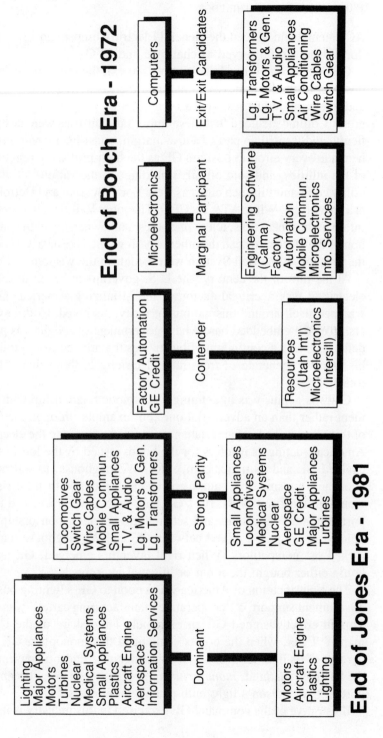

AC patents, and formed the General Electric Company in 1892. For the next thirty years Coffin served as chairman and CEO.[15]

Coffin's second critical decision was to exit the utility business. A careful observer of public policy, Coffin noted increasing regulation of the railroad and telegraph industries. Antitrust legislation was gaining support in Congress. Coffin concluded that these impacted industries were destined for difficulty and wanted no part of a low-margin, quasi-public enterprise. Instead, he made every effort to position GE as the high-profit, nonregulated supplier of the utilities, and sold off GE's holdings in the various "Edison" public utility companies in such cities as New York, Boston, and Detroit.[16] GE was at a crossroads. While AT&T's CEO, Theodore Vail, was integrating forward into switches, networks, telephone poles, and ownership of the phones in each home, GE elected to head the other way. It would take nearly a century before the breakup of the Bell System would confirm the wisdom of Coffin's path.

At the turn of the century, the U.S. government began to recognize that electricity was a critical factor in industrializing America. GE carefully wrapped itself around this national priority. As noted, Coffin avoided ownership of the embedded base where government oversight was probable. He defined instead a continuum of businesses that ranged from products that, in his words, "generate or transmit" electricity to those that "illuminate or rotate."[17]

Coffin's genius was in defining a symbiotic relationship with the government rather than an adversarial one. For example, through the first decades of this century, federal and state governments supported the electrification of America—acting as insurers for the bonds issued by the local utilities. This enabled GE and its major competitor, Westinghouse, to sell power generation and transmission equipment to the utilities with little risk that they would go bankrupt.[18] By 1911 GE had, with government and judicial support, extended its patents and secured government sponsorship of its technology. A duopoly evolved between GE and Westinghouse that effectively locked out competitors. When rival inventors emerged, GE and Westinghouse either bought them out or litigated interminably.[19]

The electrification of America was a boon to GE's lighting business. With government support, a "cooperative manufacturing cartel" was established. This in effect assigned GE an extremely large share of the U.S. lighting market. Later, when the courts challenged this monopoly, GE licensed 20 percent of its lighting business to Westinghouse under a consent decree. As the business matured, *manufacturing process* technology became more important than Edison's light bulb patents themselves.[20]

Illustrative of the command GE exercised in this industry is its imposition of the practice of selling light bulbs to retailers on consignment. The advantage of this arrangement was that it foreclosed discounting (since GE and Westinghouse owned the bulbs until they were sold—at which time the dealer received a commission). This practice, the forerunner of present-day "racking," persisted until 1971 and is only slightly less prevalent today.[21] So secure and lucrative was GE's hold on the lighting market that during the Great Depression when volume fell to half, revenues decreased only by 10 percent. GE's lighting business has been, and is, a virtual "mother lode." It has proven an unparalleled source of revenues and profits. To this day, more than half of all light bulbs sold in America are GE's, and Lighting's margins are extraordinarily high.[22]

Coffin's successor, Gerald Swope, extended GE's strategic horizon to include products and pricing and, in terms of our pendulum idea, continued to build upon Coffin's momentum. During Swope's tenure, 1923–1939, GE was a leading innovator in the electrical field as well as the dominant manufacturer in its various product lines. Swope coined the term "benign cycle" to capture the mutually reinforcing relationship among (1) large and small electrical appliances—such as ranges, refrigerators, toasters, lamps, heaters, irons, etc.—which increased demand for (2) electricity, which, in turn, (3) generated need for the utilities to purchase more power generation, transmission, and distribution equipment.[23] GE sold its housewares to generate consumption, and made its money on the big-ticket generators and transformers. In addition, GE licensed its technology throughout Europe, China, Japan, and Latin America in return for major positions in their electric companies. By 1935, GE owned 29 percent of Siemens, and 10 percent of Philips and had joint ventures in China and Japan, and throughout Latin America.[24]

Swope's vision for GE encompassed its organizational culture. The cornerstones of this culture included (1) excellence in engineering and manufacturing, (2) a solid accounting and financial control system, and (3) emphasis on the GE "family" (retreats for executives and progressive personnel policies that enlisted worker commitment and contributions to manufacturing efficiency).[25]

The integrity of GE's product lines was protected by functionally autonomous "Works" managers. The respective Works managers oversaw a geography—in effect, regional manufacturing centers, making an assortment of whatever GE assigned them to produce—but never 100 percent of any one product. Some of these factory complexes became small cities—with their own schools, parks, radio stations, and sprawling factories. At one time GE's Bridgeport Works boasted the largest group of factories under one roof in the world. Under that roof an eclectic array of products were designed and manufactured: refrigerators, housewares, small appliances, wire and cable, and so forth.[26]

The fierce independence of the respective "Works" was balanced against the sense of GE as a family and the personal loyalties that many senior executives maintained with Swope. In addition, the activities of the Works managers were monitored by GE's financial system and Swope's extensive informal intelligence network.[27]

In the 1920s Swope personally authored a number of personnel practices that were decades ahead of their time: he (1) established employee associations to ensure that worker interests were fairly represented; (2) introduced life insurance and disability insurance; (3) added the novel feature of cost-of-living increases to hourly wages; and (4) pioneered the introduction of unemployment insurance and pensions. (Swope subsequently played a central role in formulating America's Social Security program under the New Deal). On the managerial front, Swope instituted annual "off-sites" held at Association Island. All managers above the foreman level attended. Here were the not-too-distant ancestors of modern-day "team building"/ "outward bound" type of retreats: company songs were sung, interpersonal frictions softened, and esprit de corps enhanced.[28]

Precarious Vitality

By the close of Swope's tenure, GE had a moderate degree of fit, through the fine-tuning of strategy, systems, and the soft S's described earlier, and also a high degree of split (with the Works operating with a great deal of independence). The trouble facing GE was that the monolithic Works obscured business opportunities for certain products and technologies that were submerged under their wing. Plastics was a small unit within Transformers; Refrigerators had somehow grown up in Wire and Cable. Finance tied GE together from an accounting and control standpoint, but, as noted earlier, it was personal loyalty to Swope, not a give-and-take process, that held the planets in orbit. True, this system did produce contention and much of it was channeled constructively—mostly because of the shared vision of GE as a family and Swope's stature and persuasive powers. Swope's failing was in not adequately institutionalizing a system for sustaining constructive tension once he stepped down.

Inattention Yields Imbalance

The GE Board named Charles Wilson as Swope's successor in 1940. Wilson served through 1952. So closely knit was GE's relationship to the government during this period that Wilson was lent to Washington as head of the

War Mobilization Board. During Wilson's absence, Swope returned briefly from retirement and served as president—largely in a caretaker role.[29] This left GE somewhat in limbo during the war and resulted in a strategy and leadership vacuum. The finely tuned balance was lost.

When an organization has "constructive tension" in the best sense, it is really humming. A dynamic interplay prevails in which the forces at play generate self-questioning and intensity. This is not a static situation; it is an ever-changing flux of forces in dynamic equilibrium. In such circumstances, analogous to the earth and its sister planets orbiting around the sun, one can easily entertain the illusion that the system is perfectly in sync and is best left alone. But as with the solar system, there is always decay—and occasionally a discontinuous event, like a meteor colliding with a planet. During Wilson's tenure, both "decay" and "discontinuity" were impacting the GE system. "Decay" occurred gradually as a result of Wilson's inability to sustain the strong personal relationships that Swope had built with the Works managers. Wilson lacked Swope's magnetism, and his prolonged absences on government projects exacerbated the problem. Gradually, the respective Works became more independent and insular. Culturally GE shifted from being one "family" to a collection of sects with common ancestry.

Masking the above-noted vulnerabilities was the "discontinuity" of World War II and its aftermath: the war effort flooded GE with orders; in many segments, the company sold all it could produce. After the war, like many American companies, GE derived a further boost from postwar demand. The Marshall Plan underwrote the reconstruction of Europe—a further boost to demand for power generation and heavy industrial equipment.[30] While some of the dynamic forces responsible for GE's past vitality were slipping away, GE celebrated its golden years. Wilson floated on the rising tide of America's industrial preeminence.

THE CORDINER ERA

The long interval beginning with World War II and flowing through the postwar recovery had drawn GE into many wartime technologies—aircraft engines, nuclear energy, and aerospace. No real "strategy" had been required. Insatiable demand created an environment in which it was easy to succeed. But the early fifties brought reversals—both in the marketplace and in the public arena. Under the Truman and Eisenhower administrations, the government began to reverse its previously benign position toward GE.

Antitrust infractions were investigated and the responsible individuals brought to trial: GE was the target of over fourteen suits and lost the majority of them.[31] The first signs of world competition in consumer appliances and power generation equipment began to appear.

Former Harvard historian and current head of GE's executive development, James Baughman, observes:

> World War II had drawn GE into atomic energy, jet engines, radar, aerospace and a variety of other technologies it had never pursued before. This created two hazards for GE top management in the decades ahead. First, since its inception, GE had a "make" (rather than "buy") mentality. From Coffin's day there was a distrust of being "captive" to suppliers. The Works integrated backward. It was a one hundred and ten percent do-it-yourself tradition. This propensity was magnified in engineers tantalized by new post-war technologies. Thus came the tendency for GE to (a) get into everything, and (b) try to do it all in-house. These tendencies toward diversification and self-sufficiency were justifiable, but by the end of the Wilson era, had begun to generate real strains upon the functional organization that Swope had created.[32]

In the face of these challenges, GE's new CEO sought to reposition GE's portfolio. In particular, Cordiner targeted consumer goods as a hot growth area in the postwar environment. He utilized the now-famous GE logo to enhance brand identity, changed GE's slogan to "Progress is our most important product," and endeavored to build a strong marketing capability.[33] Later in his tenure he embarked on ambitious programs in the capital goods sector, funding GE's foray into computers and nuclear power. These became major cash drains.[34]

Postwar General Electric is a story about two revolutionary, and two evolutionary, CEO's. The revolutionaries were Cordiner and Welch. The evolutionaries were Borch and Jones. Cordiner came to GE having previously been president of Schick. He served as assistant to the president under Swope and Wilson. Hired for his marketing background, he believed that GE needed a strong product/market focus. By the time he became CEO, frustrating interactions with the Works convinced him that the only way to achieve his aim was to break them up entirely and replace them with smaller, more focused units.[35]

Postwar conditions warranted a repositioning of GE, and by the time that Cordiner became CEO, change was overdue. But Cordiner's response, as we shall see, was somewhat precipitous. Within a month of taking charge, he began to dismantle a good deal of what Swope had created. A champion of the "organization as machine" mindset of his day, Cordiner viewed decentralization (i.e., split) as *the* primary remedy to GE's ills.[36]

So Cordiner broke up the Works and decentralized. But he did not stop there. Over a twenty-month interval he changed the jobs of 2,000 senior executives, discontinued the tradition of Association Island, endorsed the concept of interchangeable "professional managers" (as a rationale for moving Cordiner loyalists into businesses with which they were unfamiliar), and installed administrative machinery to muscle his reforms down into the ranks.[37]

Cordiner sought to stay on top of this extensive decentralization by imposing a new concept "invented" jointly by Peter Drucker and GE, called "management by objectives." Each GE general manager was made responsible for a "profit center" and expected to achieve his "hurdle rates": 7-percent return on sales and 20-percent return on investment. The numerical targets were applied literally. Says one senior executive of that era: "The focus was on numbers, not plans; you made your numbers or lost your job."[38]

One undesirable result of Cordiner's "hurdle rates" was that they conditioned GE managers to "make their numbers"—even when unrealistic. This was particularly onerous because Cordiner's overuse of profit centers narrowed the P&L units down to very small, single businesses, even projects. This meant that there were no aggregates (i.e., cash-generating projects *and* cash-consuming projects) to balance one another. Under the circumstances, "making one's numbers" often sacrificed a unit's long-term future—yet this became the norm. This short-term tendency lowered management's resistance to "harvesting" a business; it is implicated in GE's postwar track record of selling short on some businesses (such as Mobile Communications) which, because of aggressive harvesting, never realized their potential.[39]

Cordiner did not operate alone. His impact was greatly magnified by two lieutenants—Harold Smiddy, a management specialist, as his chief of staff, and Lemuel Boulware, a GE Public Relations executive who expanded from that role into Government and Employee Relations. Each of these men left a lasting mark on GE's character.[40]

In the service of Cordiner's vision, Smiddy implemented the program that broke GE's traditional organization into almost a hundred product departments. Then, to rein it all in, Smiddy engineered complex linkage systems and procedures that (1) relied on stringent financial accounting and controls to keep track of the separate business units, (2) established a hierarchy of reporting relationships to ensure executive oversight, and (3) instituted a process of reviews that established checks and balances against possible excesses of delegated authority. In sum, Cordiner's approach epitomized an "engineered" approach to organizational change. He sought to "hard-wire" the relationship between split and fit through interlocking controls. Regrettably, as we have discussed, healthy equilibrium in organizations is always dynamic, never static or mechanistic. Earlier quoted GE historian Baughman states:

> Cordiner got decentralization without sufficient discretion. The rules were so comprehensive the P&L units didn't feel decentralized. Smiddy promulgated eight Blue Books—procedural manuals that tried to anticipate every situation. Another Smiddy tenet was "one over one." The idea was straightforward: there are certain kinds of decisions which you don't want one layer making unilaterally. These include capital commitments, budget increases, hiring/firing, performance appraisals, and salary reviews. The philosophy was sound. There are many situations where two heads are better than one. The intention was to have the P&L unit go to the boss ten percent of the time, and exercise discretion ninety percent of the time. In practice, however, next-layer approval was required far too often; and, as decentralization bred layer upon layer, as many as nine "one-over-one" approvals might be required to act.[41]

Baughman continues:

> Cordiner and Smiddy implemented their decentralization program like a zoning commission. They believed in symmetry and order: all buildings needed to be the same height. This translated into uniformity in pay, organizational structure, span-of-control, practices and policies, regardless of a business unit's size or the maturity of the product line. Everything was cross-footed—policies and procedures linked vertically and horizontally. You were locked in; the columns and rows balanced in every cell. GE's engineering- and finance-dominated cultures were particularly receptive to this orderly approach. The precepts from the Cordiner era were so powerful that even to this day they will fill any vacuum.[42]

Smiddy's counterpart, Boulware, was equally potent on the Communications front. Boulware pioneered the concept of "stake-holder relations." This "take the high ground" approach involved aggressively positioning one's company in a favorable light before rank-and-file employees, the press, and the general public. Boulware's philosophy went hand in glove with Smiddy's—both presumed a strong central control orientation.[43]

Take, for example, Boulware's highly effective system for "getting out in front on issues" with respect to GE's union and employees. Boulware did not believe the unions should convey GE's story. He championed the view: "If management is doing its job, you don't need unions." In pursuit of this objective, he felt it perfectly acceptable to engage in union avoidance— using climate surveys, attitude surveys, strategic communication, and other proactive programs. Boulware's slogan, etched into GE's Employee Relations to this day, taught all managers to *"Do right voluntarily in the best interest of all the stakeholders"* (employees, management, stockholders, and customers).[44] States one source: "You lost your job in those days if you had a union petition in your nonunionized plant."[45]

Not surprisingly, the arsenal of techniques that Smiddy and Boulware employed gave impetus to excess. The good news is that all this had impact, and the bad news is that it went too far—primarily because of the unrelenting rigor and lack of compassion with which the techniques were imposed. Cordiner communicated his belief that the Works were "natural enemies" of his plan. His style, itself, was a factor. Five feet two inches tall, he was seen by many as somewhat cold and aloof, and openly conceded that he didn't care if people were hurt if they got in his way. "Not the kind you'd want to hang out with after hours," is the way one GE veteran puts it.[46]

Like a great many managers, Cordiner saw himself "here" and wanted to get "there." The shortest distance between two points being a straight line, he set out to achieve his objective. If there is a lesson to be learned from this account, it should be the fallacy of "straight-line" thinking. Cordiner's limitation, and it is often so with senior executives, is that he focused on his script for change and didn't think through the second- and third-order effects (i.e., what would happen *after* what he wanted to happen was achieved). Like the freeway builders of the 1950s, he bulldozed a path through "ethnic neighborhoods" (i.e., the Works) and "historical landmarks" (i.e., the culture), dividing the GE community in the process.

Cordiner's declaration of war upon the Works disrupted the power structure of the manufacturing elites and, to a lesser extent, impacted the engineering cadre. It led to an attrition of a very large number of his key middle- and top-level managers over a ten-year period.[47] This loss of leadership weakened areas of traditional strength. Despite his intention to establish Marketing as an important area of GE competence, it did not emerge as a serious force within the culture.[48] Finance remained unscathed—no longer balanced by the formidable Works. In place of Association Island, Cordiner established Crotonville, a management training center. Some regarded it as a brainwashing facility; participants either hewed to the company line or were terminated.[49] An alternative view is that the facility sought, in the words of its current director, "to burn Cordiner's new approach into the collective consciousness of the management ranks."[50] In this regard it was highly effective. GE borrowed its faculty from outside sources—Peter Drucker, Chris Argyis, and a host of professors from Harvard Business School had a hand in shaping its curriculum. This symbiotic relationship with outside management experts has continued to the present day and is one reason the media so often refers to GE. Experts familiarized with GE at Crotonville often refer journalists to their client. Thus GE finds itself in another "benign cycle" that reinforces its role as the pioneer of the newest management ideas put into practice.[51]

Among the most serious consequences of Cordiner's efforts was the politization of GE. Under attack, the Works managers bitterly resisted, ultimately taking their differences to a showdown before the Board. Cordiner narrowly won.[52] Smiddy's role as Cordiner's enforcer created an environment of "fear and favorites."[53] One senior executive at the time recalls: "Smiddy came to be perhaps the most feared man in the company. Managers either liked him or hated him. There was no middle of the road." Commenting on the internecine struggle, this executive continues: "One reason for the slow attainment of Cordiner's [bottom-line revenue] goals was that GE had an enormous number of strong-charactered managers. [They] blocked change, did not willingly release power, and held up true decentralization."[54]

As has been noted, Cordiner achieved a great deal of structural and procedural change. But his ultimate failure was that he did not get the entrepreneurial behavior he sought. His approach was so intensely focused on breaking the loyalties within the Works that it severed many effective working relationships and undermined trust.

THE PRICE OF RENEWAL?

Framed in a historical context, Cordiner's measures succeeded in shocking GE out of its post–World War II complacency. It can be argued that this radical surgery was necessary to awaken GE to new competitive realities. The insular Works managers, left to their conservative traditions, might easily have ignored inroads of foreign and domestic competition, and the growing importance of consumer markets. But Cordiner might have achieved the same result without recourse to such extremes.

One final outgrowth of Cordiner's reforms was that Finance became an extremely powerful function. Charged with administering Smiddy's system, it often exercised the "tiebreaking" vote in decision making.[55] Manufacturing was particularly impacted. Decentralization of the Works splintered Manufacturing into smaller units. Ideally, this enabled Engineering and Manufacturing to concentrate on a single product. In a few cases (Aircraft Engine and Plastics), this theory held true. But to the misfortune of most businesses, line management was not strong enough to orchestrate an effective tension between Finance and the other disciplines. More typically, the pecking order was sorted out on a Darwinian basis, with Finance the usual victor.

When all the dust had settled, Cordiner's organizational machinery was staggering under its own weight. GE's growth had come to a complete halt. Revenues stagnated at $5 billion.[56] Revolutionary change that had begun with a bang ended with a whimper.

We regard certain periods of history, such as the Italian Renaissance or the late nineteenth century in Vienna, as eras of great vitality. Contrast these with periods immediately following the upheavals in Russia in 1918 and in China after the Cultural Revolution. All were periods of great change. The difference is that the golden eras flourished in an atmosphere of debate, but things never became so ideological that one prevailing view extinguished all others. In contrast, the postrevolutionary periods were times of single-mindedness. Cordiner, Smiddy, and Boulware typified the latter malady. Seeking "consistency," they imposed a dogma of decentralized profit centers, quantifiable hurdle rates, professional management, and so forth, with punctilious thoroughness. There was conflict all right, but without constructive tension. They did not create or acknowledge the need for debate because they only wanted it one way. In fact, they saw virtue in eradicating any countervailing thrust that might be deemed "opposite" to their intentions.

Chapter Three concluded with a schematic representation of the seven domains of contention depicted in a "planetary diagram." The relative size of the planets indicates the degree to which one end of the continuum overshadows the other. As suggested in Figure 7–2, the degree to which either planet overlaps the "chaos" or "overcontrol" zones indicates excess.

Applying this schematic representation to the Cordiner era visually summarizes the points made in the preceding paragraphs. We see the overemphasis on (1) mandatory systems, (2) a muscle-bound "management," (3) hard minded values, and (4) the emergence of one dominant financial elite. All of these factors tilt toward overcontrol. While such a schematic representation cannot be taken literally, it enables us to capture these complex relationships and assess their overall tendency.

In 1959, several very senior GE executives were found guilty of price-

FIG.7–2

Carrying a Good Thing Too Far:
GE In the Cordiner Era

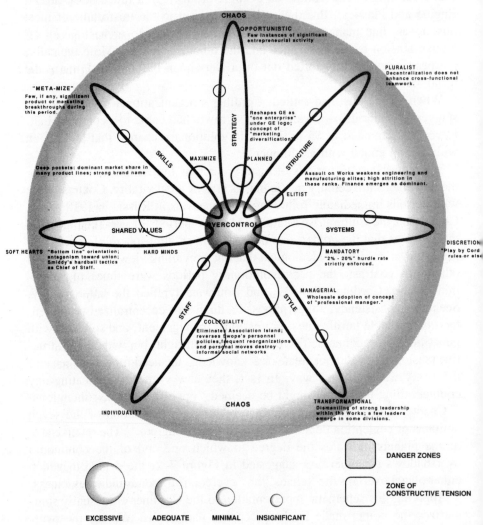

CHAOS

OPPORTUNISTIC
Few instances of significant entrepreneurial activity

PLURALIST
Decentralization does not enhance cross-functional teamwork.

"META-MIZE"
Few, if any, significant product or marketing breakthroughs during this period.

Reshapes GE as "one enterprise" under GE logo; concept of "marketing diversification"

SKILLS   **STRATEGY**   **STRUCTURE**

MAXIMIZE   PLANNED

Deep pockets: dominant market share in many product lines; strong brand name

ELITIST

Assault on Works weakens engineering and manufacturing elites; high attrition in these ranks. Finance emerges as dominant.

OVERCONTROL

SHARED VALUES   **SYSTEMS**

SOFT HEARTS   "Bottom line" orientation; antagonism toward union; Smiddy's hardball tactics as Chief of Staff.

HARD MINDS

DISCRETION
"Play by Cord rules or else"

MANDATORY
"2% - 20%" hurdle rate strictly enforced.

MANAGERIAL
Wholesale adoption of concept of "professional manager."

STAFF   **STYLE**

COLLEGIALITY
Eliminates Association Island; reverses Swope's personnel policies; frequent reorganizations and personnel moves destroy informal social networks

CHAOS

TRANSFORMATIONAL
Dismantling of strong leadership within the Works; a few leaders emerge in some divisions.

INDIVIDUALITY

DANGER ZONES

ZONE OF CONSTRUCTIVE TENSION

EXCESSIVE   ADEQUATE   MINIMAL   INSIGNIFICANT

SYMBOLS: SIZE OF SPHERES SUGGESTS THE RELATIVE EMPHASIS GIVEN TO EACH OF THE POLARITIES

fixing. It was widely believed that Cordiner's pressure to achieve the "hurdle rates" created a context in which such behavior became all too tempting. While both GE and Westinghouse executives were prosecuted, Westinghouse stood by its managers, kept them on the payroll, and let them quietly serve out their careers. GE's executives were abruptly terminated. Cordiner was incredibly angry that this incident had marred his tenure, and he readily sacrificed the transgressors.[57] But others at GE took note—many who had joined up with Cordiner's reforms no longer felt they could trust the company. Cordiner's scapegoating was seen as a breach of faith. It cast a shadow that did not dissipate and hastened his early retirement.

THE BORCH ERA

Cordiner did not play a major role in choosing his successor. Against the backdrop of the price-fixing scandal, the Board selected Fred Borch, former president of GE's lighting business.[58] It is noteworthy that the Board did not select someone in Cordiner's (or Smiddy's!) mold and perpetuate more of what was already in place. It had become obvious to many that the pendulum had swung too far. It was time to back off and restore equilibrium.[59]

As CEO, Borch undertook corrective actions. Hindsight would suggest that some were too timid and others too far-reaching. But directionally he, too, was the right man for the situation.

Borch banked on two attributes. First, he represented the old values of GE and positioned himself as a person who could heal the wounds after the tumult of the Cordiner years. Second, he had demonstrated a marketing flair in boosting lighting revenues. Such skills were badly needed to reinvigorate GE's stagnating portfolio.[60]

Borch brought a refreshing change in style. Whereas Cordiner was tight, directive, and aloof, Borch tended to be very involved. His approach was to solicit a lot of input—then work behind the scenes through subordinates to give shape to his priorities. He softened the tone (at least within the upper management echelons) with his friendliness and accessibility.

Borch's commitment to "calming the waters" was well received. Stability was called for after a period of radical change.[61] But the steady state is only desirable if it rests on a sound foundation. As noted earlier, Cordiner had destroyed a good deal of the prewar culture—its harmonious working relationships and, above all, constructive tension between Engineering, Manufacturing, and Finance. He replaced it with a coherent new culture—involving a complex matrix of decentralized units, a rigid hierarchy of levels, one-over-one reviews, control systems, and extensive proceduralization. As has been noted, the enlargement of Finance tended to overshadow other functions in most businesses.

Borch's program to "calm the waters" did not deal with these issues comprehensively. He reorganized a lot. He gave *line* managers greater say in corporate resource allocation deliberations and reemphasized the recruitment of engineering talent.[62] So far so good.

With 20/20 hindsight, Finance needed to be taken down a peg, along with its numbers-obsessive reward and control systems. Some of Swope's personnel programs needed to be reinstated to rekindle employee trust and commitment. Energetic efforts were needed to depoliticize the environment and ensure that "due process" was observed in matters impacting on individuals and their careers. But like many CEOs of this age, Borch fell short in these areas. (The 1950s and 1960s was a period of booming economic expansion; the management paradigm focused on keeping the reins on galloping growth through controls and layers of management.) Borch lacked an understanding of the specific techniques one must utilize to fine-tune organization behavior.

When all was said and done, most of Borch's efforts to "change the culture" amounted to persuasion. The exception, as noted above, was an early effort at restructuring. Concluding that the P&L units were not succeeding because they were too big, he nearly doubled their number to over 300.[63] This excess of *split* created businesses within businesses. For example, GE's refrigerator department spun off its compressor activities as a separate P&L unit. "The problem was," recalls one executive, "that we were destroying our scale economies. There was so much cross-selling between units that transfer pricing became a zoo. Borch's downsizing created nonviable cottage industries."[64] Most disappointing, GE's functional competence in sales and marketing remained weak in most businesses.

Borch was more aggressive in striving to reposition GE in fields of the future. The computer and nuclear power businesses were reemphasized as strategic priorities and received an infusion of resources. Borch also searched further afield. Current CEO Jack Welch comments:

> Borch let a thousand flowers bloom. He got us into modular housing and entertainment businesses, nurtured GE Credit through its infancy, embarked on ventures in Europe, and left Aircraft Engine and Plastics alone so they could really get started. It became evident after he stepped down that GE had once again established a foothold into some businesses with a future.[65]

MANAGEMENT CHIC

Notwithstanding the missteps, Borch, like Cordiner before him, sustained GE's image as a managerial trendsetter. Near the end of his tenure, he introduced a highly sophisticated system of strategic planning.[66] While it was a well-intentioned effort to grapple with GE's growing diversity, the intricate system was shared publicly, awed onlookers, and was given broad attention in the media. Owing to our enthusiasm for "management technology," GE remained the role model of Management Chic. Leading edge concepts such as the experience curve, value analysis, portfolio concepts, and regression-based PIMS analyses were consumed avidly by America's technique-hungry professional managers. There was, of course, merit in many of the financial tools and strategic concepts that Borch brought to bear on his far-flung portfolio. However, there was also a widespread tendency to apply such methodology excessively and simplistically. This was not an inevitability—only the consequence of "straight-line" thinking of the times.

Behind the tools and state-of-the-art techniques, there was, as suggested at the outset, both renewal and stagnation. Some of Borch's strategic thrusts paid off and reestablished avenues for future growth. The organization began to heal itself slowly after the turmoil of the Cordiner years. But many of Borch's costly acquisitions in entertainment, modular housing, personal services and education went nowhere. Further, GE's investments in computers were nearing a dead end. Growing demands of GE's nuclear and aircraft engine businesses began to represent major cash drains. Finally, fines stemming from the antitrust suits soaked up $250 million.[67] By the end of Borch's era, the seeds for some extremely important new businesses were well-planted, but debt had increased and ROI dipped to an all-time low.

As the sixties neared a close there were whispers in the corridors that GE had lost its magic. The company had gone nearly a decade with little real growth and with modest earnings. The period 1959–1966 came to be referred to inside GE as the "era of profitless prosperity."[68] GE was the same size in constant dollar sales as at the end of World War II—notwithstanding a two-decade-long postwar expansion that was the longest sustained boom in U.S. history.

Near the close of his tenure, perhaps noting a need for the corrective actions that his successor was indeed to put into place, Borch tried two "fixes." First, he hired outside consultants (McKinsey) who recommended another application of that tried and true weapon of the old paradigm, "restructuring." This time, GE underwent a massive *re*centralization—clustering its businesses in forty-three strategic Business Units. The second fix took the form of the earlier-mentioned, McKinsey-designed system of Strategic Planning. These thrusts were set in motion shortly before Borch stepped down.[69] His final act was to recommend to the Board former chief financial officer (and one-time auditor) Reginald Jones as his successor.

AIRCRAFT ENGINE—A SUCCESSFUL SUBCULTURE

An interesting microcosm of GE at its managerial best is the story of Aircraft Engine, a highly successful GE business that flourished during both the Cordiner and Borch eras. As a new business, it did not become the target of Cordiner's campaigns to dismantle the traditional Works. Borch provided sufficient autonomy and resources for it to further shape its destiny.

GE's Aircraft Engine Division was established in World War II as the manufacturer of small engines for propeller-driven training aircraft. As a cost-plus business with a reliable 10 percent return on sales, the division had been left alone, unmarred by Cordiner's decentralization efforts and exempted from the 7 percent/20 percent hurdle rates.[70] Under the leadership of Gerhard Neumann, the division developed a unique "can do" culture, dedicated to technological leadership and serving its customers. Neumann constantly stimulated internal competition within the division and established demanding engine performance goals to generate a constructive sense of crisis.[71] States one executive: "Aircraft Engine was always very different than the rest of GE. We were given latitude and autonomy. In the postwar years, GE saw us as a contribution to the nation—an act of corporate citizenship. We were not resource constrained. All our management was homegrown. We never suffered from the purges. We had legends like Neumann with great product vision who rallied people, circled the wagons, and provided focus. We performed miracles on a shoestring. This 'doing it against all odds' track record gave us a defiant sense of self-sufficiency.''[72]

By the early sixties, Aircraft Engine had grown from obscurity to commanding a 20-percent share of the military jet engine market. Two successive vice chairmen (Jack Parker and Ed Hood), each having apprenticed in the division, provided air cover at the corporate level.[73] Then under Borch, Aircraft Engine got the go-ahead to diversify away from the safe cost-plus defense programs into commercial jet engines. Now a strategic priority, GE invested $700 million in this segment over a seven-year period before the payoff began to fall in. This event is particularly noteworthy because there are few instances in GE's history in which there has been a willingness to bankroll a new business for sums of this magnitude over such a prolonged period of time.[74]

Over the past twenty years, Aircraft Engine has emerged as a star in GE's portfolio. As suggested, several factors converged to make this success possible. First and foremost, *strong* business-level leadership and continuity of personnel was in place and was willing to buck the system in pursuit of opportunities. Second, cost-plus contracts with the Pentagon gave the business relief from Finance's oversight. Third, Borch (and his vice chairmen) provided resources and personal support. For all of these reasons, Aircraft Engine was able to establish a constructive tension between the operating autonomy it needed to excel and the demands of GE's measurement-driven culture. A manager from Aircraft Engine summarizes: "At the core, GE is short-term, bottom-line oriented. If you don't meet your budget, there are no excuses. But the penalty for not meeting one's budget is more severe in other parts of GE than within our division. We have always defended our prerogatives to make sound long- versus short-term trade-offs."[75]

THE FINANCIAL ELITE

As noted earlier, an unintended consequence of the Cordiner and Borch years was that the Finance function became disproportionately influential. Prior to the 1950s, Finance was a cash accounting regime. But under Cordiner, Finance rose in stature, since (1) decentralization required beefed up control, and (2) each P&L unit needed its own manager of finance. After the price-fixing scandal, Finance became evermore vigilant, with auditing and oversight powers added.[76]

Borch made no effort to modulate this imbalance. And over the ensuing years, Finance evolved into a highly cohesive cadre. Late in the Borch era, it gained still further clout when the colateral duties of Strategic Planning and Information Systems were added to its portfolio of responsibilities.

Throughout this and prior chapters I have used the term *elites*. It is not surprising that the events just described would make an elite of GE Finance. There is, in fact, probably no more formidable example of an elite cadre in corporate America.

GE Finance had historically maintained a strong dotted-line reporting relationship to the chief financial officer and, through him, to the CEO. This paralleled its solid-line relationship between the designated financial manager and his boss within the P&L unit. By Board resolution, a manager of

Finance could not be removed without approval of higher financial management. Further, by tradition, when vacancies occurred, the Finance organization (not the line manager), determined who filled the slot. To this day, a line manager at GE cannot select, hire, or fire his financial subordinate without review and concurrence by the CFO.[77]

GE recruits its entrants into Finance from the top-tier colleges and universities. After extensive testing and interviews, the most promising are selected and proceed through the entry-level Financial Management Program (FMP). Not surprisingly, the new recruits enter feeling they are already among "the best and the brightest."[78] Yet humility is interjected into these self-confident candidates. Over the next several years, they are observed, evaluated, and ranked. Mandatory coursework parallels their on-the-job training and, at the conclusion of each module, they are tested. Participants must achieve an average score of 95 (out of 100) on tests to remain in the FMP.[79] All the while, the trainees are rotating through assignments that expose them to budgeting, cost accounting, general accounting, and other critical aspects of their profession. By the close of the third year, each trainee has seen a lot of the trenches, and his or her bosses have made assessments regarding certain crucial traits: assertiveness, presence, verbal skills, initiative, ambition, and accuracy.[80]

AUDITORS: THE ELITE OF THE ELITE

Notwithstanding the socialization process just described, GE Finance derived its distinctive cast from an even more unique feature. Through the end of the Jones era virtually *all* of GE's top 350 Finance executives passed through an even more exacting experience: all had a tour at what is known in GE as being a "traveling auditor."[81]

After three years on the job, every member of the Financial Management Program was screened again, and the top third invited to join the Auditing Staff. Selection to the Auditing Staff was a sign of high potential. Career-wise, it spelled an acceleration of responsibilities. Despite the sacrifices that would be required, few who were chosen said no. A successful tour in auditing established that one could perform at a high level, was a quick study, and had the endurance and interpersonal skills necessary to climb the corporate ladder.[82]

Life as a traveling auditor provided an intense and powerful educational experience. Auditors were assigned to a different business every three months, immersed in its details and overtime, and saw a broad cross-section of GE's businesses. Traveling auditors were on the road 250 to 300 days per year. They worked an average of 80 to 120 hours per week. Peer pressure was interjected by the simple expedient of reminding everyone that "their peers were their competition"; each year the class was ranked from first to last based on productivity and results. Only the top two-thirds survived for a second year. At the end of year three, the most highly ranked individual was awarded the top slot of Audit Staff Administrator.[83]

Needless to say, the scenario was character-building. Inductees adapted to the situation in order to survive. Enhancing the intensity, auditors were assigned to teams, with whom they were expected to eat and work. A military-like hierarchy fostered such practices as carrying one's supervisors' bags, arranging for cars, and making hotel reservations.[84]

Hard as it might be to imagine, this experience was further intensified by a variety of rituals: young auditors were (1) provided unimaginably tight meal allowances ("If you eat steak one night, you diet the rest of the week"); (2) rewarded for the *number* of discrepancies discovered in the business units under scrutiny, and (3) disciplined to write in a distinctive fashion that is both provocative and precise. As one former GE executive put it: "It's a totalitarian exposure—it's a throwback to the fifties in many ways. They manage by fear, brook no mavericks, allow no interpretations."[85]

After one year of this experience, a significant transformation had taken place. First, only the committed survived. Second, the survivors had been molded into very rigorous "Jesuits of the Financial Cause" (forming the next generation of Finance's ruling elite). Third, graduates of the auditing experience were catapulted three grade levels above their peers, who remained behind performing the blocking and tackling of general accounting. Fourth, as a member of the high-potential cadre, one could count on an "old boy network" that was stronger than any British gentlemen's club. A separate personnel unit within the Finance Fraternity tracked the 5,000 most promising individuals (Finance's total headcount exceeded 12,000 professionals and constituted 8 percent of GE's total employment). Finally, the beneficiary of this experience had not only been immersed in a substantial cross-section of GE's portfolio, but had interacted personally with senior managers at businesses and higher levels. Visibility payed off in poise and career opportunities.[86]

THE LINE VANTAGE POINT

Snapshots taken through the Cordiner and Borch eras portray an elite out of balance with its counterparts. As GE *line* managers saw it, the auditing experience instilled GE Finance with obsessiveness, risk-aversion, and a strong tendency toward control. Many, in fact, assigned GE's overcontrol in the 1970s and early 1980s to this elite and its "fanatics." A former GE executive comments: "GE's problem wasn't just the financial system. It was the Financial fraternity. These guys were zealots. They took things too far."[87]

The risk of a strong elite is that the very discipline that makes them "elite" can, if unchecked, lead an organization to excess. While it is unfair to stereotype an entire population, an informal poll of GE line managers in the early eighties conveyed their consensus that over two-thirds of the financial elite tended toward the extreme.[88] This was particularly significant because a powerful member of the Finance cadre, as part of the business unit management team, often overrode his peers (i.e., Sales, Engineering, and Marketing). This was often accomplished through the simple expedient of imposing measurement indices that delivered short-term profits.

THE JONES ERA

The emergence of an elite as dedicated and focused as GE's invariably shapes the character of an enterprise. Lacking checks and balances, it was only a question of time before Finance would emerge with direct control over GE's destiny. By the early sixties, several of Finance's more able executives had moved into line management positions. Reginald Jones was among them. Having spent twenty years in Finance and distinguishing himself on the auditing staff, he had a tour of duty in line assignments. In 1967 he returned as chief financial officer.[89]

Jones' selection in 1973 as CEO represented still another corrective swing of the pendulum. GE's current CEO, Jack Welch, states:

> Borch had gotten us into promising businesses. He planted new seeds and got us going in many directions. The era of the 1970s was more focused on controls, ROI, and cash flow. Jones brilliantly addressed these issues. He imposed staff reviews, demanded clear strategies from the business (clustered into larger units called SBUs). By the end of Jones' tenure, GE was respected by Wall Street and had enough cash to ensure strategic flexibility.[90]

Jones' foundation gave Welch the financial means to achieve the growth that GE has enjoyed in the decade that followed.

Stewardship

It is important to acknowledge at the outset that Jones was by no means one-dimensional. He was sensitive to the strains on GE's cultural fabric that had stemmed from the abandonment of shared values during the Cordiner years. Jones endeavored to ameliorate GE's relationship with its employees. He adopted a more conciliatory stance toward the union.[91]

Strategy and "Strategic" Impedance

Jones beefed up the planning staff to more than 200 professionals and applied strategic technology with great rigor. While Borch actually instituted the SBUs, it was Jones who fully implemented them. Later, faced with management overload, he superimposed six Sectors on top of the SBUs.[92]

The reclustering of GE's portfolio into forty-three SBUs added additional impedance to the system. While intended as a means to manage subsets of GE's portfolio, Sectors took on the role of an extra layer, added finance and planning staffs of their own, and strove to achieve their sector numbers. Owing to the diversification undertaken under Borch, GE was now increasingly a conglomerate. In the face of such a degree of diversification, hard-minded, top-level reviews were relied upon as a means of "stripping away fat" and piercing through "misplaced sentiment." But such reviews also tended to strip away some of the subtle aspects of what a business was about. Jones' SBU and Sector layers created exactly such problems. They imposed an overhead on GE's divisions not only in an *accounting* sense— but "overhead" in the subtle form of *compliance* with (1) planning procedures, (2) routine reports, and (3) the need to "sell" a division's plans to top management over and over again.[93]

One business journalist amplifies this latter tendency:

> Translated and amplified by his subordinates, Jones' thirst for data led to ridiculous excess. Dennis Dammerman, 43, now GE's CFO, says that the computers in one GE business spit out seven daily reports. Just one made a stack of paper twelve feet high, containing product-by-product sales information—accurate to the penny—on hundreds of thousands of items. The bureaucracy routinely emasculated top executives by overwhelming them with useless information and enslaved middle managers with the need to gather it. Old timers say that as the mastery of the facts became impossible, illusion sufficed.[94]

Layering placed GE at a disadvantage in industries in which competition was fast-moving and intense. When a GE SBU stood toe-to-toe with single product firms, it had a built-in disadvantage if it had to fight for resources through layers of skeptical staff. The SBU head's counterpart in competing firms was usually the CEO who could speak and act unilaterally.[95]

Portfolio Management

As a pioneer of the portfolio approach, GE during this era increasingly tended to view its businesses in financial terms. Inevitably, some decisions that made sense at the corporate level translated into resource allocations at the business level that jeopardized long-term competitiveness. Recalling that Jones' first objective was to grow earnings, one of his moves was to sell off the cash-draining computer and semiconductor businesses. He harvested core businesses and was highly restrictive in financing certain high-tech businesses. As noted earlier, Aircraft Engine and Plastics escaped this tightening noose.[96] However, Factory Automation (still a GE priority) and Mobile Communications (never a major thrust) were particularly affected.[97]

Mobile Communications warrants brief mention. It should be stated at the outset that this business was never regarded by GE as very important in the overall scheme of things. But as an illustration it points to the dangers of excess and, indeed, sets the stage for the corrective actions that Jones' successor, Welch, would need to set in motion.

Hindsight informs us that cellular phones are fast becoming a staple of modern communications, and that GE might have been positioned as a leading player in this exploding market. But unlike Aircraft Engine, short-comings of leadership, lack of corporate sponsorship, and underfunding contributed to GE's inability to build a significant competitive advantage in this field.

Mobile Communications was established in the late 1950s as part of Cordiner's quest for growth opportunities. The business progressed, particularly under Borch. Mobile Communications' growth is illustrative of the supportive climate Borch provided for many businesses. In 1972, Motorola held first position with a 40-percent share, while GE held on with 30 percent. Behind the two leaders were a host of smaller players.[98] With the market growing at 15 percent per year, GE was poised to exploit its strong number two position.[99] But as Jones faced the earnings pressures and swung the pendulum back, the emphasis shifted to profits. The price in many instances was market share.

By the mid-seventies, as Jones' harvesting got well underway, there was considerable consternation within the business unit. Line management knew that its core product was increasingly vulnerable and passionately appealed for investment dollars. Their appeals fell on deaf ears. Inevitably, Motorola attacked with a cheaper *and* technologically superior product, and by 1976, GE had fallen to a weak number two position. Its market share declined to 17 percent. Japanese competitors began to enter the fray. As Welch entered the scene as the next CEO, Mobile Communications was relegated to the status of a divestiture candidate, and was sold to Siemens in 1989.[100]

As we have seen repeatedly, the recourse to excess (i.e., "pendulum swings") introduces the seeds of stagnation as surely as it evokes renewal. On the positive side of the ledger, Reginald Jones did succeed in getting GE's financial house in order. As he stepped down, returns were strong and the company was widely admired. The price paid, as noted, stemmed from aggressive harvesting and the strong controls imposed to achieve his results. Mobile Communications is illustrative of the downside—a process that had become so extreme that it killed young businesses. "During Jones' tenure, GE was financially strong," comments a former member of the Strategic Planning staff. "But it was a dull, unexciting company. We were an organization in decline—and that was not recognized."[101]

THE WELCH ERA

Current CEO Jack Welch was a surprising choice as Jones' successor. His nomination reaffirms the corrective pattern we have seen at GE. Jones appears to have recognized that GE's portfolio needed the magic touch of an operating executive. While Jones might have favored an individual with a conservative nature more like his own, the situation required bold initiatives. Welch was one of the few successful in-house entrepreneurs at GE. He had almost singlehandedly built a highly successful two-billion-dollar business in the most unlikely of fields—plastics. (At GE, it is called Engineered Materials.) From there, Welch was promoted to Group head, where he repeated his earlier success by overseeing the turnaround of GE's dying medical diagnostics business. He fought the internal battles necessary to invest in CAT-scan technology and established GE as a world leader in medical imaging. Still later, as vice chairman, he began transforming GE Capital from a financier of refrigerators and turbines into a financial services powerhouse. Today it is the nation's fourteenth largest lending institution. In short, Welch stood almost alone (alongside his counterpart in Aircraft Engine, retired Gerhard Neumann) in his demonstrated ability to grow businesses *despite* GE's controls. And Welch had done it three times.[102]

The organizational imbalances that Welch inherited from Jones were in most respects continuations from the Borch and Cordiner eras. Jones, having placed such extreme emphasis on strategic planning, created a climate in which entrepreneurial initiative was the rare exception. One former executive recalls his reasons for leaving GE:

It seemed to me that if something wasn't done, GE would die. We were living off the half life of our businesses. My division could have coasted for another five to ten years. But the truth was we were in trouble. True, we were still growing at twelve percent a year and generating nine-percent profit—an engine of earnings! So the easiest course was to cut costs and lay off people, and that's what we did. All the while, we were mortgaging our future.[103]

Welch's first priority was to turn the declining portfolio around, while trying to win the confidence of employees and Wall Street. Welch is not the kind of CEO who marches forward with a lock-step plan, but with hindsight some patterns are clear. First, like Jones, he focused a great deal of attention on earnings. Right or wrong, that was how Wall Street would keep score. Welch felt it essential to earn credibility in this domain in order to have the latitude to maneuver. For GE overall, revenues were declining in constant dollars (and that would not change in the short term). But Welch moved aggressively to divest weak holdings and squeeze out costs. Utah International was sold off for $2.9 billion. Between 1981 and 1986, Welch eliminated 130,000 jobs, a 25-percent reduction of the total GE work force. (Percentage-wise, this is a greater reduction of GE's head count than during the Great Depression.) Head count cuts alone generated $6.5 billion in savings.[104]

A downsizing of this order of magnitude generates trauma, insecurity, and distrust—particularly since the purges of the Cordiner era and buttoned-down conservatism had inculcated the GE culture with an austere, "old testament" quality. Welch's moves generated an angry undercurrent among employees. He found himself in an ironic situation: In his earlier days as a division head, his style of leadership had generated high morale and instilled a common vision. Yet he now faced one of those inescapable dilemmas of being where the buck stops. Welch states: "I didn't *start* with a morale problem. I *created* it! The leader who tries to move a large organization counter to what his followers perceive to be necessary has a very difficult time. I had never had to do this before. I had always had the luxury of building a business and being the cheerleader. But it was clear that we had to reposition ourselves and put our chips on those businesses that could survive on a global scale."[105]

At Ford, Petersen and Poling had been able to harness the many rank-and-file initiatives and fix the business—and were widely praised for doing so. Welch was not the beneficiary of such acclaim. There was no perceived crisis. Further complicating the matter, he was operating at the *corporate* (not business unit) level. The only viable alternative, as he saw it, was to take actions to shock GE's businesses out of their complacency. Welch gambled on things turning out well enough so that he could right prior wrongs later on. Reactions to his belt-tightening were immediate and vociferous. He was nicknamed Neutron Jack (alluding to the neutron bomb that eliminates people but leaves the buildings standing). *Fortune* awarded him the dubious honor of being one of America's ten toughest bosses.[106] A quote, published in *Fortune,* from an executive within GE's core captures the mood in the trenches at the time:

> Morale stinks. People are looking for jobs or waiting for nice severance packages. They talk openly about it. I'm skeptical about Welch's ability to do more than cut costs. I don't see the greatness that everybody says is there. I could understand if out of this devastation came something we could all look to as the course of the future. But I see a void.[107]

It is easy to talk in the abstract about "renewing a culture" or "restoring constructive tension." But when a CEO takes decisive action to save a company (especially one that most people don't realize is in trouble yet), when one's contemplated actions will create despair in the lives of employees, when damaging quotes appear in the press, the temptations to back pedal become very great. No element is more critical to the task of leadership (and, sadly, more lacking among many CEOs) than courage. Welch *has* courage. His head-count cuts heightened anguish. Some might argue that he should have enlisted the businesses in a thorough-going self-examination (through which both lower level employees and top management would own the solution and share responsibility for it). But this, as we have seen, takes three to five years—too long an interval, in Welch's view. Whichever way he turned there were risks. Words like "leadership" or "courage" only derive meaning when one must commit the army to battle without certainty that the battle can be won. Such choices are made in the heart and the stomach—not in the head. They are not "strategic decisions" made under detached and antiseptic conditions.

Welch proceeded to squeeze and divest. The cash generated enabled him to experiment. He made a large number of small acquisitions. Some were unsuccessful and were divested a few years later. But earnings grew, and GE's stock price reflected investor confidence in their strategy. Given the long time-frame needed to grow new businesses without acquisitions, he became convinced that his best bets were in the businesses in which GE was already number one (or in a strong number two position) and in which acquisitions could build upon preexisting strengths. Here, at least, he could defend from a position of strength. He conceptualized GE's portfolio as falling into three circles (Core, Services, and High Technology) and placed several businesses outside the circles (Mobile Communications, House-wares, TV and Audio, and Consumer Electronics). The latter were divestiture candidates. Finally, he used his largest reserves of cash for two major acquisitions to beef up those portions of GE's portfolio he was going to bank on. RCA was acquired (primarily for NBC and its defense and aerospace portfolio); Employee Reinsurance Company was purchased to further strengthen GE Capital.[108] Overnight, GE's revenues increased by 30 percent.

In the years since, further acquisitions have strengthened the three circle concept. GE ranks first in the world in two-thirds of its key businesses. Under Welch, with inflation removed, real earnings per share growth have averaged 7.6 percent; this is in stark contrast to 4.9 percent under Jones and 1.6 percent under Borch.[109]

Phase I: Communicating the Strategic Vision
In Welch's words, "The decade of the 1980s imposed two distinct challenges. In the first phase, through 1986, we had to pay attention to the 'hardware'—fixing the businesses. In the second phase, from 1987 well into the 1990s, we have to focus on the 'software.' Our sustained competitiveness can only come from improved productivity—and that requires the bottom-up initiatives of our people."[110]

With regard to phase I, Welch devoted a large portion of his calendar time to meeting with employees of all levels. These were not the typical sanitized sessions choreographed by the PR department. Rather, they were frank interchanges about the state of the businesses, with a lot of give and take. Welch often shocked and refreshed these audiences with his candor and breathtaking bluntness. His messages: (1) Competitiveness—"be number one or a strong number two in your business or get out"; (2) Realism—"don't finesse the numbers, tell it like it is, address the harsh realities of your situation"; (3) Excellence—"we must be the best at what we do"; and (4) Entrepreneurship—"take a swing, take risks, we will not punish a well-reasoned and well-executed failure."[111]

In these endeavors, Welch was guided by a deeply felt philosophy. "Good business leaders create a vision," he states. "They articulate the vision, passionately own the vision, and relentlessly drive it to completion. Above all else, good leaders are open. They go up, down, and around their organization to reach people. They don't stick to established channels. They're informal. They're straight with people. They make a religion out of being accessible. They never get bored telling their story."[112] Welch pooh-poohs those who fret about the "fragility" of organizations. "Tell people the truth," he asserts, "because they know the truth anyway." "Striving to win businesses isn't something to fear; it gives you the chance to reshuffle the deck and opens opportunities. What determines your destiny is not the hand you're dealt but how you play the hand."[113]

Welch's messages made sense to many who heard him. But transformation is more than exhortation. Through the mid-eighties, Welch's relentless pressures to reposition the winning businesses, exit the marginal ones, and reduce costs generated a countercurrent of risk aversion and anxiety. Typifying the situation in 1985, one middle manager observed: "Jack says, 'Take a swing—if you miss you're OK.' But when you sandwich that message together with the other signals in the system, it plays: 'Take a swing, miss, and you're gone.' People still feel the risks are not equal to the rewards."[114] Philip Kantz, currently CEO of Itel and until 1988 a senior officer of GE Capital (one of GE's most aggressive divisions), further captures the discrepancies between Welch's intentions and actualities:

> What I found [at GE in the mid-eighties] was everything that Jack abhors. Instead of decisions being made by a liberated and empowered middle management, all decisions—save an individual's preference for lunch—were made by the Unit's CEO. The spirited repartee in which Welch engages his executives to advantage by pushing the boundaries of their knowledge of, and commitment to, a project were instead viewed as personal affronts to authority.
>
> In my own business unit, attempts to ignite productivity by clearing the decks of mediocre (long-tenured) performers were met with resistance at the top. Despite what was happening at Corporate, at GECC change was not really viewed as either necessary or positive.[115]

Phase II: Cultural Transformation

As the eighties wore on, Welch became increasingly aware that there was only so much that he could accomplish with strategic repositioning. Ever self-questioning and open to experimentation, he searched for additional ways to breathe life and ownership into the ranks below. One important "laboratory" was his own Corporate Executive Council—initially composed of sector and group heads and presidents of each of the business units. Observing time and again how the group and sector layers between himself and the businesses filtered communication and slowed up decision-making, he eliminated them. Hearing from his business heads that they were fettered by too many controls, he raised sign-off limits, dramatically reduced the number of reports and indices, chopped away at headquarters staff, and embarked on a long overdue campaign to redirect the Finance and Auditing staff from naysayers to supporters of line management.

"People always overestimate how complex business is," Welch states. "This isn't rocket science; we've chosen one of the world's more simple professions. Most global businesses have three or four critical competitors, and you know who they are. And there aren't that many things you can do with a business. It's not as if you're choosing among 2,000 options."[116]

One of Welch's great gifts as a communicator is to cut through complexity and distill an issue to its essence. He achieved this in the early 1980s with his "Three Circle Strategy"—giving coherence to GE's portfolio and letting each business know where it stood. He needed an encore in 1986 as he sought to transform the organization more fundamentally. One clear obstacle to renewal was GE's entrenched system of controls. Welch describes how his campaign to correct this problem unfolded: "By 1986, I decided we had to do away with a lot of the intricate numbers and details that were causing us to miss the forest for the trees. A good place to begin was with the CEC, by radically changing the process of review for our fourteen key businesses. Each business was asked to prepare a one-page answer to five questions. It was to be written in the most compelling Churchillian prose—without buzz words, clichés, or industry jargon."

Welch's five key questions remain intact today. They are simple, hard-minded, and to the point:

1. What are your market dynamics globally today, and where are they going over the next several years?
2. What actions have your competitors taken in the last three years to upset those global dynamics?
3. What have you done in the last three years to affect those dynamics?
4. What are the most dangerous things your competitors could do in the next three years to upset those dynamics?
5. What are the most effective things you could do to bring your desired impact on these dynamics?[117]

Welch continues:

For a large organization to be effective, it must be simple. For a large organization to be simple, its people must have self-confidence and intellectual self-assurance. Insecure managers create complexity. Frightened, nervous managers use thick, convoluted planning books and busy slides filled with everything they've known since childhood. Real leaders don't clutter. People must have the self-confidence to be clear, precise, to be sure that every person in their organization—highest to lowest—understands what the business is trying to achieve. But it's not easy. You can't believe how hard it is for people to be simple, how much they fear being simple. They worry that if they're simple, people will think they're simple-minded. In reality, of course, it's just the reverse. Clear, tough-minded people are the most simple.

We've had managers at GE who couldn't change, who kept telling us to leave them alone. They wanted to sit back, to keep things the way they were. And that's just what they did—until they and most of their staffs had to go. That's the lousy part of this job. What's worse is that we still don't understand why so many people are incapable of facing reality, of being candid with themselves and others.

We took out management layers. Layers hide weaknesses. Layers mask mediocrity. I firmly believe that an overburdened, overstretched executive is the best executive because he or she doesn't have the time to meddle, to deal in trivia, to bother people. Remember the theory that a manager should have no more than six or seven direct reports? I say the right number is closer to ten or fifteen. This way you have no choice but to let people flex their muscles, let them grow and mature. With ten or fifteen reports, a leader can focus only on the big important issues, not on minutiae.

We also reduced the corporate staff. Headquarters can be the bane of corporate America. It can strangle, choke, delay, and create insecurity. If you're going to have simplicity in the field, you can't have a big staff at home. We don't need the questioners and the checkers, the nitpickers who bog down the process, people whose only role is to second-guess and kibitz, the people who clog communication inside the company. Today people at headquarters are experts in taxes, finance, or some other key area that can help people in the field. Our corporate staff no longer just challenges and questions; it assists. This is a mindset change: staff essentially reports to the field rather than the other way around.

Cutting the groups and sectors eliminated communications filters. Today there is direct communication between the CEO and the leaders of the fourteen businesses. We have very short cycle times for decisions and little interference by corporate staff. A major investment decision that used to take a year can now be made in a matter of days.

[Consider the format for the] Corporate Executive Council. For two days every quarter, we meet with the leaders of the fourteen businesses and our top staff people. There aren't stuffy, formal strategic reviews. We share ideas and information candidly and openly, including programs that have failed. The important thing is that at the end of those two days everyone in the CEC has seen and discussed the same information. The CEC creates a sense of trust, a sense of personal familiarity and mutual obligation at the top of the company.

We consider the CEC a piece of organizational technology that is very important for our future success.

[The CEC provides a forum] to transfer the best practices across all the businesses, with lightning speed. Staff often put people all over the place to do this. But they aren't effective lightning rods to transfer best practice; they don't have the stature in the organization. Business leaders do. That's why every CEC meeting deals in part with a generic business issue—a new pay plan, a drug-testing program, stock options. Every business is free to propose its own plan or program and present it at the CEC, and we put it through a central screen at corporate, strictly to make sure it's within the bounds of good sense. We don't approve the details. But we want to know what the details are so we can see which programs are working and immediately alert the other businesses to the successful ones.[118]

Welch believes that the over $100 million a year that GE has saved from these measures is secondary to the gains realized from opening up the system to reexamination, simplification and change.[119]

Work-Out

Welch's philosophy has evolved—it did not come down from the mount like Moses' stone tablets. But by 1988, Welch and his team began to believe they were onto something. If the process of simplification worked with his direct reports, why couldn't it cascade down through the entire organization, stripping away controls, layers, and redundancy? Welch, in tandem with his head of executive development, James Baughman, reverse-engineered what they had learned, then formalized it as a process named "Work-Out."

Work-Out shares much in common with the "Valentines" process conducted at Ford. It entails the systematic identification of productivity blocks and outdated work practices. It establishes clear contracts among the management team to eliminate them. It is facilitated by an outside consultant, one attached to each of the business units; Corporate pays the consulting bill. The six basic steps of Work-Out are shown in Figure 7–3.*

It should be noted that the Work-Out process is tailored to each business' needs. Some units focus on specific problems, others on general issues, some on functional inefficiencies, others on cross-functional cooperation. Welch describes the philosophy behind his program:

Work-Out is absolutely fundamental to our becoming the kind of company we must become. That's why I'm so passionate about it. We're not going to succeed if people end up doing the same work they've always done, if they

---

* The six basic steps of Work-Out are described in more detail in Appendix II.

FIG. 7–3

Six Steps of Work-Out

Step 1. *Tying business imperatives to ineffective work practices*

Step 2. *Enlisting involvement in the Work-Out process*

Step 3. *Overview of wasteful work practices*

Step 4. *Audit by functional groups*

Step 5. *Audit by cross-functional groups*

Step 6. *Contracting, recommendations, and wrap-up*

don't feel any psychic or financial impact from the way the organization is changing. The ultimate objective of Work-Out is so clear. We want 300,000 people with different career objectives, different family aspirations, different financial goals, to share directly in this company's vision, the information, the decision-making process, and the rewards. We want to build a more stimulating environment, a more creative environment, a freer work atmosphere, with incentives tied directly to what people do.

Work-Out is the next generation of what we're trying to do. We had to put in a process to focus on and change how work gets done in this company. We have to apply the same relentless passion to Work-Out that we did in selling the vision of number one and number two globally. That's why we're pushing it so hard, getting so involved.

Work-Out has a practical and an intellectual goal. The practical objective is to get rid of thousands of bad habits accumulated since the creation of General Electric. How would you like to move from a house after 112 years? Think of what would be in the closets and the attic—those shoes that you'll wear to paint next spring, even though you know you'll never paint again. We've got 112 years of closets and attics in this company. We want to flush them out, to start with a brand-new house with empty closets, to begin the whole game again.

The second thing we want to achieve, the intellectual part, begins by putting the leaders of each business in front of a hundred or so of their people, eight to ten times a year, to let them hear what their people think about the company, what they like and don't like about their work, about how they're evaluated, about how they spend their time. Work-Out will expose the leaders to the vibrations of their business—opinions, feelings, emotions, resentments, not abstract theories of organization and management.

Ultimately, we're talking about redefining the relationship between boss and subordinate. I want to get to a point where people challenge their bosses every day: "Why do you require me to do these wasteful things? Why don't you let me do the things you shouldn't be doing so you can move on and create? That's the job of a leader—to create, not to control. Trust me to do my job, and don't make me waste all my time trying to deal with you on the control issue."

Now, how do you get people communicating with each other with that much candor? You put them together in a room and make them thrash it out.

These Work-Out sessions, and I've already done several of them, create all kinds of personal dynamics. Some people go and hide. Some don't like the dinner in the evening because they can't get along with the other people. Some emerge as forceful advocates. As people meet over and over, though, more of them will develop the courage to speak out. The norm will become the person who says, "Dammit, we're not doing it. Let's get on with doing it." Today the norm in most companies, not just GE, is not to bring up critical issues with a boss, certainly not in a public setting, and certainly not in an atmosphere where self-confidence has not been developed. This process will create more fulfilling and rewarding jobs. The quality of work life will improve dramatically.[120]

The Ongoing Work

One of Welch's remaining challenges in transforming the culture is stepping back from the strong central leadership role he has played up thus far. In the terms of Chapter Three, he struggles to shift from a "managerial" to a "transformational" style of leadership. While Welch *has* empowered his business unit heads, he is a very visible force. He has personally master-minded and overseen the majority of GE's major acquisitions. Now the challenge for many of those businesses is to grow revenues in their own right without the intrusion of the ever-present father figure.

Another challenge arising from Welch's "managerial" approach is the fallout from his hard-minded philosophy toward people. (Recalling the Petersen-Poling combination at Ford, Welch much more closely resembles the Poling end of the continuum. Further, his closest colleague, Vice Chairman Larry Bossidy, is much more a kindred spirit than a compensating element.) For those who know Welch personally, his blunt confronting style and his steamroller drive to succeed are more than offset by his sincerity, courage, and dedication. But strong leaders cast long shadows. The majority of GE managers "see" Welch second- or third-hand. From a distance he can seem overbearing and instrumental.

John M. Trani, head of GE's Medical Systems division and a great admirer of Welch, states: "The Welch theory is those who do, get; those who don't, go."[121] And Grant Tinker, the former NBC head whom Welch tried desperately to keep, says: "I look at Jack as two guys. He's a good guy you can hang out with, a man's man. The same guy walks into an office and he's a chess player. People aren't people anymore."[122]

Perhaps mindful of these shortcomings, Welch commissioned a project to hammer out a meaningful GE value statement. "It was a brutal process," he recalls. "It began with five thousand people at GE's management development center at Crotonville with small groups sweating over every word of their proposals. By 1989, a sufficient consensus had been built to warrant its publication." The statement (see Figure 7–4) avoids many of the lofty clichés that haunt such endeavors. It distills Welch's themes down to simple pragmatic prose.

In an effort to drive these values home, GE's values were incorporated into the performance evaluation system. Beginning in 1989, the top hundred officers were rated on a scale from one to five in terms of how they supported these traits. We see Welch's fingerprints in this drive to make the values real. But as we listen to his words we catch the paradox of his iron-willed top-down approach grappling with a phenomenon that has to be internalized voluntarily. He *does* talk about and believe in GE's values—such as empowerment—but his propensity to muscle implementation through is also evident. He states:

> We had a long discussion about the proposal to rate ourselves on the values in the CEC. People said: "How can you put a number on how open people are, on how directly they face reality?" Well, they're going to have to—the best numbers they can come up with, and then we'll argue about them. We have to know if our people are open and self-confident, if they believe in honest communication and quick action, if the people we hired years ago have changed. The only way to test our progress is through regular evaluations at the top and by listening to every audience we appear before in the company.[123]

One of the paradoxes arising from GE's values surrounds the matter of company loyalty and commitment. Welch values people—but his ultimate commitment is to competitive survival.

> Like many other large companies in the United States, Europe, and Japan, GE has had an implicit psychological contract based on perceived lifetime

FIG. 7–4

GE Value Statement

BUSINESS CHARACTERISTICS

Lean
    What — Reduce tasks and the people required to do them.
    Why — Critical to developing world cost leadership.

Agile
    What — Delayering.
    Why — Create fast decision-making in rapidly changing world through improved communication and increased individual response.

Creative
    What — Development of new ideas— innovation.
    Why — Increase customer satisfaction and operating margins through higher value products and services.

Ownership
    What — Self-confidence to trust others. Self-confidence to delegate to others the freedom to act while, at the same time, self-confidence to involve higher levels in issues critical to the business and the corporation.
    Why — Supports concept of more individual responsibility, capability to act quickly and independently. Should increase job satisfaction and improve understanding of risks and rewards. While delegation is critical, there is a small percentage of high-impact issues that need or require involvement of higher levels within the business and within the corporation.

Reward
    What — Recognition and compensation commensurate with risk and performance— highly differentiated by individual, with recognition of total team achievement.
    Why — Necessary to attract and motivate the type of individuals required to accomplish GE's objectives. A #1 business should provide #1 people with #1 opportunity.

INDIVIDUAL CHARACTERISTICS

Reality

    What — Describe the environment as it is— not as we hope it to be.

    Why — Critical to developing a vision and a winning strategy, and to gaining universal acceptance for their implementation.

Leadership

    What — Sustained passion for and commitment to a proactive, shared vision and its implementation.

    Why — To rally teams toward achieving a common objective.

Candor / Openness

    What — Complete and frequent sharing of information with individuals (appraisals, etc.) and organization (everything).

    Why — Critical to employees knowing where they, their efforts, and their business stand.

Simplicity

    What — Strive for brevity, clarity, the "elegant, simple solution"— less is better.

    Why — Less complexity improves everything, from reduced bureaucracy to better product designs to lower costs.

Integrity

    What — Never bend or wink at the truth, and live within both the spirit and letter of the laws of every global business arena.

    Why — Critical to gaining the global arenas' acceptance of our right to grow and prosper. Every constituency: share-owners who invest; customers who purchase; community that supports; and employees who depend, expect, and deserve our unequivocal commitment to integrity in every facet of our behavior.

Individual Dignity

    What — Respect and leverage the talent and contribution of every individual in both good and bad times.

    Why — Teamwork depends on trust, mutual understanding, and the shared belief that the individual will be treated fairly in any environment.

employment. People were rarely dismissed except for cause or severe business downturns, like in Aerospace after Vietnam. This produced a paternal, feudal, fuzzy kind of loyalty. You put in your time, worked hard, and the company took care of you for life.

That kind of loyalty tends to focus people inward. But given today's environment, people's emotional energy must be focused outward on a competitive world where no business is a safe haven for employment unless it is winning in the marketplace. The psychological contract has to change. People at all levels have to feel the risk-reward tension.

My concept of loyalty is not "giving time" to some corporate entity and, in turn, being shielded and protected from the outside world. Loyalty is an affinity among people who want to grapple with the outside world and win. Their personal values, dreams, and ambitions cause them to gravitate toward each other and toward a company like GE that gives them the resources and opportunities to flourish.

The new psychological contract, if there is such a thing, is that jobs at GE are the best in the world for people who are willing to compete. We have the best training and development resources and an environment committed to providing opportunities for personal and professional growth.[124]

The interesting quality of Jack Welch is that he is an ever-growing, ever-evolving character. Welch of the early 1980s regarded terms like "empowerment" and "transformation" as California talk.[125] By mid-decade, having seen the limits of his hard-wired strategy for change, he began to shift. There were, of course, good bottom-line reasons for doing so. Welch seeks to increase GE's productivity to 6 percent per year. (It has averaged 4.5 percent per year across his tenure thus far.) Tiny changes in growth have a phenomenal effect on profits. A single percentage point increase in productivity translates into an extra $300 million in pretax income.[126] But the additional 1.5 percent in productivity improvements is not likely to come from simple top-down moves such as automation and edicted staff cuts. Rather, it is believed that this next important increment must come from voluntary behavior—in Welch's words, "liberating and empowering middle managers and reaching the 300,000 souls still on the GE payroll. . . . It has nothing to do with whips and chains and taking heads out," he continues. "We're trying to unleash people to be self-confident, and so to take on more responsibility."[127]

Welch's comments highlight an important distinction noted earlier in this chapter. Ford, teetering on the brink of bankruptcy, enlisted the "collective genius" of its lower level workers and managers from the onset. Its crisis was everywhere evident. As of this writing, Work-Out, GE's most far-reaching vehicle to enlist employee involvement to date, has only penetrated three layers down at best. (Programs like Employee Involvement and Chimney Breaking have barely gotten off the ground at GE.) Given persistent efforts, GE believes it *may* achieve wholehearted worker commitment by the mid-nineties. While GE might be further ahead had it rolled out employee involvement programs sooner, it is unquestionably harder to enlist the rank and file when no crisis exists to mobilize them.

The opening paragraphs of this chapter enumerated the central features of the new paradigm. It entails (1) a holistic approach to organizational change, (2) harnessing (not suppressing) conflict and contention as sources of renewal, and (3) enlisting employees as colleagues in the change process, thereby drawing upon their full energies and resources. This is in contrast to the more traditional model that (1) approaches organizational change in a sequential, piecemeal fashion, (2) attacks problems as a mechanical (rather than organic) endeavor (i.e., apply enough force to overcome resistance to change), (3) emphasizes control and direction from above, and (4) tends to regard people somewhat instrumentally—as factors of production who can be driven or incented toward specific ends.

Welch and GE is the story not only of a company but a leader undergoing a transformation. Over his tenure, we see a shift from the old mindset to the new. As summarized in Figure 7–5, GE has accomplished a great deal strategically and economically.

Paralleling these events, his gradual reforms at the CEC level along with processes such as Work-Out have *begun* to address GE's most serious cultural problem: pervasive overcontrol. "We found in the eighties that speed increases in an organization as control decreases," he asserts. "We had constructed over the years a management apparatus that was right for its time, the toast of the business schools. Divisions, strategic business units, groups, sectors, all were designed to make meticulous, calculated decisions and move them smoothly forward and upward. This system produced highly polished work. It was right for the seventies . . . a growing handicap in the early eighties . . . and it will be a ticket to the boneyard in the nineties."

Welch continues:

> So we got rid of it . . . along with a lot of reports, meetings and the endless paper that flowed like lava from the upper levels of the company. When we did this we began to see people . . . who for years had spent half their time serving the system and the other half fighting it . . . suddenly come to life, making decisions in minutes, fact to face, on matters that would have once produced

FIG. 7–5

GE Entering the 90s

Leadership Businesses

How a Dozen GE Businesses Rank

	...in the U.S.	...and in the world
Aircraft engines	First	First
Broadcasting (NBC)	First	Not applicable
Circuit breakers	First tied with Square D and Westinghouse	First tied with Merlin Gerin, Siemens, Westinghouse
Defense electronics	Second behind GM's Hughes Electronics	Second behind GM's Hughes Electronics
Electric motors	First	First
Engineering plastics	First	First
Factory automation	Second behind Allen-Bradley	Third behind Siemens and Allen-Bradley
Industrial and power systems turbines, meters, drive systems, power transmission controls	First	First
Lighting	First	Second behind Philips
Locomotives	First	First tied with GM's Electro-Motive
Major appliances	First	Second behind Whirlpool tied with Electrolux
Medical diagnostic imaging	First	First

Profitable		
	Early 80s	*Late 80s*
Operating Margin	9%	11–12%
ROE	17–18%	19–20%
Annual EPS Growth	5–10%	15–17%

Strong Market Position
— High Entry Barriers
— Huge Backlogs / Installed Base
— Extensive Distribution
— Growing Parts and Service

Cash Flow		
	Early 80s	*Late 80s*
Operations	$2.8	$4.5
Capital Spending	1.9	1.9
Dividends	0.8	1.2
Free Cash Flow	0.1	1.4

FIG.7–6

Reestablishing Vitality In the Welch Era

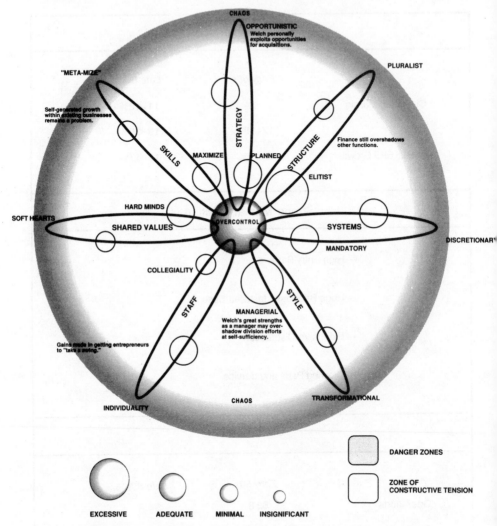

months of staff gyrations and forests of paper. But this transformation, this rebirth, was largely confined to upper management. In the nineties we want to see it engulf and galvanize the entire company.[128]

Throughout his tenure he has harnessed conflict and established a healthy dialectic. Welch advocates "constructive contention."[129] While he has not instituted a formal system of contention management, he personally exemplifies a willingness to gain from contention in almost every encounter. As shown schematically in Figure 7–6, more than any predecessor since Swope, Welch has brought the various paradoxical trade-offs that management entails into a dynamic synthesis.

Transformation is an ongoing process. Petersen at Ford talks of a twenty-year endeavor; Welch believes the cultural transformation of GE is just beginning and will require enormous persistence and hard work through the balance of the century. But if Welch is to steward the company until his retirement in the year 2000, he himself must continue to grow. As will be addressed in Chapter Ten, the matter of how top managers evolve so as to enable their corporations to do so is a major, and often overlooked, stumbling block. This far Welch has done a remarkable job of growing in pace with the needs of his company. The future is certain to challenge him as fully as has the recent past.

CHAPTER EIGHT

Living Dangerously: Citicorp
and Hewlett-Packard

The two preceding chapters have bracketed two approaches toward organizational renewal. Ford, under crisis conditions, reaped the gains of a mobilized workforce. By initiating change on many fronts, it transformed itself into a culture where constructive tension and continuous learning prevail. General Electric is two stories in one. From Cordiner through Jones, we saw how the seeds of stagnation are planted when *excess* is employed as the primary technique of renewal. Pendulum swings destroy one organizational competence as they build another. Under Welch, we see an exceptional executive seeking transformation under non-crisis conditions. Focusing for the first five years on strategic repositioning and thereafter on in-depth cultural change, we have noted a partial transformation, less profound than at Ford in that change has not yet reached far enough down to empower the rank-and-file employee and lower levels of management.

There are other alternatives to the paths charted by Petersen and Welch. This chapter will focus on two well-respected companies—Citicorp and Hewlett-Packard. Both have achieved remarkable success to date. Each is living dangerously in terms of its overreliance on one end of the contention continuum.

HARD MINDS

Citicorp is the largest bank-holding company in the United States. Its distinct character began to take shape in 1970 when Walter Wriston became chairman. Wriston, who transformed the bank from a humdrum commercial lender into an innovative purveyor of everything from mortgage financing and insurance to electronic banking services, deftly circumvented the regulatory barriers that had kept Citicorp from getting into investment banking and expanding across state lines.[1]

Citicorp illuminates two significant aspects of split, fit and contend. First, Citicorp uses contention better than most companies by living dangerously (i.e., emphasizing the "hard" at the expense of the "soft"). Second, Citicorp fosters a great deal of fit and split.

Many other institutions, such as Harry Grey's United Technologies or Harold Geneen's ITT, have fostered a driven, hard-minded atmosphere. But they didn't last for long. The remarkable achievement at Citicorp is that it has avoided the self-destructive tendencies that we have seen at other firms. How is this accomplished? From its earliest years, Citicorp interjected just enough of the soft side to keep the hard in check. Originally, this was achieved through interpersonal rather than institutional means. Walter Wriston joined forces with Arnold Spencer, the vice chairman. Wriston pushed for results. Spencer emphasized people concerns and kept a watchful eye out for excesses. Spencer was far from the low-power eunuch that one frequently finds in the Human Resource functions scattered across America. Rather, he commanded Wriston's respect and succeeded in modulating Wriston's push for a more competitive culture.[2] His successors, all fast-track line management candidates (not HR professionals), have followed in Spencer's footsteps.

Below the office of the chairman, Wriston brought in a team of aggressive "young tigers," all of whom came from outside the gentlemanly banker fraternity. One was Larry Small, an analyst from Ford Motor Company, who today runs the commercial bank. Small is an intense, tightly wired executive with little time for the niceties of protocol.[3]

Wriston's second acquisition was John Reed, today the chairman of Citicorp. Reed, another Ford recruit, won his spurs at Citicorp in the early seventies by streamlining Citicorp's "back office": the operating group that processed checks. Wriston believed that the bank's long-term profitability hinged on bringing the back office costs under control. Reed's model for the effort, brought from Ford, was to consider the back shop as a *factory* processing transactions instead of vehicles. "By automating and reorganizing the division," one source recalls, "Reed kept costs stable while transaction volume was growing fifteen percent a year. In the process, he gained a reputation for brashness, for seeking results no matter whom he hurt." After six months on the job, Reed concluded that 65 percent of his managerial team, and many of his workers, were redundant. Over a five-year period, Reed slashed head count from 2,400 to 600. Many of the displaced employees landed on the street.[4]

RELENTLESS SYSTEM, CONFRONTATIONAL STYLE

As chairman and CEO of Citicorp, there has been little mellowing of this intensity. Among Reed's first moves as chairman was a crackdown on expenses. Costs had been increasing at a rate of 24 percent per year. Reed set the goal of bringing the expense growth rate to below 10 percent (in effect, slightly lower than revenue growth rates).[5]

What makes Citicorp distinct is how this thrust was translated down into the ranks. Larry Small circulated a memo to the twenty top division heads that said: "We have too many people doing too much unnecessary, bureaucratic activity, too many studies, too many reports, too many management information systems, too many staff functions, too many improbable relationships . . . I'm telling you right now that the day of reckoning has arrived . . . We either spend for the future while we meet our desired growth rates or we don't. No one here is getting paid to have it the easy way. We must become one of the world's models of cost management . . . We have to become fatter and leaner."[6] The tone communicates the hard edge of Citicorp: intimidating, blunt, direct, and demanding.

These sound like overdetermined measures in the extreme: massive layoffs of employees, near impossible stretch targets for expense reduction, and confrontational harangues by top management. But the counterpoise to these hard attributes is provided by Citicorp's Human Resource function. Citicorp's comprehensive and contemporary human resource policies modulate the excessive pressure and capricious treatment of employees, and thus help keep Citicorp's intensity constructive.[7] Citicorp has long been a national leader in in-house executive education. This may not strike the reader as all that significant until one understands that the engine that drives the Citicorp system is the drive and skill of its managers. Managers from first-level supervision through mid-career are drilled at skills in motivating, in communicating, and in managing conflict. They are trained to provide performance feedback in a constructive way, which, as we will see later, is a pivotal ingredient in Citicorp's chemistry. Citicorp training is not the usual "gentle exposure to new ideas" sessions that are provided in many companies. Instead, managers understand that one needs to genuinely master these skills to survive.[8]

Do these HR efforts achieve an effective tension? The answer is: *barely*. "Citicorp is Darwinian," remarks one senior executive. "Yes, we have strong personnel policies, and we practice them in good faith to a certain degree, but we are obsessed with results. So, if you scratch very deeply, you will see we are willing to tolerate people who are occasionally total bastards, but determined to make the hard decisions no matter what their impact on people."[9]

HR systems, then, do not really explain Citicorp's ability to manage on the edge. Looking further, we can see an intricate system of rewards and beliefs that are tuned to drive performance.

As a general rule, organizations that put a great deal of pressure on results are risk-adverse. Such was the case at ITT under Geneen, and at United Technologies under Harry Grey. Yet Citicorp has a strong track record for innovation. Innovators tend to stay at Citicorp, and a great amount of risk-taking occurs. How can this tendency coexist in the face of so much bottom-line pressure? How does creativity live side by side with Citicorp's nearly religious observation of its Management by Objectives system?*

A senior vice president in the consumer bank gives us a partial answer. "Citicorp moves decisions down. This is an extremely important aspect of the bank, and its impact is far-reaching. An individual in his or her late twenties is handed major responsibility. You can run your business, your department, or be on a team that's running a business. With this extraordinarily strong tradition of pushing decision-making down, young individuals *have* to make decisions and are weaned on that tradition. Here is our engine of innovation. We genuinely empower them. We don't get in their way and undermine them with bureaucracy and excessive financial controls."[10]

A second factor in Citicorp's system is more ephemeral. Citicorp's footing among U.S. banks has always been secure. Yet somehow the institution continually seeds a gnawing question among all of its managers: "What have you done for us today?" The implication is that no matter what you've accomplished, there is more to be done. Executives engage in a never-ending quest to "prove themselves." One does not coast; no position is secure.[11]

This focus on what has been left undone points to a third factor. One wins by anticipating what bosses will ask for. At Citicorp, one informal rule of survival is to make the hard decisions fast (even if the solution is imperfect). The culture eschews the tendency to study things too long or to stand in the way of action.[12]

"Our corporate office is obsessive about initiative," says one consumer credit executive. "One learns the hard way that no one above you ever makes an 'aside,' or 'a throw-away comment.' If Reed or one of the group heads says: 'Gee, it would be interesting if we thought about X,' you can be

---

* Managers are expected to achieve each of their five mandatory MBOs each year, and relief is rarely given. Pass/fail evaluations assess whether a manager met his or her goals, and the system countenances no excuses, shadings, or qualitative rationalizations.

damn sure that within two weeks they'll want your position paper on X. So as an act of self-defense, you learn to pick up these asides and get into motion. You know that today's aside is tomorrow's direct order, and they'll be following up soon and looking for results."[13]

Another middle manager reinforces this view: "In order for middle managers to survive or be perceived as outstanding, you must make *preemptive* moves. When you sense a glimmer of a trend among management that has not yet reached full-fledged policy, you know you need to get ahead of them on it. You need to be on top of things and prepared. Good managers do the preemptive work. They develop the capacity to see around corners in order to stay ahead of the game. They have a wonderful sense of where the winds are blowing."[14]

A fourth factor involves rewards: Citicorp understates verbal support and compliments. Although generous promotions and pay increases are awarded to those that merit them, there are not a lot of strokes. We see again a carefully orchestrated contradiction. Citicorp creates a climate that is questioning and nonaccepting. The underlying behavioral message is always conditional acceptance.[15] Says one executive: "One of the very prevalent, and somewhat neurotic, qualities of Citicorp is that it's a culture in which you really need to let people know how good you are. As a result, the people with high ambitions—and that is the top third—really work hard at positioning themselves in ways that other companies might view as offensive."[16]

A fifth factor stems from Citicorp's propensity to assign tasks with overlapping jurisdictions. Pat Flaherty, director of Human Resources observes:

> There is a lot of creative tension here over jurisdictions. Things are organized by function, market, or product. Many of these impact on the same customers. No one here has a clear territory, or clear ownership of a total activity. This tends to keep people on their toes. You're aware that all of your colleagues are nibbling away at opportunities too, and if they can come at what you do from another direction and do it well, and make a buck, they're going to get the license and permissions to pursue that. We don't just assign a territory to one person and say: "Everything that has anything to do with this is yours." We just don't let one person have a mandate and then fall asleep.[17]

A sixth clue to understanding the Citicorp puzzle centers on the forced ranking of all employees two times a year (after which the bottom 10 percent are culled out).[18] Consider the impact of this procedure. First, it drives measurement (and Citicorp drives detailed measures, including P&L accountability, down to a lower level than any other commercial bank). If a manager knows he or she will be asked to engage in one of the most difficult of all tasks, it is a great deal easier if MBOs are tightly defined and measurement systems are sharp-edged and in place. The forced ranking system and a tight measurement system go hand in hand. Second, such procedures reveal managers who can make tough people decisions. The system self-selects for managers who can give straight feedback, and endure the anguish surrounding decisions to terminate the bottom 10 percent (some of whom may be trying their best to succeed). These are the casualties of a Darwinian meritocracy. Third, this drill, imposed on a semiannual basis, chains executives to one of the most difficult of all managerial tasks—playing god in the life of an employee. Citicorp instills a cold discipline; those who survive as managers learn to handle this role. One develops emotional calluses, suppresses second thoughts, and adopts a clinical attitude toward the hurts of others—much as physicians and nurses do in the emergency ward of a big city hospital.

This discipline has far-reaching consequences on other aspects of managerial conduct. Most companies foster decisions only when necessary, and the tendency to lean away from, rather than into, decisions causes a lot of trouble. Citicorp forces its people to *step into* decisions. Echoing a point made earlier, one upper-level manager comments: "One of the things that makes Citicorp successful is that we make those tough decisions early. We may get the reputation of being cutthroat, or brutal, or heartless, but our managers understand that they're paid to decide, to act, and are not expected to optimize in every dimension."[19]

MANAGING ON THE EDGE

Self-renewal at Citicorp is the result of constructive tension. As shown in Box 8–1, it works because a sufficient "dialectic" occurs as the result of (1) managing the expectations of those who work in this pressure-cooker environment, (2) selecting for, and building, the necessary skills to survive, and (3) rewarding those who produce. Citicorp's "tough but just" handling of people dispenses a reliable (albeit harsh) type of frontier justice. One executive comments:

> Everyone understands that achieving one's performance objectives matters. The heat gets turned on when you falter. The system may be hard-hearted, but rarely unfair. And on the positive side, Citicorp pays above-average wages for the industry and provides incentives which reward the best for excelling.

BOX 8–1.

Hard Minds: Citicorp Bold Abstractions, Detailed Organizations

Comprehensive Human Resource Systems	Darwinian Organizational Climate
Risk-Taking Encouraged; Strong Record of Individual Initiative	Five Mandatory MBOs; Pass/Fail Evaluation Concept
Highly Secure Institution among U.S. Banks	Pressure for Managers to Do More: "What Have You Done for Citicorp Today?"
Large Systems-Driven Corporation	Culture Evokes Propensity of Managers to "Stand Into" Decisions

Finally, there is an unwavering, almost ruthless, form of honesty at work that spares no one or no issue from scrutiny. From top to bottom, Citicorp is a hard-driven place in which results are measured, and results count.[20]

The risk to Citicorp stems from what it takes to sustain this dynamic instability. A top Citicorp executive observes: "We're encouraged to break away and defy the parameters. You really have a bunch of kite fliers, and like kites, they tend to go where they please and catch different currents. J. P. Morgan Guaranty has well-defined behavioral norms. At Morgan people climb the ladder. At Citicorp they're more apt to skip rungs. Morgan probably needs less coherent leadership because the culture itself sustains direction. At Citicorp the reverse is true. It's so competitive and culturally diverse that without a very strong leader with a very strong vision, we have strong centrifugal tendencies."[21]

Another executive comments: "This place is organized chaos. We start a lot of things and only ten to twenty percent of them survive. A lot don't work out. A lot of other companies with a more rigorous management style wouldn't allow that. But around here, we build things and blow them up, then start again. Part of the reason for these fluctuations is that we move managers around rather rapidly, perhaps too much, and that lends to some of the discontinuity."

The turmoil takes a toll: "There are big costs associated with our chaos," says a senior vice president. "There are a lot of politics here and a lot of energy spent dealing with politics."[22]

Are there other risks for Citicorp? Citicorp has an elite status and is recognized as a leader in its industry. This elitism is part of the draw for this cadre of intense executives who cast their lot with the company. If this were to change, would Citicorp lose its appeal? Among its current top management, do we see future leaders? Wriston was charismatic and combative, charming when he needed to be, and above all, a visionary in the field of banking. His successors—Reed and Small—are hard-minded, but less visionary, more one-dimensional. Wriston focused on the horizon and drove expansion. Reed keeps a closer eye on the pressure gauges, focusing on the details of execution and the control machinery. Without a renewal of its strategic positioning, will the bonds of this tightly wound system begin to fray? If Citicorp, with its great geographical and product diversity, loses its coherent self-concept, if it falls back from a leading edge of the industry, will the self-sacrifices that employment there entails begin to be questioned? Will the high performers exit?

SOFT HEARTS

In 1985, Hewlett-Packard was ranked by a *Fortune* magazine survey as one of the two most highly admired companies in America. Like Citicorp, Hewlett-Packard lives dangerously, but HP does so at the "soft" end of the continuum.[23]

Hewlett-Packard is governed by a powerful set of corporate strictures. First put into writing in 1957, these policies spell out specific commitments between the company and its employees. These include (1) the commitment to help employees share in the company's success through a generous stock option program; (2) job security (i.e., no layoffs) based on satisfactory performance; (3) recognition of individual achievement; (4) maintaining a climate that helps people gain a sense of satisfaction and accomplishment from their work; and (5) fostering initiative and creativity by allowing individuals the freedom of action.[24]

Founded in 1939 by Bill Hewlett and Dave Packard, two Stanford engineers, Hewlett-Packard's first product was an improved audio oscillator used to test sound equipment. For the first twenty years, HP's products were primarily electronic testing and measuring instruments for engineers and scientists. Then, in the early seventies, Hewlett-Packard virtually created the hand-held calculator market. Since then, it has moved into computers, medical devices, electronic testing equipment, and instrumentation for chemical analysis and solid-state components. By 1989, Hewlett-Packard, with over 7,000 products, had revenues of 9.8 billion.[25]

HP's guiding strategic principle has been to provide customers with devices superior to any competitive offering in performance, quality, and overall value. To this day, HP corporate strategy is pursued with three measures in mind: (1) getting the highest return out of the company's most important asset, its people, (2) getting the best output from a given technology, and (3) giving the customer the best performance for the price paid.[26]

Today, Hewlett-Packard, with 84,000 employees worldwide, has fifty-two product divisions. Nearly half are engaged in businesses directly related to computers. The organization fosters highly decentralized divisions that operate much like independent businesses. "One of the rarest qualities among entrepreneurs," states one long-time HP employee, "is the capacity to build a coherent organization, all the while continuing to bring on a stream of new inventions and meet demands of manufacturing, sales, and the customer's needs in the marketplace. HP's two founders had this gift. They were committed to building a company that retained the energy and entrepreneurial spirit of their early efforts. In a highly imaginative fashion, they crafted an institution that did this.[27]

HP adopted a set of organizational principles that fostered high levels of accountability and entrepreneurial responsiveness. Each time a product line reached $20 million in sales (or division head count exceeded 1,500 employees), a new division was created. The divisions were like entrepreneurial subsidiaries—responsible for their own marketing and manufacturing. Corporate-wide functions such as personnel and finance (and, to an extent, sales) were provided, but kept to a bare minimum.[28]

Throughout the seventies, HP's strategy, and its related principles of organization, served it exceedingly well. Along with success came a more elaborate codification of HP's earlier-named set of values—which came to be called the "HP Way." It embraced four precepts: (1) business practices should include no long-term borrowing, and market expansion through product leadership, (2) people practices, as noted earlier, should include trust, respect, and individual dignity, profit-sharing, and employment security, (3) management practices should include an open-door policy, management by walking around, accessibility and openness to dialogue with subordinates, and (4) conflict was managed by basically avoiding it and by touching bases and building consensus. As these values became more explicit, Hewlett-Packard became equally vigilant about the sorts of people it sought to attract, and the type of performance it sought to reward. Operating from the basic assumption that given proper incentives, good people want to do a good job, the company recruited people who fit the model—and it worked. Through 1982, sales grew at 20 percent per year compounded, and profits increased at an annual rate of better than 25 percent. Then, in 1983, HP began to falter. While it has since regained some of its earlier momentum, the hazards of living dangerously continue to stalk its future.[29]

HP's vulnerabilities were exposed through one of its greatest successes— its entry into the computer business. Graduating upward from its earliest entry into the hand calculator segment, HP subsequently introduced two successful minicomputers, the HP 3000 and the HP 6000. By 1989, 65 percent of HP's revenues were derived from the sale of computers.[30]

But HP's reliance on the revenue stream from its computer business drew it relentlessly into the vortex of a highly competitive industry. The availability of increasing amounts of computing power at low cost meant that competitors with general-purpose computers and tailored software could provide an alternative to specialty-instrument functions. Hewlett-Packard, historically a specialty-instrument supplier, needed to match this threat with its own computing and software products—each of which, given HP's tradition, was created by a separate and highly independent division.

As computers encroached into the traditional-instrument business (which HP had historically served with hardware rather than with software-intensive solutions) integration became more essential. Terminals need to be compatible with displays, which in turn need to be compatible with memories, circuit boards, and the logic unit itself. These systems required higher-order integration to speak to one another efficiently and easily. HP's separate divisions working as autonomous units didn't perform this task very effectively.

A December, 1982 *Business Week* cover story discussed these problems, and described some of the company's attempts to achieve the overall coordination of its twenty-two information processing divisions. The account called attention to a problem that HP's ideology of decentralization had blocked it from acknowledging: widespread difficulty in performing cross-divisional projects. There was resistance to stepping up to this problem since "recentralization" might dampen HP's entrepreneurial spirit.

Public attention now forced management to do something. With some hesitation, management clustered the separate computer divisions under the umbrella of a loosely coupled Systems Group. The man placed in charge was Paul Ely. Ely was unusual among HP's managers for his aggressiveness and willingness to deal with contention directly. He was bent on translating the structural merger into an operating reality. Predictably, his actions toward these ends evoked tensions and turfism. Opponents labeled him "Silicon Valley's Jack Welch" and mobilized behind the banner of the HP Way. Ultimately, top management flinched. HP's new CEO, John Young, feared that Ely might be sacrificing the HP Way by addressing the business imperatives too quickly.

The events that were now to unfold at HP are highly instructive in our inquiry into stagnation and renewal. A false impression may have been created thus far in that stagnation might seem like an invisible virus that strikes healthy organizations without warning and for no reason. Such is not the case. In the corporate body as in the human body, vulnerability to infection is enhanced when resistance is low. Organizations lower their resistance when (1) they live in excess for prolonged periods of time, and (2) when they hide from harsh realities.

In the early 1980s, HP faced both of these perils. (It has not altogether escaped them to this day.) As we have previously noted, its excesses lay in its attachment to the HP Way and its underlying humanitarian ideology. Greatly compounding the risks was top management's loss of nerve in the face of needed change. Ely's efforts to force true integration generated more heat than Young wished to endure. But not wishing to back down openly, he obfuscated—and reorganized. A choreography of self-deception ensued. What appeared to be more was in fact less. Ely's computer group was broken into five subgroupings: one for computers and operating software, a second for data communication, a third for terminals and personal computers, a fourth for factory marketing, and a fifth for field marketing. The position of Chief Operating Officer was established under CEO Young. Ely, who had been in charge of over half of HP's revenue stream, was the natural choice for the slot. But he was passed over and in his place a dark-horse candidate, Dean Morton, was chosen. Morton is a soft-spoken consensus builder, thoroughly steeped in the HP Way of doing things. Ely, demoted to running a small fraction of his former business, left HP soon thereafter.

What was represented as a redoubled effort to bring HP's computer efforts into common focus was a de facto return to the status quo. Cost overruns, postponement of product introductions, and missed opportunities would flow from these developments. To be sure, HP enjoyed some offsetting successes in the ensuing years. But the point of this episode is not so much an indictment of management as it is an illustration of the characteristic obfuscations through which companies hide from hard truths. Stagnation stalks those who seek to spare themselves from unpleasantness. Courage and controversy are the unwritten imperatives of the executive's job description.

Today, HP's computer activities, while operating somewhat more coherently, are still (in the view of most of HP's general managers) far from an integrated business. HP still markets entire lines of desktop computers which use different operating systems and don't talk to each other. Engineers from different divisions argue endlessly on behalf of their versions. When compromises are made in order to connect one element of a system to the other, they can result in cumbersome software which begrudgingly bridges the products of the participating divisions but which leaves the "product integrity" of the respective contributors intact. The Spectrum computer with its RISC architecture was three years late in introduction and largely missed the window of opportunity. As initially scheduled, the Spectrum minicomputer could have dominated its segment in which it is now one of several offerings. It is crowded still further by the widening role of workstations.

At Citicorp, we saw an underlying bias toward decision-making which was drilled into managers through the rigors of their semi-annual personnel reviews. At Hewlett-Packard, there is no such bias. Rather, one finds a people-oriented value system which appears to have taken on a life of its own. Employees of all levels tend to view employment securing as guaranteed by the HP Way—"security" in their *current* job.

These policies translate into higher costs. Each HP employee represents about a $600,000 commitment (the present value of the average salary over the average career). This totals up to a $50–60 billion exposure for 84,000 employees. When placed alongside HP's market value and revenues, the full implications of lifetime job security for 84,000 people become clear. HP's very generous and supportive programs inhibit attrition. Employees with over fifteen years of experience rarely leave—around 2 percent per year.[31] There's nothing wrong, of course, with the commitment to people, provided that hard-minded thinking surrounds it. For example, DEC and IBM are far better at curtailing hiring *before* a surplus situation arises. But HP, with fifty-two quasi-independent divisions and a weak centralized HR function, has not been particularly successful in pursuing such a policy. Autonomous divisions do their own hiring. Informal networks exist for shifting surpluses in one business to shortages in another, but there are no policies or sanctions to enforce workforce rebalancing.

The danger, then, is that the HP Way—for all its humanistic appeal—is becoming a maladaptive ideology of job security and autonomy. Employees at all levels tend to view employment security as more of a right than a privilege. When offered an opportunity to move (requiring an extra fifteen-mile commute to another facility), many refuse relocation yet remain on the payroll.[32] This has unquestionably contributed to some divisions becoming less competitive. The number of HP's product lines losing money has increased. And HP's tradition of divisional autonomy means that it is left in the hands of the affected division management teams to scale themselves down—an unlikely scenario, given human nature.[33]

The need to act on these problems is regarded by the separate divisions as enormously important. Concerns repeatedly surface among task forces, at management council meetings, and at other forums. While the problem has been identified, top management has been reluctant to address these matters aggressively for fear of breaking its psychological contract with its employees.

The HP Way also imposes a dysfunctional protocol for managing conflict. They have a term for it: *terminal niceness*. This refers to the HP tendency to be nice to everyone while inwardly reserving the right of one's independent judgment (and the latitude not to join in a team effort) even though one appears to be going along when decisions are made. Thus, HP's conflict management style, quite unlike the hardball practices at Citicorp, leads to a lot of smoothing and avoidance. No one loses face and discussions are always kept on a rational plane. The dialogue is always constructive. Visitors are always impressed with how positive HP's atmosphere is. But in the last analysis, the discussants can and often do choose to go their own separate ways, leaving issues essentially unresolved.

Terminal niceness plagues HP's problem-resolution process from the lowest level right up to the deliberations of Hewlett-Packard's management committee. And it is further exacerbated by a culture which cultivates "independence of mind." Esoteric debates on fine points are used to avoid closure, when such closure might encroach on the autonomy of one or more of the individuals involved. The general manager of one HP division summarizes: "I think this company's real difficulty has to do with leadership. It was more evident several years ago, when the reorganization of the computer business was long overdue. It was poorly executed. They left people hanging too long and it really didn't address the problems. Groups and sectors were created as a superstructure over the still autonomous divisions. And we're still only partially effective." Another comments: "Have you ever attended an Executive Committee meeting? It's an embarrassment. They just discuss things and there's never any closure, never any decisions. Then people go off and do what they want to do."[34]

Says one senior executive: "HP's much-discussed team play pertains primarily to behavior *within* divisions. HP has much less of a team approach within whole product groups and even less so across the company as a whole."[35] In some crucial product lines, such as workstations (where Hewlett-Packard was undoubtedly best positioned of any company in Silicon Valley to define and build a system for engineers and scientists), an enormous and lucrative window of opportunity was missed simply because the scope of the workstation product extended beyond the charter of any single division. HP had the concept on the drawing boards. It was a well-designed and marketable product idea. But no single business unit could undertake the project alone and all were hesitant to endure the contention and compromises that would arise if several divisions joined forces.

A division manager states:

> Missing the workstation market was a big setback for us. It was very clear to this company for a long time that we had an opportunity in the CAD/CAM area. But unfortunately the necessary ingredients for a successful CAD/CAM offering were spread around a half-dozen divisions. We had no one like Bill Hewlett on the scene who could recognize CAD/CAM for its potential and make sure that the resources were pulled together under one roof. Instead, our activities remained diffuse and fragmented.[36]

Here we see the costs of imbalance and too much split.

Another senior division head states:

> Hewlett-Packard's strategy has been inherently opportunistic. We have always been superb at scrambling for small opportunities as seen by each of the

FIG. 8–1

SOFT HEARTS: Hewlett-Packard
Net Sales per Employee

1980 Constant Dollars End-of-Year Employees

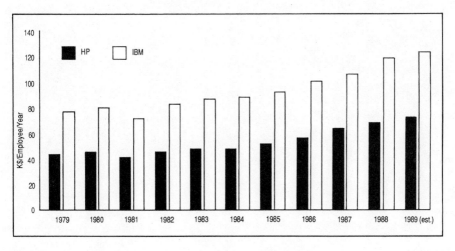

entrepreneurial divisions. Where we get into trouble, is when there's a strategic shift and the strategic opportunity cuts across the capabilities of several divisions. Such was the case with the workstations. It took a larger strategic view to see that opportunity, estimate the revenue potential, and correct the way that we were organized to pull off a competitive product. We dropped the ball.[37]

Figure 8–1 compares HP's sales per employee with IBM's. The high degree of autonomy among HP's divisions and its commitment to people increasingly exposes the firm to an uncompetitive position. Unless the softhearted side of HP is coupled with hard-mindedness, further trouble lies in store.

The tale of HP is unfolding and HP's performance remains solid. Nevertheless, HP illustrates the risks of a values system taken to extremes. In this regard, HP is not an exact parallel to Citicorp. Citicorp has succeeded in striking a dynamic tension that, while precarious, remains intact and effective in its competitive world. In contrast, HP's excesses in the direction of honoring people and humanistic values are proving inappropriate in its competitive environment. There is a pressing need for Hewlett-Packard to reestablish effective contention, to exercise some of the hard-mindedness one sees at Citicorp, to redefine values like *job security* and *autonomy* to make business sense as well as humane common sense.

CHAPTER NINE

The Two Faces of Learning: General Motors and Honda

Ultimately, organizational vitality and adaptiveness depend on "learning." Fit, split, contend, transcend, and the domains of contention are only vehicles by which companies drive themselves into the self-examination that true learning entails. There are, in fact, two types of learning: little "l" learning (incrementally improving upon a base of prior performance) and Big "L" Learning (shifting the context of the baseline itself). This distinction relates to the terminology *maximize* and *metamize* introduced in Chapter Three. Little "l" learning maximizes; Big "L" Learning meta-mizes. It is essential for organizations to do both.

General Motors and Honda provide concrete examples of the intricate machinery that inhibits or stimulates learning. General Motors' "maximizing" approach ultimately turned inward upon itself.* Honda's blend of "maxi" and "meta" learning has helped the company escape the perils of size, middle age, and success.

Some readers may balk at the comparison of two firms so different in size and maturity. Let me quantify these disparities at the outset. General Motors ranks thirty-first among the manufacturing companies of the world; Honda ranks eighty-fifth.[1] General Motors is in its eighth generation of leadership since Alfred Sloan; Honda is in its fourth. Table 9–1 contrasts the two firms along a variety of dimensions.

Surprisingly, though, these contrasts almost miss the point. The choice of

---

* Throughout this chapter, examples will be drawn from General Motors to illustrate the dangers of a closed, inward-looking culture. Clearly, as a large and complex company, GM provides many positive counterexamples—although few will deny that during much of the decade of the eighties it lost position and momentum with respect to all major competitors. Since the appointment of Robert C. Stempel as president in 1987, this situation has shown some modest signs of correcting itself.[2]

TABLE 9–1.

General Motors and Honda:
Comparisons and Performance Indicators*

	General Motors	Honda
Sales	$102 billion	$24 billion
Assets	$87.4 billion	$14.3 billion
Market Valuation	$23.1 billion	$12.6 billion
Profit of % Sales	3.5%	3.6%
U.S. Market Share	36.1%	7.3%
Number of Employees	700,000	58,320
Capital Expenditures in Core Business (1930–88)	$50 billion	$9.2 billion
Average Cost/Vehicle	$10,170	$8,670
Labor Productivity: Total Employee Hours/Vehicle Produced (adjusted for vertical integration)	92	31
R&D Expenditures (1986)	$3.7 billion	$670 million
Number of Patents Issued (1986)	300	300
Product Development Cycle	6 years	3 years
International Presence	39 countries	19 countries

* All data 1988 unless otherwise indicated

these two firms as illustrations of organizational learning is based on the fact that one far outperforms the other. General Motors is struggling with its institutional metabolism; Honda is thriving with the brisk heartbeat of a Seiko watch.

Before examining these companies and their learning processes in detail, it is useful to have a framework. Eight specific factors influence an organization's capacity for learning. These are:

1. The extent to which an elite group or single point of view dominates decision-making
2. The extent to which employees are encouraged to challenge the status quo
3. The induction and socialization of newcomers
4. The extent to which external data on performance, quality, consumer satisfaction, and competitiveness are cultivated or suppressed
5. The equity of the reward system and distribution of status and privilege
6. The degree of empowerment of employees at all levels

7. The historical legacy and folklore
8. The integrity of contention management processes—particularly with respect to surfacing hard truths and confronting reality

The following sections will address these processes in turn.

GENERAL MOTORS

Finance's Hegemony

In the golden era, General Motors' CEO Alfred Sloan, installed an abundance of checks and balances that prevented the excesses of one discipline dominating another. Engineering, Manufacturing, and Finance were of co-equal status. The product divisions—Chevrolet, Pontiac, Buick, Oldsmobile, and Cadillac—each competed for market share and fermented diversity with styling changes and marketing innovations. General Motors thrived.[3]

By the early 1960s, this beautifully choreographed arrangement had begun to change. GM's financial orientation began to gain preeminence, ultimately overshadowing rival functions. John DeLorean's *On a Clear Day You Can See General Motors* traces this development in detail.[4]

Most industry experts agree that in the 1980s GM lost momentum. Market share alone dropped 15 percent, GM's automotive styling lost leadership, patents declined, and there was an exodus of top-flight executives.[5] Many, including former Vice Chairman Elmer Johnson, trace this in part to the prevalence of a single point of view. He states:

> Finance exerts a tremendous dominance over our entire organization. I'm not just talking about the number of our chairmen that have been selected from Finance, but the degree to which Finance infiltrates all of our other functions. Our head of personnel is from Finance, our head of public affairs is from Finance, heads of Pontiac, Buick, and Oldsmobile as well. (Of course, Alan Smith, our chief financial officer, comes from that function.) Of the forty top guys in this company, at least twenty-five percent are from Finance. The difference between the career paths of these individuals and the rest is that Finance people not only occupy the top slots in Finance, but the other disciplines as well. Over time, this has led us to become fixated on volume (and revenues) at the sacrifice of the other considerations. There were not enough highly placed executives with other backgrounds to keep a healthy debate alive.[6]

The emergence of one dominant elite drives an organization toward excess, and it narrows the frame in which learning occurs. A plant manager comments: "GM has become less and less a manufacturing company. We manufacture things, true, but that's not what our culture is anymore. Our culture is Finance, and Finance is dominant. The Finance guys regard the manufacturing side as drones. They peer in on our numerous problems and say, 'Manufacturing is all screwed up. Why promote them? What can we learn from them?' They don't realize how lopsided we've become. Over a number of decades, our top management has lost sight of what business we're in."[7]

Corporations are inevitably political entities, and, as such, are crucibles for ambition. As the quest for power is a sensitive matter, its exercise is often concealed. Commencing with former Chief Financial Officer Frederick G. Donner's appointment as chairman in 1958, Finance engineered an unbroken succession of its alumni to the chairmanship.[8] But this ascendancy to power has been masked by dutiful obeisance to "the tradition of Alfred Sloan," "the importance of manufacturing," and "the autonomy of the divisions." While securing a majority of key executive slots, Finance went to considerable lengths to downplay its power.[9] As will be seen, widespread discrepancies between fact and myth impeded General Motors' learning system. This, in turn, contributed significantly to the company's difficulties in coming to terms with itself.

Learned Helplessness

Social systems can create double binds. At General Motors, many executives feel they are simultaneously exhorted to exercise initiative and undermined from doing so. GMers have coined a phrase for the psychic consequences that flow from double signals: learned helplessness.[10]

Mort Meyerson was, until 1987, the president of EDS, and served on General Motors' Executive Committee from 1984 through 1986. He comments on the ways in which "team play" was employed as a weapon against dissent.

General Motors has evolved a system which restricts subordinates from challenging the status quo. It's like the Manchu dynasty in the latter stages of its decay. And I mean *really* like the Manchu dynasty—including eunuchs. There have been a great many senior executives in General Motors who have had their balls cut off. And worse, they seem to have accepted their fate in order to play some residual role in the declining empire. An associate of mine, still a senior executive at General Motors, told me a story. Once, as a promising and fast-rising mid-career executive, he had been asked to make a presentation on a capital budgeting item that he strongly opposed. He disagreed with his boss who favored it. Pressed to make the presentation, the younger executive declined, saying that he could not do so because he did not believe in what was being recommended. Laying out his objections, he concluded: "I'm really not the right guy. I don't have my heart in it." His boss countered with a grisly anecdote about a stallion offered the choice of being made a gelding or shunted off to the meat factory. The implication was clear. One either accepted diminished integrity or was no longer considered "on the team." There was a moral to his story. That senior executive was in effect coaching *me* that I, too, needed to yield and get on the team.[11]

A GM plant manager echoes a similar refrain (and, interestingly, adopts a similar metaphor):

> Only castrated production guys who play the game get promoted to the top. GM's best manufacturing guys tend to get the shitty jobs, as contrasted to slicker guys who keep their nose clean. The ones that don't make it are more confronting, decisive, risk-taker types—and typically far better managers. But straight talk rattles the guys at the top. Our best plant managers tend to be outspoken about the things that get in their way and this puts a cap on their career prospects.[12]

The point here is that learning systems take shape in forms that are unseen or undiscussable. Management needs to continually face the emergent rituals, many of which can significantly aid or detract from learning and adaptiveness. It should be acknowledged here that General Motors has many sound patterns of behavior. The problem is that in the eighties its unhealthy patterns have tended to overshadow the constructive ones.

Rituals of Humiliation

"Learned helplessness" is communicated in part by social routines that subtly teach ambitious managers to be compliant. A fast-track, mid-career executive points to the small things that figure into this "induction process."

> GM has a ritual of humiliation. The fourteenth floor [where GM's top executives reside] has three dining rooms, and each has evolved intricate subtleties. The visitor is made aware that one's eating habits are being scrutinized. Do you pick your bacon up with your fingers? Do you push all of your food onto your fork with a piece of bread? These things count against you. The net effect is that it keeps you anxious and pliant, which is just what they want.[13]

Another former manager, and long-time observer of GM, adds:

> As you move up the ladder you have to agree to be humiliated as a rite of
> progression. Everyone gets the things they cared about, are committed to, or
> believed in, taken away. It's the price one pays for proving one's loyalty. You
> become a victim in this process, but you end up identifying with the aggressor.
> By the time you're one of the top executives of the corporation, you are ready
> to be the aggressor yourself.[14]

Rituals of Avoidance

General Motors has a well-evolved routine for conflict management. But for
the most part, General Motors suppresses conflict rather than harnesses it.
Two factors in GM's social system contribute to this pattern. First, Finance
so overshadows other functions that the checks and balances that might be
provided by the lesser disciplines are lost.[15] Second, the "committee process," instituted by Alfred Sloan as GM's primary vehicle for decision-
making, has become sterile and ritualized. Contention has little avenue for
expression. Former Vice Chairman Elmer Johnson describes the situation:

> Sloan set up a vast framework of interlocking committees and policy groups.
> These include the Marketing Policy Group, Price Review Committee, Sales
> and Service Policy Group, the Materials Management Policy Group, Industrial
> Relations Policy Group, Personnel Administration Development Policy Group,
> and so forth.
>
> Product Policy Group (PPG) focuses on such issues as model changeovers,
> styling thrusts, and the capital investments that should be tied into it. There are
> deep divisions within PPG between the Sales people, who fear they can't sell
> everything, and the Financial planners, who are optimistic and want to spread
> our fixed cost by pushing volume on dealers. The Finance guys always prevail,
> and drive us into an overproduction situation. These are not productive
> discussions.[16]

Privilege and Rewards

At General Motors, status is clearly defined, and protocol closely observed.
A middle manager in GM's Cadillac division states: "There is a saying at
GM that 'Executives rule.' This pertains to our cultural tradition which
assumes that privilege and status are perquisites of rank; deference and
obedience are expected from subordinates."[17]

GM's monetary rewards system is one of its most blatant forms of privilege. While reformed slightly in the past several years, it continues to
perpetuate significant disparities and ill will. The senior executives in a

Japanese company receive a total compensation package that is ten times that of the hourly worker on the line; at General Motors, the differential is over fifty times.[18] Not surprisingly, these differentials alienate top management from those who work for them. The following comments by a mid-level GM executive underscore this point:

> There is real arrogance at the senior levels of General Motors. The bonus system alienates leadership from the rank and file. In 1987, the salaried and hourly employees in GM's U.S. automotive operations (comprising a vast proportion of the company) received no profit-sharing bonus. At face value, this was to be expected. We lost share that year and barely broke even. On the other hand, GM as a corporation reported profits based on (1) accounting changes and (2) profits from EDS and GMAC. So our top executives granted themselves bonuses. Their rationale, of course, is that their performance is based on *corporate* results. This sounds reasonable until one gets into the details. EDS makes money because they charge Automotive Operations exorbitant fees—and thus profit at our expense. GMAC charges the Automotive Group at market rates to finance cars. Facing the enormous glut of unsold cars that year, the only way we could move them was through discount financing. Our incentives generated a windfall for GMAC. They lent at the full market rate, and Automotive Operations made up the difference (since the customer was only paying interest rates of two and a half percent). The problem is that these same top executives who were rewarded with bonuses were those responsible for overpricing and overproducing the product. We were left holding the ball.[19]

Financial incentives have great appeal when they work, but at General Motors, problems have arisen because the old systems reward "volume," and the new rhetoric stresses quality. In the 1950s and 1960s, it made sense to maximize production; GM could sell all it made. Bonuses that could double or triple salary were tied to meeting yearly "build numbers." The problem is that in today's market GM needs quality more than quantity.

A former GM manager underscores this point:

> The most serious disconnects surround the talk about quality. We lack commitment. The real issue is always "the count": "Make your numbers." So repeatedly we leave it to the dealer to rebuild our vehicles, or we do it in our own yard after they came off the assembly line. Our plant is only working two shifts, five days a week, but our repair operation works three shifts, seven days a week, trying to repair the cars that have been poorly put together on the line. There are problems with supplier's materials. Everyone games the specs. We impose unrealistically tight tolerances, the suppliers know it, so they manu-

facture below specs and know we'll still put them through production. The workers know it, and the managers know it, but they won't stop the line. They just let the cars be built and then try to fix them as best they can afterwards.[20]

Empowerment

At General Motors, CEO Roger Smith complains openly that his 10,000 "frozen" middle managers are GM's greatest obstacle to change.[21] At the hourly level, GM has not been successful in forging a true partnership with the UAW. The rank and file see GM's managerial approach little changed from a decade ago.[22] This was a major source of contention with former board member Ross Perot. Perot asserts:

> Roger is wrong. We've got terrific people at every level of GM. I'm completely sold on them. If you could ever create an environment where you tap their full potential, GM will carry the day. GM cannot win by massive capital spending. GM cannot win by massive staff involvement. GM cannot win by doing the things they have been doing in the past. Management must get involved directly with customers, employees, dealers, and stockholders, breaking down these long-standing adversarial relationships.[23]

Not only Perot, but Roger Smith's Japanese partners at GM's venture with Toyota in Fremont, California, seem to share a similar view. "As regards cultural change and human relations," says Kan Higashi, executive vice president of the GM/Toyota venture, "GM top management (i.e., Roger) simply hasn't gotten the idea yet."[24]

Reinforcing Folklore

Many executives equate "folklore" with the "grapevine"—and indeed, the two terms share much in common. "Folklore" conveys important morals or lessons; the "grapevine," in contrast, is more like the six o'clock daily news. It informs people about "what's really going on."

Like it or not, the back channel, or "grapevine," is with us to stay. Like a Greek chorus, it creates the feeling tone or ironic commentary behind the central actors on stage. We can pay attention to the Greek chorus—as the audience does—or ignore it. But make no mistake, it is always there. The social engineering of continuous learning requires us to take it into account.

As a general proposition, the "grapevine" is a pretty good litmus test of trust. If a company walks like it talks, the grapevine tends to be diminutive and positive. If inconsistencies abound, it thrives—often with strong undercurrents of cynicism. Folklore, however, can flourish in both healthy and unhealthy environments. It is especially important because it teaches. Folklore contains parables from the past that guide everyday conduct in the present.

Most companies have a rich legacy of folklore. Stories such as the iconoclastic behavior of Mr. Honda and the courageous campaign of current CEO Kume (who had a head-on confrontation with Mr. Honda—and won—on the merits of the water-cooled engine) give assurance to those who would follow in their footsteps.[25]

General Motors, too, has generated its legacy of folklore. During the period 1985–1987, in which this research was conducted, much of what was heard cast doubt on the efficacy of leadership. The two examples that follow, while possibly apocryphal, illustrate the ways in which folklore can take hold within a company and how it subsequently shapes the lens through which management's sincerity is assessed.

Open Parking

When Buick City reopened in 1985, GM emphasized its renewed commitment to a "worker-management partnership." True to this philosophy, the prime parking spots closest to the entryway of the facility no longer bore the names of the top five plant executives. Ostensibly, Buick City was now in step with one of the egalitarian practices of the industry then in vogue—open parking. But the folklore reported it differently.

Every morning at 5:30 a.m., five designated blue-collar employees arrive ahead of their shift and park their cars in those five prime slots. Around 8:00 a.m., they leave their spots on the assembly line, go out into the parking lot, and sit in their cars until the top managers arrive. On cue, they pull out their cars to accommodate the executive's vehicles.[26]

Just-in-Time

A second example of folklore pertains to GM's commitment to "Just-in-Time" inventory (a system by which in process inventory is eliminated between workstations). A material factor in this story is that Buick City had won its bid for a major refurbishing over a plant in Wisconsin. The latter had a much more congenial labor force. But under the sponsorship of Lloyd Royce, then a possible candidate for the presidency of General Motors, Buick City was given the go-ahead on the basis of its central location to suppliers. Thus it was that "Just-in-Time" emerged as a priority program in the new plant to exploit supplier proximity. Royce's name was on the line to boot.

Just-in-Time assumptions were accordingly built into Buick City's remodeling plans. The floor plan was laid out so that the aisles could no longer accommodate the levels of inventory that had lain there in the past. The factory would no longer carry the cushion of spare materials that could bail out a station if the operation upstream failed.

But the "folklore" on GM's commitment to Just-in-Time interjected a cynical counterpoint. Reportedly, in a grove of trees one mile away from the Buick City plant stands a warehouse. The facility, owned by GM until just before the plant's reopening, was sold and then leased back to Buick City. No longer carrying the GM logo, and operating under independent warehouse management, the facility now stores the hundreds of millions of dollars of Buick City's in-process inventory that no longer fits in the plant itself. The in-process inventory is there just the same—albeit now less conveniently situated and requiring a short truck ride when problems on the line occur.[27]

INTEGRITY AT RISK

Throughout much of this decade, General Motors' learning system has been in gridlock. Its machinery screens out any information at odds with its beliefs. As we saw at the Fremont plant as described in Chapter Three, to use just one example, what there was to be learned was subverted.[28]

One General Motors executive put it bluntly: "Let's face it—at GM we are literally applauded for being able to cover up problems. In contrast, at Fremont they made them heroes when they stopped the line or pointed out an inconsistency or discrepancy. You can't understand the significance of this change until you've worked in both worlds."[29]

SUMMARIZING THE GM EXPERIENCE

Although General Motors has had its share of problems, a great deal of healthy little "l" learning has occurred there. Quality has steadily improved.[30] The GM-10 cars, while late, have provided a moderate counterthrust to Ford's Taurus.[31] Buick City, slow to get started, is now a successful plant.[32] There is little doubt, in fact, that GM is beginning to pull out of its long slumber. The point here, then, is not to prophesy General Motors' destiny and decline, but rather to highlight in a vast and complex organization those factors that imperil learning. These are what the danger signs look like. In this respect, the illustrations chosen have been admittedly slanted toward the negative. It must be added, however, that General Motors was a particularly fertile ground for this purpose. There was no scarcity of executives during this research who were willing to come forward and express their concern about a learning system that suboptimized, and that was contributing powerfully to their company's loss of energy and momentum. This telling quote by one such committed, yet concerned, middle-level executive provides an apt conclusion:

> When you look at GM as an outsider, it seems that some of the things we're doing are crazy. But if you look closely you discover that everyone here is in a lifeboat, and no one is courageous enough to jump out. You have to realize that the system we've got today has been good to everybody. It rewards managers very, very well. In addition, all of our inefficiency means that during boom times the hourlies double their salaries with overtime—which takes care of them, too. We have hourly employees at GM making $40,000 a year, and they need that income to support the standard of living they have become accustomed to. In fact, one of the few worker complaints from our venture with Toyota in Fremont, California, is that they really have to live on their straight-time salary. They don't work overtime. Another factor: When you truly empower employees, and initiate from the bottom up, it takes away the legitimacy of privileges. For one, it reduces the importance of the salaried ranks—and arguably even their numbers. It casts doubts on the appropriateness of a variety of management's perquisites. Managers have mahogany offices not bullpens. They park in heated garages in the winter. They have separate cafeterias with catered services. And they have large bonuses. I'm quite sure that if you took a survey among GM executives at all levels, you would find that they would not wish to give those things up, and yet those are the very things which are at stake, and which would have to be relinquished if we were to adopt a system analogous to those which we see at Toyota or Honda. In summary, the inefficiencies of the General Motors system are very beneficial for people. They do a lot of "good" for us.[33]

HONDA

Passing reference has been made to Honda throughout this book. It is the quintessential example of a learning organization. It demonstrates the capacity for both little "l" learning and Big "L" Learning—breakthrough innovation, leading-edge engineering, low-cost manufacturing, and brilliant marketing. Finally, Honda has a remarkable track record of agility and adaptiveness—executing a late but successful entry into the automotive field, scoring a come-from-behind victory in the "motorcycle wars" with Yamaha, responding brilliantly to stringent U.S. automotive pollution controls with the CVCC engine. Honda is the gold medalist of the "industrial pentathlon."[34] No other enterprise is truly world-class in all five categories, and it is for this reason that many regard Honda as the best-managed company in the world.

But preeminence is a fragile thing. Ascendancy must be earned each day. Indeed, the challenge of continuously striving to remain number one exacts so great a price that no human institution can bear it eternally. Honda most assuredly will not remain on top forever. But the inevitability of decline need not consign us to a fatalistic acceptance of our current levels of ignorance. Our objective is akin to the endeavors that have increased human life expectancy. Steady progress in disease control, pharmaceuticals, diagnostics, surgical transplants, and an enhanced understanding of diet and exercise have nearly doubled life expectancy in eighty years. In a parallel vein, close study of the mechanisms through which companies such as Honda do as well as they do, for as long as they do, can help other organizations realize similar attainments.

Honda employs ingenious means to trigger self-questioning and learning. At the little "l" end of the learning continuum are the dedicated efforts of Honda's many employees. How do we make manifest this "secret weapon"?

Values

As strange as it sounds, all learning (whether the maxi- or meta- variety) stems from values. Virtually all of Honda's top executives share this view. That's because the first step in creating an atmosphere for learning is to enlist the hearts and minds of employees and tie them to the company's purposes.

Julian Jaynes, the Princeton psychologist, describes human consciousness as a "metaphor-making machine."[35] In this context, the organizations through which we express ourselves can be "metaphors" that make meaning in our lives. A short-order cook at McDonald's might think beyond "making hamburgers" and see himself as serving society by providing appealing and affordable meals to families of all income levels. A researcher at Merck defines the laborious work behind test tubes in terms of "saving lives." The significance of this metaphor making is that it has extraordinary potential to bridge human and organizational purposes. Thus it is that some organizations succeed in redefining unpleasant tasks, and calling upon employees to set aside personal needs in the name of a shared mission.

If you know what a company stands for, and are convinced that it will abide by those beliefs (even when it is inconvenient to do so), you are shielded to a large degree from what employees fear most in organizations: capriciousness. Employees usually want more than paychecks and job security. There is abundant evidence that employees can handle bad news, face harsh business realities, and accept necessary sacrifices. But employees are intolerant of organizations that don't walk the way they talk. They are quick to spot dual standards, inequities, and managers that lack the courage to address the real problems their companies face.[36]

We tend to put a lot of ourselves into our jobs—more than most people are willing to acknowledge. A great deal of our personal identity comes from work. When we are used, ignored, underutilized, betrayed, or discarded, it tends to hurt a lot. Most organizations commit all of these sins— most often through carelessness and inattention rather than malice. Over time, employees build up defenses against caring too much, investing too much, trying too hard. A solid set of values doesn't eradicate all hazards of organizational life, but it does assure us that insofar as possible, the organization will be true to its word. In an imperfect world, such assurances matter a great deal.

A sense of crisis can further intensify shared values. We saw this at Ford. But we need not wait upon bankruptcy or competitive disaster to invoke a sense of crisis. Honda creates a sense of crisis by halving the best-case product development cycle on some products. In the manufacturing arena, instead of expecting 3-percent improvement in productivity, it shoots for 30 percent. These targets often stress the system to the breaking point.[37]

Breakdowns and Breakthroughs

There is a second point to these observations. Honda has found that *breakdowns* produce *breakthroughs*. Couched in our learning terminology, employees learn with a little "l" until they squeeze all they can out of the existing system, methodology, or paradigm. When that is insufficient to reach the target, a breakdown occurs that, under the right conditions, opens the way for Big "L" Learning—the "meta" possibilities.

The Ideology of "Quality"

"Crisis" also aligns individual and organizational purposes because it can both move hearts and provide *concrete* focus. Still, "crisis" does not fit all situations, and can be overused. What are the alternatives? Many companies have struggled with this question. Regrettably, most efforts to generate compelling alternatives come across as vague or grandiose.

One of the most durable survivors of this quest for a compelling source of alignment is "quality." Quality can be a compelling value in its own right. It is robust enough to pertain to products, innovations, service standards, and caliber of people. Most people interpret it rather narrowly, in terms of eliminating errors or defects. "Quality," as I will use the term, is not simply a desirable attribute, but an organizational discipline. In this latter respect, few concepts are more widely misunderstood.[38]

When "quality" is defined as a systematic process or discipline, it ties values with a more familiar concept: "strategy." While this may seem a contrived association at first glance, firms that successfully embrace quality invariably define a process that encompasses R&D; extends to the customer; entails competitive analysis, resource allocation, and implementation and operations; and relies on objective data for corrective feedback.[39] The result provides competitive advantage in areas in which a company seeks to differentiate itself. This is the purpose of "strategy."

What, then, is the difference between quality and strategy? The pursuit of quality has greater motivational appeal. It is hard to enlist passionate commitment among employees to a strategy. The goal of "penetrating markets via price or feature differentiation" may quicken the pulse of MBAs—but it leaves most employees cold. "Strategy" is too cerebral. It doesn't enlist every person in every job to make a distinct contribution. In contrast, "quality," like "crisis," appeals to people because they can relate to it. Everyone at every level can do something about it and feel the satisfaction of having made a difference. Making products that work, or providing first-class service, is something we can identify with from our own experience. Equally significant, "quality" can be *quantified*, and progress tracked against goals. This has intrinsic appeal to engineering, operations, finance, and other numbers-oriented groups who only tend to take things seriously when they can be pinned down.

Quality serves as a counterweight to the seductive pull of financial objectives. It is widely acknowledged that exclusive reliance on financial measures can compromise a company's long-term future. Quality reestablishes a constructive tension. When quality is the tiebreaker (as is the case at companies such as Ford and Honda), any employee or department, however low its status, can be assured of a hearing if quality is at risk. States one Honda executive: "If you make 'quality' the king, everyone bows to the sovereign. If you make 'objective data' its handmaiden, numbers speak with a powerful voice. Objective facts act as an equalizer; they minimize the human tendency to personalize conflicts when problems surface. We worship quality around here because it motivates, equalizes, and involves."[40]

Trust

Honda's near religious adherence to certain values makes organizational life more predictable. Employees at all levels of Honda—both in the United States and Japan—regularly report that Honda's values (as enumerated in Figure 9–1) are brought to bear once or twice a week in determining how a particular problem should be solved, or how a person should be treated.[41] It is the everyday presence and continuity of these values that generates trust. Trust is the outgrowth of a psychological contract between company and employee. Honda recognizes that trust is slow to accumulate, and quick to dissipate.

Empowerment is the third link in Honda's chain aligning the individual and the corporation. Values and trust establish the preconditions that encourage individuals to think, experiment, and improve. It follows that learning organizations share, above all else, an abiding commitment to people and a faith in the human capacity to find a better way. Once employees know what an organization stands for, and believe that it is sufficiently trustworthy to warrant their commitment and effort, they begin to truly extend themselves. If management provides employees with the tools, understanding, and latitude to make a difference, great things are possible. This is a distinguishing characteristic at Honda.[42]

One notices this at Honda's automotive plant in Marysville, Ohio, where blue-collar American autoworkers demonstrate a zeal to perform day in and day out that far surpasses their brethren in most American-run facilities.[43] Once values and trust enlist this type of commitment, empowerment permits the individual to transform commitment into contribution. One sees a wave of ideas take shape—drop by drop. This is the mechanism through which gradual improvements add up to awesome competitive advantage.

Honda's commitment to its employees is rooted in the philosophy of cofounder Takeo Fujisawa. While largely inactive in company affairs from the late 1970s, when he retired, until his death in 1989, Fujisawa's legacy is very much alive. Progressive even by Japanese standards, Fujisawa believed that the enduring source of Honda's success was its employees. The task of management was to release and channel their ideas (i.e., harness their initiative as engines of learning). Fujisawa rarely issued orders or gave directions. His style was to ask probing, Socratic questions, forcing employees to think independently.[44] His approach was akin to Michelangelo's view of sculpting. Traditional sculptors approach their block of granite believing that a shape does not exist until their chisel creates it. Michelangelo believed the figure was already in the stone before he touched it. His task was to peel away the enshrouding marble and set it free. Honda regards

FIG. 9–1

HONDA

HONDA MOTOR CO., LTD.
Company Principle

"Maintaining an international viewpoint, we are dedicated to supplying
products of the highest efficiency yet at a reasonable price for
worldwide customer service."

HONDA MOTOR CO., LTD.
Management Policy

☐ Proceed always with ambition and youthfulness.
☐ Respect sound theory, develop fresh ideas, and make
   the most effective use of time.
☐ Enjoy your work, and always brighten your working atmosphere.
☐ Strive constantly for a harmonious flow of work.
☐ Be ever mindful of the value of research and endeavor.

HONDA MOTOR CO., LTD.
Operating Priorities

In all areas of manufacturing
operations, Honda of America Manufacturing, Inc.,
observes the following priorities:
1. Safety
2. Quality
3. Production

HONDA MOTOR CO., LTD.
Operating Principles

Quality In All Jobs
Learn, Think, Analyze, Evaluate, and Improve

Reliable Products
On Time, with Excellence and Consistency

Better Communication
Listen, Ask, and Speak Up

1988 SLOGAN
"Quality for the world from our hands and minds."

the manager's primary role as "freeing employees from the block of granite." Whereas traditional managers might seek to *engineer* output from employees, Honda's approach is to *discover* latent ideas and initiatives and give them full rein.[45]

At the Honda factory in Marysville, Ohio, employees experience a work environment that demands a great deal of them, but concomitantly goes to great lengths to take them and their ideas into account. "The Honda Philosophy is a way of life," says production staff member, Pat Sparks. "It is characterized by closeness, communication, and frankness at all levels. Honda employs thinking people, creative people. We want people to sound off. Honda is the only organization I know of where the only limitations are the limitations you place upon yourself."[46]

Extensive research has documented that when there is a problem, 80 percent of the time the core issues will reside in the system.[47] Because the employees most intimately involved with the system are best able to spot its flaws, they need to be empowered to initiate fixes. "Empowerment" in this sense means more than just doing one's job better; employees need to look at the system that effects *how* the job is done. Empowerment is necessary because the workers have to push back on the system—often requiring, in turn, that their superiors realign processes to better serve their subordinates. This shift in the locus of initiative redistributes power in the traditional boss-subordinate relationship. Who is working for whom? At Honda, it is very clear that the boss's job is to free up his subordinates.[48] The motto "To lead is to serve" is a deeply internalized ethic of the Honda Way. Contrast this to "Rank has its privileges" at General Motors.[49]

Honda executives frequently point out that the assembly line worker is the most important employee in the company.[50] If we accept Honda's statistic that 80 percent of problems stem from systems deficiencies (i.e., not worker *in*efficiencies), the central tenets about managing come into question. Improvements come from the bottom as often as they come from the top. It follows, therefore, that the manager's job content is different at a company such as Honda. We usually think of "management" as setting goals and ensuring that they are met. This is the rationale for Management by Objectives. But MBOs are seen as inhibitors to learning (especially Big "L" Learning) at Honda because they drive for results largely *within* the existing system. According to one plant manager at Honda, Marysville: "If the system is eighty percent of the problem, MBOs distract us from improving the system and subtly confine efforts to 'optimizing' that which is suboptimal."[51]

The Learning System at Honda

Once the golden triad of (1) enduring values, (2) trust, and (3) empowerment are in place, an organization can begin to learn. The introduction to this chapter noted nine ingredients of a learning system. Honda has been extraordinarily imaginative in the mechanisms it has employed toward these ends. In no small measure, this was the contribution of cofounder Takeo Fujisawa. Although a results-oriented manager (he twice saved the company from bankruptcy),[52] he had a knack for crafting the "softer" dimensions of an enduring enterprise. Several examples illustrate the point.

Three Tribes

Fujisawa made innovative use of organizational forms. Obsessed with the importance of maintaining Honda's leadership in automotive engineering and design, Fujisawa championed the idea of spinning off Honda R&D as a *separate,* wholly owned company with its own president. (Through transfer pricing, Honda R&D negotiates "contracts" for projects with its sister organizations in the Honda family, "selling" its services on a time-and-materials basis.) Fujisawa's idea was a radical one; his colleagues found it so extreme that he encountered a great deal of internal opposition. In a rare exception to his general practice of collaborative decision-making, he first persuaded, then cajoled, and eventually ordered his organizational change.[53] Later he spun off Honda Engineering (responsible for all of Honda's proprietary manufacturing machinery) as a second stand-alone entity. This positioned Honda Manufacturing (with the Sales, Marketing, and Administration functions) as the third leg of the stool.[54] Predictably, these "three tribes," as they are called, generate a great deal of constructive tension.[55] Whereas at General Motors, one elite and one point of view (Finance) holds sway, Honda is continually stimulated by these groups, each of which pushes and prods the organization from a different vantage point. To this day, all three maintain a distinct identity, have great pride in what they do, and are highly respected in their own right among competitors around the world.[56]

Heretics and Heroes

Both Soichiro Honda and Takeo Fujisawa viewed Honda's technological leadership as the key to Honda's sustainable competitive advantage. A legendary example of their commitment to this principle involved Tadashi Kume, a bench engineer who became embroiled in a conflict with Soichiro Honda over the merits of air- versus water-cooled engines. Mr. Honda (wrongly) believed that air cooling was the key to the future. As the debate intensified, Kume went on strike for a month, taking refuge in a Zen monastery in Shikoku. Kume's convictions compelled Fujisawa to weigh the dispute on its technical merits—not on the unequal status of the protagonists. Ultimately, this led to the company's recommitment to the watercooled engine. Kume's courage and persistence resulted in Honda's breakthrough CVCC engine—and launched him on a career that has made him Honda's current CEO.[57]

The Design of Design Teams

Assembling, challenging, and managing design teams is an important component of Honda's learning system. It has evolved to the status of an art form. Specifics help. Faced with the need for a small, inexpensive breakthrough car for the Japanese market in 1978, Honda's top management selected a multidisciplinary group from Sales, Engineering, Design (R&D), and Manufacturing. So far, not much new—but the next step was a big one. The team members were all iconoclastic youngsters with very little industry experience. The *average* age was twenty-seven! Compounding the risk and the pressure, the team received the CEO's personal assurance that there would be no interference with their deliberations. In return, he set high expectations. This was communicated by a simple act: he rejected their first three product concepts as "too conventional and ordinary."[58]

An executive comments on the factors that drove this highly successful team, and that have since evolved into Honda's formula for such project groups. "We control the *task* of researchers quite tightly, but loosen *controls*. Ideas with great potential often emerge. We monitor the creative breakthroughs carefully, and when they look promising we move fast to develop them. Too much freedom doesn't work. But we take the chance of giving young researchers basic goals and responsibilities, and then letting them go by themselves. In other words, we put them upstairs, remove the ladders, and say, 'You have to figure out a way to get down.' Then we set fire to the first floor. I think human beings display their greatest creativity under these circumstances."[59] The team created the extraordinarily successful Honda City, which became a top-selling automobile in Japan.

Idea Contests and Innovation

Still another idiosyncrasy of the Honda culture is its Idea Contests. Honda pioneered a notion that has since caught on in Japan, and that has been replicated by other companies. The Idea Contest is held bi-annually at the Suzuka testing track. Like a science fair, employees are given time and funds to build prototypes of projects that would not get funded through normal channels.[60]

Problem Finding

A fifth factor hinges on Honda's approach toward problem identification. Fujisawa believed the most important trait of a good manager was the ability to ask the right questions. This predisposition towards questions (as opposed to answers) has cultural roots. "In the East," observes consultant Maurice Cohen, "there is a deep reverence for questions. In Japan, for example, this shows up in everything from Zen koans to Toyota's Five 'Whys.' In the West, and more specifically in the United States, 'answers' are what we worship. Look at the popularity of TV shows and games such as Jeopardy, Wheel of Fortune and Trivial Pursuit. "Getting-the-answers" is a national pastime. This makes it very hard for us to live with the questions for very long. We're impatient, want closure, and so we frequently solve the symptoms and not the problem."[61]

Fujisawa was a master of Socratic dialogue. Yet as his company expanded, he encountered the limitations of his own reach. He felt, increasingly, that the next generation of managers was growing soft in its ability to question in a penetrating manner. In the 1950s, ever vigilant of ways to stem this tide, Fujisawa learned of the Kepner Tregoe Method. Kepner Tregoe is a Princeton, New Jersey, based firm dedicated to improved decision-making skills; it teaches a structure for thinking systematically and getting to the root cause of problems. (Their studies show that only 12 percent of decisions made in U.S. companies are soundly researched and decided.) Fujisawa experimented with these techniques and liked what he saw. Subsequently, the methodology was licensed and drilled into all managerial-level employees.[62] One executive observes: "Kepner Tregoe enables us to perpetuate Fujisawa's style of problem finding. It gets you beyond superficial impressions to root causes. You learn to examine alternatives without a built-in bias toward the most convenient or familiar solution."[63] Here, of course, is a driving force for Big "L" Learning.

This technique has since been termed the Honda Rational Thinking Process. Ed Buker, plant manager of Honda, Marysville, comments: "We use it constantly; it becomes second nature to the way we think. The Honda Rational method serves us in much the same way as Toyota's 'Five Whys.' Toyota teaches that the question 'Why?,' asked five times, usually brings you pretty close to the heart of the matter. In a similar vein, our approach teaches that if you ask the right questions, the answers take care of themselves."[64]

Raising the Bar

External benchmarks are invaluable in shaking up internal complacency and exposing problems. Honda tracks all types of performance data: the J. D. Power Survey of customer satisfaction, warranty claims, dealer suggestions, service and repair records, and focus groups and other specialized user surveys. To add to this, top managers spend half their time in the field, at plants and dealer outlets. Statistical samples are better interpreted when put in the context of first-hand experience.

Many companies give lip service to competitive benchmarks. What sets Honda apart is its leadership's close personal involvement with this goal. Until returning to Japan in 1988, Shoichiro Irimajiri, former president of Honda America, and currently a contender to become the next CEO, performed a monthly rite that exemplifies Honda's obsession with concrete external comparisons. Irimajiri was an ever-present figure on the assembly floor at Honda's facility in Marysville, Ohio. On the third Thursday evening of every month, Irimajiri would assemble the top thirty plant managers around a workbench and personally disassemble a competitor's part—a carburetor, a shock absorption system—and then compare its inner workings with Honda's counterpart. Plant management evaluated the strengths and weaknesses of the alternative designs. Shortcomings, along with suggestions for improvement, were sent to Honda R&D in Japan.[65]

Waigaya

All organizations develop a repertoire for managing conflict. Unfortunately, most smooth over conflict or avoid it. When conflict is inescapable, "shootouts" occur. There is little productive synthesis. This need not be the case. Appropriate routines or systems can value conflict and train employees to view disagreements as opportunities for learning and creativity.

Not surprisingly, Honda has established a set of skills and routines for managing conflict constructively. Most can be lumped under what Honda calls "waigaya" (why-guy-ya). Like the English term "hub-bub," it's a phonetic encapsulation of the noise Japanese make when in vocal disagreement. The benefit of such a term is that it institutionalizes a complex process. By virtue of having a name, and being acknowledged as a desirable phenomenon, Honda's contention management system can be passed on as part of the corporate heritage.[66]

Waigaya's philosophical underpinnings are revealed in the words of Honda's cofounder Takeo Fujisawa:

> My taste in music has changed from Wagner and Mozart to Stravinsky and Bartòk. Modern music sounds discordant at first—the instruments seem to be

playing independently. But you can hear a harmonious formulation if you listen carefully. This is an important lesson for managing contemporary organizations.[67]

In a subsequent interview he expanded on the same theme:

> I like Bartòk and Stravinsky. It's a discordant sound—and there are discordant sounds inside a company. As president, you must orchestrate the discordant sounds into a kind of harmony. But you never want too much harmony. One must cultivate a taste for finding harmony within discord, or you will drift away from the forces that keep a company alive.[68]

Honda's waigaya sessions entail a protocol. The most significant feature is that rank is disregarded. This is a necessity for seniority-conscious Japanese who tend to address their elders politely. Waigaya permits subordinates to speak frankly and directly; sessions can be initiated by seniors and subordinates alike. Waigaya contributes to straight talk, direct disagreement, questioning, and challenging. How striking is the contrast when we recall General Motors' patterns of humiliation, "castration," learned helplessness, and the subversion of an honest facts base.

The trick, of course, is to channel such dialogues productively. Many readers have experienced "gripe sessions" that led nowhere, and left participants frustrated and discouraged. The differentiating factor between a positive and negative outcome turns on the skill of the participants. Do they listen to one another? Is objective data used to support assertions? Do people disagree without being disagreeable? Above all, is someone present skillful at facilitating the session so as to surface thoughts and feelings present and *then* move toward constructive action? "To involve people in waigaya sessions," comments Hiroshi Nakajima, an analyst at Yamaichi Research Institute, "is unique in itself, but I think what makes it work at Honda is management's skill at consolidating the differing opinions into one plan. This works at Honda because they really share a common set of values. They love cars and motorcycles, love to get their hands dirty, and have strong beliefs in what the company stands for."[69]

Soichiro Honda's individualism, and Takeo Fujisawa's skill at translating behavior into institutional forms, established a learning system that is rare even by Japanese standards. As we have seen, Honda discourages hierarchy, grants responsibility to young employees, and supports contention. Today, Honda struggles to preserve this spirit even as the company grows larger. Current president, Tadashi Kume, observes: "If you don't make daily effort, people tend to agree with executives because they have a big influence. So I tell people that if the president says a crow is white, you have to argue back that a crow is really black." He often alludes to his infamous quarrel with Mr. Honda over the air-cooled engine. Mr. Kume exhorts Honda employees to follow his example, flaunting the Japanese convention that a junior employee should not question his senior. "If juniors don't rebel against their seniors," he continues, "that means there is no progress."[70]

HOLDING THE CENTER

These practices all foster initiative and learning at Honda. Nevertheless, there is always the risk of "overdetermination." A major challenge for Honda's highly charged learning system is not to self-destruct.

A Legacy of Leadership

Fujisawa, ever mindful of these dangers, instituted several checks and balances. The first entailed complementary skills at the leadership level. He and Mr. Honda demonstrated that technology and business disciplines could be married in a successful CEO/president partnership. This pairing of talents was replicated in their choice of successors. Over the subsequent generations, this legacy has ensured that the pairing at the top provides the right blend of complementary talents.[71]

A second ingredient to this equation was to ensure the preeminence of R&D. As a means of reinforcing this thrust, Soichiro Honda and Fujisawa established the tradition of drawing Honda's CEOs from the R&D subsidiary.[72] In their view, the career path from president of the R&D company to CEO of Honda, if properly managed, would elevate R&D yet militate against R&D's most likely excesses—overpricing, overdesigning, and overcommitting resources of the parent organization on ill-proven ideas. By making it explicit that the president of R&D will become heir of the entire enterprise, those aspiring to this position are groomed to think in terms broader than R&D's interests. Thus far, it has worked. And there is a dividend. The R&D experience enables Honda's CEOs to assess technology realistically. Further, they can make tough decisions on technology without a demoralizing R&D backlash. As former members of the R&D community, they are not as readily seen by the rank and file as "selling out" to the bottom line.

Cross-Training

Honda's third vehicle for integration and multi-disciplinary learning is its extensive cross-training. Each Honda manager must exchange jobs (for a two-week period) with a counterpart in another function on a yearly basis. Most frequently this entails exchanging R&D engineering and manufacturing personnel with their counterparts in sales. In addition, each of Honda's designers (located in the R&D company) spends *three* months a year attending dealer shows and automotive conventions around the world. This represents the commitment of one-quarter of each designer's time to face-to-face contact with dealers and customers. It effectively indoctrinates designers with a marketing outlook.[73]

Cross-Functional Teams

Earlier we noted that design teams at Honda are composed of youngsters prone to break with the status quo and who are "green" enough to contemplate leapfrog technology. These groups are orchestrated in such a fashion as to not only *generate* initiatives, but to *weave* conflicting views and disciplines together. The principal ingredients of this process are (1) framing project goals in a dramatic way that challenges engineers, (2) creating the right blend of personalities and expertise—including people from unorthodox disciplines who are unfamiliar with the core technology (these individuals force the group to look at the problem differently), (3) use of parallel project teams and engendering competition between them, (4) a system of regular project reviews that relies on the group's critique of itself, and (5) closing off nonproductive projects using particular techniques so as to avoid having the participants lose face.[74]

Musical Chairs

A dramatic example of Honda's ingenuity in reintegrating its potentially divergent parts can be seen in certain routines that shape the behavior of the forty top executives. Early in his tenure as president, Fujisawa decided that he was more productive on his feet than at his desk. Increasingly, he spent his days "making the rounds," pulling a chair up to the desk of each subordinate, asking questions, and working along with them on the projects at hand. As the company grew, he added other senior executives to play this role. To encourage this behavior, he made sure that there were always fewer desks and offices available than executives. As a result, desks had to be shared. With no office or desk to call one's own, top executives were forced to be out and about. They became, in effect, itinerant facilitators, problem-solvers, and on-the-scene decision makers.[75]

To this day, the top forty directors and managing directors of Honda are housed in a single open area with only *six* individual desks and five large circular conference tables. While the room has forty chairs, they are arranged around the conference tables where one's work gets done alongside others. Each person has one file drawer, and there are only eleven secretaries.[76] As in Fujisawa's day, the intent is to prevent top executives from getting too settled at headquarters. Equally important, the proximity imposed by the conference tables causes the seniors to interact. Protocol encourages each of the top forty executives to spend at least two weeks in the field each month.[77] It is in the sales offices and factories that their presence and perspective adds the most value. In the field, they serve occasionally as decision-makers and problem-solvers, but more often as listeners and facilitators.[78] Back at headquarters, they are a focal point for joint collaborative activities and major policy decisions.

One senior executive observes: "Mr. Fujisawa worked closely with the architects and directors in this layout. In fact, he felt this office configuration was his last hurrah. He was very pleased with the result. The setup encourages communication. An executive says hello, and then remembers to add, 'By the way . . .' It often triggers conversations which bring up contentious issues that might have been overlooked or avoided. And the close proximity virtually ensures that everyone overhears what others are up to. In a very concrete way, this layout helps all members of the executive team remain in the mainstream of what's going on."[79]

GETTING THERE FROM HERE

This review of Honda reveals numerous mechanisms that readers may strive to emulate. But there are two dangers. First, as seen in earlier chapters, if such mechanisms are applied piecemeal or superficially, they are largely destined to fail. Second, as noted in the discussion of General Motors, the very mechanisms that promote a strong culture easily turn inward and shut an organization off from external realities.

The critical ingredients, so present at Honda and absent at General Motors, are: (1) a deeply ingrained habit of self-questioning, (2) obsessive attention to external measures, (3) a drive to do things better than the best in the industry, and (4) a well-tuned system for managing the contention that the previous three factors tend to generate. What is most likely to be missed in this portrayal of a successful learning system is our tendency to focus on the specifics of *what* Honda has done, and not on the underlying philosophy and orientation of individuals that fuels this process. A key factor, then, is the "maxi" and "meta" types of learning that *individual* executives do as they grow in pace with their organizations. Fujisawa exemplified these traits—an executive who, throughout his career, continued to evolve in step with the needs of his company. By way of contrast, we see few such examples in contemporary General Motors. Let us now turn to investigate this personal dimension of the learning and renewal equation.

CHAPTER TEN

Conclusion: ''The Question'' Is the Answer

Organizations are more complicated than we generally realize. I have used the terms *fit, split, contend,* and *transcend* to label their increasing levels of complexity. The first two of these stages, fit and split, are the easiest to understand. Internal consistency, or fit, is important to the smooth functioning of an organization. Decentralization and other measures aimed at giving units autonomy and functional integrity, or split, are also valuable. Split sharpens focus on particular products, markets or technologies.

But the forces for coherence (fit) find themselves in a tug of war with the forces for autonomy and initiative (split). If we permit these to contend with one another by honoring the importance of opposites, we tap into a source of energy that can keep a company alive. Contention is an ingredient of organizational life. Our mistake has been to ignore, suppress, or undermanage it. I have identified several dimensions of contention that arise in organizations. These correspond to the levers that managers commonly use to improve performance. When a number of these levers are used simultaneously and a constructive tension is achieved, organizational performance tends to improve. This can trigger the next stage—transformation. True transformation of organizations requires a critical mass of change initiatives.

Ford and General Electric illustrate this dynamic. Several points are noteworthy. *First,* transformation requires an attack on many fronts. On the hard side, both GE and Ford engaged in strategic repositioning and a dramatic trimming of their cost structure. On the soft side, Ford far more than GE enlisted employees in streamlining workflow, improving productivity and increasing a sense of ownership and participation.

Second, different situations pose significantly different leadership challenges. Ford, in crisis and at the brink of bankruptcy, mobilized employees down to the hourly level. Jack Welch, at General Electric, had to "manufacture" a crisis in an environment where employees did not share his sense of urgency and resisted his initiatives. As of this writing, and nearly a decade after Welch took charge, General Electric's transformation has not reached as deeply as Ford's into the organization's rank and file.

Serendipity has been a *third* factor in the transformation of these two companies. Neither Petersen nor Welch had a master plan. Only in hindsight can we string unconnected events into a coherent form. The danger of a rational, after-the-fact account, however, is that it tempts us to try to over-engineer a process that is to a significant degree unpredictable. While we can learn from Ford and General Electric (and reverse-engineer the techniques which they perfected through trial and error), neither our plans nor our organizations have to perfectly match our models for transformation to take place. All that is essential is courage, persistence, and top management's openness to learning, both personal and organizational.

Transformation is not the only road to sustained success. Citicorp and Hewlett-Packard have sustained constructive tension and retained their vitality, albeit precariously. Each company tends toward extremes—Citicorp with its driven, social-Darwinian environment, and Hewlett-Packard with its "soft" organizational philosophy and strong commitment to people. The question here is whether these companies can remain on the brink of excess without becoming overdetermined. Both have a narrow, ideological commitment to *their* way of doing things. This mindset easily sacrifices flexibility and inhibits management from continuously redefining the culture to fit the changing situation.

Our primary objective has been to understand the anatomy of revitalization. As with human anatomy, companies have nervous systems which, while subtle and complex, are essential to understanding the total phenomenon. Chapter Nine, using General Motors and Honda to show how companies can learn, delved into such a nervous system. At General Motors we saw a company that, despite a strong market position, able executives and engineers, and vast financial resources, is largely paralyzed by a learning system that has turned inward upon itself. Its elites are out of balance, constructive tension is lacking, and many of the norms that prevail there dampen debate and initiative. At Honda, in contrast, we saw one of the best-managed companies in the world. Through the codification of its behavioral quirks, Honda has woven a fabric of beliefs and practices that encourages employees to reexamine assumptions and chip away at defect rates, cycle time, and inefficiencies. Honda points us toward the next frontier of management: one in which the social system is finely tuned to become a precise instrument for adaptation and continuous learning.

There is a moment at the top of a ferris wheel. You've ridden up looking at the reassuring structure of steel girders. But now it disappears. You gasp as you are thrust into the sky and begin the descent on the outer circumference. That moment in this book has come. We have caught glimpses of an important truth about organizations. Their transformation is tied to the growth of those who manage them.

THE QUESTION IS THE ANSWER

Change did not find its way into Honda, Ford, and General Electric through quick fixes. It happened when each company's leadership adopted new ways of thinking. Fujisawa's, Petersen's, and Welch's contributions were in direct proportion to their personal development. The concept is straightforward on an intellectual level, but it is hard to live with.

Managers are not a random cross-section of the population. Rather, they gain satisfaction from dealing with concrete tasks and making things happen. Peel the onion back a bit further and we find individuals who made promises to themselves at eighteen, twenty-one, and twenty-eight to reach the goals they had set. They set their sights high, devoted their energies, and through effort and determination succeeded at what they set out to do. There is nothing wrong with achievers and achievement; organizations owe much to those who have the courage and commitment to extend themselves. But a lifetime of setting and achieving goals shapes individuals as products of a musclebound willpower. They come subtly but inexorably to believe that they are masters of their own destiny.[1] It is no surprise, then, that these tendencies are widely applied to the organizations they manage, and explain our great appetite for techniques, control systems, and results.

Our study of Honda's Fujisawa, Ford's Petersen, or GE's Welch, however, suggest that these traits are not enough. These men grew with their jobs. Their growth was fueled by the habit of inquiry. Each problem they solved created the opportunity to solve the next problem that their last solution created. They displayed the characteristic of not just "having-the-answers" but of "living-in-the question."[2] They ask questions not merely to generate *answers* but to reveal *what is possible*. Rather than just "solve problems, they altered their relationship with problems to create larger opportunities for themselves and their companies.

Jack Welch knew that there were no easy answers when he traumatized

GE. He knew that though his cuts were essential to put GE on solid footing, he would have to cross his own burned bridges later when he sought to revitalize a frightened and demoralized organization. Fujisawa made R&D a separate tribe, realizing that eventually its independence would have to be reined in. We, too, need to develop a view of our work that is larger than the problems we face on the job.

A pattern has surfaced throughout the preceding chapters. Life doesn't follow straight-line logic; it conforms to a kind of curved logic that changes the nature of things and often turns them into their opposites.[3] Problems, then, are not just hassles to be dealt with and set aside. Lurking inside each problem is a workshop on the nature of organizations and a vehicle for personal growth. This entails a shift; we need to value the *process* of finding the solution—juggling the inconsistencies that meaningful solutions entail.

Where does this take us? Change, personal or organizational, has often been thought of as something one should embark on prudently, by small steps. Ford, the most dramatic example of a large-scale systems change in several decades, succeeded by a different route.

But changing everything does just that. It changes everything. It's nice when it works, but it is high risk, high reward. With discontinuous change, leadership leaps into the unknown. The one thing that is sure is that what's going to happen will affect people's lives—and very likely, the life of the organization. These choices are abstract; their results cannot be predicted. A general, about to capture a hill, may know that one-quarter of his men will die. He just doesn't know which quarter. When an executive, electing to *transform* an organization, can't get there with safe and reversible steps, he or she plows forward, altering old values, breaking the psychological contract with the past. Transformation is the managerial equivalent of a Rubic's Cube. If you go left first and right second, you come out in a different place than if you had moved right first and left second. The whole entity shifts.[4]

Contention and Creativity

Erik Hoffer has said, "The most gifted members of the human species are at their creative best when they cannot have their way."[5] Creativity and adaptation are born of tension, passion, and conflict. Contention does more than make us more creative. It makes us whole, it propels us along the journey of development. Psychologist Robert Johnson observes, "No aspect of the human psyche can live in a healthy state unless it is in tension with its opposite. Power without love becomes brutal; feeling without strength becomes sentimental."[6] Harold Geneen, having built ITT into this nation's largest conglomerate, stumbled because he failed to cultivate healthy opposites in both his own thinking and his organization's. This limitation in the thinking of leadership is most often the root cause of a company's demise.

There is no shortage of paradox and contention in the world around us. Trouble is, most people shield themselves from reality in one way or another. Staying in touch with what is *really* going on is the best way to force oneself to grow. The signs in the Las Vegas casinos have it right: *"You must be present to win."* The reason for being on the shop floor isn't to interfere, but to get grounded. Recall Fujisawa's managerial philosophy. He didn't deny himself a desk for show. He did it because he believed that by staying in touch with his organization he could more readily spot its deficiencies and his own.

Getting grounded is essential because it draws us into experience. If our experiences are far enough out of whack with our beliefs, we are forced to update our thinking. True, this is hard work, and we usually avoid it as long as possible. But experience usually prevails; *it is easier to act ourselves into a better mode of thinking than to think ourselves into a better mode of acting.* In Honda's early days, Fujisawa's behavior in asking probing questions of his subordinates led to a patterned way of thinking—The Honda Rational Thinking Method. Jack Welch's question-and-answer sessions with hundreds of employee groups drove him to articulate GE's Three Circle Strategy—which has since become a way of thinking.

Facing "reality" is a powerful stimulus for change. Remember your first times on a bicycle. How, you wondered, can I possibly balance on two narrow tires? The question made sense applied to the bike as a stationary object. But when you got on the bicycle, you *rode* it. *Experiencing* balance triggers a eureka: your mind shifted from a "stationary" to a "moving" concept of balance.

What had been missing before we rode the bicycle wasn't information (we had seen other kids on bicycles before) or knowledge (all this can be explained in physics); what was missing was doing it. We acted our way into the new paradigm by suspending disbelief and trying something that was counterintuitive. Trouble is, as we grow up, we don't allow ourselves enough space for *not knowing*.[7]

As life goes on, we increasingly live in our perception of what's "right," "wrong," "impossible," etc. instead of in what's real. Fortunately, life has a way of bringing us up short—if we are wise enough to take advantage of it. In the course of most careers—and lives—it inevitably happens that we clearly fail. This can be traumatic—and it is doubly so when we place too much faith in will. Not only do we lose the thing we wanted, but our whole frame of reference (i.e., that we can achieve any goal if we try hard enough) is shattered. Such setbacks, though, can stimulate self-questioning. The tragedy of adult life is that we are much more likely to fulfill our perceptions about how the world works than we are to fulfill our goals, ideals, and visions.[8] And this in turn shapes the destiny of our organizations. Think of Rolm, Tandem, Atari, and People Express and the other New Age companies that have fallen by the wayside. They were failed not by their vision and ideals but by managers who couldn't grow as the business did.

Realizing our possibilities as persons isn't about knowledge or information—it's about our own potential. This is not to say that education and study and discipline don't matter. They are necessary, but insufficient. The hazard is assigning too much importance to conscious intention. Most people are at their best when they are in a relationship with what is going on. Take your golf or tennis swing. When it is right, you are "in the groove." The growth that comes from working closely with master executives like Welch, Fujisawa, and Petersen stems from watching a person at home with his individuality. These are men who have fashioned a world in which being themselves matches their organization's needs. That's why they are hard to imitate. The trouble with "how to" books and biographies of famous executives (like *Iacocca* and *Trump: The Art of the Deal*) may be that they tantalize us with tips to make us more successful,[9] and distract us from our *own* possibilities. What's missing in these "how to" books and biographies is that people who really make things happen are standing in a different place.

This discussion brings us to a final point, namely that life is all about one's choice of paradigms. To the degree that you do not distinguish between the two, the possibility you are is confined by the *paradigm* you are. We see this behavior in a great executive like Jack Welch. Unlike his predecessors, Welch, who was appointed CEO at age forty-five, will probably occupy his position for twenty years. His first decade has done much to revitalize the company, but he needs a second act. Rather than doing an encore, Welch is reflecting on his managerial assumptions and their limitations and trying to enlarge his paradigm. Petersen does the same. Fujisawa did it over an entire lifetime.

The limitations we face in applying the ideas of this book are that none of the ideas work unless we do. As the German philosopher Martin Heidegger puts it: "We stand within the realm of that which hides itself."[10] Our quest isn't just a New Management Paradigm of the Nineties but a way of thinking that is continually open to the next paradigm and the next and the next. . . .

Employee Involvement at Ford

The hourly Employee Involvement process (EI) evolved into an eight-step model at Ford.

1. *Union and management commitment and support.* In Ford's case, this was confirmed by the participation of Pestillo and the union's leadership, and by their sharing of sensitive internal data. EI was formalized in the collective-bargaining agreement, and the company issued a policy statement on EI.

2. *Establishing a joint steering committee.* This entity was cochaired by the union leader and the plant manager.

3. *Diagnosis of problem areas for productive collaboration.* Here it was found useful to employ external consultants as well as to utilize an employee questionnaire. The major consulting firms had little success in selling their services to these joint committees. They were too dressed up, didn't talk straight, and were too conceptual. Ford ended up hiring smaller firms who did their homework, who were free-lancers, and whose rates were more competitive. The consultants worked with the Steering committees. While ostensibly engaged in identifying problem areas, they often contributed to building relationships and levels of trust. They helped the committee smoke out the points of conflict. They formally reported their findings to the Steering Committee (which was itself involved in some demanding encounters trying to become a group). The Steering committees met twice a month for a couple of months with a facilitator.

4. *Select pilot projects.* The selection was based on the diagnosis. During the diagnostic phase, the Steering committees were always canvassing for

volunteers. They developed some criteria: (a) don't start in a place that's apt to fail, (b) don't take on a problem when you don't have control over the key variables, (c) involve the plant controller on the Steering Committee to educate him on participation. (This helped reposition finance from its potential role of naysayer and watchdog.)

5. *Preparation of the organization.* The automotive industry generally, and Ford, in particular, were very austere in terms of staffing for change efforts of this type. Budgets had to be built from scratch to hire facilitators, train participants, and otherwise support the problem-solving groups. It cost $200,000 per plant to kick off the program in the first year. By far the largest cost was overtime associated with freeing people up. But this and R&D were the *only* things Ford spent money on. (Recall, it was losing $3.5 billion over this same time frame.) Overtime costs for EI (paid to hourly workers) totaled in the $1–2 million range during the first start-up year.

6. *Launching the pilot.* As noted, all of the candidate projects were volunteers. The Steering committees sought two or three voluntary problem-solving groups per plant whose identified problem areas were (1) challenging, (2) meaningful, and (3) had a reasonable chance of success.

Each pilot project needed a facilitator. The Steering committees initially drafted low-level facilitators from production supervision and quality control, and fifty or sixty from industrial relations staff jobs. They said: "Guess what? You're going to be the change agent." This first round of recruiting represented pretty careless staffing. Many didn't want to do it—didn't believe they could change anything. They were a pretty skeptical bunch. Remember, a plant manager at Ford is a grade 16. The facilitators were grade 6—equivalent to first-line supervisors. They felt they were brick #2945 at the base of a huge bureaucratic pyramid. Today the facilitator jobs (still grade 6) are highly sought after. People are waiting in line.

Initially, the facilitators reported directly to the plant manager. Now they report to the Steering committees. Ford has both hourly and salaried facilitators. They receive six to eight weeks of solid facilitation training each year. They travel nationally. Ford has seventy projects (i.e., living experiments) underway in each plant. This requires a lot of in-house facilitation capability.

A key first step in the "launch pilot" stage is venting—allowing participants to let off steam and see that it is legitimate to talk straight and say things out loud. But inevitably the group turns (with the facilitator's assistance) to the *key* step: moving on the complaints, arraying them as data, and deciding which you can do something about at your level. The triggering insight that leads to this breakthrough reads like this: "The whole world isn't filled by problems that have to be solved *above* your level. There is more to be done besides bitching." In time, each group identifies and prioritizes the things they believe they'll have some success in resolving.

These "buy-in" sessions were successful. In addition, Ford provided training sessions in three key skill areas:

1. Meeting management.
2. Problem-solving (not as sophisticated as the Japanese because Ford's people weren't as educated). The Japanese will wrestle with a problem for six months. Americans like closure, fast—and measure the sincerity of the plant manager by how quickly their ideas get implemented.
3. Listening.

Many of Ford's pilot projects and improvements were, and are, two-bit, small-time improvements. But they added up, and had enormous implications for quality of work life, as well as productivity. The employees got more data—quality data, performance data—which got them thinking about what they were doing and prioritizing, what was important, as plant management always had done. Now first-line managers and hourly employees began thinking this way. They were no longer victims.

When Ford embarked on EI, no one could use the word *productivity*. To many, the term meant "line speed-up," "screwing the worker," and so on. So, every effort was made to avoid that word. *Quality* was the goal all could agree on.

Today, most plants have problem-solving groups, and they generate their own projects. They are now comfortable with inviting managers in to generate ideas. However, there is a strong norm against a manager trying to manipulate a group by giving them "homework," or telling them what they have to do.

From the onset, the UAW insisted that EI projects stay outside the union's turf (i.e., health and safety issues). In fact, a lot of these issues get discussed. It used to be that any legitimate improvement in health or safety was used by the union to justify its existence—and by management as a negotiating chip. No one wanted the problem-solving groups in this territory. Now, a lot of low-level problems (such as oil slicks, dangerous machinery) get handled through the EI process.

When these groups really work, they strike a balance between economic and people issues.

7. *Evaluating and fine tuning.* This step is the major responsibility of the Steering committees. At Ford, EI just gathered steam. It is felt that if management had tried to evaluate it first, it would have evaluated the wrong things. They would have used regression equations. The academics who came to look at Ford's EI program were cynical about its impact—no matter how Ford measured it. The sponsors remembered all of the futile, brute empiricism of the 1960s—like trying to assess Headstart or Heroin Recidivism. That seemed unproductive. They looked for surrogate and motivationally valid indices. For example: Does management double the EI budget the second year? Is there a reduction in grievances? These involve very costly, no-win litigation procedures. (About 5 percent of Ford grievances are filed by employees who are trying to screw the system. These continue, but eliminating the other 95 percent, which involve the vast majority of the employees—who are not interested in playing games—is viewed as an incalculable saving.)

Ford believes that if they had devised measures before they started, they would have focused on what the group did during the one hour per week at the formal EI sessions and the payoff from those efforts. What they wouldn't have looked at is what the employees did the other thirty-nine hours a week. In fact, it is felt that the EI process has caused a dramatic, and indeed staggering, improvement in quality. The one hour a week in EI leverages the other thirty-nine hours a week, resulting in vastly improved performance. Climate surveys show that participants in EI groups swing from 30-percent believers to 80- to 90-percent believers in quality over a twelve-month experience. Ford's quality improvement has been 59 percent over three years, based on external audits. (Prior to that, quality improved 2 to 3 percent per year). Another measure: Ford has a good number of plant managers who have no predisposition to assign credit to EI. Many are notorious for building careers by taking credit for what *they* have done. A good many of these individuals are saying: "These are changes that I can't claim credit for. These belong to the guys on the plant floor."

8. *Generalization and diffusion.* Generalizing and spreading EI across an entire plant involves improving facilitator skills and getting management to change how it manages across an entire plant. Employees gauge the sincerity of management by the review process: (1) Is it timely? and (2) Are the suggestions either turned down or accepted? Ford had to establish an intermediate level, below the Steering Committee, to handle the flood of employee initiatives in the large plants. These review boards are staffed by managers. In general, middle managers bring a unique competence to the

table: How to position suggestions to obtain top management buy-in; how to use data to make a convincing case. Ford found that these intermediate review boards boosted the odds of an EI team's suggestions being implemented. Middle managers know how to touch bases and massage things through the system.

Diffusion at Ford has encountered an additional problem. In 1979 and 1980, the plants were way below capacity, and workers were hungry for overtime. Participation in EI didn't come at the cost of not doing something else. Today, with the plants booming again, it is much tougher for everyone to participate on problem-solving teams and put in additional EI overtime. The solution has taken a variety of forms. Basically, Ford went beyond EI. They use workers on all task forces in launching new cars, buying machinery, installing robotics, reconfiguring a plant, and so on. In short, ad hoc arrangements are appearing as part of the normal way of doing business. EI is becoming less a label and more a way of life in the company routine.

The Work-Out Process at General Electric

Step 1. *Tying Business Imperatives to Ineffective Work Practices*

The first hour of the Work-Out process is devoted to a review of the business strategy. It is essential to begin the process here since Work-Out is dedicated to enhancing a business's ability to achieve its strategy. This review addresses the major opportunities in the business and presents an update on the actions of the major competitors, the gaps, and current programs to close the gaps.

Step 2: *Enlisting Involvement in the Work-Out Process*

The question then asked is, "How much more effective would you be in achieving this strategy if all the impedances to your performance were eliminated?" The consensus from the ensuing discussion is usually 30 to 50 percent—a nontrivial number. The task for participants now becomes clear: How do we identify and eliminate the wasteful work practices?

Step 3: *Overview of Wasteful Work Practices*

Groups of five or six managers generate lists of wasteful work practices. Each is detailed in several paragraphs and these sheets (one for each practice) are posted on the wall. Subsequently, like practices are gathered together. The entire group assembles and each practice targeted for streamlining or elimination is discussed. If it is a complex matter entailing study, three questions are addressed. First, who needs to be involved to solve this? Second, what exactly are we trying to accomplish? And third, what resource data do we need to do it right?

Step 4: *Audit by Functional Groups*

Attendees now break into functional groups. The task is to identify internal impedances to their own work and those they impose on others. Findings are presented when participants reassemble. A process similar to that described in Step 3 ensues.

Step 5: *Audit by Cross-Functional Group*

Participants are now organized into cross-functional teams. The task is to identify specific work processes, procedures, and controls that hinder teamwork or that favor one function at the expense of others. Flip charts, posted on the wall, bear the name of each function, department, or division. Participants affix to the appropriate function the identified problems that most closely belong to it.

Step 6: *Contracting, Recommendations, and Wrap-Up*

Clear and specific *contracts* are now made for the elimination or streamlining of each work practice and the goals sought. Within two months, each function must report back to all participants on its recommendation on every work practice that was assigned to it. The business unit head presides at this session and is expected to agree with proposals or decline them for clearly stated reasons. These recommendations are compiled in a summary report. For a large business unit—such as GE's aircraft engine or appliance business—it is usually thirty to forty pages. A part-time staff person manages the paperwork.

Notes

INTRODUCTION

1. John Paul Newport, Jr., "A New Era of Rapid Rise and Ruin," *Fortune,* April 24, 1989, p. 77.
2. For a discussion of this general topic, see R. K. Clark, R. Hayes, and C. Lorenz, eds., *The Uneasy Alliance: Managing the Productivity-Technology Dilemma* (Boston: Harvard Business School Press, 1985), pp. 1–10; especially Richard E. Walton, "From Control to Commitment: Transforming Workforce Management in the United States," in *The Uneasy Alliance,* pp. 237–265.
3. W. R. Ashby, *An Introduction to Cybernetics* (New York: John Wiley & Sons, 1956); also Leonard Silk, "On Managing Creativity," *Business Month,* April 1989, p. 76.

CHAPTER ONE
UNLOCKING THE MYSTERY OF SELF-RENEWAL

1. Thomas Kuhn, *The Structure of Scientific Revolutions* (Chicago: University of Chicago Press, 1962); also Peter F. Drucker, *The Age of Discontinuity* (New York: Harper & Row, 1968), p. 141.
2. Kuhn, *The Structure.*
3. Thomas J. Peters and Robert H. Waterman, *In Search of Excellence* (New York: Harper & Row, 1982), pp. 19–24.
4. For a general discussion of this period of European history, see Barbara W. Tuchman, *A Distant Mirror* (New York: Knopf, 1978), pp. 25–39. Also Matt Clark, "Plagues, Man and History," *Newsweek,* May 9, 1988, pp. 65–66.
5. For a discussion of research methodology, see Richard T. Pascale, "Perspectives on Strategy: The Real Story Behind Honda's Success," *California Management Review,* Vol. XXVI, No. 3 (Spring 1984), p. 58.

6. Thomas Woodard, unpublished McKinsey staff paper for Network Systems, AT&T, Feb. 10, 1988.

7. As discussed in footnote, approximations of "popularity" are based on the frequency with which each of these fads was mentioned in *The New York Times, The Wall Street Journal* and the *Reader's Guide to Periodical Literature.* Owing to the increased amount of business reporting, a subjective "inflationary adjustment" was introduced for the periods 1975–80, 1981–85, and 1986–90.

8. John A. Byrne, "Business Fads: What's In—and Out," *Business Week,* Jan. 20, 1986, p. 53.

9. Wickham Skinner, "The Taming of Lions: How Manufacturing Leadership Evolved, 1970–1984," *The Uneasy Alliance,* pp. 78–79. Also see Alfred D. Chandler, Jr., *Strategy as Structure* (Cambridge, Mass.: MIT Press, 1962), and *The Visible Hand* (Cambridge, Mass.: Harvard University Press, 1977).

10. John Byrne, "Business Fads," pp. 51–61.

11. Jeremy Main, "The Trouble with Managing Japanese Style," *Fortune,* April 2, 1984, p. 50.

12. There is a great deal of commentary on this problem. See, e.g., James O'Toole, "Sic Transit Excellence," *Across the Board,* October 1986, pp. 5–7; also Ralph H. Kilmann, *Beyond the Quick Fix* (San Francisco: Jossey-Bass, 1984), and Robert B. Reich, *Tales of a New America* (New York: Times Books, 1987).

13. Paul R. Lawrence and Davis M. Dyer, *Renewing American Industry* (New York: Free Press, 1983), p. 51.

14. Roger Smith estimates that GM spent $60 billion on acquisitions, new plant, and automation; Roger Smith, "The U.S. Must Do as GM Has Done," *Fortune,* Feb. 13, 1989, p. 72. As of 1988, the market value of Nissan was $27 billion; Honda, $13.3 billion; and Toyota, $54.2 billion; source, "The Global 1000," *Business Week,* July 17, 1989.

15. See, e.g., the largely positive and optimistic account for People Express based on research by J. Richard Hackman, "The Transition that Hasn't Happened," *Managing Organizational Transitions,* John R. Kimberly and Robert E. Quinn, eds. (Homewood, Ill.: Richard D. Irwin, Inc., 1984); likewise see the generally optimistic outlook toward GM's transformation based on research in Rosabeth Moss Kanter, *The Change Masters* (New York: Simon and Schuster, 1983), p. 350. For examples of the media missing the boat, see Carrie Dolan, "Rolm's Merger Could Fulfill Its Dream of Fighting ATT on Equal Footing," *Wall Street Journal,* Sept. 27, 1984, p. 3; also P. Nulty, "People Express:

Champion of Cheap Airlines," *Fortune,* March 22, 1982, pp. 127–28; also P. Bernstein, "Atari and the Video Game Explosion," *Fortune,* July 27, 1981, pp. 40–46; S. H. Brown, "Fun Makes Money for Warner Communications," *Fortune,* April 4, 1974, pp. 120–25; "Warner Communications' Golden Possession," *Financial World,* Feb. 20, 1974, p. 15.

16. Otis Port, "Innovation in America," *Business Week,* July 1989, pp. 15–16.

17. There is a vast literature on the importance of coherence for successful organizational functioning. The classics include E. J. Miller and A. K. Rice, *Systems of Organization* (London: Tavistock Publications, 1967), and James D. Thompson, *Organizations in Action* (New York: McGraw Hill, 1967); also see Richard T. Pascale and Anthony G. Athos, *The Art of Japanese Management* (New York: Simon and Schuster, 1981), pp. 80–82.

18. The landmark work explicating the rationale for split (i.e., differentiation) as well as fit (integration) is Paul R. Lawrence and Jay W. Lorsch, *Organization and Environment* (Homewood, Ill.: Richard D. Irwin, Inc., 1969). More contemporary discussions usually focus on the advantages of splitting up large organizations. See Peters and Waterman, *In Search,* and George Gilder, *The Spirit of Enterprise* (New York: Simon and Schuster, 1984); also John A. Byrne, "Is Your Company Too Big?," *Business Week,* March 27, 1989, pp. 84–94.

19. While the literature on conflict and its management is abundant, no book has explicitly advanced a model that *embraces* conflict as a source of organizational renewal. Several books treat conflict and how it can be channeled constructively. For a refreshing treatment of the subject, see Thomas Crum, *The Magic of Conflict* (New York: Simon and Schuster, 1987); also see David A. Lax and James K. Sebenios, *The Manager as Negotiator* (New York: Free Press, 1986).

20. Several recent books build the case for transformation. See especially Robert E. Quinn and Kim S. Cameron, eds., *Paradox and Transformation* (Cambridge, Mass.: Ballinger Series, a subsidiary of Harper & Row, 1988). Also Kimberly and Quinn, *Managing.* For the interesting statistic "only 1/2 of one percent of American companies" are transformed, see Otis Port, "Innovation," p. 18; also see the pathbreaking discussion, Stanley M. Davis, "Transforming Organizations: The Key To Strategy Is Context," *Organizational Dynamics,* Winter 1982, pp. 64–80. Other good discussions of organizational transformation are covered in Kanter, *The Change Masters,* pp. 58–65; also Ikujira Non-

aka, "Creating Organizational Order out of Chaos: Self Renewal in Japanese Firms," *California Management Review*, Spring 1988, pp. 59–73: also Ralph H. Kilman and Teresa Joyce Corlin, *Corporate Transformation* (San Francisco: Jossey-Bass, 1988).

21. The argument for a coordinated attack on many fronts as a precondition for transformation is contained in Kanter, *The Change Masters*, pp. 278–306 and 350.

22. A vast number of accounts of Honda support this view. See Ikujiro Nanaka, "Toward Middle-Up-Down Management," *Sloan Management Review*, Spring 1988, pp. 9–18; also see charts in Marvin B. Lieberman, "Learning by Doing and Dynamic Industrial Competitiveness," *INSEAD Research Symposium on Issues in International Manufacturing*, Sept. 1987 [Honda outperforms all firms on the four indices utilized]. Also Stewart Toy et al., "The Americanization of Honda," *Business Week*, April 25, 1988; also Gary Vasilash, "Honda Is World-Class in Ohio," *Production*, July 1988; also John Merwin, "A War of Two Worlds," *Forbes*, June 16, 1986, pp. 101–6; also Faye Rice, "America's New No. 4 Automaker—Honda," *Fortune*, Oct. 28, 1985, pp. 30–33; also Steven Thompson, "The Rise and Rise of Honda," *Auto Week*, Feb. 13, 1989.

23. Internal competitive data provided by Honda, Tokyo, March 9, 1987, and also see Ken-Ichi Imai, Ikujiro Nanaka, and Hirotaka Takeuchi, "Managing the New Product Development Process: How Japanese Companies Learn and Unlearn," Clark et al. *The Uneasy Alliance*, pp. 333–75, and Richard J. Schonberger, *Japanese Production Techniques* (New York: Free Press, 1982).

24. A variety of excellent studies have reported on the system which drives innovation at Honda. See Koichi Shimokawa, *Honda's Entry into the World Wide Automotive Market* (Cambridge, Mass.: Harvard Business School Press, 1978), pp. 305–13. See also Roxanne Guillemette, "Innovation in Japan," unpublished dissertation, June 1987. Also Brian Dumaine, "Speed," *Fortune*, Feb. 17, 1989, pp. 54–59.

25. J. D. Power, *Annual Automotive Survey* (Westlake, Calif.: J. D. Power Publications, 1986, 1987, 1988).

26. Henry Scott Stokes, "Honda, the Market Guzzler," *Fortune*, Feb. 20, 1984, pp. 105–8; also Honda internal data based on Honda, Tokyo interviews.

27. Interviews at Honda, Tokyo, Sept. 29, 1988, March 9–11, 1987; America Honda Sales, Compton, Calif., Feb. 7, 1987; Honda, Marysville, June 9, 1987; interview with Shoichiro Irimajiri, president, American Honda, April 15, 1988, Palo Alto, Calif.

28. Interview with Takeo Fujisawa, Tokyo, Japan, March 16, 1987; also see Tetsua Sakiya, *Honda's Motor: The Men, the Management, the Machines* (Tokyo: Kodansha, 1982).
29. Interview with Fujisawa, March 16, 1987; also see Sakiya, *Honda's Motor*.
30. Interview with Fujisawa, March 16, 1987; also see Sakiya, *Honda's Motor*.
31. Frederick W. Taylor, *The Principles of Scientific Management* (New York and London: Harper, 1929); for an excellent and balanced discussion of Taylor's ideas, see Kim B. Clark and Robert H. Hayes, "Recapturing America's Manufacturing Heritage," *California Management Review*, Summer 1988, pp. 15–20.
32. Interview with Konosuke Matsushita, Osaka, Japan, Sept. 3, 1982.
33. This assertion is based upon three factors: IBM's size (revenues, assets, number of employees), its continued high ranking in the major polls of "most admired companies," and the extended period (65 years) over which it has held its leadership position. See D. Quinn Mills, *The IBM Lesson* (New York: Times Books, 1988); also Patricia Sellers, "America's Most Admired Corporations," *Fortune*, Jan. 7, 1985, pp. 18–30; Cynthia Hutton, same title, *Fortune*, Jan. 6, 1986, pp. 16–27; Carol Davenport, same title, *Fortune*, Jan. 30, 1989, pp. 68–94. (These rankings are based on polls of 8,000 senior executives, outside directors, and financial analysts. Eight attributes were scaled 0 (poor) to 10 (excellent). IBM held the top spot 1982–83, ranked no. 2 in 1986, dropped out of the top ten in 1987–89 during restructuring and is trending toward the top position.)
34. William O. Ingle, casewriter, "The IBM 360: Giant as Entrepreneur," Harvard Business School case study (Cambridge, Mass.: Harvard Business School Case Services, 1968).
35. James Chposky and Ted Leonis, *Blue Magic: The People, Power, and Politics Behind the IBM Personal Computer* (New York: Facts on File, 1988), p. 206.
36. Interviews at IBM, Armonk, New York, May 26, 1982 and Dec. 4, 1985; also Richard T. Pascale, "Recruitment and Socialization at IBM," unpublished, November 3, 1983.
37. Interviews at IBM, 1982 and 1985.
38. Aaron Bernstein, "How IBM Cut 16,200 Employees Without an Ax," *Business Week*, Feb. 15, 1988, p. 98.
39. The best-known example is Donald Estridge, late president of Entry Systems Division, and his team. See Chposky and Leonis, *Blue Magic*.
40. Interviews at IBM, Dec. 4, 1985, May 19, 1986, and Sept. 9–10, 1987.

41. Interviews at IBM, 1985, 1986, 1987.
42. Mills, *The IBM Lesson*.
43. Other scholars have grappled with these shifts from an older model to a future one. See Kanter, *The Change Masters,* pp. 42–43, especially chart on traditional vs. emerging design factors.
44. Douglas McGregor, *The Human Side of Enterprise* (New York: McGraw-Hill, 1960); also Douglas McGregor, *The Professional Manager* (New York: McGraw-Hill, 1967).
45. William B. Ouchi, *Theory Z* (Reading, Mass.: Addison-Wesley, 1981).
46. I am indebted to Anthony G. Athos for this example.
47. See for example Thomas J. Peters and Nancy K. Austin, *A Passion for Excellence* (New York: Random House, 1985); also Thomas J. Peters, *Thriving on Chaos* (New York: Random House, 1988); and Thomas J. Peters and Robert H. Waterman, *In Search of Excellence*.
48. Peters and Waterman, *In Search of Excellence*.

CHAPTER TWO
THE FIT/SPLIT PARADOX

1. Pascale and Athos, *The Art of Japanese Management*. Underlying the more general treatment of Japanese management in this book are a considerable number of technical papers written by Richard Pascale and his coauthors over several years. Listed in chronological order, these are:

"Made in America (Under Japanese Management)," with William Ouchi, *Harvard Business Review,* Sept.–Oct. 1974.

"The Adaptation of Japanese Subsidiaries in the United States," *Columbia Journal of World Business,* Vol. 12, No. 7 (Spring 1977).

"Communication and Decision Making Across Cultures: Japanese and American Comparisons," *Administrative Science Quarterly,* April 1978.

"Personnel Practices and Employee Attitudes: A Study of Japanese and American Managed Firms in the United States," *Human Relations,* Vol. 31, No. 7 (1978).

"Zen and the Art of Management," *Harvard Business Review,* March–April 1978.

"Communication, Decision Making and Implementation among Managers in Japanese and American Managed Companies in the United States," with Mary Ann Maguire, *Sociology and Social Research,* Vol. 63 (1978), No. 1.

"Comparison of Selected Work Factors in Japan and the United States," with Mary Ann Maguire, *Human Relations,* Vol. 31, No. 7 (July 1980).

2. For a discussion of the Seven S's see Pascale and Athos, *The Art,* pp. 80–82; also Robert H. Waterman, *The Renewal Factor* (New York: Bantam Books, 1987), p. 57.
3. Robert Johnson, "Fast-Food Chains Draw Criticism for Marketing Fare as Nutritional," *Wall Street Journal,* April 6, 1987, p. 27.
4. Interviews at Federal Express (internal competitive analysis of UPS), Memphis, Tenn., Feb. 14, 1989. Also see Kenneth Labich, "Big Changes at Big Brown," *Fortune,* Jan. 18, 1988, pp. 56–64; also Daniel Machalaba, "United Parcel Service Gets Deliveries Done by Driving Its Workers: But Its Vaunted Efficiency's Now to Be Challenged by an Automated Rival," *Wall Street Journal,* April 22, 1986, pp. 1 and 26.
5. Interviews of McDonald's franchisees, February–March 1987; also Robert Johnson, "McDonald's Combines a Dead Man's Advice with Lively Strategy," *Wall Street Journal,* Dec. 18, 1987, pp. 1 and 13; also see Penny Moser, "The McDonald's Mystique," *Fortune,* July 4, 1988, pp. 112–16.
6. Chposky and Leonis, *Blue Magic,* p. 209. For a broader discussion of the pros of split, see Michael Tushman and David Nadler, "Organizing for Innovation," *California Management Review,* Spring 1986, Vol. 28, Nov. 3, pp. 74–92; also Bill Saporito, "Companies that Compete Best," *Fortune,* May 22, 1989, p. 39, and Robert B. Reich, "Entrepreneurship Reconsidered: The Team as Hero," *Harvard Business Review,* May–June 1987, pp. 77–83.
7. Jeremy Main, "The Winning Organization," *Fortune,* Sept. 26, 1988, p. 50, and Joel Dreyfuss, "Reinventing IBM," *Fortune,* Aug. 19, 1988, pp. 30–39.
8. Alfred Chandler, *Strategy and Structure.*

9. E. L. Ginzberg and George Vojta, *Beyond Human Scale: The Large Corporation at Risk* (New York: Basic Books, 1985). Also anon., "Centralization vs. Decentralization," unpublished internal study of 26 companies. (McKinsey Organizational Practice, Yountville, Calif., Organizational Effectiveness Workshop, Nov. 16–21, 1980.) McKinsey tracked 18 client companies in the aftermath of decentralization; two thirds recentralized within five years and did not feel that they realized major benefits from decentralization. For a discussion of how split led to overreliance on financial reporting, see Kim B. Clark and Robert H. Heyes, "Recapturing America's Manufacturing Heritage," *California Management Review*, Vol. 30, No. 4 (Summer 1988), pp. 27–31.

10. E. F. Schumacher, *Small Is Beautiful* (New York: Harper & Row, 1973).

11. Gifford Pinchot III, *Intrapreneuring* (New York: Harper & Row, 1985).

12. Ginzberg and Vojta, *Beyond Human Scale*.

13. Michael J. Piore and Charles F. Sabel, *The Second Industrial Divide* (New York: Basic Books, 1984).

14. Peter F. Drucker, *The Age of Discontinuity*, pp. 54–57 and 188–211.

15. Table 2–1 is based on three sources: Intel internal data; SIA Public Information: "Crisis in a Critical Industry," Washington, D.C., Sept. 28, 1988; and Data Quest, March 7, 1989. Also see Richard Foster, *Innovation* (New York: Summit Books, 1986), p. 133.

16. National Science Foundation, "International Science and Technical Data Update" (Washington, D.C., National Science Foundation, 1984).

17. Telephone interviews at Dana, May 27, 1987.

18. Interviews at 3M, St. Paul, Minn., Jan. 24, 1986. Also see Russell Mitchell, "Masters of Innovation," *Business Week*, April 10, 1989; anon., *Our Story So Far* (St. Paul: Minnesota Mining and Manufacturing Co., 1977); and Virginia Huck, *Brand of the Tartan: The 3M Story* (New York: Appleton-Crofts, 1955).

19. Interview with Dean Tombs, former VP at Texas Instruments, March 10, 1987; also see "Texas Instruments Show U.S. Business How to Survive in the Eighties," *Business Week*, Sept. 18, 1978; and Eugene W. Helms, "The OST System for Managing Innovation at Texas Instruments," an address to the Armed Forces Management Association, April 7, 1971.

20. Peters and Austin, *A Passion*, p. 187.

21. Interviews at Hewlett-Packard, July 1985, December 1985, January–February 1986, and April 1988.

22. Interviews at HP, 1985, 1986, 1988. Also see Bro Uttal, "Delays and Defections at Hewlett-Packard," *Fortune,* Oct. 29, 1984, p. 62; Bro Uttal, "Mettle Test Time for John Young," *Fortune,* April 29, 1985, pp. 242–48; and Peter Waldman, "Hewlett-Packard, Citing Software Snag, Will Delay New Computer Six Months," *Wall Street Journal,* Sept. 26, 1986, p. 2.

CHAPTER THREE
VECTORS OF CONTENTION

1. This point is argued by M. L. Tushman and E. Romanelli, "Organization Evolution: A Metamorphosis Model of Convergence and Reorientation," *Research in Organizational Behavior,* Vol. 7, B. Staw and E. Cummings, eds. (Greenwich, Conn.: JAI Press, 1985). Some authors propose that a new paradigm is emerging to replace the "old." One limitation of such discussions is that the new paradigm is posited to be the opposite of the old rather than (as proposed in the book) inclusive of the old plus something more. See D. Clark, "Emerging Paradigms in Organizational Theory and Research," in *Organizational Theory and Inquiry: The Paradigmatic Revolution,* Y. Lincoln, ed. (Beverly Hills, Calif.: Sage, 1986). See also Jeffrey D. Ford and Robert W. Backoff, "Organizational Change In and Out of Dualities," pp. 81–121; also Chris Argyris, "Crafting a Theory of Practice," pp. 255–278, and Quinn and Cameron, Paradox and Translation: A Framework For Rethinking Organization and Management," pp. 289–308, all in Quinn and Cameron, *Paradox and Transformation.*
2. The argument made here is succinctly stated by Kenwyn K. Smith, "Rabbits, Lynxes, and Organizational Transitions," Kimberly and Quinn, *Managing Organizational Transitions,* p. 272. He states:

> For the past three decades there have been many attempts to understand planned organizational changes and, since Ashby (1956), Katz and Kahn (1966), Miller and Rice (1967), Thompson (1967) and von Bertalanffy (1968), a rich set of metaphors have been borrowed from open systems theory. In many ways it would make sense for us to attempt to formulate our images of transitions in terms congruent with the systems theory we learned to apply from the biological sciences: inputs, throughputs, and exports; the cyclical nature of system activities; the concept of dynamic homeostasis; the tendency of systems to become increasingly differentiated; and the view that systems are equifinal

(Katz and Kahn, 1966). These basic concepts, fruitfully augmented by the role of boundary systems as articulated by Rice (1969) and elaborated by Alderfer (1976), would seem the most logical place to start.

But there's a snag.

Since the late 1960s there has been a quiet revolution taking place in scientific thought, especially as it relates to evolution and the dynamics of change. Long-standing beliefs in principles such as the "survival of the fittest" have crumbled. Hence, if we wish to draw on metaphors from man's knowledge of the universe and from theories of evolution it is necessary first to appreciate the theories that are replacing those we've relied on for years. Although these new theories are still in their embryo they contain great potential for radically different types of thinking. I refer to the theory of dissipative structures developed first by Prigogine (1967) in the field of chemistry but now applied to a wide range of disciplines, from biology to sociology, from embryology to consciousness (Jantsch, 1976; Bateson, 1979; Jantsch, 1980).

Also W. R. Ashby, *An Introduction to Cybernetics* (New York: John Wiley & Sons, 1956); D. Katz and R. L. Kahn, *The Social Psychology of Organization)* (New York: John Wiley & Sons, 1966); E. J. Miller and A. K. Rice, *Systems of Organization;* Thompson, *Organizations;* Ludwig von Bertalanffy, *General Systems Theory, Foundations, Development, Applications* (New York: Braziller, 1968); I. Prigogine, "Order Through Fluctuation: Self Organization and Social System," *Evolution and Consciousness,* E. Jantsch and C. H. Waddington, eds. (Reading, Mass.: Addison-Wesley, 1976); E. Jantsch, *The Self Organizing Universe* (New York: Paragon Press, 1980).

3. Prigogine, *Order Through Fluctuation,* and Jantsch, *The Self Organizing Universe.*
4. This finding conforms to the discussion by Stuart Albert, "A Delete Design Model for Successful Transitions," in Quinn and Cameron, eds., *Paradox and Transformation,* p. 169; also K. Smith, "Rabbits," p. 279.
5. Ford's turnaround is discussed in Chapters Five and Six of this volume. A discussion of IBM's revitalization is presented in Mills, *The IBM Lesson.* For DEC, see R. Pascale, "Interviews at DEC," unpublished working paper, Cambridge, Mass., July 16–Feb. 22, 1988. For Federal Express, see Brian Dumaine, "Turbulence Hits The Air Couriers," *Fortune,* July 21, 1986, pp. 101–6; Larry Reibstein, "Federal Express Faces Challenges to Its Grip on Overnight Delivery," *Wall Street Journal,* Jan. 8, 1988, pp. 1 and 8; Dean Foust, "Why Federal Express Has

Got Overnight Anxiety," *Business Week,* Nov. 3, 1987; Scott Ticer, "Why Zap Mail Got Zapped," *Business Week,* Oct. 15, 1986, pp. 48–49. For Honda, see Sakiya, *Honda's Motor,* pp. 94–99.

6. For more theoretical treatment of dialectic and trialectics, see Michael P. Thompson, "Being Thought and Action," in Quinn and Cameron, eds. *Paradox and Transformation,* pp. 125–35; also see Jeffrey D. Ford and Robert W. Bockoff, "Organization Change In and Out of Dualities and Paradox," pp. 81–121.

7. See, in particular, Henry Mintzberg and James A. Waters, "Of Strategies, Deliberate and Emergent," unpublished (McGill University, January 1983); also Henry Mintzberg, "Crafting Strategy," *Harvard Business Review,* July–August 1987, pp. 65–75; also Daniel J. Isenberg, "The Tactics of Strategic Opportunism," *Harvard Business Review,* March-April 1987, pp. 92–97. For a good overall description of the strategy-making process, see Joseph L. Bower, *Managing the Resource Allocation Process* (Cambridge, Mass.: Division of Research, Graduate School of Business Administration, Harvard University, 1970).

8. Lawrence and Lorsch, *Organization and Environment.*

9. See Robert Quinn and John Kimberly, "Paradox, Planning and Perseverance: Guidelines for Managerial Practice," in *Managing Organization Transitions,* pp. 295–314.

10. For this breakthrough notion of strategy as context, see Stanley M. Davis, "Transforming Organizations: The Key to Strategy Is Context," *Organizational Dynamics,* pp. 64–80.

11. Davis, "Transforming Organizations," p. 65. Also Robert A. Burgleman, "Corporate Context and the Concept Strategy," unpublished (Palo Alto: Stanford Graduate School of Business Administration, 1988).

12. This account is represented in Pascale, "Perspectives on Strategy: The Real Story Behind Honda's Success," *California Management Review,* p. 52; also Sakiya, *Honda's Motor,* p. 73.

13. Pascale, "Perspectives," p. 52.

14. Pascale, "Perspectives," pp. 52–53.

15. Pascale, "Perspectives," pp. 52–53.

16. Pascale, "Perspectives," p. 53.

17. Pascale, "Perspectives," pp. 54–56.

18. Pascale, "Perspectives," p. 56.

19. Pascale, "Perspectives," pp. 56–57.

20. Interviews at Honda. See Chapter One, note 20.

21. Pascale and Athos, *The Art,* pp. 58–78.
22. Interview with Paul Van Orden, senior VP, General Electric, Fairfield, Conn., Feb. 20, 1986.
23. Marriott Annual Reports, 1985–1988.
24. For example, see "Woo the Secretary and Win the Boss," *Business Week,* Sept. 11, 1965; "Hyatt International: Growth Through Management Services," *Cornell Hotel & Restaurant Quarterly,* February 1977, pp. 36–43; anon., Hyatt Hotels, "Putting Out The Welcome Mat for a Broader Clientele," *Business Week,* Oct. 13, 1983, pp. 68–70; and Ford S. Worthy, "The Pritzkers," *Fortune,* April 25, 1988, pp. 164–78.
25. Marriott internal memo, April 1984.
26. Interview with former staff member of Marriott New Product Development Group, November 1985; also see press releases four years later confirming the long delay and roll-out that was foreseen in 1985 memo. Also Roger Lowenstein, "Marriott Is Planning to Invest $500 Million to Launch Nationwide Chain of Low-Priced Motels," *Wall Street Journal,* Sept. 8, 1988, p. 4.
27. Interviews at Honda. See Chapter One, note 20.
28. Interview with former AT&T senior executive, New York, Nov. 1987.
29. Interviews with current and former Macy's sales personnel, San Francisco, October 1988; also see Isadore Barmash, "Macy's Loaded with Debt Loses $19 Million in Quarter," *New York Times,* Dec. 15, 1988, pp. C1 and C2; also Manu Parpia, "Macy's California," Harvard Business School case study (Cambridge, Mass.: Harvard Business School Case Services, August 1986); also John Greer, "Macy's Tough Battle to Stay on Top," *San Francisco Chronicle,* Dec. 15, 1986, pp. 19–26; and Martha Groves, "A New Face for Bullocks: Macy's Raises Eyebrows by Trying to Recast Chain into Own Image," *Los Angeles Times,* Feb. 23, 1982, Part 4, p. 1.
30. Interviews with Nordstrom's sales and managerial personnel, San Francisco, Oct. 15, 1988.
31. Interviews at Macy's. See note 29.
32. Interview with Marriott Hotel management, Los Angeles, Jan. 8, 1987.
33. Interview with Marriott management, Jan. 8, 1987.
34. Warren Bennis and Bert Nanus, *Leaders: The Strategies For Taking Charge* (New York: Harper & Row, 1985), p. 21.
35. Remarks by R. S. Miller to Financial Executive Institute, Chicago, Jan. 19, 1984; also Alexander L. Taylor, "Iacocca's Tightrope Act," *Time,* March 21, 1983, pp. 50–61; Steven Flax, "Can Chrysler Keep Rolling Along?," *Fortune,* Jan. 7, 1985, pp. 34–39.

36. Interviews at Chrysler, Detroit, March 5, April 21, and Oct. 5, 1983, and Jan. 19, 1989.

37. Interviews at Chrysler, 1983 and 1989.

38. Interviews at Chrysler, fall 1988.

39. Interviews at Intel, Santa Clara, Calif., Aug. 27–30, 1986, Nov. 18, 1986, fall 1988.

40. Interviews at Intel, 1986 and 1988. See also a variety of articles and Intel releases: John Markoff, "Powerful New Chip Ready to Be Introduced," *New York Times,* Feb. 27, 1989, p. C1, and Richard Brandt and Otis Port, "Intel: The Next Revolution," *Business Week,* Sept. 26, 1988. For further insight into Grove's philosophy and style, see Andrew Grove, *High Output Management* (New York: Random House, 1983); and Andrew Grove, *One-on-One with Andy Grove: How to Manage Your Boss, Yourself, and Your Co-Workers* (New York: G. P. Putnam's Sons, 1987).

41. Interviews at Intel, fall 1988.

42. Interviews at Intel, fall 1988.

43. Interviews with Konosuke Matsushita and others of Matsushita Electric Co., Osaka, Japan, September 1982. For a good biography of Thomas Watson, Jr., see Robert Sobel, *IBM: Colossus in Transition* (New York: Times Books, 1981); also Thomas Watson, Jr., "A Business and Its Beliefs," McKinsey Foundation Lecture Series, Graduate School of Business, Columbia University (New York: McGraw Hill, 1963); also "The Greatest Capitalist in History," *Fortune,* August 31, 1987, pp. 24–35.

44. Interviews at Ford Motor Company, Dearborn, Michigan, July 19, 1988; also Gregg Easterbrook, "Ford Revs Up," *Washington Monthly,* October, 1986, and Robert England, "Ford Shifts Gears for Road to Riches," *Insight,* July 13, 1987.

45. Sakiya, *Honda's Motor.*

46. Interviews at Hewlett-Packard, Palo Alto, Calif., fall 1985.

47. Interviews at Sun Microsystems, Palo Alto, Calif., July 12–27 and Aug. 11, 1989; also see Brenton R. Schlender, "Computer Maker Aims to Transform Industry and Be a Giant," *Wall Street Journal,* March 18, 1988, pp. 1 and 7; also Stuart Gannes, "Sun's Sizzling Race to the Top," *Fortune,* Aug. 17, 1987, pp. 88–91.

48. Interview with David Quarmby and David Sainsbury, London, May 24, 1989.

49. Interviews with Jack Welch, Fairfield, Conn., September 1989.

50. Interviews at Apple, Cupertino, Calif., April 8 and May 20, 1988; also

see Brian O'Reilly, "Apple Computer's Risky Revolution," *Fortune,* May 8, 1989, pp. 75–84.

51. Interviews at Hewlett-Packard. See note 46.
52. Interviews with Ross Perot and Mort Meyerson, Dallas, spring 1986, and interviews at corporate offices, Detroit, May 29–30, 1986.
53. Interviews at AT&T, Basking Ridge, New Jersey, fall 1987.
54. Chapter Nine includes an extensive discussion of the dark side of socialization. See also Richard T. Pascale, "Recruitment and Socialization at Proctor & Gamble," unpublished working paper, Nov. 3, 1982.
55. Interviews at Apple, April 8 and May 20, 1988.
56. Interviews at Apple, April 8 and May 20, 1988.
57. Erik Jacobsen, *NUMMI: A Model in Human Relations,* thesis written at Buick-Oldsmobile-Cadillac (Detroit: GMI Engineering and Management Institute, Sept. 12, 1986).
58. Karl Weick, *The Social Psychology of Organizing* (Reading, Mass.: Addison-Wesley, 1969).
59. See Robert Rehder, "Organizational Transformation: The GM Fremont Plant," unpublished (University of New Mexico, June 1986); also interviews with GM employees and executives, Palo Alto, winter–spring 1986, and Detroit, May 29, 1986.
60. Interview with Steven Bera, former GM employee and Manager of Materials an NUMMI, July 27, 1986.
61. Interview with Bera.
62. Interviews with GM executives and employees.
63. Steven Bera, "The Japanization of Steve," unpublished working paper (Detroit, spring 1985); also interview with Bill Barton, GM manager assigned to NUMMI, Fremont, Calif., April 28, 1987; and Jacobsen, *NUMMI,* pp. 12–14.
64. Jacobsen, *NUMMI* pp. 13–14. For a more general discussion supporting this anecdote, see Marvin Lieberman, "When Does Union-Management Cooperation Work? A Look at NUMMI and GM-Van Nuys," unpublished paper for conference Can California Be Competitive and Caring?, UCLA, May 6, 1988.
65. Interviews with employees and executives.
66. J. A. Langenfeld, "NUMMI Management Practices: A Report of the General Motors Study Team," unpublished, April 9, 1986.
67. David J. Morrow, "How to Quit Losing in the Olympics," *Fortune,* April 29, 1989, p. 266.
68. Pascale and Athos, *The Art,* pp. 192–99.
69. Pascale and Athos, *The Art.*

70. Conversation with Tom Woodard, Basking Ridge, N.J., spring 1988.
71. Anthony Biano, "The Sad Saga of Western Union's Decline," *Business Week,* Dec. 14, 1987, pp. 108–14.
72. Stanley M. Davis, *Future Perfect* (Reading, Mass.: Addison-Wesley, 1987), pp. 16–20.
73. See Don Dunn, "So You Wanna Be in Pictures?," *Business Week,* Aug. 22, 1988, pp. 102–3; Ron Grover, "Michael Eisner's Hit Parade," *Business Week,* Feb. 1, 1988, p. 27; Bill Powell, "Hollywood's New Hardline," *Newsweek,* Aug. 15, 1988, p. 40; and Charles Leersen, "How Disney Does It," *Newsweek,* April 3, 1989, pp. 49–54.
74. Dean Rotbart and Laurie D. Cohen, "About Face: The Party Isn't Quite So Lively as Recruiting Falls Off," *Wall Street Journal,* Oct. 6, 1986, p. 1; also Kate Ballen, "Get Ready for Shopping at Work," *Fortune,* Feb. 15, 1988, pp. 95–98.
75. Interviews at Hewlett-Packard.
76. Interviews at Coca-Cola, Atlanta, spring 1986.
77. Excerpts from Japanese haiku: Murakami Kijo, "On Buddha's Face . . . ," *Modern Japanese Haiku, An Anthology,* Makoto Ueda, ed. (Toronto: University of Toronto Press, 1976), p. 91.
78. Interviews with officers at J. P. Morgan, New York, spring and July 1984.
79. This argument is made in part by Miller and Freisen, who note that "no type of structure can remove the need for periodic restructuring"; see Danny Miller and Peter H. Freisen, "Momentum and Revolution in Organizational Adaptation," *Academy of Management Journal,* Vol. 23, December 1980, pp. 591–614; also Miller and Freisen, "Structural Change and Performance," *Academy of Management Journal,* Vol. 25, No. 4, December 1982, pp. 867–92.

CHAPTER FOUR
DISTURBING EQUILIBRIUM

1. See Kuhn, *The Structure of Scientific Revolutions;* also see Fritjof Capra, "Paradigms and Paradigm Shifts," presentations and discussions from a symposium sponsored by the Elmwood Institute, Big Sur, Calif., Nov. 29–Dec. 4, 1985, reprinted in *ReVISION,* Vol. 9, No. 1 (Spring 1986), p. 11.
2. For a helpful and extremely readable discussion of paradigms see Joel

Barker, *Discovering the Future: The Business of Paradigms* (St. Paul, Minn.: ILI Press, 1985), pp. 20–22.

3. There are a wide number of contemporary books on modern physics. One of the most provocative and readable is Gary Zukav, *The Dancing Wu Li Masters* (New York: Morrow, 1979), pp. 18–41.

4. Zukav, *The Dancing Wu Li,* pp. 77–78, 281–285; also Daniel Garber, "Science and Certainty in Descartes," in Michael Hooker, ed., *Descartes* (Baltimore: Johns Hopkins Press, 1978).

5. Zukav, *The Dancing Wu Li,* pp. 77–78; also David Bohm, *Quantum Theory* (New York: Prentice Hall, 1951).

6. Zukav, *The Dancing Wu Li,* pp. 255–83.

7. Zukav, *The Dancing Wu Li,* p. 28.

8. Fritjof Capra, *The Turning Point* (New York: Simon and Schuster, 1982), p. 15; also see Capra, *The Tao of Physics* (Berkeley: Shambala, 1975).

9. Rosabeth Moss Kanter, *Commitment and Community: Communes and Utopias in Sociological Perspective* (Cambridge, Mass.: Harvard University Press, 1972).

10. This point is well argued in Skinner, "The Productivity Paradox," pp. 63–101; also George Lodge and Bruce Scott, "Rules of the Game," *Harvard Business School Bulletin,* June 1984, pp. 53–64; and Norman Jonas, "Can America Compete?," *Business Week,* April 20, 1987, pp. 45–47. Also see statement by Robert H. Hayes, "It's like congratulating ourselves for finishing a race second to last," in Richard I. Kirkland, Jr., "America on Top Again," *Fortune,* April 15, 1985, p. 138.

11. *Made in America,* the report of MIT's Commission on Industrial Productivity (Cambridge, Mass.: MIT Press, 1989).

12. Michael J. Piore and Charles F. Sabel, *The Second Industrial Divide* (New York: Basic Books, 1984), pp. 134, 222–23, and 247.

13. Richard Rosecrance, *The Rise of the Trading State* (New York: Basic Books, 1986), pp. 143–49; also Piore and Sabel, *The Second.*

14. A great many sources reaffirm the point. See Rosecrance, *The Rise,* p. 145, and Piore and Sabel, *The Second,* pp. 134–37; also Drucker, *The Age of Discontinuity,* pp. 3–41, and Alfred D. Chandler, "From Industrial Labs to Departments of R&D," *The Uneasy Alliance,* pp. 53–61.

15. See, e.g., Chandler, *Visible Hand*; also Piore and Sabel, *The Second,* p. 49.

16. Piore and Sabel, *The Second,* p. 49.

17. Chandler, *Visible Hand.*

18. Drucker, *The Age of Discontinuity*, pp. 82–83.
19. Drucker, *The Age;* also Chandler, *Visible Hand.*
20. Drucker, *The Age.*
21. Drucker, *The Age;* also Nathan Rosenberg, "The Commercial Exploitation of Science by American Industry," Clark et al., *The Uneasy Alliance*, pp. 14–51.
22. Piore and Sabel, *The Second*, pp. 52–72; also Rosenberg, "The Commercial," p. 51.
23. Chandler, *Visible Hand.*
24. Chandler, *Visible Hand;* also Rosenberg, "The Commercial."
25. Chandler, *Visible Hand.*
26. See Robert H. Hayes and Kim B. Clark, "Exploring the Sources of Productivity Differences at the Factory Level," Clark et al., *The Uneasy Alliance*, pp. 151–99; also Walton, "From Control," pp. 237–77.
27. Walton, "From Control."
28. Walton, "From Control."
29. Walton, "From Control." See also Pascale and Athos, *The Art*, pp. 177–99.
30. Chandler, *Visible Hand;* also Piore and Sabel, *The Second*, pp. 111–20.
31. Chandler, *Visible Hand.*
32. Chandler, *Visible Hand.*
33. Walton, "From Control," p. 237.
34. Piore and Sabel, *The Second;* also Rosecrance, *The Rise.*
35. This table is drawn from over twenty sources. For an overview, see John Jewkes, *Sources of Invention* (London: Macmillan; New York: St. Martin's Press, 1958); J. D. Bernal, *Science and Industry in the 19th Century* (London: Routledge and Kegan Paul, 1953); Victor S. Clark, *History of Manufactures in the United States* (New York: McGraw-Hill, 1929); Edward De Bono, *Eureka* (New York: Holt, Rinehart and Winston, 1974); Anthony Feldman and Peter Ford, *Scientists and Inventions* (New York: Facts on File, 1979); Valerie-Anne Giscard D'Estaing, *Second World Almanac Book of Inventions* (New York: Ballantine Books, 1986); Ernst Frank Carter, *Dictionary of Invention* (New York: Philosophical Library, 1967); Gerhard O. Mensch, *Stalemate in Technology* (Cambridge, Mass.: Ballinger Publishing Company, 1975); and Rosenberg, "The Commercial," pp. 19–51.
36. See Drucker, *Age of Discontinuity*, pp. 8, 18–19, 25, and 31; also Jeanne McHugh, *Alexander Halley and the Makers of Steel* (Baltimore: Johns Hopkins University Press, 1980), pp. 108, 258; Rosenberg, "The Commercial," p. 27; Kenneth Warren, *The American Steel Industry,*

1850–1970 (Oxford: Clarendon Press, 1973), pp. 255–57; De Bono, *Eureka,* p. 40; Roger Lushington, *UK Plastics Industry, Special Report #103* (London: Economist Intelligence Unit Ltd., June 1981), p. 9; Vernon Herbert and Attilio Bisio, *Synthetic Rubber* (Westport, Conn.: Greenwood Press, 1985), pp. 4–5; and Charles W. Parry, *Alcoa: A Retrospection* (New York: Newcomen Society of the U.S., 1989), pp. 8–13.

37. T. Wasson, ed., *Nobel Prize Winners* (New York: H. W. Wilson Co., 1987).
38. Rosecrance, *The Rise,* pp. 73–85.
39. Rosenberg, "The Commercial," p. 25.
40. Rosecrance, *The Rise,* pp. 86–106.
41. Skinner, "The Taming," p. 74.
42. Skinner, "The Taming," p. 75; also see Drucker, *Managing in Turbulent Times,* pp. 4–5.
43. Skinner, "The Taming."
44. Chandler, *Strategy and Structure.*
45. Chandler, *Visible Hand.*
46. Piore and Sabel, *The Second,* pp. 133–63, 184–93.
47. Wasson, *Nobel prize winners.*
48. Intel internal documents. Also see William J. Broad, "Novel Technique Shows Japanese Outpace Americans in Innovation," *New York Times,* March 7, 1988, pp. 1 and 7; and John Huey, "Executives Assess Europe's Technology Decline," *Wall Street Journal,* Feb. 4, 1984, p. 32; and Gene Bylinsky, "The High Tech Race: Who's Ahead," *Fortune,* Oct. 13, 1986, pp. 26–27.
49. Rosecrance, *The Rise,* pp. 18–20.
50. Rosecrance, *The Rise.*
51. Chandler, *Strategy and Structure.*
52. Interviews at Frito-Lay, Dallas, April 30–May 1, 1987.
53. Max Weber, *The Theory of Social and Economic Organization,* trans. A. M. Henderson and Talcott Parsons (New York: Oxford Univ. Press, 1947).
54. See Henry Fayol, *Industrial and General Administration,* Part II, Chap. I, "General Principles of Organization" (Paris: Dunod, 1925); Luther Gulick, "Notes on the Theory of Organizations," in *Papers on the Science of Administration,* Luther Gulick and Lyndall F. Urwick, eds. (New York: Institute of Public Administration, Columbia University, 1937); and Lyndall F. Urwick, "Organization as a Technical Problem," in *Papers.*

55. See Michael Masuch, "Vicious Circles in Organizations," *Administrative Science Quarterly,* March 1985, pp. 14–33.
56. Taylor, *The Principles.*
57. For an excellent discussion of why it is wrong to split intelligence from brute effort, see Robert H. Hayes and Ramchandrin Jaikumor, "Manufacturing Crises: New Technology, Obsolete Organizations," *Harvard Business Review,* September–October 1988, pp. 81–83; also Kanter, *The Change Masters,* pp. 156–205.
58. Chester I. Barnard, *The Functions of the Executive* (Cambridge: Harvard Univ. Press, 1968).
59. See F. J. Roethlisberger and William J. Dickson, *Management and the Worker* (Cambridge, Mass.: Harvard Univ. Press, 1939); also Elton Mayo, *The Human Problems of Industrial Civilization* (New York, Macmillan, 1933).
60. Interviews at Sony TV manufacturing facility, San Diego, Calif., March 19, 1975.
61. Herbert A. Simon, *Administrative Behavior* (New York: Free Press, 1945), and Richard M. Cyert and James G. March, *A Behavioral Theory of the Firm* (Englewood Cliffs, N. J.: Prentice-Hall, 1963). For a general discussion of these works and their relevance to company problems, see Ikujiro Nanaka, "Creating Organizational Order Out of Chaos: Self Renewal in Japanese Firms," *California Management Review,* Spring 1988, pp. 57–75.
62. Simon, *Administrative Behavior.*
63. James G. March and Herbert A. Simon, *Organizations* (New York: John Wiley & Son, 1958).
64. Simon, *Administrative Behavior.* This point is also made in Joseph Bower, "Planning Within the Firm," *American Economic Review,* May 1970, pp. 187–88.
65. See Fritjof Capra, *The Turning Point;* also Kenneth Boulding's introduction to Mark Davidson, *Uncommon Sense: The Life and Thought of Ludwig von Bertolanffy, Father of General Systems Theory* (Los Angeles: T. P. Torcher, 1985), p. 18.
66. Capra, *The Turning Point.*
67. Capra, *The Turning Point;* also Zukav, *The Dancing Wu Li.*
68. Karl E. Weick, quoted in Peters and Waterman, *In Search,* p. 7; also see Karl E. Weick, "Educational Organizations as Loosely Coupled Systems," *Administrative Science Quarterly,* Vol. 21 (1976), pp. 120, 193, and 202; also see Nanaka, "Creating," p. 58.
69. Lawrence and Lorsch, *Organization.*

70. Lawrence and Lorsch, *Organization.*
71. Quinn and Cameron, "Paradox and Translation."
72. Robert F. Quinn and John R. Kimberly, "Paradox, Planning and Perseverance: Guidelines for Managerial Practice," pp. 295–313; Robert F. Quinn and David F. Anderson, "Formalization as Crises: Transition Planning for a Young Organization," pp. 11–28, both in *Managing Organizational Transition,* Kimberly and Quinn, eds. (Homewood, Ill.: Irwin, 1984).
73. Steven Jay Gould and Niles Eldridge, "Punctuated Evolution: The Tempo and Mode of Evolution Reconsidered," *Paleobiology,* Vol. 3 (1977), pp. 154–57. See also S. J. Gould, *The Panda's Thumb* (New York: Norton, 1982); also W. Graham Astley, "The Dynamics of Organizational Evolution," working paper no. 304, unpublished (The Wharton School, December 1983).
74. Davidson, *Uncommon Sense,* p. 91; also Gould, *The Panda's Thumb,* pp. 154–57.
75. See K. Smith, "Rabbits," pp. 278–80; also L. Margolis, *Origin of Eukaryotic Cells* (New Haven: Yale Univ. Press, 1970); also Louise Young, *The Unfinished Universe* (New York: Simon and Schuster, 1986), p. 123.
76. Davidson, *Uncommon Sense,* p. 18.
77. See, e.g., Katz and Kahn, *The Social Psychology,* Miller and Rice, *Systems,* and Peter M. Blau and W. Richard Scott, *Formal Organizations* (San Francisco: Chandler Publishing, 1962).
78. K. Smith, "Rabbits," pp. 275–77.
79. K. Smith, "Rabbits," pp. 273–77.
80. K. Smith, "Rabbits," p. 289.
81. K. Smith, "Rabbits," pp. 289–92.
82. W. V. Quine, *The Ways of Paradox and Other Essays* (Cambridge: Harvard Univ. Press, 1966); also see Jeffrey D. Ford and Robert W. Bockoff, "Organizational," pp. 95–104.
83. Peter Elbow, *Embracing Contraries* (New York: Oxford Univ. Press, 1987).
84. Jerome S. Bruner, *On Knowing* (Cambridge: Harvard Univ. Press, 1962), pp. 18–19.
85. Elbow, *Embracing,* p. 241.
86. Kim S. Cameron, "Effectiveness as Paradox: Consensus and Conflict in Conceptions of Organizational Effectiveness," unpublished paper delivered at Radical Workshop on Organizational Design, Monterey, Calif., 1984, pp. 17–19.

87. A. Rothenberg, *The Emerging Goddess* (Chicago: Univ. of Chicago Press, 1979).
88. Elbow, *Embracing*, pp. 243–52.
89. Elbow, *Embracing*, pp. 147–48.
90. T. S. Eliot, "East Coker," *The Complete Poems and Plays, 1904–1950* (New York: Harcourt, Brace & World, 1971), pp. 123–29.
91. Charles Lindbloom, "The Science of Muddling Through," *Public Administration Review*, spring 1959.
92. James G. March, "Footnote to Organizational Change," *Administrative Science Quarterly*, Vol. 26 (1981), p. 575.
93. Karl E. Weick, "Educational Organizations as Loosely Coupled Systems," p. 120; also Karl E. Weick, "RePunctuating the Problem," in *New Perspectives on Organizational Effectiveness*, P. S. Goodman and J. M. Pennings, eds. (San Francisco: Jossey-Bass, 1977), p. 146.
94. Danny Miller and Peter H. Freisen, "Structural Change and Performance: Quantum Versus Piecemeal-Incremental Approaches," *Academy of Management Journal*, Vol. 25 (1982), No. 4, pp. 867–92; also Danny Miller and Peter H. Freisen, "Momentum and Revolution in Organizational Adaptation," Vol. 23 (1980), No. 4, pp. 591–614; also Danny Miller, "Evolution and Revolution: A Quantum View of Structural Change in Organizations," *Journal of Management Studies*, 1982, No. 19, pp. 130–51.
95. Miller and Freisen, "Momentum and Revolution," pp. 593–94.
96. Steven C. Wheelwright and Robert H. Hayes, "Competing Through Manufacturing," *Harvard Business Review*, January–February 1985, pp. 99–109.
97. Wheelwright and Hayes, "Competing"; also Wickham Skinner, "The Productivity Paradox," *Harvard Business Review*, July–August 1986, pp. 56–58, discusses why the "incremental approach" has not worked in manufacturing and why transformation is needed.

CHAPTER FIVE
CRISIS AND TRANSFORMATION: FORD

1. The financial ramifications of the Ford turnaround are best captured in the Annual Reports of the Ford Motor Co. 1980–88. For excellent close-in reporting of the turnaround, I have drawn extensively upon Gregg Easterbrook, "Ford Revs Up."
2. Robert Lacey, *Ford: The Men and the Machine* (New York: Ballantine,

1986), pp. 607–23. Also David Halberstam, *The Reckoning* (New York: Macmillan, 1987), pp. 537–38.

3. (Quoting a Ford toolmaker.) See the excellent coverage of Ford's turn-around based on shop floor interviews in Robert England, "Ford Shifts Gears for Road to Riches." Also see Jeremy Main, "Ford's Drive for Quality," *Fortune,* April 18, 1983, p. 62, quoting Tom Ryan, Ford Louisville industrial-relations manager: "The Plant was filthy; workers and supervisors shouted at each other—workers were AWOL two to three days a week."

4. Refer to table of 1988–91 wages in Wendy Zellner, "Smiling Fender to Fender," *Business Week,* Oct. 5, 1987, p. 39. Also see James Brian Quinn and Penny C Paquette, "Ford: Team Taurus," a case study, Amos Tuck School of Business Administration, Dartmouth College, 1988, p. 1.

5. England, "Ford Shifts," p. 11.

6. England, "Ford Shifts."

7. David Halberstam, *The Reckoning,* pp. 234–59.

8. Lee Iacocca (with William Novak), *Iacocca.*

9. James Danziger, interview with David Halberstam, *Interview,* December 1986, pp. 1 and 2, "pernicious influence of bonus system"; also Halberstam, *The Reckoning,* and Easterbrook, "Ford Revs," p. 89.

10. Easterbrook, "Ford Revs," p. 84.

11. Easterbrook, "Ford Revs." Also interview with Petersen.

12. Interview with Lewis Veraldi, Vice President, Car Programs Management places cost of Taurus at $3.2 billion; other published sources estimate $3.0 billion. See Ann B. Fisher, "Ford Is Back on the Track," *Fortune,* Dec. 23, 1985, pp. 18–22.

13. Easterbrook, "Ford Revs," p. 86.

14. See Amy Borrus, "The Global 1000," *Business Week,* July 17, 1989, pp. 139–40; also Reed Abelson and Rahul Jacob, "The Fortune 500," *Fortune,* April 24, 1989, p. 354.

15. Interviews at Ford Motor Co., Dearborn, Aug. 1–2, Oct. 3–5, Oct. 30, 1983; June 12, 1984; Jan. 5, May 29, Aug. 31, Oct. 27, 1987; July 18–19, Dec. 8, 1988; Aug. 4, Nov. 10, 1989; also Peter Nulty, "Ford's Fragile Recovery," *Fortune,* April 2, 1987, pp. 42–48; also Brian Dumaine, "Donald Petersen: A Humble Hero Drives Ford to the Top," *Fortune,* Jan. 4, 1988, pp. 23–24.

16. See Rebecca Fannin, "The Road Warriors," *Marketing and Media Decisions,* March 1987, p. 60.

17. Moriz survey data quoted in Jeremy Main, "Detroit's Cars Really Are

Getting Better," *Fortune,* Feb. 2, 1987, pp. 93 and 96. Also see J. D. Power and Associates data reported in William J. Hampton, "Why Image Counts," *Business Week,* June 8, 1987, p. 135.

18. Paul Ingrassia and Bradley A. Stertz, "Ford's Strong Sales Pose Agonizing Issue of Additional Plants," *Wall Street Journal,* Oct. 26, 1988, pp. 1 and 10. Also Dumaine, "Donald Petersen," pp. 23–24, and 1988 Annual Report. Also John Holusha, "Ford Had Record Net of $4.6 Billion for 1987," *New York Times,* Feb. 19, 1988, p. 25.
19. Fannin, "The Road Warriors," p. 65.
20. Easterbrook, "Ford Revs," p. 89; also Fisher, "Ford Is Back," p. 21.
21. Numerous sources address this topic. See William N. Marbach et al., "Cars of the Future," *Business Week,* Oct. 28, 1985, p. 85 (comparing performance of Ford 1976 and 1986 vehicles). Also Ford Annual Reports, 1980–89.
22. See James B. Treece et al., "Will the Auto Glut Choke Detroit?," *Business Week,* March 7, 1988, p. 56, and Charles Burck, "Ford's Mr. Turnaround: Phillip Caldwell," *Fortune,* March 4, 1985, p. 84.
23. Main, "Detroit's Cars."
24. For survey data, see "UAW-Ford: Employee Involvement Survey Report," Education and Personnel Research Department, Detroit, Sept. 15, 1982; and Raymond H. Johnson, HRD briefing paper, "Salaried Personnel Opinion Survey," Dearborn, 1988; also interviews at Ford; also James B. Treece et al, "Can Ford Stay On Top?," *Business Week,* September 28, 1987, p. 81. For an excellent overview on the general proposition of teamwork, see Robert B. Reich, "Entrepreneurship Considered: The Team as Hero," *Harvard Business Review,* May–June, 1987, pp. 77–83.
25. Interview with William Broussard, outside facilitator to Ad Hoc Committee, Basking Ridge, N.J., July 28, 1987.
26. Peter F. Drucker, *Management: Tasks, Responsibilities, Practices* (New York: Harper & Row, 1973), pp. 430–32.
27. Interviews at Ford.
28. Interviews at Ford.
29. J. Richard Hackman, "The Transition That Hasn't Happened," in *Managing Organizational Transitions,* John Kimberly and Robert Quinn, eds. (Homewood, Ill.: Irwin, 1984).
30. Quinn and Paquette, "Ford Team," p. 4.
31. Easterbrook, "Ford Revs," p. 90.
32. Interview with Robert Mueller, former internal Ford facilitator for white-collar Employee Involvement, NAAO and the Ad Hoc Commit-

tee, Dec. 19, 1988; also implied in Dale D. Buss and Masayoshi Kanaboyashi, "Wrong Road? Critics Fault Ford Plan to Produce Small Cars with Mazda of Japan," *Wall Street Journal* (June 23, 1986), pp. 1 and 8.

33. Interview with Mueller; interviews at Ford.
34. Interviews at Ford.
35. Interviews at Ford; also John Bussey and Bridgett Davis, "Ford Cost Cutting Move Is a Strike Issue," *Wall Street Journal,* Aug. 8, 1988; and Fannin, "The Road Warriors," p. 62.
36. Interviews at Ford.
37. Elie Humbert, *Carl G. Jung: The Fundamentals of Theory and Practice* (Wilmette, Ill.: Chiron Publications, 1984), pp. 103–4.
38. Easterbrook, "Ford Revs," p. 90; also Halberstam, *The Reckoning,* pp. 234–59.
39. Interviews at Ford, quoting Drucker (who characterized the old Ford as "corrupt") and William Abernathy ("Ford . . . where politics ran rampant . . . a lot of pot shot artists . . . sixteen rats and 15 holes . . . "), Stanford University, Oct. 31, 1983.
40. See North American Automotive Operations, "Japanese Business Practices: Study Findings of the 1981 Ford Task Force," unpublished white paper, Aug. 17, 1981, pp. 3–10; also Raymond H. Johnson, "Driving Forces for Participative Management and Employee Involvement," paper presented at the Academy of Management Symposium, Aug. 12, 1984, Boston, in *Cultural Change Within a Large System* (Detroit, Ford Motor Co., 1984), Sec. II, pp. 1–2.
41. Karen L. Cornelius and C. Douglas Hincker, "Early Initiatives: The 8-Step Model of Planned Change," Academy of Management Symposium, Sec. III, p. 2; also interviews with Savoie.
42. Interviews at Ford.
43. Interviews at Ford.
44. Interviews at Ford.
45. Interviews at Ford.
46. Interviews at Ford.
47. Interviews at Ford.
48. Interviews at Ford; also Pascale working notes as consultant to the Ford Change Task Force, Oct. 30, 1983.
49. Interviews at Ford.
50. Interviews at Ford.
51. Interviews at Ford.
52. Interviews at Ford.

53. Interviews at Ford.
54. Interviews at Ford.
55. Interviews at Ford.
56. Interviews at Ford.
57. Interviews at Ford.
58. Interviews at Ford.
59. Interviews at Ford.
60. Interviews at Ford.
61. Easterbrook, "Ford Revs," p. 90.
62. Interviews at Ford.
63. Paul H. Weaver, *The Suicidal Corporation* (New York: Simon and Schuster, 1988).
64. Interviews at Ford.
65. Interviews at Ford.
66. Interviews at Ford.
67. Interviews at Ford.
68. Interviews at Ford.
69. Interviews at Ford.
70. Quinn and Paquette, "Ford: Team."
71. Interviews at Ford.
72. Interviews at Ford.
73. Interviews at Ford.
74. Interviews at Ford; also see Raymond H. Johnson, Academy of Management Symposium, Sec. II, p. 2.
75. Briefing by William Broussard, President, King, Chapman and Broussard, Basking Ridge, N. J., July 28, 1987.
76. Interviews at Ford.
77. Interviews at Ford.
78. Interviews at Ford.
79. Interviews at Ford.
80. Interviews at Ford.
81. Interviews at Ford.
82. See Treece et al., "Will the Auto Glut Choke Detroit?," p. 56, quoting MIT study: "Ford's popular Taurus has cut production time very, very close to the 18.2 man hours per vehicle it takes to turn out Civics at Honda's pace setting plant in Marysville, Ohio . . . "
83. Interview with Broussard.
84. Interviews at Ford.
85. Interviews at Ford.
86. Interviews at Ford.

87. Interviews at Ford; also see Jeffrey T. Walsh, "Creating the Conditions for Large Scale Systems Change," in *Cultural Change Within a Large System,* Academy of Management Symposium, Sec. IV, p. 1.
88. Nancy Lloyd Badore, "The Role of Management in the Change Process," Academy of Management Symposium.
89. Interview with Bill Pilder, Basking Ridge, N. J., Aug. 31, 1987; also memo to Harold Burlingame of AT&T, Aug. 31, 1987, subject "One-on-One Consulting Intervention."

CHAPTER SIX
FORD: RESOLVING THE "DIALECTIC"

1. Hans-Georg Gadamer, *Hegel's Dialectic* (New Haven and London: Yale Univ. Press, 1976).
2. England, "Ford Shifts," p. 20; interviews at Ford.
3. Interviews at Ford.
4. Halberstam, *The Reckoning,* pp. 620–21. Also interview with Michael Naylor, Director of Strategic Planning, Detroit, July, 1986.
5. Interview with Naylor; also Halberstam, *The Reckoning.*
6. Quinn and Paquette, "Ford: Team," p. 4.
7. Interviews at Ford.
8. Interviews at Ford.
9. Interviews at Ford.
10. Interviews at Ford.
11. Quinn and Paquette, "Ford: Team," pp. 4–5; also Nulty, "Ford's Fragile," pp. 42–48.
12. Interviews at Ford.
13. Lewis Veraldi letter to Nancy Badore, July 17, 1988, p. 2; Henry Ford's preference for large cars is well documented. See Halberstam, *The Reckoning;* also Quinn and Paquette, "Ford: Team," p. 4 (which cites the 6-percent loss of Ford market share stemming from Henry Ford II's decision against small cars 1978–80).
14. This insight first appears in Ford's Japan Study Team Report, p. 6.
15. Pascale, "The Problem of Strategy"; also Otis Port, "Quality," *Business Week,* June 8, 1987, pp. 131–35.
16. Danziger, interview with Halberstam, and Halberstam, *The Reckoning;* also interview with Petersen.
17. Halberstam, *The Reckoning;* also Lacey, *Ford: The Men,* and Peter

Collier and David Horowitz, *The Fords* (New York: Summit Books, 1987).

18. Halberstam, *The Reckoning,* pp. 204–10 and 234–59.
19. Halberstam, *The Reckoning;* also Danziger, interview with Halberstam, p. 2.
20. Halberstam, *The Reckoning,* p. 330.
21. Interviews at Ford.
22. Collier and Horowitz, *The Fords.*
23. Interviews at Ford.
24. Interviews at Ford.
25. Interviews at Ford; Quinn and Paquette, "Ford: Team," p. 1.
26. Interviews at Ford.
27. Interviews at Ford.
28. Interviews at Ford.
29. Interviews at Ford.
30. Interviews at Ford.
31. Interviews at Ford.
32. Interviews at Ford; also interview with Mueller, and interview with Broussard.
33. Dale D. Buss, "Ford Is Riding High with Smart Execution and Slashed Capacity," *Wall Street Journal,* Oct. 7, 1986, pp. 1 and 30.
34. Interviews at Ford.
35. Interviews at Ford.
36. Petersen as quoted in Easterbrook, "Ford Revs," p. 90.
37. Interviews at Ford.
38. Interview with Mueller.
39. Interview with Mueller. ("———, a brilliant engineer, had a feisty, difficult personality . . . very emotional but not a team player. . . . He'd literally blow up in Ad Hoc Committee—swear, fly off the handle . . . so he was sent off to Chrysler on an amicable basis.")
40. Interview with Mueller.
41. Interviews at Ford.
42. Interviews at Ford.
43. Interviews at Ford.
44. Interviews at Ford.
45. Interviews at Ford.
46. Interviews at Ford.
47. Interviews at Ford.
48. Interviews at Ford.
49. Interviews at Ford.

50. Interviews at Ford; also see Management and Nonmanagement Performance Evaluation Forms, Industrial Relations Form 824, June 1986.
51. Interviews at Ford.
52. Interviews at Ford.
53. Interviews at Ford.
54. Interviews at Ford.
55. Interviews at Ford.
56. Andrew C. Brown, "A Surprising Ford–GM Face Off," *Fortune,* June 19, 1985, pp. 150 and 152.
57. Quinn and Paquette, "Ford: Team"; also James D. Moore, "Overview: The Ford Story" (white paper for ATT office of the Chairman based on interviews at Ford), Jan. 3, 1987.
58. Eric Gelman, "Ford's Idea Machine," *Business Week,* Nov. 24, 1986, p. 64; also James B. Treece et al., "Will the Auto Glut Choke Detroit?," p. 56; interview with Petersen.
59. Dale D. Buss, "Ford Is Riding High," p. 30.
60. Interviews at Ford.
61. Interviews at Ford.
62. Interviews at Ford.
63. Dumaine, "Donald Petersen," p. 23.
64. See Easterbrook, "Ford Revs," pp. 84–92; also Dumaine, "Donald Petersen," p. 23.
65. Easterbrook, "Ford Revs," p. 90.
66. Dumaine, "Donald Petersen," p. 23.
67. Easterbrook, "Ford Revs," pp. 84–92.
68. Dumaine, "Donald Petersen," p. 23.
69. Easterbrook, "Ford Revs," p. 86.
70. Kordick quoted in Easterbrook, "Ford Revs," p. 86.
71. Gregg Easterbrook, "Have You Driven a Ford Lately?," *Washington Monthly,* October, 1986, p. 88.
72. Easterbrook, "Have You," p. 88.
73. Easterbrook, "Have You," p. 88.
74. Easterbrook, "Have You," p. 88.
75. Ingrassia and Stertz, "Ford's Strong Sales . . . ," p. 10.
76. Iacocca, *Iacocca.*
77. Interviews at Ford.
78. Interviews at Ford.
79. Interviews at Ford.
80. Interviews at Ford.
81. Interviews at Ford.

82. Eric Gelman, "Ford's Idea Machine," *Business Week,* Nov. 24, 1986, p. 66.
83. Easterbrook, "Have You," p. 91.
84. Interviews at Ford.
85. Interviews at Ford.
86. Easterbrook, "Have You," p. 91.
87. Interviews at Ford.
88. Interviews at Ford.
89. Interviews at Ford.
90. Interviews at Ford.
91. Interview with Mueller; also Phillip Caldwell Policy Letter #B-14, Nov. 5, 1979.
92. Interviews at Ford.
93. Interviews at Ford.
94. Interviews at Ford.
95. Easterbrook, "Have You," p. 90; also interviews at Ford.
96. Interviews at Ford; for discussion of the current contribution of 20 cents an hour, see Schlesinger, "Auto Firm and the UAW Find That Cooperation Can Get Complicated," p. 20.
97. Interviews at Ford.
98. Ingrassia and Stertz, "Ford's Strong Sales," p. 56.
99. Ingrassia and Stertz, "Ford's Strong Sales," also Treece et al., "Will the Auto," p. 56.
100. Quinn and Paquette, "Ford: Team," p. 12.
101. Quinn and Paquette, "Ford: Team," p. 14; also see *Industry Week,* April 1, 1985.
102. Thomas Moore, "Would You Buy a Car From This Man?," *Fortune,* April 11, 1988, p. 72.
103. Moore, "Would You," pp. 72–74; also Alex Taylor III, "Why Fords Sell Like Big Macs," *Fortune,* Nov. 21, 1988, pp. 123–35.
104. Collier and Horowitz, *The Fords,* pp. 156–57 and 160–63; interviews at Ford.
105. Quinn and Paquette, "Ford: Team," p. 285.
106. Halberstam, *The Reckoning,* pp. 547–52; also Lacey, *Ford: The Men,* pp. 586–88, 576–601 and 689–90.
107. Interview with Mueller.
108. For a general discussion of how the Vision Statement evolved, see interviews at Ford.
109. Interviews at Ford.
110. Interviews at Ford.

111. Dale D. Buss, "Ford Is Riding," pp. 1 and 30.
112. Burck interview with Caldwell, "Ford's Mr. Turnaround," p. 84.
113. Brian Dumaine, "Speed," pp. 54–59.
114. Quinn and Paquette, "Ford: Team."
115. Marbach, "Cars of the Future," p. 89.
116. Interviews at Ford.
117. Treece et al., "Can Ford Stay on Top?," p. 78; also England, "Ford Shifts," p. 8.
118. Interviews at Ford.
119. Interviews at Ford.

CHAPTER SEVEN
THE PENDULUM PRINCIPLE

1. *Enantiodromia* is a philosophical term coined by Heraclitus, who conceived of the universe as a conflict of opposites but ruled by eternal justice. Carl Jung, *Letters,* Bollinger Series XCV (Princeton: Princeton University Press, 1975), Vol. II, p. 157.
2. Reed Abelson and Rahum Jacob, "The Fortune 500," *Fortune,* April 24, 1989, p. 354.
3. Ann Borrus et al., "The Global 1000," *Business Week,* July 17, 1989, p. 140.
4. See Ronald G.Greenwood, *Managerial Decentralization* (La Crosse, Wisc.: Hive Publishing, 1982); also see James P. Baughman, "Problems and Performance of the Role of Chief Executive of the General Electric Company, 1892–1974," mimeographed discussion paper, July 15, 1974.
5. Greenwood, *Managerial,* p. 111.
6. Interview with John F. Welch, Jr., Fairfield, Connecticut, June 1, 1988.
7. These data provided by GE internal documents. Also interviews with James P. Baughman, Manager of Executive Education, Crotonville, Conn., Feb. 16, 1989.
8. Ann M. Morrison, "C.E.O.'s Pick the Best C.E.O.'s," *Fortune,* May 4, 1981.
9. Thomas J. Lueck, "Why Jack Welch Is Changing GE," *New York Times,* May 5, 1985, Section 3, p.1.
10. Robert Barker, "Commanding General: GE's Management Merits a Premium—But How Much?," *Barron's,* Oct. 15, 1984, p. 9.

11. Frank Aguilar, "General Electric: Strategic Position 1981," a Harvard Business School Case Study (Cambridge: Harvard Business School Case Services, 1981); also Frank Aguilar, "General Electric: 1984" (Cambridge: Harvard Business School Case Services, 1985).

12. Interviews with William E. Rothschild, former Executive Staff in Charge of Strategic Planning, Fairfield, Conn., February 16, 1983.

13. See Harold Passer, *The Electronic Manufacturers* (Cambridge: Harvard University Press, 1953); also W. E. Fruhan, "GE 1970" a Harvard Business School case study (Cambridge: Harvard Business School Case Services, 1970).

14. Passer, *The Electronic.*

15. Passer, *The Electronic;* also Greenwood, *Managerial,* p. 13.

16. Passer, *The Electronic;* also Baughman, interviews.

17. Interviews with Baughman.

18. Interviews with Baughman.

19. Interviews with GE's Lighting executives, NELA Park, Cleveland, Ohio, December 12, 1983; also see 1953 Ted Quinn, head of GE's Lamp, quoted in Greenwood, *Managerial,* p. 77.

20. Interviews with GE's Lighting executives, 1983.

21. Interviews with GE's Lighting executives.

22. Interviews with GE's Lighting executives.

23. Interview with William E. Rothschild.

24. Interview with Rothschild.

25. Greenwood, *Managerial.*

26. Interview with Donald E. Kane, former member Executive Management Staff, General Electric, Feb. 16 and July 20, 1989; also see Kane, "Resizing the Structure," unpublished staff paper for top management, August 12, 1985.

27. Interview with Kane.

28. Greenwood, *Managerial,* pp. 15–16.

29. Greenwood, *Managerial,* pp. 15–16.

30. Interview with Baughman.

31. Greenwood, *Managerial,* p. 87.

32. Interview with Baughman.

33. Greenwood, *Managerial,* pp. 17–18.

34. Greenwood, *Managerial,* p. 111.

35. Greenwood, *Managerial,* p. 18; also interviews with Baughman.

36. Interview with Baughman; also interview with Kane.

37. Greenwood, *Managerial;* pp. 18–19, 98–101.

38. Interview with Kane. Also Greenwood, *Managerial,* pp. 59–65.

39. Interview with Baughman; interview with Kane.
40. Greenwood, *Managerial,* pp. 98 and 124.
41. Interview with Baughman.
42. Interview with Baughman.
43. Interview with Baughman.
44. Interview with Baughman.
45. Interview with Kane.
46. Interview with Kane.
47. Vice Chairman Jack S. Parker, New York, July 1, 1970, quoted in Greenwood, *Managerial,* p. 99.
48. Interview with Paul Van Orden, General Electric, Fairfield, Conn., Feb. 20, 1986.
49. Interview with Rothschild, Feb. 16, 1983.
50. Interview with Baughman.
51. Interview with Baughman.
52. Greenwood, *Managerial.*
53. Greenwood, *Managerial,* p. 98.
54. Greenwood, *Managerial,* p. 98.
55. For a detailed account of how the finance fraternity grew to be feared and powerful, see Greenwood, *Managerial,* pp. 101–111.
56. Greenwood, *Managerial,* pp. 111–112; also Annual Reports 1950–65.
57. Greenwood, *Managerial.*
58. Interview with Kane.
59. Interviews with John F. Welch, Jr., CEO of GE, Fairfield, Conn., Sept. 16 and Oct. 8, 1983; July 17, August 15 and Sept. 29, 1984; August 28, 1985; and June 1 and 13, 1988.
60. Interview with Kane.
61. Interview with Kane.
62. Interview with Kane.
63. Interview with Baughman.
64. Interview with Baughman.
65. Interviews with Welch.
66. Interviews with Welch.
67. Greenwood, *Managerial,* p. 111, estimates $100 million. Subsequent 1983 GE internal analysis by strategic planning staff estimates $250 million net. Interview with Rothschild.
68. Interview with Kane. Numerous published reports discussed Borch's reasons for taking early retirement at age 62 and focused on GE's loss of momentum. See ''GE's New Strategy for Faster Growth,'' *Business Week,* July 8, 1972, pp. 52–54.

69. See Borch comments on the McKinsey study in Aguilar, "General Electric, Strategic," pp. 3–8.
70. Interviews with executives of Aircraft Engine, Lynn, Mass., March 21, 1983.
71. Gerhard Neumann, *Herman the German* (New York: Morrow 1984).
72. Interviews with executives of Aircraft Engines.
73. Interviews with executives of Aircraft Engines.
74. Interviews with executives of Aircraft Engines.
75. Interviews with executives of Aircraft Engines.
76. Interview with Baughman.
77. Interview with Baughman.
78. Interviews with executives of GE Finance, Fairfield, Conn., February 16, 1983, December 3–7, 1984, and November 6, 1985.
79. Interviews with executives of GE Finance.
80. Interviews with executives of GE Finance.
81. Interviews with executives of GE Finance.
82. Interviews with executives of GE Finance.
83. Interviews with executives of GE Finance.
84. Interviews with executives of GE Finance.
85. Interviews with executives of GE Finance.
86. All details of this paragraph from interviews with executives of GE Finance.
87. Interview with a former GE senior line manager, April 10, 1986.
88. Interviews with executives of various GE business units, 1983–86; also see anon., "Executive Opinion Survey Report," prepared for Officers Meeting, July 1985.
89. "GE's New Strategy," *Business Week,* pp. 52–54.
90. Interviews with Welch.
91. Interviews with Welch.
92. "GE's New Strategy, *Business Week,* p. 56.
93. Richard T. Pascale, "The Problem of 'Strategy,' " keynote address delivered at the Strategic Management Society Annual Conference, Boston, Mass., October 16, 1987.
94. Stratford P. Sherman, "The Mind of Jack Welch," *Fortune,* March 27, 1989, p. 42.
95. Interview with executives of GE's Major Appliance Business, Louisville, Ky., December 1983.
96. Interviews with executives of Aircraft Engines; interviews with Welch.
97. Interviews with executives of Factory Automation, Charlottesville, Va.,

and with executives of Mobile Communications, Lynchburg, Va., July 18, 1984, and Sept. 5, 1985.

98. Interviews with executives of Mobile Communications.

99. Interviews with executives of Mobile Communications.

100. Interviews with executives of Mobile Communications.

101. Interview with Rothschild.

102. See Russell Mitchell, "Jack Welch: How Good a Manager?," *Business Week,* Dec. 19, 1987, p. 94; Mark Potts, "GE's Welch Powering Firm into Global Competitor," *Washington Post,* Sept. 23, 1984, pp. G1–10; also see Sherman, "The Mind," pp. 39–50.

103. Interview with Rothschild.

104. See Peter Petre, "What Welch Has Wrought at GE," *Fortune,* July 7, 1986, p. 43.

105. Interviews with Welch.

106. P. Nulty, "America's Toughest Bosses," *Fortune,* Feb. 27, 1989.

107. Petre, "What Welch," p. 43.

108. Janet Guyon, "Combative Chief: GE's Jack Welch," *Wall Street Journal,* Aug. 4, 1988, pp. 1 and 4; Petre, "What Welch"; also see Peter Petre, "Jack Welch: The Man Who Brought GE to Life," *Fortune,* Jan. 5, 1987, p. 77; also William Glasgall, "General Electric Is Stalking Big Game Again," *Business Week,* March 16, 1987, pp. 112–14.

109. Sherman, "The Mind," p. 39.

110. Interviews with Welch.

111. Interviews with Welch.

112. Noel Tichy and Ram Charan, "Speed, Simplicity, and Self-Confidence," *Harvard Business Review,* Sept.–Oct. 1989.

113. Interviews with Welch.

114. Interviews with GE business unit heads, various East Coast locations, from February 1983–February 1986.

115. Philip C. Kantz, "Letters to the Editor," *Fortune,* April 24, 1988, p. 338.

116. Tichy and Charan, "Speed, Simplicity."

117. Interviews with Welch.

118. Tichy and Charan, "Speed, Simplicity."

119. Interviews with Welch.

120. Tichy and Charan, "Speed, Simplicity."

121. Interview with John M. Trani, Lynchburg, Va., Sept. 5 and Oct. 13, 1985 and April 12, 1986.

122. Guyon, "Combative Chief."

123. Tichy and Charan, "Speed, Simplicity."
124. Tichy and Charan, "Speed, Simplicity."
125. Interviews with Welch.
126. Sherman, "The Mind," pp. 40 and 46.
127. Sherman, "The Mind," p. 46.
128. John F. Welch, Jr., "Management in the Nineties," speech to Bay Area Council, San Francisco, Ca., July 6, 1989.
129. Interviews with Welch; also interviews with Kane; also Mitchell, "Jack Welch," p. 94.

CHAPTER EIGHT
LIVING DANGEROUSLY: CITICORP AND HEWLETT-PACKARD

1. See Edward Boyer, "Citicorp: What the New Boss Is Up To," *Fortune,* Feb. 17, 1986, pp. 40–44, also Sarah Bartlett, "John Reed's Citicorp," *Business Week,* Dec. 8, 1986, pp. 90–95, and Robert E. Norton, "Citibank Woos The Consumer," *Fortune,* June 8, 1987, pp. 48–54.
2. Interviews with Citicorp, New York, March 7 and 25, 1986, April 27–8, 1986, and July 3, 1986.
3. Boyer, "Citicorp," p. 40–44; also see Daniel Hertzberg, "Citicorp Leads Field in Its Size and Power . . . and Arrogance," *Wall Street Journal,* May 11, 1984, pp. 1 and 16.
4. John A. Seeger, "First National City Bank A & B," a Harvard Business School case study (Cambridge, Mass.: Harvard Business School Case Services, 1975); also Boyer, "Citicorp," p. 40.
5. Boyer, "Citicorp," p. 42.
6. Boyer, "Citicorp," p. 42.
7. Interviews with Citicorp.
8. Interviews with Citicorp.
9. Interviews with Citicorp. Also see Hertzberg, "Citicorp Leads," pp. 1 and 16.
10. Interviews with Citicorp.
11. Interviews with Citicorp.
12. Interviews with Citicorp.
13. Interviews with Citicorp.
14. Interviews with Citicorp.
15. Interviews with Citicorp.
16. Interviews with Citicorp.

17. Interview with Pat Flaherty, VP, Human Resources, New York, April 28, 1986.
18. Interview with Flaherty. This practice of culling out the bottom 10 percent is not practiced by all groups within the bank. The rigor with which it is carried out in those areas which follow this procedure has had a widespread impact on the culture of the bank as a whole.
19. Interview with Ira Rimmerman, Group Vice President, Citicorp International Consumer Products Group, New York, July 3, 1986.
20. Interview with Rimmerman.
21. Interview with Rimmerman.
22. Interview with Rimmerman.
23. Patricia Sellers, "America's Most Admired Corporations," *Fortune,* p. 19.
24. Dick Hackborn and Don Harris, "The Hewlett-Packard Way," undated internal Hewlett-Packard publication.
25. See Chris Lee "Training the H.P. Team," *Training,* March 1989, pp. 29–31; also Bro Uttal, "Mettle Test."
26. Interviews at Hewlett-Packard, Palo Alto, California, fall 1985.
27. Interviews at HP.
28. Interviews at HP.
29. Interviews at HP.
30. Jonathan B. Levine, "Mild Mannered H.P. Is Making Like Superman," *Business Week,* March 7, 1988, p. 110.
31. Bruce Karney, "Employee Productivity: How Does H-P Stack Up?" case study for HP executive education (Palo Alto: January 10, 1986). Also see L. Greenhalgh, R. McKersie, and R. Gilkey, "Rebalancing the Workforce at IBM," unpublished working paper #1718-85, October 1985.
32. B. Karney, "HP's Human Assets," a case study for executive education (Palo Alto, January 10, 1986).
33. Interviews at HP, 1985.
34. Peter Waldman, "Hewlett-Packard, Citing Software Snag, Will Delay New Computer Six Months," *Wall Street Journal,* Sept. 26, 1986, p. 2; see also John Young quote: "We have been running at less than full speed for the last three years," in Richard Brandt, "H-P May Have Come Up with a Winner," *Business Week,* June 1, 1989.
35. Brandt, "H-P May."
36. Jonathan B. Levine, "Hewlett-Packard's Screeching Turn Toward Desktops," *Business Week,* September 11, 1988, p. 106.
37. Interviews at HP.

CHAPTER NINE
THE TWO FACES OF LEARNING: GENERAL MOTORS AND
HONDA

1. Amy Borrus et al., "The Global 1000," *Business Week,* July 17, 1989, p. 140; also see Susan E. Kuhn and David J. Morrow, "The Fortune International 500," *Fortune,* July 31, 1989, p. 291; and Reed Abelson and Rahul Jacob, "The Fortune 500," April 24, 1989, p. 354.
2. See, e.g., James B. Treece, "It's Time for a Tune-Up at General Motors," *Business Week,* Sept. 7, 1987, pp. 22–25.
3. See Alfred P. Sloan, *My Years at General Motors* (Garden City, N.Y.: Doubleday, 1963), and J. Patrick Wright, *On a Clear Day You Can See General Motors* (New York: Avon Books, 1979); also Charles G. Burck, "Will Success Spoil General Motors?," *Fortune,* Aug. 22, 1983, pp. 98–100.
4. Wright, *On a Clear Day,* pp. 6–11, 47–57, and 63–85.
5. A large number of books and articles make the point. See Joseph B. White and Bradley A. Stertz, "Auto Makers Drive into a Mess as Plants Expand and Sales Fall," *Wall Street Journal,* Aug. 7, 1989, pp. 1–2; Treece, "It's Time"; Richard M. Donnelly (GM manager of manufacturing components), "Competitiveness Overview," unpublished internal staff paper, 1986; "GM: Not Yet a Perfect 10," *Fortune,* July 4, 1988, p. 14; Jacob M. Schlesinger and Bradley A. Stertz, "GM 10 Cars Are Off to a Sluggish Start," *Wall Street Journal,* June 17, 1988, p. 17; Jacob M. Schlesinger and Joseph B. White, "Shrinking Giant," *Wall Street Journal,* June 6, 1988, pp. 1 and 14; James B. Treece and Robert Ingersoll, "GM Faces Reality," *Business Week,* May 9, 1988, p. 122; Albert Lee, *Call Me Roger* (New York: Contemporary Books, 1988); Paul Ingrassia, "Detroit Paradox: GM's Market Share Declined Last Year Even as Net Set a Mark," *Wall Street Journal,* Feb. 15, 1989, pp. 1 and 10; Alex Taylor III, "The Tasks Facing General Motors," *Fortune,* March 13, 1989, pp. 52–58; James B. Treece et al., "Motor City Madness: GM Leads Detroit Toward a Costly New Car Glut," *Business Week,* March 6, 1989, pp. 22–23; Jerry Flint and Laura Jeraski, "Fiddling with Figures While the Sales Drop," *Forbes,* Aug. 24, 1987, pp. 32–35; finally, Faye Rice, "America's New No. 4 Automaker—Honda," *Fortune,* Oct. 28, 1985, p. 30.
6. Interview with Elmer Johnson, Executive Vice President in charge of operating staffs, General Motors, Detroit, July 22, 1986.

7. Interview with Ernest Schaffer, Plant Manager, GM Pontiac Trans Am facility, Van Nuys, Calif., June 12, 1986.
8. Wright, *On a Clear Day*. Also see Thomas Moore, "Make or Break Time for General Motors," *Fortune*, Feb. 15, 1988, pp. 32–37.
9. Wright, *On a Clear Day*. Also interviews with executives of GM, Van Nuys and Fremont, Calif., and Detroit, April–July 1986.
10. Interviews with middle managers at GM, Detroit, July 21, 1986.
11. Interview with Mort Meyerson, President, EDS, Dallas, April 9, 1986.
12. Interview with Steven Bera, Arthur Young manufacturing practice, and former manager of materials, NUMMI, July 27, 1986.
13. Interview with Bera.
14. Interview with a former GM executive, Boston, Mass., March 21, 1986.
15. Interviews with senior executives of GM. Also, Cory Reich, "The Innovator," *New York Times Magazine*, April 21, 1989, p. 75.
16. Interview with Elmer Johnson.
17. Interview with GM personnel executive, April 4, 1988; interviews with GM executives, Detroit, July 21–22, 1986, and George Getschow, "Some Middle Managers Cut Corners to Achieve High Corporate Goals," *Wall Street Journal*, Nov. 8, 1979, pp. 1 and 19.
18. Shawn Tully, "American Bosses Are Overpaid," *Fortune*, Nov. 7, 1988, pp. 121–136; also John A. Byrne et al., "Who Made the Muster and Why: Executive Compensation Scorecard," *Business Week*, May 2, 1988, p. 57.
19. Interview with GM personnel executive. Also see Amanda Bennett, "GM's Bonus Flop: 'The Timing Was Wrong,' " *Wall Street Journal*, Nov. 7, 1988, p. 1; Wendy Zellner, "Back to Butting Heads with the UAW?," *Business Week*, May 8, 1988, p. 118. For a somewhat more optimistic account, see Jacob M. Schlesinger and Paul Ingrassia, "People Power: GM Woos Employees by Listening to Them, Talking of Its 'Team,' " *Wall Street Journal*, Jan. 12, 1989, pp. 1 and A7.
20. Interview with Dennis Pauley, former GM plant manager, Fiero plant, Pontiac, Mich. (currently VP and plant manager, Mazda, Flatrock, Mich.), July 19, 1986.
21. See Anne B. Fisher, "GM Is Tougher Than You Think," *Fortune*, Nov. 10, 1986, p. 60; also see Daniel Pedersen, "Perot to Smith: GM Must Change," *Newsweek*, Dec. 15, 1986, p. 58.
22. Wendy Zellner, "GM's New 'Teams' Aren't Hitting Any Homers," *Business Week*, Aug. 8, 1988, pp. 46–47; also see Bennett, "GM's Bonus."

23. Lunch with Ross Perot, Dallas, Sept. 23, 1986. Also see Jon Lowell, "Perot's Rx for GM," *Ward's Auto World,* November 1986, p. 35.

24. John Bussey and Mike Tharp, "NUMMI Auto Venture Termed A Success," *Wall Street Journal,* May 20, 1986, p. 6.

25. Sakiya, *Honda's Motor,* pp. 152–166.

26. Interviews with employees at Buick City facility, Mich., May 29, 1986.

27. Interviews with employees, Buick City.

28. Jacobsen, Erik. "NUMMI: A Model in Human Relations," thesis written at Buick-Oldsmobile-Cadillac (Detroit: GMI Engineering and Management Institute, September 12, 1986), p. 8; also Langenfeld Study, April 6, 1986; Langenfeld, J. A. "NUMMI Management Practices: A Report of the General Motors Study Team," unpublished report, April 9, 1986, and sampling procedures as described in interviews with managers of NUMMI, Fremont, Calif., March 20–April 20, 1986.

29. Jacobsen, "NUMMI," p. 92.

30. Alex Taylor, "The Tasks," p. 53; for a generally optimistic account, Roger Smith, "The U.S. Must Do as GM Has Done," *Fortune,* Feb. 13, 1989, pp. 70–72.

31. Taylor, "The Tasks," pp. 53 and 58. The picture for GM 10 cars is very mixed. See White and Stertz, "Auto Makers," p. A2; also Schlesinger and Stertz, "GM 10," p. 17; also R. Smith, "The U.S. Must Do."

32. Treece, "Motor City Madness," pp. 22–23. Also R. Smith, "The U.S. Must Do."

33. Interviews with Ed Battinger and team assigned to design the GM production system, "The War Room," GM Technical Center, July 21, 1986. Also see Ross Perot, "How I Would Turn Around GM," *Fortune,* Feb. 15, 1988, pp. 44–49.

34. A great many sources extoll the virtues of Honda. Honda cars were named two of the top three in J. D. Power & Associates Consumer Satisfaction Index, Santa Monica, Calif., 1988; the Honda Accord was named one of *Car & Driver* magazine's "Ten Best Cars in the World" (Feb. 9, 1989), making it the only seven-time winner of this honor in history; Gary S. Vasilash, "Honda Is World Class in Ohio," *Production,* July 1988; Tom Incantalupo, "How Honda Won Respect," *Newsday Business*, Sept. 27, 1987; Jerry Flint, "Nobody Likes Us Except the Customer," *Forbes,* Oct. 19, 1987; James Risen, "Honda: The Americanization of an Auto Maker," *Los Angeles Times,* Oct. 12,

1987; see also *1989 Motorcycle Statistical Annual* (Costa Mesa, Calif.: Motorcycle Industry Council, 1989). For additional background on the motorcycle wars, interviews with Mich Aneha, former Honda manager, Palo Alto, Calif., May 3 and 20, 1988; "1988 World Motorcycle Statistics," *Honda* (Tokyo: Honda Motor, Ltd., May 1988). Honda soared to a place as the number one foreign manufacturer of luxury cars in the three-year period 1986–88 (interview with Honda, Palo Alto, May 12, 1989); also Alex Taylor III, "Luxury Cars: New Leaders in an Upscale Upheaval," *Fortune*, April 10, 1989, p. 72. Honda's legacy of breakthroughs in automotive technology is summarized in "The Story of Honda," *Honda* (Tokyo: Honda Motor, Ltd., May 1988), pp. 47–49. Honda leads in engineering: see Alex Taylor III, "Here Come Japan's New Luxury Cars," *Fortune*, Aug. 14, 1989, p. 62.

35. Julian Jaynes, *The Origin of Consciousness in the Breakdown of the Bicameral Mind* (Boston: Houghton Mifflin, 1976), pp. 52–56.

36. Thomas F. Boyle, "Loyalty Ebbs at Many Companies as Employees Grow Disillusioned," *Wall Street Journal*, July 11, 1985, p. 25; Nanaka, "Creating Organizational Order Out of Chaos," pp. 61–63; also Lieberman, "When Does Union-Management Cooperation Work?" Also Tadashi Kume, "The Challenging Spirit," unpublished speech to Automotive Manufacturers Association, Detroit, Sept. 26, 1988, pp. 1–2; also Robert N. Bellah, "Religion and the Technological Revolution in Japan," University Lecture in Religion, Arizona State University, Feb. 19, 1987, p. 7.

37. Interview with Soichiro Irimajiri, President of Honda Manufacturing Co., U.S., Palo Alto, Calif., April 15, 1988. Also see Nanaka, "Creating Organizational," p. 66. Motorola borrows this breakthrough approach from the Japanese; see Ronald Henkoff, "What Motorola Learns from Japan," *Fortune*, April 24, 1989, pp. 164–68.

38. See Nanaka, "Creating Organizational," p. 66. Also interviews with plant management team, Honda manufacturing facilities, Marysville, Ohio, June 9, 1987. For an excellent discussion, see Masaoki Imai, *Kaizen: The Key to Japan's Competitive Success* (New York: Random House, 1986). Also interviews with Komatsu executives, Osaka, Sept. 28, 1988, and Shigeru Mizuno, *Company Wide Total Quality Control* (Hong Kong: Asian Productivity Organization, 1988).

39. For a general outline of Honda's strategy: "Elements of Honda's Strategy," unpublished white paper, 1987.

40. Interviews with Ed Buker, plant manager, Honda, Marysville, in Maui, Hawaii, June 16, 1988.

41. Interviews at Honda, Marysville; also "Honda People," an internal Honda handbook on the Honda Way, undated.
42. Interviews at Honda. Also, see Kanter, "Dilemmas of Participation," *The Change Masters*, pp. 56–59, 241–77.
43. Interviews at Honda, Marysville; also Shin Okubo, "The Honda Approach to Productivity," speech to Baldwin-Wallace College, Berea, Ohio, March 2, 1987.
44. Interviews with Takeo Ueda, President, Honda Foundation, Tokyo, June 2, 3 and 19, 1980; July 7, 1980; Sept. 10, 1982; Feb. 6 and March 3, 1987. Also interviews with Honda executives, Tokyo, June 2, 1980, and Sept. 10, 1982.
45. For this metaphor I am indebted to Stanley Davis, "The Key to Strategy Is Context."
46. Interviews at Honda, Marysville.
47. Interview with Robert King, President, Goal/QPC, Tokyo, Sept. 27, 1988; also see Imai, *Kaizen*.
48. Interviews at Honda, Tokyo, June 2 and July 7, 1980, Feb. 7 and March 9, 1987, and Sept. 26, 1988; and interviews at Honda, Marysville.
49. Interview with Irimajiri. This issue is argued more generally in Kanter, *The Change Masters*, pp. 56–59; and Walton, "From Control to Commitment."
50. Interview with Irimajiri. Also interviews at Honda, Marysville. For a general elaboration on this philosophy, see Jacobsen, Chap. 1–2.
51. Interviews at Honda, Marysville.
52. Sakiya, *Honda's Motor*.
53. Interview with Takeo Fujisawa, Tokyo, March 16, 1987; also interview with Ueda; also "Man Behind the Scenes: Takeo Fujisawa," *Honda Today*, No. 68 (April 1989), pp. 11–14.
54. Interview with Fujisawa.
55. Interview with Fujisawa. Also interview with Honda executives, Tokyo.
56. Interview with Fujisawa, also "Everyone is Equal in the Presence of Technology," Honda white paper, Technology Research Dept., undated.
57. Sakiya, *Honda's Motor*, pp. 152–66.
58. For an excellent account of the city design process, see Nanaka, "Toward Middle-Up-Down Management," *Sloan Management Review*, Spring 1988, pp. 9–10; also Imai, Nanaka, and Takeuchi, "Managers the New Product."

59. Nanaka, "Toward Middle."
60. Interviews at Honda, Tokyo; also "Idea Contests," *Honda Today,* No. 62 (December 1987), pp. 1–18.
61. Interview with Maurice Cohen, President, JMW, Inc., Carmel, Calif., July 8, 1989.
62. Interviews with Fujisawa; also interviews with Ueda.
63. Interviews with Fujisawa; also interviews with Ueda.
64. Interview with Edward Buker, Marysville, Ohio, June 9, 1987.
65. Interviews at Honda, Marysville.
66. Interviews at Honda, Marysville; also interviews at Honda, Tokyo.
67. Interviews with Fujisawa.
68. Interviews with Fujisawa.
69. Susan Chira, "In Tokyo, Its Chief Welcomes Dissent," *New York Times,* June 15, 1987, p. C1.
70. Chira, "In Tokyo."
71. Interview with Fujisawa.
72. Interview with Fujisawa.
73. Interviews at Honda, Tokyo.
74. Interviews at Honda, Tokyo. For a general discussion of the notion of cross-functional design teams, see Richard S. Rosenbloom and Michael A. Cusumono, "Technological Pioneering and Competitive Advantage," *California Management Review,* Vol. XXIX, No. 4 (Summer 1987), pp. 51–76.
75. Interviews at Honda, Tokyo.
76. Interviews at Honda, Tokyo.
77. Interviews at Honda, Tokyo.
78. Interviews at Honda, Tokyo.
79. Interviews at Honda, Tokyo.

CHAPTER TEN
THE "QUESTION" IS THE ANSWER

1. These thoughts stem from a talk given by Anthony G. Athos, Johnson and Johnson Workshop, Orlando, Florida, April 1979.
2. Werner Erhard, "On Transformation and Productivity: An Interview," *ReVISION,* Norman Bodek, ed., Vol. 7, No. 2, 1984, pp. 30–38. In addition, there are numerous articles in the popular press on the virtues of a questioning orientation in the decade ahead. See, e.g., Brian Du-

maine, "What the Leaders of Tomorrow See," *Fortune,* July 3, 1989, pp. 48–62.

3. Goldian Vanden Broeck, *Less Is More: The Art of Voluntary Poverty* (New York: Harper & Row, 1978).

4. I am indebted to Professor Howard Stevenson of the Harvard Business School for this metaphor.

5. Leonard Silk, "On Managing Creativity," *Business Month,* April 1989, p. 11.

6. Robert A. Johnson, *We* (New York: Harper & Row, 1983), p. 23.

7. An interesting case for "not knowing" is made by Helen M. Luke, *Dark Wood to White Rose, A Study of Meanings in Dante's Divine Comedy* (Pecos, New Mexico: Dove Publications, 1975), pp. 95–102; also see Martin Heidegger, *Discourse on Thinking* (New York: Harper & Row, 1966), pp. 54–55, and Martin Heidegger, *On The Way to Language* (New York: Harper & Row, 1971), p. 70; Stephen Levine, *A Gradual Awakening* (Garden City, N.Y.: Anchor Press/Doubleday, 1979), p. 39.

8. Erhard, "On Transformation," p. 34

9. Lee Iacocca (with William Novak), *Iacocca,* (New York: Bantam Books, 1983), and Donald J. Trump (with Tony Schwartz), *Trump: The Art of the Deal* (New York: Warner Books, January, 1989).

10. Heidegger, *Discourse on Thinking,* p. 55.

Sources

INTERVIEWS

Mich Aneha
Bill Barton
Edward Battinger
James P. Baughman
Steven Bera
William Broussard
Edward Buker
Maurice Cohen
Pat Flaherty
Takeo Fujisawa
Tobi Hynes
Shoichiro Irimajiri
Elmer Johnson
Donald E. Kane
Robert King
Konosuke Matsushita
Mort Meyerson

Robert Mueller
Dennis Pauley
Ross Perot
Bill Pilder
David Quarmby
Ira Rimmerman
William E. Rothschild
David Sainsbury
Ernest Schaffer
Richard L. Schneider
Dean Tombs
John M. Trani
Takeo Ueda
Paul Van Orden
John F. Welch, Jr.
Thomas Woodard

BOOKS

Ashby, W. R. *An Introduction to Cybernetics* (New York: John Wiley & Sons, 1956).

Barker, Joel. *Discovering the Future: The Business of Paradigms* (St. Paul, Minn.: ILI Press, 1985).

Barnard, Chester I. *The Functions of the Executive* (Cambridge: Harvard University Press, 1968).

Bennis, Warren, and Bert Nanus. *Leaders: The Strategies for Taking Charge* (New York: Harper & Row, 1985).

Bernal, J. D. *Science and Industry in the 19th Century* (London: Routledge and Kegan Paul, 1953).

319

Bertalanffy, Ludwig von. *General Systems Theory, Foundations, Development, Applications* (New York: Braziller, 1968).

Blau, Peter M., and W. Richard Scott. *Formal Organizations* (San Francisco: Chandler, 1962).

Bohm, David. *Quantum Theory* (New York: Prentice Hall, 1951).

Bruner, Jerome S. *On Knowing* (Cambridge, Mass.: Harvard University Press, 1962).

Capra, Fritjof. *The Turning Point* (New York: Simon & Schuster, 1982).

————. *The Tao of Physics* (Berkeley: Shambala, 1975).

Carter, Ernst Frank. *Dictionary of Invention* (New York: Philosophical Library, 1967).

Chandler, Alfred D., Jr. *Strategy As Structure* (Cambridge, Mass.: MIT Press, 1962).

————. *The Visible Hand* (Cambridge, Mass.: Harvard University Press, 1977).

Chposky, James, and Ted Leonis. *Blue Magic: The People, Power, and Politics Behind the IBM Personal Computer* (New York: Facts on File, 1988).

Clark, R. K., R. Hayes, and C. Lorenz, eds. *The Uneasy Alliance: Managing the Productivity-Technology Dilemma* (Boston: Harvard Business School Press, 1985).

Clark, Victor S. *History of Manufactures in the United States* (New York: McGraw-Hill, 1929).

Collier, Peter, and David Horowitz. *The Fords* (New York: Summit Books, 1987).

Crum, Thomas. *The Magic of Conflict* (New York: Simon & Schuster, 1987).

Cyert, Richard M., and James G. March. *A Behavioral Theory of the Firm* (Englewood Cliffs, N.J.: Prentice-Hall, 1963).

Davidson, Mark. *Uncommon Sense: The Life and Thought of Ludwig von Bertalanffy, Father of General Systems Theory* (Los Angeles: T. P. Torcher, 1985).

Davis, Stanley M. *Future Perfect* (Reading, Mass: Addison-Wesley, 1987).

De Bono, Edward. *Eureka* (New York: Holt, Rinehart and Winston, 1974).

Drucker, Peter F., *The Age of Discontinuity* (New York: Harper & Row, 1968).

————. *Management: Tasks, Responsibilites, Practices* (New York: Harper & Row, 1973).

Elbow, Peter. *Embracing Contraries* (New York: Oxford University Press, 1987).

Fayol, Henry. *Industrial and General Administration,* Park II, Chapter I, "General Principles of Organization" (Paris: Dunod, 1925).

Feldman, Anthony, and Peter Ford. *Scientists and Inventions* (New York: Facts on File, 1979).

Foster, Richard. *Innovation* (New York: Summit Books, 1986).

Gadamer, Hans-Georg. *Hegel's Dialectic* (New Haven and London: Yale University Press, 1976).

Gilder, George. *The Spirit of Enterprise* (New York: Simon & Schuster, 1984).

Ginzberg, E. L., and George Vojta. *Beyond Human Scale: The Large Corporation at Risk* (New York: Basic Books, 1985).

Giscard D'Estaing, Valerie-Anne. *Second World Almanac Book of Inventions* (New York: Ballantine Books, 1986).

Gould, Stephen Jay. *The Panda's Thumb* (New York: Norton, 1982).

Greenwood, Ronald G. *Managerial Decentralization* (La Crosse, Wisc.: Hive Publishing Co., 1982).

Grove, Andrew. *High Output Management* (New York: Random House, 1983).

―――. *One-on-One with Andy Grove: How to Manage Your Boss, Yourself, and Your Co-Workers* (New York: G. P. Putnam's Sons, 1987).

Halberstam, David. *The Reckoning* (New York: Macmillan & Co., 1987).

Heidegger, Martin. *Discourse on Thinking* (New York: Harper & Row, 1966).

―――. *On the Way to Language* (New York: Harper & Row, 1971).

Herbert, Vernon, and Attilio Bisio. *Synthetic Rubber* (Westport, Conn.: Greenwood Press, 1985).

Huck, Virginia. *Brand of the Tartan: The 3M Story* (New York: Appleton-Crofts, Inc. 1955).

Humbert, Elie. *Carl G. Jung: The Fundamentals of Theory and Practice* (Wilmette, Ill: Chiron Publications, 1984).

Iacocca, Lee (with William Novak). *Iacocca* (New York: Bantam Books, 1983).

Jantsch, E. *The Self Organizing Universe* (New York: Paragon Press, 1980).

Jaynes, Julian. *The Origin of Consciousness in the Breakdown of the Bicameral Mind* (Boston: Houghton Mifflin, 1976).

Jewkes, John. *Sources of Invention* (London: Macmillan; New York: St. Martin's Press, 1958).

Johnson, Robert A. *We* (New York: Harper & Row, 1983).

Jung, Carl. *Letters* (Princeton: Bollinger Series XCV, Princeton University Press, 1975).

Kanter, Rosabeth Moss. *Commitment and Community: Communes and Uto-*

pias in Sociological Perspective (Cambridge: Harvard University Press, 1972).

————. *The Change Masters* (New York: Simon & Schuster, 1983).

Katz, D., and R. L. Kahn. *The Social Psychology of Organization* (New York: John Wiley & Sons, 1966).

Kilman, Ralph H. *Beyond the Quick Fix* (San Francisco: Jossey-Bass, 1984).

Kilman, Ralph H., and Teresa Joyce Corlin. *Corporate Transformation* (San Francisco: Jossey-Bass, 1988).

Kimberly, John R., and Robert E. Quinn, eds. *Managing Organizational Transitions* (Homewood, Ill.: Richard D. Irwin, Inc., 1984).

Kuhn, Thomas. *The Structure of Scientific Revolutions* (Chicago: University of Chicago Press, 1962).

Lacey, Robert. *Ford: The Men and the Machine* (New York: Ballantine, 1986).

Lawrence, Paul R., and Davis M. Dyer. *Renewing American Industry* (New York: Free Press, 1983).

Lawrence, Paul R., and Jay W. Lorsch. *Organization and Environment* (Homewood, Ill.: Richard D. Irwin, Inc., 1969).

Lax, David A., and James K. Sebenios. *The Manager as Negotiator* (New York: Free Press, 1986).

Lee, Albert. *Call Me Roger* (New York: Contemporary Books, 1988).

Levine, Stephen. *A Gradual Awakening* (Garden City, N.Y.: Anchor Press/ Doubleday, 1979).

Lincoln, Y., ed. *Organizational Theory and Inquiry: The Paradigmatic Revolution* (Beverly Hills, Calif: Sage, 1986).

Luke, Helen M. *Dark Wood to White Rose, a Study of Meanings in Dante's Divine Comedy* (Pecos, New Mexico: Dove Publications, 1975).

Lushington, Roger. *UK Plastics Industry, Special Report #103* (London: Economist Intelligence Unit Ltd., June 1981).

March, James G., and Herbert A. Simon. *Organizations* (New York: John Wiley & Son, 1958).

Margolis, L. *Origin of Eukaryotic Cells* (New Haven, Conn.: Yale University Press, 1970).

Mayo, Elton. *The Human Problems of Industrial Civilization* (New York: Macmillan, 1933).

McGregor, Douglas. *The Human Side of Enterprise* (New York: McGraw-Hill, 1960).

————. *The Professional Manager* (New York: McGraw-Hill, 1967).

McHugh, Jeanne. *Alexander Halley and the Makers of Steel* (Baltimore: Johns Hopkins University Press, 1980).

Mensch, Gerhard O. *Stalemate in Technology* (Cambridge, Mass.: Ballinger Publishing, 1975).

Miller, E. J., and A. K. Rice. *Systems of Organization* (London: Tavistock Publications, 1967).

Mills, D. Quinn. *The IBM Lesson* (New York: Times Books, 1988).

Mizuno, Shigeru. *Company Wide Total Quality Control* (Hong Kong: Asian Productivity Organization, 1988).

Motorcycle Industry Council. *1989 Motorcycle Statistical Annual* (Costa Mesa, Calif.: 1989).

Neumann, Gerhard. *Herman the German* (New York: Morrow, 1984).

Ouchi, William B. *Theory Z* (Reading, Mass.: Addison-Wesley, 1981).

Parry, Charles W. *Alcoa: A Retrospection* (New York: Newcomen Society of the U.S., 1989).

Pascale, Richard T., and Anthony G. Athos. *The Art of Japanese Management* (New York: Simon & Schuster, 1981).

Passer, Harold. *The Electronic Manufacturers* (Cambridge, Mass.: Harvard University Press, 1953).

Peters, Thomas J. *Thriving On Chaos* (New York: Random House, 1988).

Peters, Thomas J., and Nancy K. Austin. *A Passion for Excellence* (New York: Random House, 1985).

Peters, Thomas J., and Robert H. Waterman. *In Search of Excellence* (New York: Harper & Row, 1982).

Pinchot, Gifford, III. *Intrapreneuring* (New York: Harper & Row, 1985).

Piore, Michael J., and Charles F. Sabel. *The Second Industrial Divide* (New York: Basic Books, 1984).

Power, J. D. *Annual Automotive Survey* (Agoura Hills, California: J. D. Power & Associates, 1986, 1987, 1988).

Quine, W. V. *The Ways of Paradox and Other Essays* (Cambridge, Mass.: Harvard University Press, 1966).

Quinn, Robert E., and Kim S. Cameron, eds. *Paradox and Transformation* (Cambridge, Mass.: Ballinger Series, Harper & Row, 1988).

Reich, Robert B. *Tales of a New America* (New York: Times Books, 1987).

Roethlisberger, F. J., and William J. Dickson. *Management and the Worker* (Cambridge, Mass.: Harvard University Press, 1939).

Rosecrance, Richard. *The Rise of the Trading State* (New York: Basic Books, 1986).

Rothenberg, A. *The Emerging Goddess* (Chicago: University of Chicago Press, 1979).

Sakiya, Tetsua. *Honda's Motor: The Men, the Management, the Machines* (Tokyo: Kodansha, 1982).

Schonberger, Richard J. *Japanese Production Techniques* (New York: Free Press, 1982).

Schumacher, E. F. *Small Is Beautiful* (New York: Harper & Row, 1973).

Simon, Herbert A. *Administrative Behavior* (New York: Free Press, 1945).

Sloan, Alfred P. *My Years at General Motors* (Garden City, N.Y.: Doubleday, 1963).

Sobel, Robert. *IBM: Colossus in Transition* (New York: Times Books, 1981).

Taylor, Frederick W. *The Principles of Scientific Management* (New York, London: Harper, 1929).

Thompson, James D. *Organizations in Action* (New York: McGraw Hill, 1967).

Trump, Donald J. (with Tony Schwartz). *Trump: The Art of the Deal* (New York: Warner Books, 1989).

Tuchman, Barbara W. *A Distant Mirror* (New York: Knopf, 1978).

Urwick, Lyndall F., and Luther Gulick, eds. "Organization as a Technical Problem," in *Papers on the Science of Administration* (New York: Institute of Public Administration, Columbia University, 1937).

Vanden Broeck, Goldian. *Less Is More: The Art of Voluntary Poverty* (New York: Harper & Row, 1978).

Warren, Kenneth. *The American Steel Industry, 1850–1970* (Oxford: Clarendon Press, 1973).

Wasson, T., ed. *Nobel Prize Winners* (New York: H. W. Wilson Co., 1987).

Waterman, Robert H. *The Renewal Factor* (New York: Bantam Books, 1987).

Weaver, Paul H. *The Suicidal Corporation* (New York: Simon & Schuster, 1988).

Weber, Max. *The Theory of Social and Economic Organization,* translated by A. M. Henderson and Talcott Parsons (New York: Oxford University Press, 1947).

Weick, Karl E. *The Social Psychology of Organizing* (Reading, Mass: Addison-Wesley, 1969).

Wright, J. Patrick. *On a Clear Day You Can See General Motors* (New York: Avon Books, 1979).

Young, Louise. *The Unfinished Universe* (New York: Simon & Schuster, 1986).

Zukav, Gary. *The Dancing Wu Li Masters* (New York: Morrow, 1979).

ARTICLES

Abelson, Reed, and Rahul Jacob. "The Fortune 500," *Fortune,* April 24, 1989.

Albert, Stuart. "A Delete Design Model for Successful Transitions," in *Paradox and Transformations,* Robert E. Quinn and Kim S. Cameron, eds. (Cambridge, Mass.: Ballinger Series, Harper & Row, 1988).

Argyris, Chris. "Crafting a Theory of Practice," in *Paradox and Transformation,* Robert E. Quinn and Kim S. Cameron, eds. (Cambridge, Mass.: Ballinger Series, Harper & Row, 1988).

Ballen, Kate. "Get Ready for Shopping at Work," *Fortune,* Feb. 15, 1988.

Barker, Robert. "Commanding General: GE's Management Merits a Premium—But How Much?," *Barron's,* Oct. 15, 1984.

Barmash, Isadore. "Macy's Loaded with Debt Loses $19 Million in Quarter," *New York Times,* Dec. 15, 1988.

Bartlett, Sarah. "John Reed's Citicorp," *Business Week,* Dec. 8, 1986.

Bennett, Amanda. "GM's Bonus Flop: 'The Timing Was Wrong,' " *Wall Street Journal,* Nov. 7, 1988.

Bernstein, Aaron. "How IBM Cut 16,200 Employees Without an Ax," *Business Week,* Feb. 15, 1988.

Bernstein, P. "Atari and the Video Game Explosion," *Fortune,* July 27, 1981.

Biano, Anthony. "The Sad Saga of Western Union's Decline," *Business Week,* Dec. 14, 1987.

Borrus, Amy, et al. "The Global 1000," *Business Week,* July 17, 1989.

Bower, Joseph. "Planning Within the Firm," *American Economic Review,* May 1970.

Boyer, Edward. "Citicorp: What the New Boss Is Up To," *Fortune,* Feb. 17, 1986.

Boyle, Thomas F. "Loyalty Ebbs at Many Companies as Employees Grow Disillusioned," *Wall Street Journal,* July 11, 1985.

Brandt, Richard. "H-P May Have Come Up with a Winner," *Business Week,* June 1, 1989.

Brandt, Richard, and Otis Port. "Intel: The Next Revolution," *Business Week,* Sept. 26, 1988.

Broad, William J. "Novel Technique Shows Japanese Outpace Americans in Innovation," *New York Times,* March 7, 1988.

Brown, Andrew C. "A Surprising Ford-GM Face Off," *Fortune,* June 19, 1985.

Brown, S. H. "Fun Makes Money for Warner Communications," *Fortune,* April 4, 1974.

Burck, Charles. "Ford's Mr. Turnaround: Phillip Caldwell," *Fortune,* March 4, 1985.

———. "Will Success Spoil General Motors?," *Fortune,* Aug. 22, 1983.

Buss, Dale D. "Ford Is Riding High with Smart Execution and Slashed Capacity," *Wall Street Journal,* Oct. 7, 1986.

Buss, Dale D., and Masayoshi Kanaboyashi. "Wrong Road? Critics Fault Ford Plan to Produce Small Cars with Mazda of Japan," *Wall Street Journal,* June 23, 1986.

Bussey, John, and Bridgett Davis. "Ford Cost Cutting Move Is a Strike Issue," *Wall Street Journal,* August 8, 1988.

Bussey, John, and Mike Tharp. "NUMMI Auto Venture Termed a Success," *Wall Street Journal,* May 20, 1986.

Bylinsky, Gene. "The High Tech Race: Who's Ahead," *Fortune,* Oct. 13, 1986.

Byrne, John A. "Business Fads: What's In—and Out," *Business Week,* Jan. 20, 1986.

———. "Is Your Company Too Big?," *Business Week,* March 27, 1989.

Byrne, John A., et al. "Who Made the Muster and Why: Executive Compensation Scorecard," *Business Week,* May 2, 1988.

Capra, Fritjof. "Paradigms and Paradigm Shifts," presentations and discussions from a symposium, sponsored by The Elmwood Institute, Big Sur, California, Nov. 29–Dec. 4, 1985, reprinted in *ReVISION,* Vol. 9, No. 1, spring 1986, p. 11.

Chandler, Alfred D. "From Industrial Labs to Departments of R & D," in *The Uneasy Alliance,* R. K. Clark, R. Hayes, and C. Lorenz, eds. (Boston: Harvard Business School Press, 1985).

Chira, Susan. "In Tokyo, Its Chief Welcomes Dissent," *New York Times,* June 15, 1987.

Clark, Kim B., and Robert H. Hayes. "Recapturing America's Manufacturing Heritage," *California Management Review,* summer 1988, Vol. 30, No. 4, pp. 15–20, 27–31.

Clark, Matt. "Plagues, Man and History," *Newsweek,* May 9, 1988, pp. 65–66.

Davenport, Cynthia. "America's Most Admired Corporations," *Fortune,* Jan. 30, 1989, pp. 68–94.

Davis, Stanley M. "Transforming Organizations: The Key to Strategy Is Context," *Organizational Dynamics,* pp. 64–80.

Dolan, Carrie. "Rolm's Merger Could Fulfill Its Dream of Fighting ATT on Equal Footing," *Wall Street Journal,* Sept. 27, 1984, p. 3.

Dreyfuss, Joel. "Reinventing IBM," *Fortune,* August 19, 1988, pp. 30–39.

Dumaine, Brian. "Donald Petersen: A Humble Hero Drives Ford to the Top," *Fortune,* Jan. 4, 1988, pp. 23–24.

———. "Speed," *Fortune,* Feb. 17, 1989, pp. 54–59.

———. "Turbulence Hits The Air Couriers," *Fortune,* July 21, 1986, pp. 101–106.

———. "What the Leaders of Tomorrow See," *Fortune,* July 3, 1989.

Dunn, Don. "So You Wanna Be in Pictures?," *Business Week,* August 22, 1988, pp. 102–103.

Easterbrook, Gregg. "Ford Revs Up," *Washington Monthly,* Oct. 1986, pp. 84–87.

———. "Have You Driven A Ford Lately?," *Washington Monthly,* Oct. 1986, p. 88.

England, Robert. "Ford Shifts Gears for Road to Riches," *Insight,* July 13, 1987, p. 11.

Erhard, Werner. "On Transformation and Productivity: An Interview," *ReVISION,* Norman Bodek, ed., Vol. 7, No. 2, 1984, pp. 30–38.

Fannin, Rebecca. "The Road Warriors," *Marketing and Media Decisions,* March 1987, p. 60.

Fisher, Ann B. "Ford Is Back on the Track," *Fortune,* Dec. 23, 1985, pp. 18–22.

———. "GM Is Tougher Than You Think," *Fortune,* Nov. 10, 1986.

Fisher, Lawrence M. "Hewlett-Packard Profit Down by 200% in Quarter," *New York Times,* August 18, 1989, p. C2.

Flax, Steven. "Can Chrysler Keep Rolling Along?," *Fortune,* Jan. 7, 1985, pp. 34–39.

Flint, Jerry. "Nobody Likes Us Except the Customer," *Forbes,* Oct. 19, 1987.

Flint, Jerry, and Laura Jeraski. "Fiddling with Figures While the Sales Drop," *Forbes,* August 24, 1987.

Ford, Jeffrey D., and Robert W. Bockoff. "Organizational Change in and Out of Dualities," in *Paradox and Transformation,* Robert E. Quinn and Kim S. Cameron, eds. (Cambridge, Mass.: Ballinger Series, Harper & Row, 1988).

Foust, Dean. "Why Federal Express Has Overnight Anxiety," *Business Week,* Nov. 3, 1987.

Gannes, Stuart. "Sun's Sizzling Race to the Top," *Fortune,* August 17, 1987, pp. 88–91.

"GE's New Strategy for Faster Growth." *Business Week,* July 8, 1972, pp. 52–54.

Gelman, Eric. "Ford's Idea Machine," *Business Week,* Nov. 24, 1986, p. 64.

Garber, Daniel. "Science and Certainty in Descartes," *Descartes,* Michael Hooker, ed. (Baltimore: Johns Hopkins Press, 1978).

Getschow, George. "Some Middle Managers Cut Corners to Achieve High Corporate Goals," *Wall Street Journal,* Nov. 8, 1979.

Glasgall, William. "General Electric Is Stalking Big Game Again," *Business Week,* March 16, 1987, pp. 112–14.

"GM: Not Yet a Perfect 10," *Fortune,* July 4, 1988.

Gould, Stephen Jay, and Niles Eldridge. "Punctuated Evolution: The Tempo and Mode of Evolution Reconsidered," *Paleobiology,* Vol. 3, 1977, pp. 154–57.

"The Greatest Capitalist in History," *Fortune,* August 31, 1987, pp. 24–35.

Greer, John. "Macy's Tough Battle to Stay on Top," *San Francisco Chronicle,* Dec. 15, 1986, pp. 19–26.

Grover, Ron. "Michael Eisner's Hit Parade," *Business Week,* Feb. 1, 1988, p. 27.

Groves, Martha. "A New Face for Bullocks: Macy's Raises Eyebrows by Trying to Recast Chain into Own Image," *Los Angeles Times,* Feb. 23, 1982, Part 4, p. 1.

Guillemette, Roxanne. "Innovation in Japan," unpublished dissertation, June 1987.

Gulick, Luther. "Notes on the Theory of Organizations," in *Papers on the Science of Administration,* Luther Gulick and Lyndall F. Urwick, eds. (New York: Institute of Public Administration, Columbia University, 1937).

Guyon, Janet. "Combative Chief: GE's Jack Welch," *Wall Street Journal,* August 4, 1988.

Hackman, J. Richard. "The Transition That Hasn't Happened," in *Managing Organizational Transitions,* John Kimberly and Robert Quinn, eds. (Homewood, Ill.: Irwin, 1984).

Hampton, William J. "Why Image Counts," *Business Week,* June 8, 1987, p. 135.

Hayes, Robert, and Kim Clark. "Exploring the Sources of Productivity Differences at the Factory Level," in *The Uneasy Alliance,* R. K. Clark, R. Hayes, and C. Lorenz, eds. (Boston: Harvard Business School Press, 1985).

Henkoff, Ronald. "What Motorola Learns from Japan," *Fortune,* April 24, 1989.

Hertzberg, Daniel. "Citicorp Leads Field in Its Size and Power . . . and Arrogance," *Wall Street Journal*, May 11, 1984, pp. 1 and 16.

Holusha, John. "Ford Had Record Net of $4.6 Billion for 1987," *New York Times*, Feb. 19, 1988, p. 25.

Huey, John. "Executives Assess Europe's Technology Decline," *Wall Street Journal*, Feb. 4, 1984, p. 32.

Hutton, Cynthia. "America's Most Admired Corporations," *Fortune*, January 6, 1986, pp. 16–27.

"Idea Contests." *Honda Today*, No. 62, Dec. 1987.

"Hyatt International: Growth Through Management Services," *The Cornell Hotel & Restaurant Quarterly*, Feb. 1977.

"Hyatt Hotels: Putting Out the Welcome Mat for a Broader Clientele," *Business Week*, Oct. 13, 1983.

Imai, Ken-Ichi, Ikujiro Nanaka, and Hirotaka Takeuchi. "Managing the New Product Development Process: How Japanese Companies Learn and Unlearn," in *The Uneasy Alliance*, R. K. Clark, R. Hayes, and C. Lorenz, eds. (Boston: Harvard Business School Press, 1985).

Incantalupo, Tom. "How Honda Won Respect," *Newsday Business*, Sept. 27, 1987.

Ingrassia, Paul, and Bradley A. Stertz. "Ford's Strong Sales Pose Agonizing Issue of Additional Plants," *Wall Street Journal*, Oct. 26, 1988, pp. 1 and 10.

Ingrassia, Paul. "Detroit Paradox: GM's Market Share Declined Last Year Even as Net Set a Mark," *Wall Street Journal*, Feb. 15, 1989.

Isenberg, Daniel J. "The Tactics of Strategic Opportunism," *Harvard Business Review*, March–April 1987, pp. 92–97.

Jaikumor, Ramchandrin. "Manufacturing Crises: New Technology, Obsolete Organizations," *Harvard Business Review*, Sept.–Oct. 1988, pp. 81–83.

Johnson, Robert. "Fast-Food Chains Draw Criticism for Marketing Fare as Nutritional," *Wall Street Journal*, April 6, 1987, p. 27.

———. "McDonald's Combines a Dead Man's Advice with Lively Strategy," *Wall Street Journal*, Dec. 18, 1987, pp. 1 and 13.

Jonas, Norman. "Can America Compete?," *Business Week*, April 20, 1987, pp. 45–47.

Kantz, Philip C. "Letters to the Editor," *Fortune*, April 24, 1988, p. 338.

Kirkland, Richard I., Jr. "America on Top Again," *Fortune*, April 15, 1985, p. 138.

Kuhn, Susan E., and David J. Morrow. "The Fortune International 500," *Fortune*, July 31, 1989.

Labich, Kenneth. "Big Changes at Big Brown," *Fortune,* Jan. 18, 1988, pp. 56–64.

Lee, Chris. "Training the H.P. Team," *Training,* March 1989, pp. 29–31.

Leersen, Charles. "How Disney Does It," *Newsweek,* April 3, 1989, pp. 49–54.

Levine, Jonathan B. "Hewlett-Packard's Screeching Turn Toward Desktops," *Business Week,* Sept. 11, 1988.

———. "H-P: Now No. 1 in Workstations," *Business Week,* April 24, 1989.

———. "Mild Mannered H.P. Is Making Like Superman," *Business Week,* March 7, 1988, p. 110.

Lieberman, Marvin B. "Learning by Doing and Dynamic Industrial Competitiveness," *INSEAD Research Symposium on Issues in International Manufacturing,* Sept. 1987.

Lindbloom, Charles. "The Science of Muddling Through," *Public Administration Review,* spring 1959.

Lodge, George, and Bruce Scott. "Rules of the Game," *Harvard Business School Bulletin,* June 1984, pp. 53–64.

Lowell, Jon. "Perot's Rx for GM," *Ward's Auto World,* Nov. 1986.

Lowenstein, Robert. "Marriott Is Planning to Invest $500 Million to Launch Nationwide Chain of Low-Priced Motels," *Wall Street Journal,* Sept. 8, 1988, p. 4.

Lueck, Thomas J. "Why Jack Welch Is Changing GE," *New York Times,* May 5, 1985, Section 3, p. 1.

Machalaba, Daniel. "United Parcel Service Gets Deliveries Done by Driving Its Workers: But Its Vaunted Efficiency's Now to Be Challenged by an Automated Rival," *Wall Street Journal,* April 22, 1986, pp. 1 and 26.

Main, Jeremy. "Detroit's Cars Really Are Getting Better," *Fortune,* Feb. 2, 1987, pp. 93 and 96.

———. "Ford's Drive for Quality," *Fortune,* April 18, 1983, p. 62.

———. "The Trouble with Managing Japanese Style," *Fortune,* April 2, 1984, p. 50.

———. "The Winning Organization," *Fortune,* Sept. 26, 1988, p. 50.

"Man Behind the Scenes: Takeo Fujisawa," *Honda Today,* No. 68, April 1989.

Marbach, William N. et al. "Cars of the Future," *Business Week,* Oct. 28, 1985, p. 85.

March, James G. "Footnote to Organizational Change," *Administrative Science Quarterly,* Vol. 26, 1981, p. 575.

Markoff, John. "Powerful New Chip Ready to Be Introduced," *New York Times*, Feb. 27, 1989, p. C1.

Masuch, Michael. "Vicious Circles in Organizations," *Administrative Science Quarterly*, March, 1985, No. 30, pp. 14–33.

Merwin, John. "A War of Two Worlds," *Forbes*, June 16, 1986, pp. 101–106.

Miller, Danny. "Evolution and Revolution: A Quantum View of Structural Change in Organizations," *Journal of Management Studies*, No. 19, 1982, pp. 130–51.

Miller, Danny, and Peter H. Freisen. "Momentum and Revolution in Organizational Adaptation," *Academy of Management Journal*, Vol. 23, No. 4, Dec. 1980, pp. 591–614.

———. "Structural Change and Performance: Quantum Versus Piecemeal-Incremental Approaches," *Academy of Management Journal*, Vol. 25, No. 4, 1982, pp. 867–92.

Mintzberg, Henry. "Crafting Strategy," *Harvard Business Review*, July–Aug. 1987, pp. 65–75.

Mitchell, Russell. "Jack Welch: How Good a Manager?" *Business Week*, Dec. 19, 1987, p. 94.

———. "Masters of Innovation," *Business Week*, April 10, 1989.

Moore, Thomas. "Make or Break Time for General Motors," *Fortune*, Feb. 15, 1988.

———. "Would You Buy a Car from This Man?," *Fortune*, April 11, 1988, p. 72.

Morrow, David J. "How to Quit Losing in the Olympics," *Fortune*, April 29, 1989, p. 266.

Moser, Penny. "The McDonald's Mystique," *Fortune*, July 4, 1988, pp. 112–16.

Nanaka, Ikujiro. "Creating Organizational Order out of Chaos: Self Renewal in Japanese Firms," *California Management Review*, spring 1988, pp. 59–73.

———. "Toward Middle-Up-Down Management," *Sloan Management Review*, spring 1988, pp. 9–18.

Newport, John Paul, Jr. "A New Era of Rapid Rise and Ruin," *Fortune*, April 24, 1989, p. 77.

Norton, Robert E. "Citibank Woos the Consumer," *Fortune*, June 8, 1987, pp. 48–54.

Nulty, Peter. "Ford's Fragile Recovery," *Fortune*, April 2, 1987, pp. 42–48.

———. "People Express: Champion of Cheap Airlines," *Fortune*, Mar. 22, 1982.

O'Reilly, Brian. "Apple Computer's Risky Revolution," *Fortune,* May 8, 1989, pp. 75–84.

O'Toole, James. "Sic Transit Excellence," *Across the Board,* Oct. 1986.

Pascale, Richard T. "The Adaptation of Japanese Subsidiaries in the United States," *Columbia Journal of World Business,* Vol. 12, No. 7, spring 1977.

———. "Communication and Decision Making Across Cultures: Japanese and American Comparisons," *Administrative Science Quarterly,* April 1978.

———. "Communication, Decision Making and Implementation Among Managers in Japanese and American Managed Companies in the United States," with Mary Ann Maguire, *Sociology and Social Research,* Vol. 63, No. 1, 1978.

———. "Comparison of Selected Work Factors in Japan and the United States," with Mary Ann Maguire, *Human Relations,* Vol. 31, No. 7, July 1980.

———. "Made in America (Under Japanese Management)," with William Ouchi, *Harvard Business Review,* Sept.–Oct. 1974.

———. "Personnel Practices and Employee Attitudes: A Study of Japanese and American Managed Firms in the United States," *Human Relations,* Vol. 31, No. 7, 1978.

———. "Perspectives on Strategy: The Real Story Behind Honda's Success," *California Management Review,* Vol. XXVI, No. 3, spring 1984, p. 58.

———. "Zen and the Art of Management," *Harvard Business Review,* March–April 1978.

Pedersen, Daniel. "Perot to Smith: GM Must Change," *Newsweek,* Dec. 15, 1986.

Perot, Ross. "How I Would Turn Around GM," *Fortune,* Feb. 15, 1988, pp. 44–49.

Petre, Peter. "Jack Welch: The Man Who Brought GE to Life," *Fortune,* Jan. 5, 1987, p. 77.

———. "What Welch Has Wrought at GE," *Fortune,* July 7, 1986, p. 43.

Port, Otis. "Innovation in America," *Business Week,* July 1989, pp. 15–16.

———. "Quality," *Business Week,* June 8, 1987, pp. 131–135.

Potts, Mark. "GE's Welch Powering Firm into Global Competitor," *Washington Post,* Sept. 23, 1984, pp. G1–10.

Powell, Bill. "Hollywood's New Hardline," Newsweek, Aug. 15, 1988.

Prigogine, I. "Order through Fluctuation: Sell Organization and Social

System," in *Evolution and Consciousness,* E. Jantsch and C. H. Waddington, eds. (Reading, Mass.: Addison-Wesley, 1976).

Quinn, Robert E., and David Anderson. "Formalization as Crisis: Transition Planning for a Young Organization," in *Managing Organizational Transitions,* John Kimberly and Robert Quinn, eds. (Homewood, Ill.: Irwin, 1984).

Quinn, Robert E., and Kim S. Cameron, eds. "Paradox and Translation: A Framework for Rethinking Organizations and Management," in *Paradox and Transformation,* Robert E. Quinn and Kim S. Cameron, eds. (Cambridge, Mass.: Ballinger Series, Harper & Row, 1988).

Quinn, Robert E., and John Kimberly. "Paradox, Planning, and Perseverence," in *Managing Organizational Transitions,* John Kimberly and Robert Quinn, eds. (Homewood, Ill.: Irwin, 1984).

Reibstein, Larry. "Federal Express Faces Challenges to Its Grip on Overnight Delivery," *Wall Street Journal,* Jan. 8, 1988, pp. 1 and 8.

Reich, Cory. "The Innovator," *New York Times Magazine,* April 21, 1989.

Reich, Robert B. "Entrepreneurship Reconsidered: The Team as Hero," *Harvard Business Review,* May–June 1987, pp. 77–83.

Rice, Faye. "America's New No. 4 Automaker—Honda," *Fortune,* Oct. 28, 1985, pp. 30–33.

Risen, James. "Honda: The Americanization of an Auto Maker," *Los Angeles Times,* Oct. 12, 1987.

Rosenberg, Nathan. "The Commercial Exploitation of Science by American Industry," in *The Uneasy Alliance,* R. K. Clark, R. Hayes, and C. Lorenz, eds. (Boston: Harvard Business School Press, 1985).

Rosenbloom, Richard S., and Michael A. Cusumono. "Technological Pioneering and Competitive Advantage," *California Management Review,* Vol. XXIX, No. 4, summer 1987.

Rotbart, Dean, and Laurie D. Cohen. "About Face: The Party Isn't Quite So Lively as Recruiting Falls Off," *Wall Street Journal,* Oct. 6, 1986.

Saporito, Bill. "Companies that Compete Best," *Fortune,* May 22, 1989, p. 39.

Schlender, Brenton R. "Computer Maker Aims to Transform Industry and Be a Giant," *Wall Street Journal,* March 18, 1988, pp. 1 and 7.

Schlesinger, Jacob M., and Paul Ingrassia. "People Power: GM Woos Employees by Listening to Them, Talking of Its 'Team' " *Wall Street Journal,* Jan. 12, 1989.

Schlesinger, Jacob M., and Bradley A. Stertz. "GM 10 Cars Are Off to a Sluggish Start," *Wall Street Journal,* June 17, 1988.

Schlesinger, Jacob M., and Joseph B. White. "Shrinking Giant," *Wall Street Journal,* June 6, 1988.

Sellers, Patricia. "America's Most Admired Corporations," *Fortune,* Jan. 7, 1985, pp. 18–30.

Sherman, Stratford P. "The Mind of Jack Welch," *Fortune,* March 27, 1989.

Shimokawa, Koichi. "Honda's Entry into the World Wide Automotive Market," (Boston: Harvard Business School Press, 1978), pp. 305–13.

Silk, Leonard. "On Managing Creativity," *Business Month,* April 1989, p. 76.

Skinner, Wickham. "The Productivity Paradox," *Harvard Business Review,* July–August, 1986, pp. 56–58.

―――. "The Taming of Lions: How Manufacturing Leadership Evolved, 1970–1984," in *The Uneasy Alliance,* R. K. Clark, R. Hayes, and C. Lorenz, eds. (Boston: Harvard Business School Press, 1985).

Smith, Kenwyn. "Rabbits, Lynxes, and Organizational Transitions," in *Managing Organizational Transitions,* John Kimberly and Robert Quinn, eds. (Homewood, Ill.: Irwin, 1984).

Smith, Roger. "The U.S. Must Do as GM Has Done," *Fortune,* Feb. 13, 1989, p. 72.

Stokes, Henry Scott. "Honda, the Market Guzzler," *Fortune,* Feb. 20, 1984, pp. 105–108.

Taylor, Alexander L. "Iacocca's Tightrope Act," *Time,* March 21, 1983, pp. 50–61.

Taylor, Alex, III. "Here Come Japan's New Luxury Cars," *Fortune,* August 14, 1989.

―――. "Luxury Cars: New Leaders in an Upscale Upheaval," *Fortune,* April 10, 1989.

―――. "The Tasks Facing General Motors," *Fortune,* March 13, 1989, pp. 52–58.

―――. "Why Fords Sell Like Big Macs," *Fortune,* Nov. 21, 1988, pp. 123–135.

"Texas Instruments Shows U.S. Business How to Survive in the Eighties," *Business Week,* Sept. 18, 1978.

Thompson, Michael P. "Being, Thought and Action," in *Paradox and Transformation,* Robert E. Quinn and Kim S. Cameron, eds. (Cambridge, Mass.: Ballinger Series, Harper & Row, 1988).

Thompson, Steven. "The Rise and Rise of Honda," *Auto Week,* Feb. 13, 1989.

"Ten Best Cars in the World." *Car & Driver,* Feb. 9, 1989.

Ticer, Scott. "Why Zap Mail Got Zapped," *Business Week,* Oct. 15, 1986, pp. 48–49.

Tichy, Noel, and Ram Charan. "Speed, Simplicity, and Self-Confidence," *Harvard Business Review,* Sept.–Oct. 1989.

Toy, Stewart et al. "The Americanization of Honda," *Business Week,* April 25, 1988.

Treece, James B. "It's Time for a Tune-Up at General Motors," *Business Week,* Sept. 7, 1987.

Treece, James B., and Robert Ingersoll. "GM Faces Reality," *Business Week,* May 9, 1988.

Treece, James B. et al. "Can Ford Stay on Top?," *Business Week,* Sept. 28, 1987, p. 81.

———. "Motor City Madness: GM Leads Detroit Toward a Costly New Car Glut," *Business Week,* March 6, 1989.

———. "Will the Auto Glut Choke Detroit?," *Business Week,* March 7, 1988, p. 56.

Tully, Shawn. "American Bosses Are Overpaid," *Fortune,* Nov. 7, 1988.

Tushman, Michael, and David Nadler. "Organizing for Innovation," *California Management Review,* Fall 1986, Vol. 28, Nov. 3, pp. 74–92.

Tushman, M. L., and E. Romanelli. "Organization Evolution: A Metamorphosis Model of Convergence and Reorientation," *Research in Organizational Behavior,* Vol. 7, B. Staw and E. Cummings, eds. (Greenwich, Conn: JAI Press, 1985).

Uttal, Bro. "Delays and Defections at Hewlett-Packard," *Fortune,* Oct. 29, 1984, p. 62.

———. "Mettle Test Time for John Young," *Fortune,* April 29, 1985, pp. 242–48.

Vasilash, Gary. "Honda Is World-Class in Ohio," *Production,* July 1988.

Waldman, Peter. "Hewlett-Packard, Citing Software Snag, Will Delay New Computer Six Months," *Wall Street Journal,* Sept. 26, 1986, p. 2.

Walton, Richard E. "From Control to Commitment: Transforming Workforce Management in the U.S.," in *The Uneasy Alliance,* R. K. Clark, R. Hayes, and C. Lorenz, eds. (Boston: Harvard Business School Press, 1985).

———. "Warner Communications' Golden Possession," *Financial World,* Feb. 20, 1974.

Weick, Karl E. "Educational Organizations as Loosely Coupled Systems," *Administrative Science Quarterly,* Vol. 21, 1976.

———. "Re-Punctuating the Problem," in *New Perspectives on Organi-*

zational Effectiveness, P. S. Goodman and J. M. Pennings, eds. (San Francisco: Jossey-Bass, 1977).

Wheelwright, Steven C., and Robert H. Hayes. "Competing Through Manufacturing," *Harvard Business Review,* Jan.–Feb. 1985, pp. 99–109.

White, Joseph B., and Bradley A. Stertz. "Auto Makers Drive into a Mess as Plants Expand and Sales Fall," *Wall Street Journal,* Aug. 7, 1989.

———. "Woo the Secretary and Win the Boss," *Business Week,* Sept. 11, 1965.

Worthy, Ford S. "The Pritzkers," *Fortune,* April 25, 1988, pp. 164–178.

Zellner, Wendy. "Back to Butting Heads with the UAW?," *Business Week,* May 8, 1988.

———. "GM's New 'Teams' Aren't Hitting Any Homers," *Business Week,* August 8, 1988.

———. "Smiling Fender to Fender," *Business Week,* Oct. 5, 1987, p. 39.

SPEECHES, ACADEMIC PAPERS, AND INTERNAL CORPORATE DOCUMENTS

Aguilar, Frank. "General Electric: Strategic Position 1981," a Harvard Business School Case Study (Cambridge: Harvard Business School Case Services, 1981).

Astley, W. Graham. "The Dynamics of Organizational Evolution," working paper #304, unpublished, The Wharton School, December 1983.

Athos, Anthony G. Untitled talk, Johnson and Johnson Workshop, Orlando, Florida, April 1979.

Badore, Nancy Lloyd. "The Role of Management in the Change Process," paper presented in Academy of Management Symposium, Section IV, Boston, August 12, 1984.

Baughman, James P. "Problems and Performance of the Role of Chief Executive of the General Electric Company, 1892–1974," mimeographed discussion paper, July 15, 1974.

Bellah, Robert N. "Religion and the Technological Revolution in Japan," University Lecture in Religion, Arizona State University, Feb. 19, 1987.

Bera, Steven. "The Japanization of Steve," unpublished working paper, Detroit, spring 1985.

Bower, Joseph L. *Managing the Resource Allocation Process* (Cambridge, Mass.: Division of Research, Graduate School of Business Administration, Harvard University, 1970).

Burgleman, Robert A. "Corporate Context and the Concept Strategy," unpublished paper (Palo Alto: Stanford Graduate School of Business Administration, 1988).

Caldwell, Phillip. *Policy Letter #B-14,* November 5, 1979.

Cameron, Kim S. "Effectiveness as Paradox: Consensus and Conflict in Conceptions of Organizational Effectiveness," unpublished paper delivered at Radical Workshop or Organizational Design, Monterey, California, 1984.

Cornelius, Karen L., and C. Douglas Hincker, "Early Initiatives: The 8-Step Model of Planned Change," Academy of Management Symposium, Section III, Boston, August 12, 1984.

Ford. "UAW-Ford: Employee Involvement Survey Report," Education and Personnel Research Department, Detroit, Sept. 15, 1982.

Fruhan, W. E. "GE: 1970," a Harvard Business School case study (Cambridge, Mass.: Harvard Business School Case Services, 1970).

General Electric. "Executive Opinion Survey Report," prepared for General Electric Officers Meeting, July 1985.

————. General Electric Annual Reports, 1950–1965.

————. GE internal documents.

————. "GE's New Strategy for Faster Growth," prepared for General Electric Officers Meeting, July 1985.

Greenhalgh, L., R. McKersie, and R. Gilkey, "Rebalancing the Workforce at IBM," unpublished working paper #1718-85, October 1985.

Hackborn, Dick, and Don Harris, "The Hewlett-Packard Way," undated internal Hewlett-Packard publication.

Hamermesh, R. G. "General Electric: 1984," (Cambridge, Mass.: Harvard Business School Case Services, 1985).

Helms, Eugene W. "The OST System for Managing Innovation at Texas Instruments," an address to the Armed Forces Management Association, April 7, 1971.

Honda. "Honda People," internal Honda handbook on the Honda Way, undated.

————. "Elements of Honda's Strategy," unpublished white paper, 1987.

————. "Everyone Is Equal in the Presence of Technology," unpublished white paper, Technology Research Dept., undated.

Ingle, William O., casewriter. "The IBM 360: Giant as Entrepreneur," Harvard Business School case study (Cambridge, Mass.: Harvard Business School Case Services, 1968).

Intel. Intel internal documents.

Jacobsen, Erik. "NUMMI: A Model in Human Relations," thesis written at

Buick-Oldsmobile-Cadillac (Detroit: GMI Engineering and Management Institute, September 12, 1986).

Johnson, Raymond H. "Driving Forces for Participative Management and Employee Involvement," paper presented at the Academy of Management Symposium, August 12, 1984, Boston; published in *Cultural Change Within a Large System* (Detroit, Ford Motor Company, 1984).

———. HRD briefing paper, "Salaried Personnel Opinion Survey," Dearborn, Mich., 1988.

Kane, Donald E. "Resizing the Structure," unpublished staff paper for General Electric's top management, August 12, 1985.

Karney, Bruce. "Employee Productivity: How Does H-P Stack Up?," case study for HP executive education (Palo Alto: January 10, 1986).

———. "HP's Human Assets," a case study for executive education (Palo Alto, January 10, 1986).

King, Richard. "Hewlett-Packard: Challenging the Entrepreneurial Culture," Harvard Business School case study (Cambridge, Mass.: Harvard Business School Case Services, 1983).

Kume, Tadashi. "The Challenging Spirit," unpublished speech to Automotive Manufacturers Association, Detroit, Sept. 26, 1988.

Langenfeld, J. A. "NUMMI Management Practices: A Report of the General Motors Study Team," unpublished report, April 9, 1986.

Lieberman, Marvin. "When Does Union-Management Cooperation Work? A Look at NUMMI and GM–Van Nuys," unpublished paper for conference: Can California Be Competitive and Caring?, UCLA, May 6, 1988.

Marriott. Annual Reports, 1985–1988.

McKinsey Organizational Practice. "Centralization vs. Decentralization," unpublished internal study of 26 companies, Yountville, Calif., Organizational Effectiveness Workshop, Nov. 16–21, 1980.

Miller, R. S. Remarks to Financial Executive Institute, Chicago, Jan. 19, 1984.

Minnesota Mining and Manufacturing. *Our Story So Far* (St. Paul: Minnesota Mining and Manufacturing Co., 1977).

Mintzberg, Henry, and James A. Waters. "Of Strategies, Deliberate and Emergent," McGill University, January 1983.

Moore, James D. "Overview: The Ford Story," white paper for ATT office of the chairman, based on interviews at Ford, January 3, 1987.

National Science Foundation. International Science and Technical Data Update (Washington, D.C.: National Science Foundation, 1984).

North American Automotive Operations. "Japanese Business Practices:

Study Findings of the 1981 Ford Task Force,'' unpublished white paper, August 17, 1981.

Okubo, Shin. "The Honda Approach to Productivity," speech at Baldwin-Wallace College, Berea, Ohio, March 2, 1987.

Parpia, Manu. "Macy's California," Harvard Business School case study (Cambridge, Mass.: Harvard Business School Case Services, Aug. 1986).

Pascale, R. *Interviews at DEC,* unpublished working paper (Cambridge, Mass.: July 16–February 22, 1988).

———. Memo to Harold Burlingame of AT&T, August 31, 1987, subject: "One-on-One Consulting Intervention."

———. "The Problem of 'Strategy,' " keynote address to the Strategic Management Society Annual Conference, Boston, Mass., October 16, 1987.

———. "Recruitment and Socialization at IBM," unpublished paper, November 3, 1983.

———. "Recruitment and Socialization at Procter & Gamble," unpublished working paper, Nov. 3, 1982.

———. Working notes as consultant to the Ford Change Task Force, October 30, 1983.

Quinn, James Brian, and Penny C. Paquette. "Ford: Team Taurus," a case study, Amos Tuck School of Business Administration, Dartmouth College, 1988.

Rehder, Robert. "Organizational Transformation: The GM Freemont Plant," unpublished paper; University of New Mexico, June 1986.

Seeger, John A. "First National City Bank A & B," a Harvard Business School case study (Cambridge, Mass.: Harvard Business School Case Services, 1975).

SIA Public Information. "Crisis in a Critical Industry," Washington, D.C., Sept. 28, 1988 and Data Quest, March 7, 1989.

Walsh, Jeffrey T. "Creating the Conditions for Large Scale Systems Change," in *Cultural Change Within a Large System,* Academy of Management Symposium, Section IV, August 12, 1984.

Watson, Thomas, Jr. "A Business and Its Beliefs," McKinsey Foundation Lecture Series, Graduate School of Business, Columbia University (New York: McGraw Hill, 1963).

Welch, John F., Jr. "Management in the Nineties," speech to Bay Area Council, San Francisco, Ca., July 6, 1989.

Woodard, Thomas. Unpublished McKinsey staff paper for Network Systems, AT&T, February 10, 1988.

Index

341